Religion in Contemporary Nigeria

Adonis & Abbey Publishers Ltd
St James House
13 Kensington Square,
London, W8 5HD
United Kingdom

Website: http://www.adonis-abbey.com
E-mail Address: editor@adonis-abbey.com

Nigeria:
Suites C4 & C5 J-Plus Plaza
Asokoro, Abuja, Nigeria
Tel: +234 (0) 7058078841/08052035034

Copyright 2016 © Y.A. Quadri, R.W. Omotoye&R.I. Adebayo

British Library Cataloguing-in-Publication Data
A catalogue record for this book is available from the British Library

ISBN: 978-1-909112-60-5

The moral right of the author has been asserted

All rights reserved. No part of this book may be reproduced, stored in a retrieval system or transmitted at any time or by any means without the prior

Religion in Contemporary Nigeria

Edited by

Y.A. Quadri
R.W. Omotoye
R.I. Adebayo

Preface

Religion is expected to be a springboard for the development of socio-ethical values, as it contains not only the spiritual backing to individual conduct but also an effective means of inculcating interpersonal relationships within the society. It is therefore a potent instrument for the realisation of the goal of national development. In the history of religion in Nigeria, religious groups and individuals have contributed immensely to issues of national and international understanding. Nobody can deny that the vehicle through which the art of reading and writing came to Nigeria is religion. Religion is playing this role up till now. In the same vein, religion has played a significant role in the health sector. This came in form of spiritual assistance rendered to individuals and communities to solve personal and communal challenges and through the establishment of health centres and hospitals. In the economic sector, religion also functions as a vehicle of economic growth by being a massive employer of labour.

However, in contemporary period, the spirit of nationalism, ethnicity and tribalism has dragged religion into mud, as it has been downplayed by those who believe that it is a potent instrument of polarisation, terrorism and insecurity. This is being amplified on the media, electronic and print. Looking at the opposite side of religion at the neglect of its positives is like being unjust to it in view of its multifarious positive contributions to the nation. It is therefore worrisome that information about religions generally on the wrong side given by those who are either not experts in the field or those who are biased of one religion and try to exonerate his own.

In view of the above, the idea to come up with this book titled *Religion in Contemporary Nigeria* is to provide a basic source material in one piece for students, lecturers, public commentators and the general readers interested in religion on the use and abuse of religion in Nigeria. This, to us, will guide against throwing a baby with bathwater. Also, revealing the various ways through which religion is being used as an instrument of disorganisation, polarisation, disintegration and destruction will assist in determining the extent of abuse of religion in the hand of those who claim to be practising it. Since no religion teaches these obnoxious practices, we believe that this work will further assist in determining some factors working against effective use of religion in the country. In the same token, the role of religion in the provision of the moral, psychological, social and spiritual infrastructure for the development of the nation would also be examined. We therefore anticipate that this book would provide as much as what its users would need to know about religion in contemporary Nigeria as it offers variety of articles which give insights into new developments in religious studies.

Y.A. Quadri; R.W. Omotoye; & R.I. Adebayo
Department of Religions,
University of Ilorin, Ilorin,
Nigeria.

Table of Contents

Chapter One
Religion and National Transformation in Nigeria 9

Chapter Two
Issues and Challenges of Religion in Nigeria in the 21st Century 31

Chapter Three
Ethnic and Religious Violence in Nigeria: A Proposal for Peaceful
Co-Existence 47

Chapter Four
Religious Terrorism in Contemporary Nigeria: The Implication for
National Development 61

Chapter Five
Violence in the Name of God: An Analytical Study of the
Boko Haram Insurgency in Nigeria 75

Chapter Six
Peaceful Co-Existence in a Multi-Religious Society:
An Islamic Perspective 105

Chapter Seven
The Impact of Religion in Curbing Corruption in Nigeria 135

Chapter Eight
An Exegetical Study of Psalm 122 in the Nigerian Context 151

Chapter Nine
The Growth and Expansion of Pentecostal Churches in Ilorin,
Kwara State, Nigeria 169

Chapter Ten
Prospects and Challenges of Arabic and Islamic Studies in Nigeria With
Particular Reference to Yoruba Land 199

Chapter Eleven
Inhibiting Factors Against Education of Muslim Children in Nigeria 225

Chapter Twelve
Dividends of International Islamic Organisations in Nigeria 241

Chapter Thirteen
Ethno-Religious Crisis and its Implication for National
Security and Development.. 269

Chapter Fourteen
A Comparison of Polygamy as a Concept in African Religion and Christianity
.... 283

Chapter Fifteen
The Obsession of Nigerians with Miracles in the Islamic and
Christian Religions 297

Chapter Sixteen
Traditional Religion and Ethical System of the People of
Isiala-Mbano Local Government Area of Imo State, Nigeria 323

Chapter Seventeen
The Trends of Application of Islamic Legal System in
Yorubaland of Nigeria.. 349

Chapter Eighteen
Distribution of Inheritance and Muslim Women in Kaduna and
Kano States of Nigeria 367

Chapter Nineteen
The Evolution of Izālatul- Bid ᶜah Movement in North-Eastern
Nigeria with Particular Reference to Bauchi and Gombe States...... 391

Chapter Twenty
Historical Development of Islam in Central and
Eastern Delta of Nigeria... 417

Index..445

CHAPTER ONE

Religion and National Transformation in Nigeria

Gwamna Dogara Je'adayibe
*Department of Religious Studies,
Nasarawa State University, Keffi, Nigeria
gwamnad1@yahoo.com*

Introduction

The focus of this study is centred on the tripartite issues of religion, national transformation and Nigeria. These key concepts evoke different understanding, perspectives and explanations. Religious discourse has gained global attention since 9/11 event in the United States of America. Since then, religious related events around the world have witnessed unprecedented attention and critical probing. Nigeria has joined in the frenzy of religiously induced conflicts in the last three decades. From religious identity conflicts to ethno-religious unrests, religion has emerged as Nigeria's albatross. That Nigeria is a religious nation cannot be over stated. This is manifested in its religiously saturated public space which is an everyday experience in Nigeria. John Onaiyekan a Catholic Cardinal in Nigeria puts this observation succinctly thus:

> Any casual look at our country obviously shows the all pervading presence of religion. We only need to note, for example, the number of places of worship, the volume of holy noises that are emitted everywhere, the array of religious leaders with various titles and robes and the fervor with which we not only practice our faith but at times violently confront one another. Some are wondering whether our reputation as a religious nation is something to be proud of. They suspect that there is something dubious about this record.[1]

The resultant effects of the above observation is that virtually everybody claims to be an expert on religious natters in Nigeria. With such enviable credential as the most religious nation, it is paradoxically one of the most corrupt nations in the world. The damning verdict on religion is that instead of serving as a resource for peace and stability, it has become a veritable resource for conflict and war and easy tool for manipulation by some politicians, elites and religious charlatans and bigots. It is such tendency that has portrayed religion as a negative force in Nigeria today. This study discusses the interplay of such paradoxical roles of religion in Nigeria and how religion can play a more positive role towards national transformation.

Religion: Towards A Clarification

There is no scholarly consensus on the definition of religion. Religion has meant different things to different people over time. Yet, religion is as old as human civilization. The often divergent views on religion have given rise to several perspectives, understanding and explanations. Nigosian appreciated this problem and raised diverse ways religion is understood to include emphases on the intellectual function, emotional, worship, individual experience, and social functions of religion.[2] Religion could be defined as man's attempt to relate with supernatural force(s) as part of man's search for meaning, understanding and explanation of life. Such attempt has led to man's coding of such forces under different names such as God, the "wholly other," Allah, Shekwoyi, Chukwu, Olodumare, and so on.

Religion has influenced different forms of human civilizations such as in art, architecture, music, poetry, dance, history, philosophy, politics, and so on. Miller supports this statement when he wrote that, "religion has produced the noblest monuments and the finest works of art known to humanity."³ Miller buttresses this observation further by stating that religion "like art and beauty, its meaning is very much in the eyes of the beholder."⁴

Understanding religion therefore, requires a multi-dimensional overview of its essence and manifestation. Religion has a forceful factor with the capacity to arouse deep emotions of man and passion toward obedience, commitment and total surrender. Religion creates faith which could be revolutionary, that is, with the capacity to influence change; and it could also be transformational in content and goal. When religion assumes the extreme content in its belief and practice, it leads to fanaticism, extremism, intolerance and unguarded bigotry. Religion could be used or blatantly manipulated by its adherents in order to achieve certain primordial interests. Haar notes this of religion when she wrote that, "the political manipulation of and mobilisation through religion is probably the most frequent way in which religion is used, or misused, in present times."⁵

Nigeria today is a multi-faith society. That is to say that there are many religions in Nigeria such as Christianity and Islam, adherents of African Traditional Religion (ATR), New Agers and a few Atheists. The predominant religions are Christianity and Islam (monotheistic faiths) both which are "foreign religions" in Nigeria. Thus, Onaiyekan, has indicated that "there is no country in the world which has so many Christians and Muslims living within the same nation – and living in relative peace with one another."⁶ The numerical statistical data of these two religions in Nigeria is often contested and has been a source of conflict in Nigeria.

Chapter One | Gwamna Dogara Je'adayibe, in
Y.A. Quadri, R.W. Omotoye & R.I. Adebayo (Eds)
Religion in Contemporary Nigeria
London, Adonis & Abbey Publishers

A Brief on Nigeria

A commentary on Nigeria evokes provocative and sad passions. Nigeria evolved as an independent nation state from the British colonial rule on October 1, 1960 following its amalgamation in 1914. Achebe writes that "on amalgamation, Christians – Muslims and animists alike were held together by a delicate, some say artificial lattice."[7] Some other scholars have referred to it as the colonial "artificial creation." With a population slightly above 160 million people, Nigeria is the biggest black nation in the world. Nigeria is endowed with huge human and natural resources with potentials to emerge as one of the developed nations in the world. Commenting on natural resources in Nigeria, Fatubarin lists some of those resources to include; petroleum – the black gold, natural gas, arable land, extensive hydro power and different types of solid minerals such as iron ore, gold, tin, columbite, coal, limestone, lead and zinc. Nigeria is also rich in diverse agricultural products, in the form of cash crops, food crops, livestock species, fishes and forestry resources.[8]

Nigeria is the sixth producer of oil in the world. However, a look at Nigeria and of its people today, portrays a picture of a nation that has lost its potentials for growth. Thus, many commentators on Nigeria have described Nigeria in many ways. For example, Maeir refers to Nigeria as, "This House Has Fallen."[9] For Bishop Peter A. Adebiyi, now retired Anglican Bishop of Lagos West Diocese, "Nigeria is Africa's sleeping giant."[10] Fatubarin sees Nigeria as "a land of wasted opportunities."[11] Peel, also extols Nigeria's possibilities, greatness and of its potentially deadly explosiveness.[12] Bishop Matthew Hassan Kukah says "Nigeria is one kind place. Its people think one kind, and they behave one kind."[13] In the words of Nigeria's Pop music star, Abdulkareem Idris,

Chapter One Gwamna Dogara Je'adayibe, in
Y.A. Quadri, R.W. Omotoye & R.I. Adebayo (Eds)
Religion in Contemporary Nigeria
London, Adonis & Abbey Publishers

"Nigeria Jaga Jaga, everything scatter, scatter." Nigeria is described as "a nation that has pieced its soul." In the words of Ilechuckwu, Nigeria is "a failed state that works."[14]

Scholarly discourse is not agreed on Nigeria's status today as a failed state. But global indices of failed states seem to fit Nigeria's present experience. For example, reflecting on this, Campbell states:

> Failed states are more like sick people, with diseases of varying causes, intensities, and consequences. Recovery is often slow and progress is uneven. Like ill people, failed states continue to function in various ways even while they are failing in others. This analogy fits Nigeria well.[15]

In the words of Ellis, failed states are like "broken machines."[16] Illustrating the credentials of Nigeria as a failed state to corroborate this assertion further, Achebe is instructive here thus:

> Nigeria has been doomed to witness endless cycles of inter-ethnic, inter-religious violence because the Nigerian government has failed woefully to enforce laws protecting its citizens from wanton violence, particularly attacks on non-indigenes living in disparate parts of the country.[17]

In fact, in 2011, Nigeria was ranked number 14 in the Failed States Index.[18]

Nigeria seems to be a country today that is at war with itself as the "evil men" have taken over the reins of the state. The paradoxical and negative indices in Nigeria indicate troubling scenario when compared with other nations of the world. A few of such vital statistics show the following among others:

Chapter One — Gwamna Dogara Je'adayibe, in
Y.A. Quadri, R.W. Omotoye & R.I. Adebayo (Eds)
Religion in Contemporary Nigeria
London, Adonis & Abbey Publishers

i. For many years, Nigeria has had and still has the highest mortality in the world and particularly, of maternal deaths.[19]

ii. Out of 182 countries ranked by Transparency International (IT) in 2012, Nigeria was ranked 142 as one of the most corrupt nations in the world;

iii. Since 1960s, it is alleged that Nigeria has been drained of $400 billion by its leaders.[20]

iv. In 2011, UNDP, World Bank and IMF showed that Nigeria lives below its status as one of the world's largest producer of oil, "the only major producer of oil that is known to be abysmally poor."[21]

v. More than 70% of Nigerians live below poverty level, namely, those who live less than US $1 per day.

vi. One of the poorest people in the world but have the highest paid leaders in the world.[22]

vii. Despite its huge human and natural resources, Nigeria is still plagued by natural disasters, environmental degradation, destructive accidents, and preventable diseases.

viii. Nigeria is described as the most "religious nation in the world," and also the most corrupt in the world. This is what Onaiyekan calls "a nation of superlatives."[23]

Added to the above are systemic collapse of infrastructure, moral decay, leadership failure, lawlessness (including both the led and the law makers). Nigeria can best be compared to what Amos saw of Israel, as a people, who had "turned justice into bitterness and cast righteousness to the ground" (Am. 5:7). Isaiah says, "so justice is driven back and righteousness stand at a distance, truth has stumbled in the streets, honesty cannot enter" (Is. 59:14).

For the purpose of this study, we have chosen a few issues outlined above for brief comments before we relate them to the theme of our reflection. They include, insecurity, poverty, corruption and false spirituality.

Insecurity

Nigeria's security apparatus today is on trial. To say it has collapsed is not an exaggeration. The killings of Boko Haram along with kidnappings, assassinations and armed gang attacks have left Nigeria as a dreaded place and theatre of war that is unprecedented in its history. In fact, the presence of security patrols in our cities, check points on our high ways and in public places, gives a first time traveller on the Nigerian roads, a picture of a nation under siege with itself.

Human life today has lost its sacredness. The impurity in which this has continued unabated depicts the level of our culture of lawlessness that we have found ourselves and government's failure to provide protection for lives and property for its citizens. We seem to be experiencing a similar scenario of Israel when "in those days Israel had no King, everyone did as he was fit" (Jdg. 21:25). We are likened to "a city divided against itself." And as Jesus said, "a city divided against itself cannot stand" (Matt. 12:25; Mk. 3:25).

Complicity of the state officials, including religious leaders in Nigeria shows that Nigeria is sliding towards annihilation as recent calls for break up of the country and foisting of flags by many groups such as the Boko Haram Islamic insurgents and members of the Movement for the Actualization of the Sovereign State of Biafra (MOSSOB), are indicators towards secession and self-immolation. That was why Isaiah pronounced; "woe to those who call evil good, and good evil, who put darkness for light and light for darkness, who put bitter for sweet and sweet for bitter" (5:20). They were a people who shouted peace, peace, when there was no peace (Jer. 6:14).

Poverty

As we had noted earlier, Nigeria is one of the richly endowed nations of the world, but also has the poorest people in the world. Its people have been reduced to all forms of hunger, deprivation and have become vulnerable to all forms of societal crimes. In the words of Nigerian Afro Musician, Fela Anikulapo Kuti, Nigerians are "a people who are suffering and smiling." For Adebiyi, "we have become like the cloth owner who wears rags."[24] Powell, the former United States Secretary of State, described Nigeria "as a country of marvellous scammers, blessed with wealth it had pissed away."[25]

Nigeria can be compared today to what the Psalmist wrote of Israel when he states that, "He turned rivers into desert, flowing spring into thirsty ground, and fruitful land into salt waste because of the wickedness of those who lived there" (Ps. 107:33-34). Today, the gap between the rich and the poor is so high. By the poor, we are referring to people who are without food, education, social status, shelter and hope.

It is a common experience in Nigeria to see affluent Nigerians living amidst highly impoverished citizens who are deprived and dehumanized by poverty and want. The resultant effects of poverty in Nigeria today has led to what is succinctly captured by Cuncliffe-Jones thus:

> Since Independence, tensions between Christians and Muslims have grown as Nigerians disillusioned with what the country has become, have turned more than ever to religion for their answers. And as an ever more important part of their identity, religion has become one of the great issues dividing the country.[26]

Chapter One | Gwamna Dogara Je'adayibe, in
Y.A. Quadri, R.W. Omotoye & R.I. Adebayo (Eds)
Religion in Contemporary Nigeria
London, Adonis & Abbey Publishers

In fact, a result of poverty today, most crimes and social vices easily find justification for their evil activities.

Corruption

Nigeria has been acclaimed as one of the most corrupt nations in the world. Corruption has been defined as "the misuse of public power for private benefit." Corruption has permeated every segment of Nigeria. Adebiyi states that "even the blind knows that Nigeria is a thoroughly corrupt country. Corruption flourishes in Nigeria today; it is endemic from cradle to grave. "It is noticeable in homes, markets, government offices, private organisations and even in churches."[27] The manifestation of corruption and its effects in Nigeria have reached a cancerous level which some see as a "major affliction," and one that has "handcuffed" Nigeria.

Many terms have developed to refer to corruption in Nigeria such as; "brown envelope," "settlement," "paying tribute," "apostolic blessing," "Ghana must go," "Chuwachuwa," "deal," "greasing the palm," "*kayan aiki*," "oiling," "appreciation," and so on. Similarly, different types of corruption have been identified to include; political corruption (bribery, election rigging, nepotism, cronyism and mediocrity), educational corruption (lack of funding, payment for admissions, attitude of teachers, students, parents complicity, sex for grade, examination malpractices); religious corruption, economic and financial corruption in public and private sectors.

The elite in Nigeria, namely, the educated class which Campbell refers to as the "big men," or the "*ogas*" and the "cabals" have perpetuated corruption for their selfish interests as popular pressure and protests by the civil populace remains docile, divisive and unpopular.[28] For Achebe, the problem of corruption and indiscipline in Nigeria is probably worse today than its ever been and states further that "corruption in Nigeria has passed the alarming and entered the fatal stage, and Nigeria will die if we continue to pretend that she is only slightly indisposed."[29] Today, corruption has infected religion and we now witness what Akinwale sees "as a toxic mixture of corrupt politics and corrupt religion."[30]

It could be rightly asserted that when religion is manipulated for political interests by politicians and the elites, it is corruption. When religion is used to exploit Nigerians under several guises, it is a form of corruption. When religious leaders use religion to fan bitterness and acrimony among Christians, Muslims and other religious adherents, it is a form of corruption. When people masquerade under religion to claim fake religious titles and honours, it is a form of corruption. It is such tendencies of corrupt religion that have given birth to false religiousity or spirituality that we now wish to turn.

False Spirituality

Nigeria is a religious nation with a highly conscious religious people. It is also a religiously plural society. The external show of religiousity in the public space depicts the truism of this observation. Ojo has listed some of these manifestations of religion in the public sphere to include;

i. The dominance of religious symbols and activities in the media. The media is used for propagation of their religion.
ii. The landscape is saturated with religious advertisement or religious edifices. For example, religious camp grounds and church buildings and religious billboards have dotted our major highways.

Chapter One | Gwamna Dogara Je'adayibe, in
Y.A. Quadri, R.W. Omotoye & R.I. Adebayo (Eds)
Religion in Contemporary Nigeria
London, Adonis & Abbey Publishers

iii. Sometimes, appointments into key positions in the political sector are determined on the basis of religious affiliation.
iv. The entertainment industry is becoming increasingly dominated by religious actors and symbols.[31]

Others include;

v. Religious attire of all shades are not only freely, but also proudly worn by Nigerians at private and public functions.
vi. At government and public functions, Nigerians open and close the programme of the day with prayers.
vii. The number of Nigerians that travel out annually for pilgrimage to Israel and Saudi Arabia is unprecedented. Thus, it is observed today that such pilgrimages have turned to big jamborees and pleasure trips devoid of spiritual renewal and divine encounter.
viii. Cars and lorries are often decorated with religious posters, inscriptions and images.

Other Nigeria's religious credentials and manifestations in the public space include:

i. The Redeemed Christian Church of God led by Pastor Dr. E.A. Adeboye, which has gathered the most believers in one location in the history of the church, an estimated seven million people.[32] Its Holy Ghost Annual Congress has continued to attract people around the world.
ii. Pastor Matthew Ashimolowo of Kings International Christian Centre (KICC), a Nigerian, leads one of the largest Pentecostal churches in Europe.

iii. Pastor Sunday Adelaja of the Embassy of the Blessed God for All Nations, Kiev, Ukraine, is leading a revolutionary transformation in Ukraine.
iv. Nigeria has a vibrant, large Christian presence in Africa with potential of shaping African Christianity in the future. All these are positive attributes of religion which need to be appropriated in Nigeria for its transformation.

Nigeria's external show of religiousity has been criticised as mere show of religion and spirituality, similar to the Pharisaic posturing of Jesus' day, which he condemned. In Matthew 23:1ff, Jesus described the Pharisees and the teachers of the law in many ways. He referred to them as a people who do not do what they preached (23:3). People who loved to be greeted in the market places and to have men call them "Rabbi" (23:7), as is of some religious leaders today who cherish big titles of "Arch Bishop," "General Overseer," "Founder," "Ustaz," "Sheikh," "Mallam," "Rev. Dr," and so on. The Pharisees became stumbling blocks to others, "who shut the kingdom of heaven in men's faces, you yourselves do not enter, nor will you let those who are trying to" (23:14). They were called hypocrites. They were "blind guides," namely, they were a people who majored on minor things ignoring the essentials of true religion such as love, acts of mercy and justice (23:23). They were "blind fools" (23:17), "white washed tombs," full of decay and dead men's bones (23:27). They were called "brood of vipers" (23:33). Such vices described above apply to many religious leaders today in Nigeria who have simply criminalised religion.

Reflecting on this problem, Odumuyiwa wondered why Nigeria could be a religious society but criminal at the same time. He identified main crimes in our religious society such as:

i. Adherents of all religions who fail to practise the tenets of their religions, and they demonstrate love for materialism at all cost; and
ii. Bad example from religious leaders.[33]

Odumuyiwa elaborated further on crimes committed by religious leaders and stated:

> Apart from cases of embezzlement of church, mosques or shrines' money which are common to all religious institutions and denominations, leaders also lobby for high positions in their various establishments through foul means such as – application of magical spells on their colleagues, taking such people's lives through poisoning or by maligning others through character assassination and perpetuating a lot of acts of man's inhumanity to man.[34]

Another face of religion in Nigeria is the commercialisation of religion. For example, it is perceived that to establish a Church today is an easy way towards wealth acquisition. Thus, Nigeria has witnessed the proliferation of religious institutions and the rise of religious functionaries, some, who have abandoned their original vocations and training in fields such as banking, medicine, teaching and so on, in order to establish and be head of churches. Similarly, religion has turned into a big business venture as sundry charges in form of tithes, offerings, sowing seed, and so on, are believed to attract blessings. Agang reflects on this scenario thus:

> Economic corruption stands at the centre of ethnic, religious, and political struggles in Nigeria. Thus, it is not only the politicization of religion or the mixing of religion with absolute truth claims, that is the reason for violence in Nigeria, but also the commercialization of religion.[35]

Today, what Max Romeo, the reggae musician sang of religion about three decades ago, is true of Nigeria. He had rendered the following: "Stealing, stealing, stealing, stealing in the name of the Lord. My Father's house of worship has become the den of thieves, stealing in the name of the Lord."

Thus, it could be asserted that because religion is being commercialised in Nigeria with all the sundry charges, this has further impoverished the already poverty – striken religious adherents. However, Ghandi's caution is relevant here who said, "oppression of people in the name of God is the worst form of oppression."[36]

We are witnesses today of false men of God who masquerade as angels of light but are wolves in sheep's clothing (2 Cor 11:14). We have miracle merchants, magicians, swindlers and charlatans who in the name of "anointing," have cheated unsuspecting public. In the name of politics, Boko Haram has turned religion into a chess game for criminal and ungodly (anti-religious) propaganda and manipulative rhetoric.

While some scholars see manipulation of religion in Nigeria, others see "deliberate manoeuvre of religion," which involves to move, work, negotiate, steer, guide, direct, and manipulate persons or things with dexterity.[37] Manipulation of religion involves some level of masquerading under religion. In other words, religion serves as a smokescreen by its manipulators while the real "conflict entrepreneurs" and sponsors hide behind the scenes. These have negative effects on development and transformation of Nigeria.

Religion as Tool for National Transformation

This section looks at religion as a tool for national transformation by posing pertinent questions: How can there be national transformation when religion has become a factor of conflict, division and war? How can there be national

Chapter One	Gwamna Dogara Je'adayibe, in
	Y.A. Quadri, R.W. Omotoye & R.I. Adebayo (Eds)
	Religion in Contemporary Nigeria
	London, Adonis & Abbey Publishers

transformation when religious leaders dine and wine with corrupt leaders and who have become gullible to stolen national wealth? How can there be national transformation when religion is easily manipulated and has been politicised and ethnicised by politicians and elites? How can there be national transformation when religion has become a tool for provocation and incitement by its leaders?

National transformation has become a popular catchword in Nigeria's public space today. According to Wale Oyemakinde,

> Transformation is a complete change. It denotes about turn, total twist or full scale, full circle. Transformation is about turning over to a new leaf, a new life, a new order, a new way, a new style, a new strategy, a new look, a new view, a new form, a new dispensation.[38]

Transformation involves an experience of a new beginning. It involves abandoning things that are no longer valuable or relevant.

Based on the indices we have presented in the foregoing discourse on Nigeria, the need for transformation becomes pertinent. In visioning such a transformation in Nigeria, Movement for Nigeria's Total Transformation (MNTT), anticipates "a rebirth of a new nation, where the rule of law, justice, fair play, peace and stability will be minimum conditions for social relations."[39] Fatubarin sees such a transformation as involving a holistic change, change of leadership, change of follower-ship, change for appropriate orientation; change in our politics and governance and change to godliness and holiness.[40]

Kukah has noted rightly too, that religion is "like a double edged sword."[41] Like Janus - faced phenomenon, religion is like water, it heals but it also drowns.[42] One could say that with reference to Nigeria, religion has played the negative role of almost drowning its adherents. And like snake, it has proven to be a venom that is also deadly. But religion has positive quality in which Nigeria could enjoy certain dividends, such as peace, justice, prosperity, and good governance.[43]

The contribution of faith-based Universities in Nigeria today has projected the positive image and contribution that religion could play towards national transformation. The contributions of such Universities have helped to restore functional education in Universities in Nigeria, promoted academic excellence, stabilised academic calendar, reduced strikes and brain drain, among others.[44] Universities worthy of mention include, Babcock University, Ilishan, Covenant University, Otta, Joseph Ayo Babalola University (JABU), Bowen University, Iwo, Salem University, Lokoja, Bingham University, Karu, among others.

Today, Pentecostal churches are positively impacting people's lives through social engagements motivated by religious beliefs and values in areas such as addressing urban problems of unemployment, boys and girls who are social deviants, drug addicts, armed robbers, and commercial sex workers. Others include, poverty alleviation programmes, provision of water, rehabilitation and construction of roads and provision of health services (free drugs, and counselling), new emphasis on leadership training and collaboration with government to combat corruption and the promotion of good governance.[45]

The *Save Nigeria Group* led by Pastor Tunde Bakare, a Pentecostal preacher turned politician, had organised demonstrations against corruption; bad leadership and removal of oil subsidy in Nigeria. The Catholic Bishops Conference of Nigeria have consistently drawn the attention of government towards national socio-economic and political issues that will propel Nigeria towards development, peace and

---

Chapter One | Gwamna Dogara Je'adayibe, in
Y.A. Quadri, R.W. Omotoye & R.I. Adebayo (Eds)
Religion in Contemporary Nigeria
London, Adonis & Abbey Publishers

stability, which are ingredients of national transformation. Thus, the recently launched Christian campaign on social transformation by the Christian Association of Nigeria (CAN), is an example which illustrates this point further. Outside Pentecostal and Christian circles are also other religious bodies and agencies who are similarly involved in intervention in areas of health, education and other projects that need to be encouraged and sustained.

National transformation cannot take place in Nigeria until people experience a national cleansing of the heart which comes only from God. 11 Chronicles 7:14 says "If my people who are called by my name will humble themselves and pray and seek my face, and turn from their wicked ways, then I will hear from heaven and will forgive their sin and will hear their land."

In a country like Nigeria where sin has reached unprecedented heights, only humble submission to God in repentance can bring forgiveness and healing in the land. In a country that has suffered division, ethnic strife and religious conflicts, only God's healing can restore the land and bring reconciliation and peace. Proverbs 14:34 says, "righteousness exalts a nation, but sin is a disgrace to any people."

True national transformation requires that we seek and to do justice in the society. Amos 5:24 says; "but let justice roll like a river, righteousness like a never failing stream." There is the need also to allow religion to play its revolutionary role in the Nigerian society towards national transformation. Here, the example of Pope John Paul II in Poland, Lech Walesa in Poland, Ayatollah Khomeini in Iran; and Bishop Desmond Tutu in South Africa, among others easily come to mind. These men used religion positively to lead their countries towards human dignity, development and reconciliation.

Others include, Catholic Arch Bishop Christopher Munzihirwa in Zaire who opposed Mobutu Sese Seko; Arch Bishop Luwum who opposed Idi Amin of Uganda; Catholic Arch Bishop Michael Francis in Liberia who opposed Samuel Doe; Charles Taylor and Prince Johnson; and Anglican Primate Makuba Gitari in Kenya who opposed Arap Moi.[46] We need prophetic voices in Nigeria today, namely people who are God's watchmen and not wind bags who will speak against the evils of corruption, bad governance, abuse of human rights and other societal vices. The need of the moment is to confront evil through prophetic voices which is consistent with the Biblical witness (2 Kings 13:18-22).

Nigeria needs to appropriate teachings from the various religions towards good governance in order to propel it towards greatness. We need to also develop values of transformation based on religious principles of hardwork, integrity, service, truth and accountability, which are true hallmarks of developing nations such as Malaysia, South Korea, Japan, India, China, Indonesia and Brazil, among others.

Conclusion

Religion in Nigeria has huge potentials for national transformation if properly its resources are properly harnessed and contextualised. Religion could be used to mobilise its large followership towards a revolutionary transformational agenda for national development. But religion can only play such positive role if it is removed from the corruption influences that have affected it and de-masked from its present posturing. For this to happen, both adherents of religions in Nigeria and their leaders need to exhibit sincere commitment to religious beliefs and teachings which promote values of human solidarity and common good, for a truly national transformation. This also involves that religious adherents live by what their religions teach. This is a practical way by which religion will be seen as a veritable tool for Nigeria's transformation devoid of its present posture.

References

1. Arch Bishop John Onaiyekan, "Dividends of Religion in Nigeria," Public Lecture Delivered at the University of Ilorin, 12 May, 2010, 2.
2. S.A. Nigosian, *World Religions,* (Edward Arnold, London, 1981), 2-3.
3. Ronald E. Miller, "Religion and Religions," Frank W. Klos, et al, *Lutherans and the Challenges of Religious Pluralism,* (Augsburg Fortress, Minneapolis, 1990), 3.
4. Roland E. Miller, "Religion and Religions," 4.
5. Gerrie ter Haar, "Religion: Source of Conflict or Resource for Peace?," Philip Ostein, et al (eds.), *Comparative Perspectives on Shariah in Nigeria,* (Spectrum Books Ltd, Ibadan, 2005), 309.
6. Arch Bishop John Onaiyekan, "Dividends of Religion in Nigeria," p.44.
7. Chinua Achebe, *There Was a Country: A Personal History of Biafra,* (Penguin Books, London, 2012), 2.
8. Ayo Fatubarin, *The Church and the Imperative of Change in Nigeria,* (Keynote Publishers Ltd, Ilesa, 2010), 3-4.
9. Karl Maeir, *This House Has Fallen,* (Penguin Books, London, 2000).
10. Peter Awelewa Adebiyi, *Let the Nations Hear,* (The Book Company, Lagos, 2012).
11. Ayo Fatubarin, *The Church and the Imperative of Change in Nigeria,* 4.

12. Michael Peel, *A Swamp Full of Dollars: Pipeline and Paramilitants at Nigeria's Oil Frontier,* (Bookcraft, Ibadan, 2009), xxii.
13. Matthew Hassan Kukah, "Pastors With Private Jets and Embarrassment – Bishop Kukah," *The Nation on Sunday,* (Nov. 18, 2012c), 4.
14. Cosmas Illechukwu, *Transformation Leadership: An Effective Tool For Nation Building,* (Fourthman Creations, Lagos, 2011), 29.
15. John Campbell, *Nigeria: Dancing on the Brink,* (Bookcraft, Ibadan, 2010), 138.
16. John Campbell, *Nigeria: Dancing on the Brink,* 137.
17. Chinua Achebe, *There Was a Country,* 205.
18. Chinua Achebe, *There Was a Country,* 251.
19. Danny McCain, "Mission in a Troubled World: Challenging the Church in Africa to Respond," A Paper Presented to the Theological Educators in Africa (TEA) Conference, Theological College of Northern Nigeria (TCNN), (Bukuru, 14th May, 2012), 3.
20. Bill Houston, "The Paradox of Impoverished Africa," *Ogbomosho Journal of Theology* (OJOT) Vol. XIV, 2009, p.11. see also, Chinua Achebe, *There Was a Country,* 249.
21. Peter Awelewa Adebiyi, *Let the Nations Hear,* 240.
22. Danny McCain, "Mission in a Troubled World", 4.
23. Arch Bishop John Onaiyekan, "Dividends of Religion in Nigeria," 2.
24. Peter Awelewa Adebiyi, *Let the Nations Hear,* 48.
25. Quoted in Michael Peel, *A Swamp Full of Dollars,* xxi.
26. Peter Cuncliffe-Jones, *My Nigeria: Five Decades of Independence,* Palmgrave Mcmillan, New York, 2010, 165.
27. Peter Awelewa Adebiyi, *Let the Nations Haer,* 263.
28. John Campbell, *Nigeria: Five Decades of Independence,* 185.
29. Chinua Achebe, *There Was a Country,* 249.

30. Anthony Akinwale, "Denunciation, Deconstruction and Reconstruction: Theology at the Service of Church and Society, *Ogbomosho Journal of Theology,* (Vol. XVI No. 3, 2011), 16.
31. Matthew A. Ojo, "When Did Things Fall Apart?: Reflection on Religion, Spirituality and Socio-Political Experience in Contemporary Nigeria," Onah Odey (ed.) *Religion and Nigeria Today,* (A Publication of Nigerian Association for the Study of Religion, 2010), 13-14.
32. Loren Cunnigham and Janice Rogers, *The Book That Transforms Nations,* (YWAM Publishing, Seattle, 2007), 167.
33. E. Ade Odumuyiwa, "A Religious But Criminal Society: Any Remedy?," 19th Inaugural Lecture, (Olabisi Onabanjo University, Ago-Iwoye, 2001), 8.
34. E. Ade Odumuyiwa, "A Religious But Criminal Society: Any Remedy?," 13.
35. Sunday Bobai Agang, *The Impact of Ethnic, Political, and Religious Violence on Northern Nigeria, and a Theological Reflection on Its Healing, Langham,* (Carlisle, 2011), 46.
36. Paulins Ike Ogara, *Nigeria Must Survive,* (Life Apostolate Publications, Enugu, 2011), 127.
37. S. Awoniyi, "De-Emphasizing Fanaticism in Religion as a Way of Re-Designing Nigerian Society," Ayantayo, Jacob K. (ed.) *Religion and Governance in Nigeria,* (Ibadan, 2012), 186.
38. Wale Oyemakinde, *Transformation,* (Sunlight Syndicate Ventures, Ibadan, 2012), 1.
39. *Movement For Nigeria's Total Transformation (MNTT): Its Origin and Growth and Vision and its Goals,* (Ibadan, undated), 3.
40. Ayo Fatubarin, *The Church and the Imperative of Change in Nigeria,* 15-22.

Chapter One	Gwamna Dogara Je'adayibe, in Y.A. Quadri, R.W. Omotoye & R.I. Adebayo (Eds) Religion in Contemporary Nigeria London, Adoris & Abbey Publishers

41. Matthew Hassan Kukah, "The Janus Face of Religion," Constance Chiogo Ikokwu, *Nigeria: Half a Century of Progress and Challenges,* 1st Edition, (Five Express Press, 2011a), 25.
42. Matthew Hassan Kukah, "The Janus Face of Religion," 26.
43. Arch Bishop John Onaiyekan, "Dividends of Religion in Nigeria," 26.
44. Godwin N.D. Aja and Sampson M. Nwaomah, *Private Unversity Education in Africa: Issues and Challenges,* (Babcock University Press, Ilishan-Remo, 2012).
45. Danny McCain, "Addressing Urban Problems Through Kingdom Theology: The 'Apostles in the Market Place' Model in Lagos, Nigeria," (Paper Presented in Padova, Italy, 7th June, 2012b), 3-13.
46. Stan Chu Ilo, *The Face of Africa: Looking Beyond the Shadows,* (Spectrum Books Ltd, Ibadan, 2008), 366.

CHAPTER TWO

Issues and Challenges of Religion in Nigeria in the 21st Century

Akande, Lydia Bosede
Department of Islamic, Christian, and Comparative Religious Studies,(ICCRS) Kwara State University, Malete.
Kwara State, Nigeria.
lydia.akande@kwasu.edu.ng
+2348135448801, +2348056712854

Introduction

Issues relating to religions, be it Christianity, Islam or African religion, in the development of any nation, cannot be ignored. It is in line with this opinion that this chapter examines the level of sincerity of Nigerians about religious commitment. Attempts are made to look at the historical evolution of Nigeria as a nation vis-à-vis the various indecent behaviours which had made the country to become a threat not only to her citizens but also to the international community. It is indeed an irony for a nation that is acclaimed as religious to continue to wallow in the ocean of all forms of indecency like drug trafficking, prostitution, bombing, internet frauds, etc. It also discusses how religion can be a catalyst for a decent Nigerian society and the challenges for the future.

Much of Nigeria's early history is contained in myths and legends.[1] The frame work that now bears Nigeria existed as an heterogeneous society,consisting of powerful kingdoms and regions.[2] Before her amalgamation in 1914, in 1898 in an article in the *Times Newspaper*, Flora Shaw, was said to have suggested that, the various British protectorates in the Niger be collectively called Nigeria[3]. Thus Nigeria assumed her name.

On 1st October 1960, Nigeria became independent politically as a result of the efforts of nationalists such as Herbert Macaulay, Tafawa Balewa, Obafemi Awolowo, and a host of others. The country became a Republic on 1st October, 1963, with Nnamdi Azikwe as the first president of the new nation.[4]

However, since independence, Nigeria has been ruled by various leaders of different political and religious backgrounds, some of whose regimes have been characterized with series of indecencies and woes, ranging from lack of the fear of God, economic malpractices, corruption of various degrees and lack of knowledge and purpose, thus causing the nation to sink into economic, political and religious jeopardy as contained in the words of Buah:

> The leaders placed regional interests above the common good of the country as a whole. The chief concern of several of these men was to amass wealth at the expense of the ordinary people[5]

The level of indecency and corruption experienced in the country in the first republic was insignificant compared to that being witnessed in the 21st century. A critical assessment of the country's political scene suggests or reveals that majority of the leaders assume office with an intention and opportunity to amass wealth for themselves at the expense of the poor or the less privileged. Ango Abdullahi opined that:

> No doubt corruption has eaten deep into the fabric of Nigerian Society, so much so that it is at present one of the obstacles to national development. Corruption in its various manifestations and ramifications can be described as less purity in the minds and actions of Nigerians.[6]

From the religious perspective, Nigeria is a multi-religious society with three officially-recognised religions, namely: African Religion, Islam and Christianity. Each religion is contributing its quota to the political, social, economic, educational and religious developments of the country. But despite the religious outlook of Nigerians, the lives of her citizenry do not reflect a religious society. In this regard, Christianity and other religions have a lot of challenges to face in order to make the nation a decent place for everyone to live.

Are Nigerians Truly Religious? Issues for Discussion

The fact remains that Nigerians are religious. But how sincere are they in the practices of these religions? Different denominations and sects exist in each of these religions; thus reasonable number of Nigerian populace claim to be religious people.

As religious people, Nigerians strongly believe in the sovereignty and supremacy of the Almighty God, to whom prayers, offerings, supplications and sacrifices are offered. The Christians, Muslims and Afrelists attach great importance to all these aspects of their religious practices. Different types of prayers and fasting are offered on different occasions depending on the prevailing circumstances. These include organised prayers in crusades, Sunday or Jumat worships, all night vigils and prayers on mountains. Worship centres such as Churches, Mosques, Shrines, hired shops or primary school classrooms for religious activities are very many in the country. For instance, more than five different churches can be found in one building. Religious stickers are easily and conspicuously sighted on cars, Holy Books, shops and buildings. Fasting during Ramadan period as well as religious holidays are observed, while large numbers of faithful Christians and

Muslims turn out yearly to perform the holy pilgrimages to Jerusalem and Mecca, becoming JP (Jerusalem Pilgrim) or Alhaji and Alhaja as the case may be. Visits to various camp meetings such as Christ Apostolic Church Camp ground at Ikeji, Osun State or at Odo-owa, Redeemer, Mountain of Fire and Miracles and Deeper Life camp grounds, enable one to behold very large crowd of worshippers joyfully attending to their religious obligations. Supporting this view, Onishi opined that:

> Christianity is growing faster in sub-saharan Africa than in any other place on earth. Roman Catholicism and the major protestant denominations are gaining more followers everyday but new Churches are leading the boom.[7]

Most Christian families observe daily family altars where prayers are offered and the Bible read. Civil Servants in government offices now have specified day(s) of prayer meetings. Churches and Mosques are filled on Sundays and Fridays with worshippers. Registration of new Churches is on the increase as stated by the Ministry of Internal Affairs in *Sunday Vanguard* of January 18th, 1987 that "Churches spring daily having broken up from the established ones".[8] Religious consciousness of Nigerians is encouraging. Religious exclamations like 'Praise the Lord' and 'Thank you Jesus', are not farfetched. Supporting this consciousness of Nigerians great and small, rich and poor, Rev. Fr. George Ehusani said:

> In the last few years, a new dimension has also been added to the thriving religious enterprise. It is the increase in patronage of high ranking public officials who not only openly call for and sponsor regular prayers sessions in different prayer houses, but have themselves become born-again Christians and prayer merchants, often appearing at Church Crusades and Prayer vigils with all the paraphernalia of public office, and sometimes grabbing sanctimonious homilies and earth-shaking prayers.[9]

He went further to say:

> The largest billboards in our towns and cities are those advertising upcoming religious crusades and faith healing carnivals. Religious exclamations such as 'To God be the glory,' 'Praise The Lord', and 'Alaahu Akbar', are often on the lips of Nigerians, at work or at play from the exalted members of the National Executive Council or Council of State, to the young ones who are about to sit for common Entrance Examination[10].

Hence, from all indications, Nigerians are seen to be religious. Through the stages of life religious doctrines are observed and recognised. Religious songs and choruses of various types are not far from the lips of all and sundry. It can therefore be said that in all things they are religious. However, despite the entire religious outlook that Nigerians project to the outside world, it is ironic that, religious commitment of the people is below one's expectation. It is difficult to turn those religious teachings into action. According to Nural Alkali:

> Nigeria has claimed to be among the most religious people in the world. In a recent survey conducted by the British Broadcasting Corporation, Nigeria topped the list of the countries having the highest percentage of people who believe in God, compared to 46% in the United Kingdom and only 28% in South Korea. Yet, the 2004 report of Transparency International, the Berlin based global corruption watchdog, showed that Nigeria has still maintained its permanent position as the second most corrupt country in the world after Bangladesh.[11]

Selected Social Problems in the 21st Century

A very close look at the following corrupt practices among Nigerians contradicts in totality their religious protestation. These include religious violence especially among the Christians and Muslims and the contradiction of the law of love in both the Bible and Qur'an (Hebrews 13:1, Qur'an 41: 34)

Lawal and Oyebanjo also supported this view by saying that:

> Conflicts and intolerance in religions pose a lot of danger to the lives of the people of the world in general and to Nigerians in particular which is against the teachings of the two major religions namely Christianity and Islam.[12]

Badmus further observes that "both Islam and Christianity lay down very clear and adequate regulations, if these were strictly adhered to, there would be no case of bloody clashes during preaching sessions".[13]

Pilgrims to the holy lands being involved in drug trafficking, money laundering, prostitution, advanced fee fraud, and child trafficking are on the increase. In some towns or cities, particular streets are associated with these acts. They are either Christians or Muslims. Even housewives, in order to make ends meet, get involved in these shameful practices. Arowosegbe says it succinctly thus:

> Every street of our cities is now flooded with brothels completely full of whores that have sent many men into perpetual sufferings ranging from gonorrhea, herpes, syphilis and to the most dreadful of all sexual diseases called Acquired Immune Deficiency Syndrome (AIDS).[14]

In addition, Nigerians are subjected to rigorous bodily searches at foreign airports as a result of the bad image the country has. Other nations see Nigerians as experts in burning places of worship and killing of fellow human beings during religious riots. Kidnapping of human beings for rituals is on the increase. A story was told on the Nigerian Television Authority on the popular Sunday Network programme 'News Line' by Kehinde Young Harry on Sunday 10th June, 2007 by 9:00pm, of how some men deceived a seven-year old boy to a sugarcane plantation and plucked out his eyes in an attempt to use them for rituals, rendering the boy blind for life.

In addition, cases of ministers employing magic to aid the work of God abound. Bilikisu Yusuf buttressed this point thus:

> This has fuelled the competition among prosperity preachers who in a bid to meet the aspirations of worshippers, mix ancient paganism with Christianity, they then coin agnatic messages like faith, prosperity, healing and deliverance and more and more people fervently besieged the churches for miracles and excessive urge for wealth and materialism[15].

Illicit affair between Pastors and female members of the Church is also prevalent. *The Nigerian Tribune* of Tuesday 16th January, 2007 reported Pastor of a Pentecostal Church in Awka, Anambra State who raped a 13year old member of his Church and impregnated her[16]. This is just one of the many cases of atrocities perpetrated by supposed Ministers. This was further confirmed by a former herbal healer who is now a pastor during one of his confessions:

> I have seen many things since I came in. I have seen many of the Pastors who have taken female members to different churches at midnight and made love to them for various reasons, at times, occult. Some use their churches as a base for 419 activities; many used occult and questionable powers[17].

Public officers of various cadres see embezzlement and misappropriation of public funds as the order of the day, using such stolen funds to seek important positions in the church. Related to this is the fact that, many Christians and Muslims holding one title or post in churches or mosques are involved in fraudulent acts including obtaining fake receipts for items not bought and falsifying their ages in order to stay longer in service.

Examination malpractice and cultism too have become the order of the day at all levels of our educational system. Akande submitted that:

> Cultism among youths in Nigeria has become a popular discussion in the contemporary Nigerian society. It is one of the most important social problems experienced in Nigerian educational set up. The youths have always been in the core of it. This is incredible[18].

Unfortunately, parents who are supposed to be responsible are initiators of some of these evils. Similarly, counterfeiting in drugs, food and spare parts are other evils perpetrated by some Nigerians. This of course has led to the premature deaths of many innocent Nigerians. Idleness and procrastination in places of work are common. Kumuyi observed that the "tasks are not carried out until such officers in charge are tipped off."[19] These and many others are the ungodly practices that the Holy Books frown at. For instance, Jeremiah 22:13 says "Woe unto him that buildeth his homes by unrighteousness, and his chambers by wrong: that useth his neighbour's service without wages, and gives him not for his work".

In addition to the aforementioned is the fact that Nigeria has been turned to a great asylum of human misery courtesy of Jean-Martin, the 19th century French Physician. "419", and Boko Haram, have become household names. Our daily news is full of reports of ethnic or communal clashes. Nigerians do not practise "to love tenderly, to do justice, and to walk humbly before your God" as commanded by Micah 6:8. Cases of armed robbery on high ways, banks, homes, Churches and Mosques abound almost every day. Traveling on roads has become dreadful not only at night but even in the day time. Having a child outside wedlock has become the normal practice in order to ascertain how fertile a woman is

Chapter Two	Akande, Lydia Bosede, in Y.A. Quadri, R.W. Omotoye & R.I. Adebayo (Eds) Religion in Contemporary Nigeria London, Adonis & Abbey Publishers

before she is lawfully married; a practice that is contrary to the teachings of Christianity and Islam. Sometimes a woman who is pregnant is joined to a man in a so-called Holy wedlock when the Bible clearly states in Hebrews 13:4 that "Marriage is honorable in all, and the bed undefiled...". If God's judgment is to be instant, many Nigerians both great and small who constantly exclaimed 'somebody shout Alleluia'; 'The Lord is good' and 'salam Alaikum' would have learnt their lesson in a hard way. But God is merciful and slow to anger. How can a nation recognised as very religious, be involved in all these vices when the three religions practised in the country teach people to love, respect human life and the constituted authorities?

Possible Solutions

The religious scenario in the present day Nigerian society is full of uncertainties. Issues related to these uncertainties have been highlighted. It therefore follows that Christianity and other religions more than ever before must stand up to face the challenges. They must sincerely commit themselves to the task of redeeming Nigeria and her citizens. Such a task involves the following steps:

(a) Placing adequate emphasis on the importance of worship in all religions is a vital challenge to all religious leaders and followers. For instance, the five pillars of Islam centre round the worship of Allah. These pillars are:

i. Testifying that there is no God but Allah and that Muhammad is His messenger.
ii. Performing prayers regularly (*Salat*)
iii. Paying the poor-rate (*Zakat*)
iv. Fasting during the month of Ramadan (*Sawm*) and

v.   Pilgrimage to the sacred sanctuary of Allah (*Hajj*) [20].

In African Religion, fear of God, reverence for God, sacrifices, festivals and prayers of different forms to divinities and the Supreme Being are important features of African Religion.[21] Also in Christianity, the belief in one God, Charity, Fasting and Prayers, love for God and one's fellow men[22] are principles which its adherents must adopt. The concept of worship in the three religions connote similar meanings. It thus follows that without worship, there is no religion, because worship forms a strong pillar of any true and worthy religion. Hence, when Nigerian Christians, Muslims or Afrelist are sincerely committed to their various modes of worship, Nigeria will develop.

(b)   Similar to the above is the fact that religious bodies should embark on very sound and intensive religious teachings instead of glorying in daily increase in the number of religious buildings and laying emphasis on prosperity-based sermons, thus commercialising religion. No wonder Kelly Elisha says that: "Religious leaders are doing contrary to the teachings of religions"[23].

Religious leaders today must rise up with vision and mission which should be noted in the desire to meet the challenges facing the masses. They must be pragmatic, committed and ever ready to work hard for social and economic development of Nigeria. Stephen Audu believes that:

> Leadership position is an opportunity to serve towards achieving a set objective. In Christian leadership, the leader is modeled after the example of Christ who came, not to be served, but to serve. Those aspiring for political leadership must know that authority is to be used to render qualitative service to citizens. Thus, authority should be exercised in love, justice, compassion and the fear of the Lord.

Authority and power are meant to be used to improve the welfare of the people not to impoverish them through plundering of available resources[24].

(c) Another task for religious bodies to undertake is that they should be bold enough to expose corrupt leaders and guide their followers against voting for them. Their followers should be encouraged to vote for credible leaders. The Bible, for instance, calls the Christians the light and salt of the earth (Matthew 5:13 and 14). These values of light, salt, love, selfless services, justice and equality should be reflected in every segment of Nigerians' lives. Christians, especially must stop calling politics a dirty game. If truly the game is dirty, then God expects them to join and make it clean, thereby renewing and transforming the hope of the poor and suffering Nigerians for good.

Prophet Amos in his book says "Let justice roll down like waters, and righteousness like an ever – flowing stream" (Amos 5:24). The scripture further says "righteousness exalts a nation, but sin is a reproach". This Biblical injunction therefore proves that meaningful development in Nigeria cannot be achieved through corrupt, greedy and evil-minded leaders or politicians; it can only be attained through Nigerians who are always conscious of the religious values they profess.

(d) Poverty, which has eaten deep into the fabric of Nigerian culture should be addressed not only by the government, but more importantly by the religious bodies. The causes of many of these societal vices could be traced to poverty. It needs to be noted that government is making commendable efforts in this regard through her many poverty-alleviation programmes such as "National Poverty Eradication Programme (NAPEP); Family Economic Advance Programme (FEAP), Federal Government Poverty Alleviation

Programme(PAP), and National Directorate of Employment (NDE). Akande said:

> All these programmes are arranged to eradicate poverty in Nigeria. Youths are mainly involved. Through these governmental efforts, many have been able to set up their business and become self employed, thus reducing the number of those searching for jobs.[25]

To complement Government's effort, religious bodies too must rise up to the challenges. It must be noted that some religious groups or denominations are making frantic efforts in this regard. Many of them have set up charitable homes to cater for the less-privileged, the welfare unit of most Churches and other Muslim bodies are working vigorously to rid Nigerians of all forms of poverty by offering assistance in form of finances, clothing and food. Visitations to the prison yards on regular basis for evangelism are part of these efforts. So also is the building of mission hospitals and schools by the various religious bodies. This step by the religious bodies agrees with what Apata said:

> Alleviating the condition of the poor must be in the practical sense. The Church has men who can do it successfully. The Lawyers, Engineers, Economists, Teachers and Politicians in the Church do not only have to be men of religion but also of Godliness. The Nigerian Society is of widespread poverty and outrage against human and dignity and freedom. The root causes of all these must be probed so that overcoming the evil will be easy.[26]

The danger inherent in a nation that is poverty-stricken can be expressed in the words of John F. Kennedy that, "if the poor cannot sleep because they are hungry, the rich cannot sleep because the poor are awake".[27] It is to this effect that every hand must be on deck. The task must be carried out by all and sundry - the government, religious bodies, NGOs and even individual Nigerians.

(e) The diligence, integrity, dedication, loyalty and devotion manifested by some characters in the Bible and Qur'ān should pose challenges to all. We must be honest, dutiful, dependable and loyal in our places of work showing forth the religious virtues we profess. It is only in this way that Nigerians can beautify and project to the whole world that they are truly religious.

(f) Parents must endeavour to inculcate religious ideals into their children from the cradle. These children are future leaders who will grow to handle the socio-economic, political and religious affairs of the nation. If they are not properly brought up religiously, they may be led away from the religious virtues by their peers, bad magazine, and even the daily advancement in technology. Hence, all efforts must be made to get a child's soul freed from the clutches of evil as early as possible. The Biblical injunction that says "train up a child in the way he should go and when he is old, he will not depart from it" (Proverbs 22:6) should be parents' guide.

(g) Only those of enviable and noble characters should be made to handle issues relating to the religious life of the nation. The teaching of moral education at all levels of the Nation's institutions of learning should be made compulsory. This is because "the fear of God is the beginning of wisdom" (Psalm 111:10).

Conclusion

The religious situation of Nigeria today calls for solemn reflection. In a country where unrighteousness prevails, injustice, oppression, corruption and indecency will become part of her custom. However, there is hope for a better

Nigeria if the citizens, irrespective of religious affiliations, are united and committed to hard work. This will purge or cleanse the nation of the atrocities pervading every sector of her life. Olalere is also of the opinion that, "Nigeria would be a better place to live if we are ready to cooperate with God's plan for us"[28]. Talking about a healthy Nigerian society therefore, calls for a viable political system, and better governance, which can only be facilitated if religion is practised the way it is expected to be practised.

Notes and References

1. M. Crowther, *The Story of Nigeria*, (London: Faber and Faber, 1962), 17.
2. M. Crowther, *The Story of Nigeria*.
3. F.K. Buah, *West Africa and Europe: A New History for Schools and Colleges*, (London: Macmillan Educ. Ltd., 1967), 239.
4. F.K. Buah, *West Africa and Europe*, 239
5. F.K. Buah, *West Africa and Europe*, 231
6. F. Odekunle (ed) *Nigerian: Corruption in Development*, (Ibadan: University Press, 1982), 9
7. New York Times, March 13th, 2002.
8. *Sunday Vanguard*, January 18th, 1987, 25
9. G. Ehusani, *Challenges for the Church in the 21st Century*. (Retrieved 7th March 2014) from http://georgeehusani.org/challenges for the church.
10. G. Ehusani, *Challenges for the Church in the 21st Century*.
11. N. Alkali, "Religion and Hypocrisy in a Decadent Society: A Case Study of Nigeria, *National Pilot*, (Monday 29th – Wednesday 31st May, 2006), 32.

12. L. Manzor A and Oyebanjo, O. O. *"Causes and Effects of Religious Intolerance in Nigerian Society"* A paper presented at the National Annual Conference of the National Association for the Study of Religions and Education (NASRED) (Abeokuta: 2006), 3
13. M. A. Bidmos, *Inter-Religious Dialogues: The Nigeria Experience*, (Lagos: Irede Printers, 1993), 17-30
14. I. K. Arowosegbe, "Prostitution in Nigeria", (*Sunday Tribune*, May 2nd, 1993), 3
15. B. Yusuf, "Corruption and Religious Institutions: The Score Board" in Ayodele Aderinwale (ed), *Corruption, Accountability and Transparency for Sustainable Development* (Ota: African Leadership Forum, 2007), 10.
16. *Nigerian Tribune*, "Pastor rapes, impregnates 13 year old", (Tuesday 16th January, 2007), 3.
17. B. Yusuf, "Corruption and Religious Institutions ", 186.
18. L.B. Akande, "Curbing Cultism Among Nigerian Youths: The Role of Christian Religion" in M.A. Folorunsho, I.O. Oyeneye and R.I. Adebayo (eds) *Religions and Community*, (Nigeria Association for the Study of Religion and Education, 2003), 167.
19. E.F. Kumuyi, "Seeking God's Glory on the job" in *Life Magazine for the Victorious Living*, (May 2006), 2.
20. A.R.I. Doi, *The Cardinal Principles of Islam*, (Lagos: Islamic Publications Bureau, 1974), 34-35.
21. J.S. Mbiti, *Concepts of God in Africa*, (London : SPCK. 1970)
22. B. Berkhof, *Systematic Theology*, (Michigan: W.M.B. Erdmann's Publishing Company, 1985), 19-90.
23. K.Elisha *Defection of Pilgrims*, (Lagos: Ray Power Private Radio, Nov.3.1996).
24. S. Audu "The church and the challenges of 2007 polls" in *The Guardian*, (Sunday November 19, 2006), 29.

25. L.B. Akande, "An examination of poverty in Nigeria: A Christian perspective" in P. Ade Dopamu, M.O. Adeniyi, Olalekan Dairo, Onah Odeh and Wellington O. Wutogbe Weneka (eds), *GOD: The Contemporary Discussion* (Nigeria Association for the Study of Religion (NASR), 2005), 535-536.
26. C.T. Apata, "The Nigerian church's concern for the poor :A Discussion" in Razaq 'D Abubakre, E. Ade Odumuyiwa and M.O. Opeloye (eds), *Religion and Service to Humanity,* (Nigeria Association for the Study of Religions (NASR)), 59.
27. Bolaji Akinyemi quoting John F. Kennedy in "In search of a New World Order" *Sunday Time*s August 11 2008, (Lagos: Daily Times Publication) 5.
28. O. Olalere , " Rudder" in *Nigerian Tribune*, (September 27, 1995), 6.

CHAPTER THREE

Ethnic and Religious Violence in Nigeria: A Proposal for Peaceful Co-Existence

Akinfenwa, Olubusola Bosede
*Department of Religions,
University of Ilorin, Ilorin, Nigeria*
akinfenwaolubusola@gmail.com
+2348164479208

Introduction

That Nigeria is a pluralistic society cannot be denied. This can be seen in many spheres of her national life; that is, in the multiplicity of ethnic groups, languages, culture, religion, social values and norms. Nigeria, being one of the most populous countries in Africa has so many ethnic groups. These include Hausa-Fulani, Nupe, Tiv and Kanuri in the North; Yoruba in the South-West, Igbo, Efik, Ibibio, Annang, and Ijaw in the South-East. Hausa, Igbo, and Yoruba speakers constitute the largest population in Nigeria. Three major religions in Nigeria are recognised: Islam, Christianity, and African Religion. Islam and Christianity are however the most dominant religious groups with the North and part of South-West being dominated by Muslims, while Christians dominate the South-East and South-South. The South-West contains the mixture of Muslims, Christians and adherents of African Religion. To a certain extent the three religions co-habit successfully in the South-Western part of the country.

The aim of this chapter is to trace the origin, and discuss the causes and effects, of ethnic and religious violence in Nigeria. It will also examine the role of religion in the survival of the society. It concludes on the note that religion can serve as a weapon of peace if positively used to provide lasting solution to the problem facing the society. This can only be achieved through peaceful co-existence and tolerance.

The Importance of Religion in the Survival of Human Race

Charles Kimball painted a gloomy but true picture of religion when he wrote: "It is somewhat trite, but nevertheless sadly true, to say that more wars have been waged, more people killed and these days, more evil perpetrated in the name of religion than by any other institutional force in history"[1]. This statement is true about Nigeria in the sense that religion, which is supposed to be a binding force, has now turned to a weapon of division which leads to problems such as social and political violence, insecurity and ethnicity among others. The assumption is that the tenets of most religions in the world are designed to inculcate the positive virtues of love, kindness, honesty, and forbearance in their adherents. Elements that can generate peaceful co-existence are what religions are generally known for.

The significance of religion to humanity cannot be over-emphasised. Despite the fact that religion is such a difficult word to define and understand, Dopamu opines that there is no known society where religion does not exist. From ancient days, religion has played significant roles in human understanding of the world. According to him, religion explains everything about nature and deals with all aspects of human life and activities such as history, politics, philosophy, governance, social interaction, worship and other spheres of life.[2] Above all, religion aims at the transformation of personal life through commitment to a more inclusive centre of devotion. Although countries such as Russia and China somehow opposed religion, due to the fact that they both adopted a Marxist –Leninist philosophy which rejects religion and advocates a materialist undertanding of nature, many countries give due recognition to religion. Marxism-Leninism holds that religion is an opium of the people in the sense of promoting passive acceptance of suffering on earth in the hope of eternal reward,[3] the fact remains that the existence of God cannot be denied in the universe. Religion has different connotations to different people. Although, people have expressed their views on religion from different contexts, no single definition can adequately describe the numerous religious expressions in the world.

Emile Durkheim saw religion as a "unified system of beliefs and practices relative to sacred things".[4] In Ugwu's view, religion is that part of culture composed of shared beliefs and practices which not only identify or define the supernatural and the sacred and man's relationship, but which relate them to the known world in such a way that the group is provided with moral definitions as to what is good (in harmony with the supernatural) and what is bad (contrary to the supernatural).[5]

Brein, in Akinseye maintained that religion is the whole complex of attitudes, convictions, emotions, gestures, rituals, beliefs and institution by which we come to terms with God and express our fundamental relationship with reality (God and the created order). Whoever is religious or guided by religious spirit is therefore expected to be disciplined, aspire after holiness and perfection and do things creditably and properly.[6]

However, An-na'im looks at religion as that which entrenches its own exclusivity. He says: (a) Religion can be defined as a system of beliefs, (b) practices, (c) institutions and relationships that is used by a community of believers to identify and distinguish itself from other communities. The feature of religion in this specific sense is the exclusivity of the community of believers, as defined by its own religious faith and practices, institutions, and relationships to identify and distinguish itself from other communitie.[7]

On the other hand, religion is fundamental in the affairs of societies and nations. Its importance is therefore emphasised by Mahatma Ghandhi when he wrote that "the role of religion is one, but in a multitude of forms".[8] To him, it is the same universal God that is being addressed in different languages, and worshipped in different communities. One of the most important variables that draw people together is the issue of religion. Religion addresses human existence and shares a concern with universal humanity. One of the characteristics of almost all religions is to consent and subscribe to certain practices such as norms, rites and culture of the people. All these have a common meeting point in the sense that they all emphasise what one must do to please his deity and society.

Globally, religion has produced a common bond of humanity, which cuts across cultural and linguistic lines. The positive influence of religion on the society cannot be over-emphasised in the sense that it has a pattern of holding people of the same faith together and bringing cohesion into the society. It also ensures social stability and provides basis for human conduct in Nigeria as a whole. These are in line with the fact that all religions claim to advocate peace and harmony in the society.[9]

Chapter Three	Akinfenwa, Olubusola Bosede, in Y.A. Quadri, R.W. Omotoye & R.I. Adebayo (Eds) Religion in Contemporary Nigeria London, Adonis & Abbey Publishers

A Chronicle of Ethnic and Religious Violence in Nigeria.

Ethnic and religious crises or conflicts are not new in Nigeria. They have been with the country since the advents of Islam and Christianity and their negative effects remain with the society till date. In Nigeria, experience shows that the incidence of religious violence has recently become a daily ritual often leading to destruction of lives and property. These conflicts are often generated by some groups either trying to impose their religious beliefs on others, or attempting to denigrate the validity and values of other people's religious beliefs. At times most of the conflicts arose from a situation whereby a particular group perceives its faith as superior to other people's faith.

Notable among the crises are: The 1981 Kaduna Polytechnic Muslim- Christian skirmishes; the Cross versus the Crescent conflict at the University of Ibadan; 1982 ethno-religious conflict of the Bulumkutu Christian-Muslim riot; 1984 Jimeta-Yola religious disturbances; ZangoKataf crises in Kaduna State; 1992 Kafanchan College of Education Muslim-Christian riots; 1996 Muslim- Christian clash during Easter procession in Ilorin and the July, 1999 crisis in Sagamu between Oro cultists and Hausa people living in the area.[10]

Also in the year 2000, Governor Ahmed Yerima of Zamfara state introduced the Islamic Legal Code (Sharia), which caused another religious crisis between the Muslims and non-Muslims in Northern Nigeria. The crisis later developed into ethnic and religious crisis between the North and the South-East and many lives and property were lost. In October, 2000 another ethnic conflict erupted between the Yoruba and Hausa people in Idi-Araba and Oko-Oba in Lagos State. The violence later spread to Kano where Southerners became the target. In September, 2001, there was an ethnic crisis between the Tiv and the Junkuns in Plateau State where about one hundred and sixty people lost their lives. In February, 2001, Muslims attacked Christians in Kachia and Walingo (Kaduna).[11]

The attack of al-Qaeda on the World Trade Centre in the United State of America in September 11, 2001 which caused the American Government to launch an offensive against the Taliban government in Afghanistan also led to another religious riot in Nigeria. Kano broke the calibrated key of gun powder in October, 2001, as some Islamic fundamentalists who felt that the United States of America had no reason to attack Afghanistan decided to set the city of Kano on fire.[12] The aforementioned ethnic and religious crises and many others have characterised national instability in Nigeria and the violence has indeed been a frightening phenomenon to development of the country in general.

Clement Sadjere opines that Nigeria is presently facing the problem of an Islamic religious sect, *Jama'atuAhlis Sunna Lidda'awati Wal-jihad* better known by its Hausa name "Boko Haram" (western education is a sacrilege or sin). It is a Jihadist terrorist organization based in the Northeast of Nigeria. It seeks to abolish the secular system of government and establish Sharia Law in Nigeria.[13] Currently, over one thousand lives have been lost due to their attacks in Nigeria. Though they claim that their target is government institutions and organisations such as security agencies, they often attack Churches, market places and tertiary institutions. Their attack includes the 2011 Christmas day church bombing in Suleja, Niger state; Kaduna and Maiduguri market bombings; and the

Bayero University, Kano church bombing on Sunday April 29th, 2012 among others.[14]

Causes of Ethnic and Religious Violence in Nigeria

Religious violence is a global crisis and Nigeria is not exempted from it. James Henslim agrees with this statement when he wrote that "history is filled with wars based on religion co-mingled with politics. Between the 11th and 14th centuries, Christian monarchs conducted nine bloody crusades in an attempt to wrest control of Jerusalem from the Muslims. Unfortunately, such wars are not just a relic of the past. Even in recent years we have seen Protestants and Catholics kill each other in Northern Ireland, while Jews and Muslims in Israel and Christians and Muslims in Bosnia have done the same thing".[15] Some of the causes of religious violence are hereby discussed below.

Intolerance

The Oxford Dictionary of Current English defines intolerance as unwillingness to let other people act in a different way or hold different opinions from one's own. It also means unwilling to accommodate ideas or behaviour that is different from one's own.[16] This is a situation where religious faithful are unwilling to accommodate the perceived lapses or excesses of others. This is common among Christians and Muslims in Nigeria in the sense that they both see their faiths as being superior to others which normally generate problems for their adherents. Lack of religious tolerance has manifested itself in various ways. The strong opposition to inter-religious marriage and the denial of people of the right of employment, etc. are the outcome of intolerance. A survey conducted among Christians and Muslims in Oyo State in 1983 revealed that there are deep rooted prejudices existing between them. Christians accuse Muslims of hard-heartedness, fanaticism, unforgiveness, filth, and other ofences, while Muslims on the other hand accuse Christians of idolatry, arrogance, deceit, and so on.[17]

Politics

Politics is also another factor that is responsible for ethnic and religious violence in Nigeria. Religion plays a significant role in the political stability of a nation including Nigeria; therefore, politics must be properly handled in order not to constitute problems for its citizens. The politicians sometimes hide behind religion to perpetrate evil and this often results in religious crises. They specialise in sponsoring misguided youths to create disturbances which often degenerate into massive conflicts among religious groups leading to death of innocent souls. Also when the politicians fail to fulfil their promises to the people, there is bound to be violence which will eventually disturb the peace and unity of the community. Religion seems to have played a significant role in creating tension in matters that appear to be purely political.

Economic Issues

The economic situation of a nation can also cause ethnic and religious violence. Nigerian Government had been accused of exploitation, domination, victimisation, oppression, discrimination, and marginalization among others. Different ethnic groups in Nigeria have diverse interests and demands which they want the government of the day to meet. Conflicts often occur in a situation where a particular group believes it is deprived of certain amenities or is being neglected. The breakdown of social amenities and increase in poverty rate can also aggravate violence and disturb the peace of the society.

Ignorance and Poverty

Majority of those who participate and play prominent roles in ethnic and religious violence are largely ignorant of the core tenets of their religions. Most of the times, the root and the cause of the conflict are totally unwarranted. Ignorance and poverty help to fuel religious-related violence. The fact that the Nigerian government has no concrete plan for the citizens in terms of basic needs such as education, health and shelter poses a serious threat to her stability, oneness and survival. There is high level of unemployment in Nigeria today and the youths are the most affected. Unemployment allows the youths to surrender themselves to be used to fuel religious and ethnic violence. Unemployment also allows the youths to be cajoled into taking steps that can lead to religious and ethnic violence. The youths are ready to maim or kill even under the guise of religion as a way of paying back the government that is totally insensitive to their legitimate needs. There is the saying that "a hungry man is an angry man" and this is true of the Nigerian situation where hunger, unemployment and other related issues are prevalent.

Abuse of Freedom of Expression and Fundamental Human Rights.

The Nigerian Constitution guarantees freedom of expression for every citizen of the country, but the freedom seems to have been abused by certain people of extreme religious conviction. In a situation where human rights are being violated or abused, there will always be religious uprising and violence. When religious groups fail to recognise and respect other faiths within the same society, there is bound to be religious crises and uproar emanating from the aggrieved groups.

Ethnic and Religious Violence in Nigeria: The Way Out

In a multi-ethnic and multi-religious society like Nigeria, religion can serve the noble role of preserving peace and bringing about the harmony that can move the country forward. This can be achieved through the following:

Poverty Alleviation

The poverty level in Nigeria today is alarming. This is caused by high rate of unemployment among youths of productive age. This calls for concern because if urgent step is not taken to reduce the poverty level to the minimal level the violence in the country will continue. Akpan Ekpo, the Director General, West African Institute for Financial and Economic Management, considered the Nigerian situation as scandalous. He wrote:

> The unemployment situation is not only disturbing but also becoming embarrassing and disgraceful. It has become a national crisis, which has to be addressed if the economy is to enjoy sustained growth and development with relative peace and security. The insecurity in the country-the spate of terrorist attacks, kidnappings, armed robbery and breakdown of law and order- is not unconnected with the high rates of unemployment, particularly among youths.[18]

Government should therefore create opportunities for gainful employment by ensuring that the educational system adopted in the country has a heavy dose of entrepreneurial training, especially at the lower level. The government also needs to create enabling environment for economic development.

Emphasis on Positive Element of Faith

The two religions (Christianity and Islam) causing violence in Nigeria should check themselves. The religious leaders should inculcate the spirit of good neighbourliness from the word of God in their adherents. There are lots of positive virtues which the adherents can imbibe if properly taught. The Imam and the Pastors should see themselves as representatives of God in the midst of the people. They should stop criticising each other and misinterpreting the holy books (Bible and Qur'an) and rather focus their attention on what they were called for.

Tolerance and Respect for Other Religions

Every individual in the society should tolerate and respect other people and their religion. All human beings cannot practise the same religion because God did not want it that way; therefore there is the need for religious tolerance and understanding in order to move the society forward. There are common elements that bind every member of the society together. All religions should be respected and the adherents should view themselves as common citizens within the boundaries of the nation. There is need for mutual understanding among adherents of different religions by using the truth found in their doctrines for the betterment of the society.

Interaction and Dialogue should be Encouraged.

The government should encourage interaction and dialogue of different religious groups. This is necessary because the government is at the centre of affairs in the country. This will allow tolerance among religious groups. Religious and moral education should be included and encouraged in schools. This will prepare the youths for the future and allow them to respect other people's religion.

Demarcation Between Politics and Religion

One of the major problems facing Nigeria as a nation is the people's inability to separate religion from politics. Religion is often used and seen as a strong weapon during politics; yet the majority of those seeking political offices are not religious. They merely use religion as a stepping stone to their destinations. If citizens can play politics without emotions and sentiments, then there will be a better society. Politicians should not be voted for on the basis of their religions but on their ability to perform in the office. President Goodluck Jonathan for instance was supported by Christians because of his religion in the April, 2011, election yet this ought not to be so.

Conclusion

This study has traced the origin and causes of religious violence in Nigeria and also examined the importance of religion in the society. Possible solutions to the problem were also discussed as there is the need for permanent solutions to religious violence in Nigeria. The Boko Haram sect seems to have taken over in the North, leaving tales of innocent people hacked to death or maimed for life. The middle-belt has become a war zone because of ethnic and religious violence that seem to have become a permanent feature there. The South-West is not at peace because the problem can spread to that region any moment. This calls for immediate concern from those in authority in order for peace to reign in Nigeria.

Notes and References

1. Charles Kimball, *When Religion Becomes Evil*, (Sam Francisco, Harper Sam Francisco, 2002), 1
2. A.P. Dopamu, "The History of the Changing Relationship Between Religion and Science" in *Confluence of Religions and Science*, Volume1, Journal of Local Societies Initiatives, (Ilorin: University Press, 2005), 1
3. Vladimir Lenin, in Novaya Zhizn, No. 28, December 3,1905, as quoted in *Maxists Internet Archive*. Religion is one of the forms of spirituality oppression which everywhere weigh down heavily upon the masses of the people.
4. Richard T Schaefer, *Sociology: A Brief Introduction*, (New York, MC Graw Hill, 2001), 309
5. C.O. Ugwu, "African Traditional religion and Culture: Relevance in Reconciliation in Nigeria" *Bulletin of African Religion and Culture*, (Akwa, NAARC, 1998), 18.
6. M. C. Brein, in Akinseye "The Place of Religion in Achieving National Integration and Cohesion: A Christian Overview, in P. E. Eya (ed), *Nigerian Journal of*

Research and Production *(NIJOREP)*, (Enugu State University of Science Press, 2002), 172.
7. David Mason, *Ethnicity and Social Division*, (London, Macmillan Publisher, 2002), 94
8. J.O. Omoregbe, *Comparative Religion: Christianity and other world Religions in Dialogue*, (Lagos, Joja Publishers, 1999), Xi
9. J.A. Glynn, & E.W. Steward, *Introduction to Sociology*, (New Jersey, Prince Town, 1981), 46
10. F.A. Akinseye, "Religion and Violence: A Christian Discourse" *in Religion and Democracy in the 21st Century*, R.A Akanmidu (ed), (NASR, 2010), 146
11. *News Watch Magazine*, (Vol. 34, No.17, October, 29th 2001), 42
12. Clement Sadjere, *Three Reasons Why Crisis is Always Occurring in Nigeria*. http//ezinearticles.com/?exper=clem entsadjere.
13. Clement Sadjere, *Three Reasons Why Crisis is Always Occurring in Nigeria*.
14. *The Nation Newspaper*, 30th April 2012, 14
15. James M Henslim, *Sociology: A Down-To-Earth Approach*, (Boston: Ally and Bacon, 1995).
16. Catherine Soanes (ed),*The Oxford Dictionary of Current English*, third edition, (Oxford University Press, New York, 2001), 477
17. R. A Akanmidu (ed), *Religion and Democracy in the 21st Century*, Adekunle Ajasin University, Akungba Akoko, (NASR, 2010), 153
18. Akpan Ekpo, "Nigeria and Its Growing Unemployment Crisis" in *Tell Magazine*, (February 21, 2011), 38.

CHAPTER FOUR

Religious Terrorism in Contemporary Nigeria: The Implication for National Development

Akinwumi, O. S.
Department of Christian Religious Studies,
College of Education, Ikere-Ekiti, Nigeria
+2349053221710; tunji.samakin@yahoo.com

&

Balogun, H. O.
Department of Islamic Studies,
ollege of Education, Ikere-Ekiti, Nigeria
+2348067824276

Introduction

In recent times, Nigeria has been tagged a Security-risk nation[1]. This has prompted the international communities to warn their nationalities not to live in or even travel to the country[2]. A critical examination of the present security situation in Nigeria reveals that the country is a "danger zone". In fact, one might be tempted to agree with these international communities. The various cases of religious intolerance, fanaticism and terrorism in different parts of the country, most especially the present Boko Haram imbroglio portend danger for the nation.

This Chapter examines how religious terrorism has negatively affected the overall development of this nation. This implies that religion in Nigeria no longer serves as a medium for moderating relationships and conflicts. Religion that ought to serve as "hiding place", a kind of city of refuge for the believers, has now placed a sword of Damocles on the country's development. Terrorists now hide under the umbrella of religion to unleash terror on innocent citizens. This study recommends possible solutions to the problems.

Terrorism

As observed by Thompson[3], terrorism is a global concern, which over the years has assumed a dangerous trend. Terrorism is an issue that has attracted the attention of every individual in Nigeria in recent times. According to *Macmillan English Dictionary*, "Terrorism is the use of violence to achieve political aims"[4]. *Chambers Encyclopaedia*[5] defines terrorism as a systematic and organised use of violence and intimidation to force a government, community, race, etc, to act in a certain way or accept certain demands.

Hutchinsen Encyclopaedia, as quoted by Thompson defines terrorism as systematic violence in the furtherance of political aims often by small guerrilla groups[6]. Others also define terrorism as an activity that involves a violent act or any act dangerous to human life, that is, a violation of the criminal law that appears to intimidate or coerce a civilian population to influence the policy or conduct of a government by assassination or kidnapping[7]. We can therefore infer from these definitions that a terrorist is an individual who uses violence to achieve his aim. He is always ready to take his life for a cause. He sees the destruction of other people's lives as an achievement and glory.

Origin of Terrorism

Though Christianity kicks against terrorism in its entirety, the beginning of terrorism can be traced back to the Bible. There is a form of violence according to the Old Testament account

Chapter Four	Akinwumi, O. S. & Balogun, H. O, in Y.A. Quadri, R.W. Omotoye & R.I. Adebayo (Eds) Religion in Contemporary Nigeria London, Adonis & Abbey Publishers

between Cain and Abel in Genesis chapter 4:10f. Cain, according to this biblical record, was angry with his brother, Abel, because of the rejection of his sacrifice by God. He smashed his brother, Abel, to death. Cain, having committed this act, took to his heels but the voice of God came to him thus: "... the voice of thy brother's blood crieth unto me from the ground. And now art thou cursed from the earth... "In Matthew chapter 14:10ff, we also see another form of terrorism. "And he sent, and beheaded John in the prison. And his head was brought in a charger and given to the damsel..."

There are other cases of violence in the New Testament. Herod the Tetrarch beheaded John during his birthday. In 64 AD, Emperor Nero practised terrorism[8]. He saw Christians as criminals; Christianity was then a social stigma. Consequently, many Christians were gruesomely assassinated, crucified and set ablaze. According to Olayinka as quoted by Thompson[9], for three hundred years after the Neronian persecution, the Christian faith was labelled "unlawful and treasonable religion". The popular slogan[10] then was "Give them (Christians) to the lions".

In Islam, there are also records of terrorism. Some scholars maintain that after Prophet Muhammad's revelation in 610 AD, he called his people to repent and believe in the one and only true God[11]. His message was resisted, and he was forced to leave Makkah and had to migrate to Madina for safety. At Madina his followers gathered together to fight the opposing forces. The followers won the battle and the Ka^{c}aba was purified of idols[12].

Terrorists' Activities in Nigeria

The first terrorists' activities started in the form of a riot in 1980. It was led by a man called Maitatsine in Kano. The riot started from a small enclave in Yan Awaki quarters in Kano[13]. The full names of the leader were Muhammad Marwa Maitatsine. He hailed from Cameroon and had been living in Kano as a Quranic teacher. The followers always looted and burnt properties and even maimed or killed people. According to Dauda, they were said to be drinking blood of their dead victims[14].

The Maitatsine movement opposed and rejected the use of all scientific inventions and regarded them as un-Islamic. They hated anything called socialisation and hence, they neither wore wrist watches nor put on any dress other than the Babanrigas (flowing gowns). They never used spoons (while eating) nor watched television[15]. The terrorist activities of his group extended two years later to Kaduna and Bulunkutu in Maiduguri; Jimeta in the defunct Gongola State and Bauchi in 1985 witnessed the activities of this group. It is obvious that lack of understanding and deliberate contempt for other people's religion and beliefs remained the major cause of this terrorists' activities. Can one fight for God? Fighting for God is a reflection of the weakness of such a god. A weak god is not worth serving.

Boko Haram Insurgency

The term "Boko Haram" comes from the Hausa word *Boko* meaning "Animist" western or otherwise non-Islamic Education and the Arabic word *Haram* figuratively means "sin" (forbidden). In view of the etymological meaning of Boko Haram, it is colloquially translated as "Western

Chapter Four	Akinwumi, O. S. & Balogun, H. O, in Y.A. Quadri, R.W. Omotoye & R.I. Adebayo (Eds) Religion in Contemporary Nigeria London, Adonis & Abbey Publishers

education is sin"[16]. Boko Haram is an Islamic religious sect and terrorist group, whose goal is to establish a complete Islamic State in Nigeria, including the establishment of Sharia Courts across the country[17].

The sect calls itself *Jamd'atul Ahlul Sunnah Lidda wati wal Jihad* meaning: "people committed to the propagation of the Prophet's teachings and Jihad." Boko Haram's origin is believed to have been influenced by the teaching of Maitatsine, Muhammad Marwa, a Muslim fundamentalist, who rejected the influence of the system of education imposed by the British when they conquered Sokoto Caliphate in 1903.[18]

The sect was formed by Muhammad Yusuf, a radical Islamic cleric in Maiduguri, Borno State, in the year 2002. His followers are called *Yusufiya*[19], and include hundreds of impoverished young northerners, students and professionals, many of whom are unemployed. The sect opposes not only western education, but western culture and modern science as well.

In the first seven years of its existence, Boko Haram's operations were relatively peaceful, the sect only criticised northern Muslims for participating in illegitimate and un-Islamic activities. The group became violent in 2009 when it became known to them that government had started investigating their activities. The members resolved to be arming themselves. They out-rightly defied government's ban on riding motorcycles without helmets. This led to the first deadly clashes of the group with Nigerian security forces. The incident was suppressed by the army but about seven hundred people were reportedly killed[20]. The group's founder, Muhammad Yusuf, was arrested and later killed while still in police custody. His father-in-law and other sect members were also killed in circumstances which human rights groups have called extra-judicial killings[21].

Since the assassination of Muhammad Yusuf and other members, the sect vowed to carry out persistent, uninterrupted and incessant retaliatory attacks on innocent Nigerians everywhere[22]. Boko Haram carried out the first terrorist attacks in Borno State in January 2010[23]. Many people were killed during the attack. Since then, the sect has increased the frequency and intensity of its attacks with increased sucide bombings and assassinations spreading from Maiduguri to Abuja.There were bomb attacks in several states shortly after President Goodluck Jonathan's inauguration in May 2011; many innocent Nigerians met their untimely deaths[24]. In the following month, June 2011, Nigeria Police Headquarters in Abuja was bombed. It was reported that many police officers died in the incident[25].

Boko Haram proceeded and bombed the UN building in Abuja in August 2011. Twenty-three Nigerians and foreigners were killed in the attack[26]. Also in September 2011, Babakura Fugu, brother-in-law to the late Boko Haram leader, Muhammad Yusuf, was shot dead two days after attending a peace meeting with ex-president Olusegun Obasanjo[27]. There were series of bombs and gun attacks in Yobe and Borno States in November 2011, which led to the death of many people in the area[28]. The sect, however, vowed not to hold talks with the government until all members of the sect that had been arrested were released.

Nigerians witnessed another terrible and sad event in December 2011, on Christmas Day, when the Boko Haram sect carried out another bomb attack on Saint Theresa Catholic Church in Madalla.Many innocent worshippers, including children, died in the attack[29]. In January 2012, Boko

Haram launched another bomb attack coupled with heavy gun battles in Kano. Their plan was to destroy the police headquarters. Over one hundred and fifty people were reportedly killed[30]. It was this massacre that prompted President Goodluck Jonathan to declare a state of emergency in 15 Local Government Areas in Borno, Yobe and Plateau States in the same month. The Federal Government also ordered the closure of Nigeria's borders in the North[31].

The steps taken against Boko Haram sect appear to be an exercise in futility since the sect continues to cause havoc on a daily basis. In all honesty, Federal Government seems not to know how to clip the group's wings.[32]

Causes of Religious Violence in Nigeria

Quoting the scripture out of context: Some people fail to know that every verse of the Bible or Qur'ān has historical particularity[33]. Consequently, scriptural passages are often misinterpreted. For instance, in Islam, some of the followers believe that if they are killed during religious riot or Jihad, heaven or 'Al-Janna' is their destination[34]. Some of these Muslims misinterpret passages such as:

> O you who believe when you meet those who disbelieve in battle do not turn your back on them. And whoso turns his back on them ... incurs God's wrath (Q. 8: 15-16).
> If you are slain in God's way or you die surely God's protection and His mercy are better than all that they amass. And if you die or are slain, to God you are gathered (Q. 3: 157-8)

There are also passages in the Bible that are often misinterpreted and quoted out of context. Some of these passages include: "Do not think I have come to bring peace on earth ... but sword ..." (Matthew 10: 34); "Do you think I have come to give peace on the earth? No, I tell you rather division" (Luke 12:49-50)

Some religious leaders manipulate and misinterpret these passages to incite ignorant followers, especially the youths, to rebel against constituted authority.

Lack of Religious Dialogue and Interaction

In a pluralistic society like Nigeria, when people of different religious backgrounds refuse to rub minds and cross-fertilize ideas, prejudice and rivalry will be perpetuated. The ultimate results of this will be conflict and violence.

Commercialization of Religion and Quest for Materialism

Some people because of poverty see religion as a money-making venture. Some of these people deceive the masses under the pretext that they are called by God. Whenever their victims become aware of their deception, crises always ensue.

Unfavourable Government Policies

According to Adebimpe[35], when a group of people feel that a particular government policy would work against its interest, it may resort to violence in order to register its grievances. In politics, public office holders are not usually comfortable with those who openly preach against social vices in the society. They see this as a threat to their authority and would use government machinery to stop it[36]. A classic example was the Jihad of 1804 launched against oppressive rule in Hausa Land by Uthman Dan Fodio. Consequently, the war between Fodio and the Hausa led to the establishment of Sokoto Caliphate[37].

Chapter Four | Akinwumi, O. S. & Balogun, H. O, in
Y.A. Quadri, R.W. Omotoye & R.I. Adebayo (Eds)
Religion in Contemporary Nigeria
London, Adonis & Abbey Publishers

Particularity

Adherents of different religions always claim superiority of their own religions over others. Each of these adherents see their religion as the true and only way of salvation. In Nigeria, Oke[38] maintains that Christians have claimed the uniqueness of Christ and Christianity as the only way to God. Muslims have also claimed the uniqueness of Islam as the only religion of mankind. The feeling of superiority has remained the major cause of religious conflict in Nigeria.

Religious Terrorism: The Implication for National Development

The very concept of development can be described as the constant improvement in the quality of life in a nation through the improvement of the productive capacities of individuals. It can as well be defined as a multidimensional phenomenon that exerts positive influence on the overall social, economic, political and cultural spheres of societal life. It is concerned with the science of progress, it is associated with a society devoid of rancour and acrimony, a society without violence, a nation without the social problems of hunger, disease, ignorance, unemployment, inadequate housing and insecurity. The task of national development is therefore reducing conflicts to its barest minimum while laying a solid foundation for economic development and political advancement.

A critical look into the concept of development as analysed above, reveals that Nigeria is far from developed or, to use a conventional term, is developing. The religious intolerance, fanaticism and terrorism being currently witnessed in Nigeria has caused havoc that has negatively affected national development.

Religious terrorism has made the security agents appear inept. There is a growing perception that the police and their allied organisations are weak, corrupt and poorly-trained. The security agents are viewed as cowards who are unable to arrest, dismantle and bring to justice, a group that has contributed to the nation's problem. This perception, whether true or not, will most likely have a negative impact on the trust and confidence people repose in the security agents which will in turn affect the expected national development.

The incessant security challenges in the country portrays the president as weak and incompetent. This perception may lead to military intervention, which is undesirable. Persistent bombing may lead to retaliation. Boko Haram activities, for instance, may provoke one or two other groups or individuals to avenge the killing of their brethren or the bombing of their churches. If the bombings and counter-bombings persist, the country may witness another civil war.

In most cases, those who are lucky to escape death are usually displaced from their original abode and become refugees elsewhere[39]. Some of the displaced individuals may lose their sources of income since they cannot continue with their former profession in their new environment. The effect of this is poverty.

The displacement of people as a result of crises also affects the continuation of government's economic activities in the affected areas. This has a rippling effect on the development of the people and the nation. The 'terrorist' attacks continue to dent the image of Nigeria. This scares away foreign investors who might have helped to develop the country's economy. No investor would risk investing in a country where violence is rampant.

The violence in the country, as observed by Thompson[40], may lead to the emergence of social miscreants and criminals who, by their access to weapons become terrors to their immediate community and the larger society. In Thompson's explanation[41], after the crisis, it is always difficult to retrieve such weapons. Since most of these people are originally jobless, they will find solace in terrorism.

Conclusion and Recommendations

From the foregoing, we can see that national development implies changes for a better society or quality life-style. This kind of development is required in all fields of human endeavours. However, it cannot be achieved in a society where there are lawlessness, acrimony, anarchy, arson, rancour and breach of peace. Religious intolerance, fanaticism and terrorism have shattered the existing peace and security in Nigeria. Life is no longer sacrosanct, as security cannot be guaranteed.

The nation seems to be galloping towards implosion. It is saddening that Nigeria is enmeshed in this situation that has dented her image. Peace and security can only be possible when the positive role of religion is acknowledged and practised. It is in the light of the above conclusion that the following recommendations are made.

There is nothing inherently bad about religion. Except people, especially the adherents of different religions are sufficiently sensitised and conscientised to use religion positively, peace will elude Nigeria. The much needed national development will then be a mere illusion.

Adherents of all religions should have mutual respect for; and understanding of others' religious beliefs and culture. Nigerians must be impartial and all groups in the country must be treated equally.

Seminars and symposia should always be organised by different religious groups and there should be inter-religious dialogue. This will enhance peaceful co-existence.

The opportunists who advance their own personal interests at the expense of the national interest in the name of religion should desist. Religious leaders should be embodiments of tolerance.

Religious institutions are to be encouraged to avoid the deliberate use of arms in resolving conflicts or disputes arising from inter-religious relations.

Government should be just on religious matters. The trouble makers should be severely dealt with as this will serve as deterrent to others. Above all, Nigerians should be ready to demonstrate to the outside world the capability to transcend their difficulties or turn these difficulties to opportunities.

Notes and References

1. E. O. Olayinka, "The Roles of Religious Education to Peace, Security and National Development", in Adeniji, A. A., Adeyemo S. A. and Adeniji D. R. (Eds) *Peace, Security and National Development.* (Ibadan: Remo Ind. Printers, 2007), 237.
2. E. O. Olayinka, "The Roles of Religious Education to Peace, Security and National Development", 238
3. E. O. Thompson, "Music as panacea for Religious Terrorism", in Folorunso, M. A., Oyeneye, I. O. and Adebayo R. I. (Eds) *Religions and Modernity.* (Ijebu-Ode: Alamsek Press Ltd. 2007), 407.

4. *Macmillan, English Dictionary for Advanced Learners* (2nd Edition). (Oxford, Macmillan Publishers Limited).
5. A. Rober, *Chambers Encyclopaedic English Dictionary.* (Bartholomew: Harpe Collins Publishers Limited, 1994).
6. E. O. Thompson, "Music as panacea for Religious Terrorism", 407.
7. E. O. Thompson, "Music as panacea for Religious Terrorism", 407.
8. E. O. Thompson, "Music as panacea for Religious Terrorism", 408.
9. E. O. Thompson, "Music as panacea for Religious Terrorism", 408.
10. E. O. Thompson, "Music as panacea for Religious Terrorism", 409.
11. M. O. A. Abdul, *An Introduction to the study of the Qur'ān.* (Lagos: Islamic Publications Bureau. 1974), 63.
12. M. O. A. Abdul, *An Introduction to the study of the Qur'ān,* 63
13. G.O. Dauda, "Islamic and Religious Tolerance: A Case Study of Nigeria's Public Uprisings 1980-1992", *Journal of Arabic and Religious Studies.* Department of Religions, University of Ilorin. (Vol. 10, 1983), 18.
14. G.O. Dauda, "Islamic and Religious Tolerance", 18
15. G.O. Dauda, "Islamic and Religious Tolerance", 18
16. www.africa-spectrum.org 2010
17. U.Y. Yusuf, *The Manipulation of Religion in Nigeria. 1977-1987.* (Kaduna: Vanguard Printers and Publishers Limited. 1987), 2.
18. U.Y. Yusuf, *The Manipulation of Religion in Nigeria,* 2.
19. S. Robert, *Africa South of the Sahara: A Geographical Interpretation.* (New York: Guilford Press, 2004).
20. *ThePunch,* August 13th, 2011, *14*
21. *ThePunch,* 14
22. T. Toyin Falola, *Violence in Nigeria: The Crisis of Religion, Politics and Secular ideologies.* (Rochester, Rochester Press, 1998).
23. www.africa-spectrum.org 2010

24. *www.thenationonlineng.com* Aug 2011
25. *www.thenationonlineng.com* Aug.2011
26. *The Nation*, Saturday, August 27th 2011, 1-6
27. *www.thenationonlineng.com* September 2011
28. *The Punch*, November 9th 2011, 2
29. *The Nation*, December 26th 2011, 2-7
30. *The Punch*, Sunday January 22nd 2012, 2-5
31. *The Punch*, Saturday 21st January 2012
32. www.africa-spectrum.org 2010
33. O. Orebiyi and A. O. Dairo, *Contextualization and Exegesis: An Introduction*, (Ile-Ife: Amat-Printing and Publishing Company, 2000).
34. R. O.Oke, "Religion: Panacea to violence and conflict in Nigeria", in Adeniji A. A., Adeyemo, S. A. and Adeniji D. R. (Eds) *Peace, Security and National Development*. (Ibadan: Remo Ind. Printers. 2007), 174
35. I. A. Adebimpe, and A. O. Ogunsola, "Ethno-Religious Violence in plural society: A case study of Nigeria", in Folorunso M. A., Oyeneye, I. O and Adebayo R. I. (Eds). *Religion and Modernity*. (Ijebu-Ode: Alamsek Press Limited. 2007), 396
36. M. O. A. Abdul, *An Introduction to the study of the Quran*,116
37. M. O. A. Abdul, *An Introduction to the study of the Quran*, 117
38. R. O. Oke, "Religion: Panacea to violence and conflict in Nigeria", 171.
39. *The Punch*, (Sunday January 22nd 2012), 2-5
40. Thompson E.O, "Music as panacea for Religious Terrorism", 407.
41. Thompson E.O, "Music as panacea for Religious Terrorism", 399.

CHAPTER FIVE

Violence in the name of God: An Analytical Study of the Boko Haram Insurgency in Nigeria

Akanni, Abdul Hakeem
Department of Religious Studies
Olabisi Onabanjo University
Ago-Iwoye, Nigeria
akanniakeem2050@gmail.com
+2348033561743

Introduction

Since the Boko Haram crisis began in Nigeria in 2008, various tools and approaches have been employed in analysing it with a view to proffering solutions to it. People of different walks of life including professionals and experts have expressed views and opinions about the group, its nefarious activities and ways of curtailing them. Public and political analysts, social critics and commentators, security experts, media practitioners, among many others have spoken and also written extensively about the group that one would think that the crisis would have ended. While some had recommended a clamp down on the group, others have called for dialogue with it. Some have even recommended amnesty for its members as done for the youths of the Niger Delta. That then would mean that further, better and perhaps more comprehensive analyses would be required for the unfortunate experience to be stalled. It is against this background that this study is carried out to further analyse the group so as to understand it and the possible reason(s) behind its activities with a view to proffering practicable and lasting solution(s) to the crisis associated with it. The analysis, this time around, is theologically done from the Islamic point of view, using the Qur'ān as the main source of reference. This is because the group, rightly or wrongly is associated and identified with Islam and analysing it and its nefarious activities within the context of the religion's divine book will help a great deal in understanding the problem and in proffering solution(s) to it.

Boko Haram and Its Activities

Boko Haram is a name by which a group responsible for most of the recent bombings and killings especially in northern Nigeria is known to the public. "Boko" is a Hausa word meaning "Western/formal education" or "Western ideology" or "Westernisation" in its entirety[1]. In classical Hausa language, it means "deception" because of the experience of the people of the region with the colonial masters who used western/formal education to lure them into accepting Christianity[2]. "*Haram*", on the other hand is an Arabic word which means "prohibited", "forbidden" etc[3]. "Boko-*Haram*", therefore, would mean either "Western/formal/secular education is Islamically prohibited or forbidden" or "Evangelism deceptively camouflaged as western education is Islamically unacceptable" or both[4].

The Group, popularly known as "Boko Haram" calls itself *Jamā'atu Ahlus Sunnah li'd Da'wah wal Jihād* meaning "People Committed to the Propagation of the Prophet's Teachings and Striving in the Cause of Allah". It started like any other group formed by Muslims to advance the cause of Islam. The formation of the Group or any of such in Islam is hung on the verse of the Glorious Qur'ān which urges Muslims to constitute themselves into a group for the purpose of enjoining good on people and forbidding evils for them. The verse reads:

> Let there arise among you (Muslims) a group of people inviting to all that is good, enjoining what is right, and forbidding what is wrong. They are the ones to attain felicity (Qur'ān 3:104)

This verse has been the motivating factor for Muslims, not only in forming groups, societies or associations, but also in striving to correct societal ills. They see themselves as duty bound to do so particularly that the verse ends with the description of those who do so as "ones who attain felicity". Going by its official name, "Boko Haram" could not have otherwise been formed. Evidence on its founder and the activities of the group, prior to its militarization, point at this. Muhammad Yusuf, who founded the Group, for example, was said to have been a member of the Islamic Brotherhood of Shaykh Az-Zakizaki in Kaduna[5]. But when later the Group was accused of *Shi'ah*[6] tendencies and consequently broke into two, Muhammad Yusuf joined the *Tajdid*[7] group. He was said to have later found the teachings of the *Tajdid* group also unpleasant and therefore founded his own group which he called *"Jama'atu Ahlus Sunnah li d Da'wah wal Jihād"*.

A cardinal preaching of the Group is that western education is the main cause of corruption, which to them is the mother of all the problems facing the country. They hold further that if Muslims were to attain felicity, they should avoid it (i.e. western education). Before long, many of those who listened to his sermons withdrew from school, many stopped sending their children and wards to school and those who had acquired one certificate or another burnt them. A revolution against western education had started. The irony of the matter is that the founder himself was a university graduate.

A number of Islamic scholars were said to have challenged Muhammad Yusuf's preaching against western education in public lectures, drawing his attention to the socio-political and economic implications of his position especially on the people of Northern Nigeria who are educationally disadvantaged compared with their counterparts in other parts of the country. One of those scholars was Shaykh Ja'far Muhammad Adam who eventually was assassinated in 2006 in controversial circumstances. While some have alleged that his death was the price he had to pay for criticising the government of the day, others have attributed it to his stern opposition to the Group's position on western education[8].

The Group came into prominence and public notice in 2008 during the regime of late President 'Umaru Musa Yar'Adua. While details of the circumstances surrounding its militarisation remain sketchy and may perhaps remain so due to the killing of the foundation members of the Group who would know, its founder was said to have claimed in a *tafsir*[9] video tape that some mobile policemen attacked and injured some members of the Group and would not also allow families and friends to visit them in the hospital where they were receiving treatment. He was said to have further claimed that attempts by members of the Group to visit the injured in the hospital attracted the brutality of the police and several members of the Group were killed. The founder also said that while those killed were being taken for burial, the policemen also attacked them and further killed some of his members. He then vowed never to take kindly to this as he and members of his Group were determined to fight back[10]. The Group made good its threats by attacking police formations in Maiduguri, Borno State where its headquarters is and where the unfortunate incident started.

As a Yoruba adage would say: *agbe f' oba kii jebi*, meaning "no fault is found with actions taken as a government official", the then President Musa Yar'Adua, acting on intelligence report ordered a clampdown on members of the Group. Though he did not live to see the outcome of his decision, this further aggravated the crisis as members of the Group were (and are still more) determined to fight on. More than six years into the crisis, the battle rages on with casualties on both sides. The Group had lost its founder and many of its foundation members as well as their family members, the government and people of Nigeria have equally lost many of their loved ones in one attack of the Group or the other since the attacks are no longer limited to military formations and government establishments. Attacks are now targeted at getting as many casualties as possible by freely using guns and bombs in schools, markets, worship places, motor parks among other places.

An inventory of some of the nefarious activities associated with or for which the Group claims responsibility include: Bauchi prison break of 7th September, 2010; Abuja attack of 31st December, 2010; Yola jailbreak of 22nd April, 2011; series of bombings in some states in northern Nigeria on 29th May, 2011; bombing of Nigeria Police Force Headquarters, Abuja, on 16th June, 2011; and bombing of a beer parlour at Maiduguri on 26th June, 2011. Others include bombing of the All Christian Fellowship Church at Suleja on 10th July, 2011; killings of a Muslim cleric (Liman Bana) in Maiduguri on 12th

August, 2011; bombing of the United Nations' Building at Abuja on 26th August, 2011; series of attack at Damaturu on 4th November, 2011; and series of bombings across some states of the northern Nigeria on 25thDecember, 2011. To show that the Boko Haram crisis is not near ending or easily solvable as people would think, the Group also claims responsibilities for the series of killing and bomb attacks in many states of northern Nigeria between 5th and 28th January and between 8thand 16thFebruary, 2012. In January 2013, an attack was made on the entourage of the Emir of Kano and members of his family just as scores of people died in Kano as a result of two bomb explosions allegedly carried out by Boko Haram members at motor parks during the Easter holidays of March 2013. About one hundred and eighty-five people were said to have also died in the fracas between members of the Group and government forces in Maiduguri in April, 2013.[11]

The nature and dimensions of the attacks of Boko Haram have made it difficult for analysts, commentators and even experts to describe the Group and what it stands for, moreso that a good number of the attacks were suicidal. When the attack was on the church, Christian leaders were often quick to say that the Group was targeting Christians with a view to Islamising the country and the Muslims reacted by debunking the allegation. While the 'debate' was on, the Group would shift its attacks to the Muslims. No sooner would the Muslims claim they were vindicated that the Group would attack people from the eastern part of the country who had settled and are residents in the north. Analysts and commentators would then interpret the Group's action and mission as aiming at the disintegration of the country. When the attack was on government establishments and security institutions, people read political meanings into it claiming it was a ploy of politicians of northern extraction to destabilise President Goodluck Jonathan Southern-led government which the former had earlier objected to.

At times, the Group hacked down certain individuals including politicians and leading Islamic scholars of the region. Some of the attacks were even carried out in the month of Ramadan in which Muslims worldwide fast and which they hold in very high esteem. In short, the Group's activities have defiled all forms of description. No sooner would one perfectly describe the situation than happenings and events necessitated a modification of the description. Although, peace talks are already being initiated, it suffices to note that the only *fair* description of the Group and its activities is the media usage of the phrase "the nefarious activities of the fundamentalist militant Islamist sect- Boko Haram". The description is said to be fair because the activities of the Group are truly nefarious as hundreds of innocent lives and property had been wasted on the one hand and on the other hand, the Group was formed by supposedly Muslims and, rightly or wrongly, claims to have the advancement of the religion of Islam as its mission. Unfortunately too, members of the Group are consequently seen by a larger portion of the society as fighters and martyrs of Islam. What meaningful interpretation can one read into the activities of this vicious Group which is identified so fairly with a religion that claims "peace" as its motto? In other words, why would members of the Group do what they are doing and believe they are justified in their faith more so that other practitioners of the faith have disowned and disassociated themselves from them?[12] Explanations for this are sought in the relevant Islamic concepts of *da'wah* (Invitation to Islam), *Jihād* (striving in the cause of Allah), warfare and martyrdom. While *da'wah* and *Jihād* are the reasons for the formation of the Group as the name indicates, warfare and martyrdom are the two concepts that describe their activities and aspirations.

Theological Bases for the Activities of Boko Haram

One distinguishing feature between Islam and other religions is the prominence attached to law in its practice. Although only the bases of the laws are laid in most cases while subsidiary legislations are left to jurisprudence as time went on and as occasions demanded, there is virtually nothing done in the religion or by a Muslim that there is no law supporting it. Hence, there are laws guiding all Muslims' actions including Invitation to Islam (*da'wah*), striving in the cause of Allah (*jihād*), warfare and martyrdom. What are these laws and how do they explain the activities of the Boko Haram?

Da'wah in Islam

Every religion has a mechanism for spreading its message and winning converts. The Bible, for example, quotes Jesus Christ as advising his disciples not to take with them gold, silver or money, not even slippers when on evangelical mission as the one for whom they worked would provide for them. They were however, to find out who was worthy in any town they entered and stay with him and whoever would not receive them or their preaching, they should shake the dust of their feet in his house as a testimony against him or the town, adding: "Truly, I say to you, it shall be more tolerable on the day of judgement for the land of Sodom and Gomorrah than for that town" (Matthew 10:5-15). This, with modern understanding, has been the principle guiding evangelical activities of today's Christians.

In Islam too, there is a mechanism for evangelical activities and there are also rules guiding them. The concept is called *da'wah*, defined by Raji as "the propagation of the message of Allah through which Muslims understand their religion better and the non-Muslims are exposed to the beauty of Islam"[13]. Oladimeji opines that *da'wah* is "any duty performed by any Muslim for the purpose of inviting others to the religion of Islam, because if *da'wah* is to invite non-Muslims to the fold of Islam, what other name could be given to efforts on maintaining faith of the Muslims"[14]. Other interesting definitions of *da'wah* include those of Afolabi, Yusuf, Racius and Gulush. While Afolabi sees it as "efforts made to maintain faith in Allah and keep away from disbelief,"[15] Yusuf defines it "as embarking on public enlightenment activities that will project Islam as it truly is and how it should be practised".[16] For Racius, it is "the explanation and practical action that lead to conversion"[17]. Gulush however, views *da'wah* as "practical or communicative efforts to divert people's attention to Islam", seeing its scope as covering three basic elements of Islam; namely faith (*'aqā'id*), Islamic Law (*Sharī'ah*), and morals (*akhlāq*).[18] According to him, faith and its articles constitute the inner actions and foundation for Islamic principles and ideologies while the other pillars of Islam: Sa*lāt* (Ritual Prayer), Sa*wm* (fasting), *Zakāt* (Islamic tax) and Ha*jj* (Pilgrimage to Makkah) are the outer actions physically demonstrated. Both the inner and the outer actions are however governed by certain rules and regulations known as the *Sharī'ah*. In other words, *Sharī'ah* regulates the relationship between mankind and their creator and makes it the basis for any kind of relationship with other creatures, living and non-living things. According to Gulush, it is this relationship that becomes the product of both inner and outer actions of man otherwise called morals (*akhlāq*).[19] Regardless of what each of these definitions emphasises, the goal of *da'wah* according to all of them is to ensure peace in man's relationship with God and fellow creatures, which is what "Islam" means both as a word and as a religion.

The methodology of practising *da'wah* is however what makes it whatever every Muslim takes it to be. Saying that there is no compulsion in religion (Qur'ān 2:256), the Qur'ān advises Muslims on how to carry out *da'wah* thus:

> Invite to the way of your Lord with wisdom and good exhortation, and argue with them in a way that is best...(Qur'ān 16:125)

According to this verse, *da'wah* may take the form of sermons, lectures, question and answer sessions, discussions, dialogues and debates. Other methods include book writing, organising conferences, workshops, seminars, training and having good character.

Another relevant verse of the Glorious Qur'ān on *da'wah* is that which sees it as the best act a Muslim could engage in. It says:

> Who is better in speech than one who invites to the way of Allah, works righteousness, then says: I am among the Muslims. (Qur'ān 41:33)

Another is that which says:

You are the best community of people produced evolved for mankind (because) you enjoin what is right and forbid what is wrong and believe in Allah (Qur'ān 3:110)

These verses and similar ones in the Glorious Qur'ān have helped to shape the opinions of Muslims about *da'wah* so much that many, including members of the Boko Haram consider it duty bound to engage in *da'wah*, stretching its meaning. Hence, some consider it as *fard al'ayn* (i.e. a compulsory duty for every individual) while others take it as *fard kifāyah* (i.e. a collective duty which, once embarked upon by some, exempts others from being held responsible). *Da'wah*, therefore, is not the duty of certain professionals but of all Muslims, though some are encouraged to take it as a profession. Every individual is expected to engage in it as much as he/she can and anywhere one finds oneself including markets, offices, and motor parks. The establishment of the *Jama'atu Ahlus Sunnah li dDa'wah wal Jihād* otherwise known as Boko Haram therefore is an effort in the direction of *da'wah*.

Jihād (Striving in the Cause of Allah)

The dictionary meanings of the word *"Jihād"* include endeavouring, striving, labouring, taking pain, to overwork, to overtax, to go out of one's way to concentrate on something, to fight or to struggle.[20] Generally, the word *"Jihād"* means unceasing efforts made by a Muslim towards self-improvement and self-purification. Technically however, it means to struggle to the utmost of one's ability to please Allah and advance His cause.[21] The Qur'ān talks about it when it says:

> And if anyone strive (with might and main), they do so for their own souls; for God is free of all needs from all creation. (Qur'ān 29:6)

"*Jihād*" also means the individual and collective duty of Muslims to struggle against all forms of evil, corruption, injustice, tyranny, oppression and even unbelief committed by or against Muslims or non-Muslims.[22] The Qur'ān urges Muslims to help God's cause by extending the frontiers of godliness in all ramifications when it says:

> Had it been Our Will, We could have sent a warner to every people. Therefore, listen not to the unbelievers, but strive against them with the utmost strenuousness with it (i.e. the Qur'ān) (Qur'ān 25:51&52)

Muslim theologians have argued that the struggle enjoined by God in this and similar verses involves both peaceful and armed struggle. Yusuf Ali for example, interprets "it" in the last verse quoted above as referring to the Glorious Qur'ān, saying "the man of God pays no heed to carping critics who reject Faith. He wages the biggest *Jihād* of all, with the weapon of God's Revelation".[23] Those who hold this opinion about *Jihād* rely on verses of the Qur'ān like Q27:80-81 which read:

> Indeed, you will not make the dead hear, nor will you make the deaf hear the call when they have turned their backs retreating. And you cannot guide the blind away from their error. You will only make hear those who believed in our verses; so they become Muslims.

Thus, one form of *Jihād* is the peaceful one.

Other Muslim theologians however believe that though *Jihād* principally entails peaceful struggle, it also entails armed struggle if necessity demands it. Among the verses of the Glorious Qur'ān relied on by this group is that which says:

Fight them until there is no more oppression (*fitnah*) and until religion (i.e. worship) is acknowledged to be for God (alone). But if they cease, then there is to be no aggression except against the oppressors. (Qur'ān 2:193).

Consequently, *Jihād* can be peaceful as well as forceful either to fight an oppressive government denoted in the verse by the phrase "until there is no more oppression (*fitnah*)" or to advance the cause of Islam also described in the verse as "until religion (i.e. worship) is acknowledged to be for God (alone)". Going by the meaning of the last quoted verse, *Jihād* is therefore a tool for effecting social, political, economic and even religious changes. Hence, Prophet Muhammad is reported to have answered a man who asked him what kind of *Jihād* is best thus: "A word of truth before an oppressive ruler".[24] He also identified other forms of *Jihād* to include *hajj* and service to one's parents.[25] He however described "striving against oneself for the sake of Allah" as the best form of *Jihād* and in interpreting this, Muslim scholars have said that as long as (the servant of God) does not first strive against his own evil tendencies in obedience to God's commands, it is not possible for him to succeed in striving against the enemies in the outside world.[26]

Warfare in Islam

The claim Islam makes to be a comprehensive and complete way of life would not permit it to leave any aspect of human life unregulated. That is why it has issued legislations on all aspects of human endeavours including war which is the direct opposite of what it stands for - i.e. peace. Instructions to the early Muslims on how to relate with their neighbours who challenged their rights to existence and freedom of religion formed the bases of legislation on war and warfare in Islam. The Prophet Muhammad and his few followers had been challenged and persecuted by the unbelievers of Makkah on the basis of the new faith they practised to the extent that they had to flee from their place of birth for refuge.[27] These unbelievers of Makkah would not also allow them to practise their newly found religion in their new home as emissaries were not only sent to the governments of the host communities to reject the Muslim asylums but wars were also waged on them.[28] Even when an agreement was reached to keep and maintain peace in the community for a specific number of years, the unbelievers would still not keep to the agreement.[29] It was then that Allah ordered the Muslims to resist the persecution of their enemies. The Qur'ān recounts this when it says:

> To those against whom war is made, permission is given (to fight), because they are wronged; and verily God is Most Powerful for their aid. They are those who have been expelled from their homes in defiance of right, (for no cause) except that they say, "Our Lord is God"...(Qur'ān 22:39&40)

Even at that, the Muslims, for so many reasons including the fear of being few in number were reluctant in going to war with the unbelievers. The Qur'ān attests to this when it says:

> Fighting has been enjoined upon you while it is hateful to you. But perhaps you hate a thing and it is good for you; and you love a thing and it is bad for you. And Allah knows, while you know not. (Qur'ān 2:216)

It was then necessary for God to encourage the Muslims to fight since He so desired. Hence, God addressed them as follows:

And why should you not fight in the cause of God and of those who, being weak, are ill-treated (and oppressed)? — men, women, and children, whose cry is : " Our Lord, rescue us from this town, whose people are oppressors, and raise for us from Thee one who will protect, and raise for us from Thee one who will help". Those who believe fight in the cause of God and those who reject Faith fight in the cause of Evil. So fight ye against the friends of Satan; feeble minded is the cunning of Satan (Qur'ān 4:75&76)

The address to encourage them continues:

Will you not fight people who violated their oaths, plotted to expel the Apostle, and took the aggressive by being the first (to assault) you? Do you fear them? Nay, it is God Whom you should fear, if you believe. Fight them, and God will punish them by your hands, cover them with shame, help you (to victory) over them, and heal the breasts of the believers. (Qur'ān 9:13&14)

The address even involved threats to punish them if they would not oblige Him of His request. Allah said further:

If you do not go forth, He will punish you with a painful punishment and will replace you with another (set of) people; and you will not harm Him at all. And Allah is over all things competent (Qur'ān 9:38&39)

God however attached conditions to the permission given to fight and ways of going about it. For example, He specifies those who such fight should be directed at so that the permission does not appear to be an open licence to violence. He says:

O ye who believe! Fight the unbelievers who gird you about, and let them find firmness in you; and know that God is with those who fear Him. (Qur'ān 9:123)

It must be noted that the fight permitted, according to the above verse is not against all unbelievers but against *only* those who make life uncomfortable and unbearable for Muslims among them. Besides, the permission is granted on the condition that the enemies are the first to launch the attack on Muslims. Again, God urged the Muslims to be firm and persevere in the battle against the unbelievers. He further says:

> And fight them on until there is no more tumult or oppression and there prevails justice and faith in God ... (Qur'ān 2:193)

Other conditions are that no fighting should occur in the Sacred Mosque at Makkah (Qur'ān 2:191) and the Sacred Months of Dhul Hijjah, Dhul Qa'adah, Muharram and Rajab unless initiated by them (Qur'ān 2:194) and that women, children, the elderly, trees bearing fruits and animals are to be spared[30]. The fight should also be suspended by Muslims as soon as the unbelievers sue for peace. The Qur'ān says:

> But if they cease, let there be no hostility except to those who practise oppression (Qur'ān 2:192&193).

The Qur'ān however permits Muslims to collect ransom from their war captives and also to grant asylum to whoever seeks it from them even if he/she were to be from the unbelievers. The relevant verses read:

> Therefore, when you meet the unbelievers (in fight), smite at their necks, at length, when you have thoroughly subdued them, bind a bond firmly (at them); thereafter (is the time for) either generosity or ransom until the war lays down its burdens... (Qur'ān 47: 4)
> If one amongst the pagans asks thee for asylum, grant it to him, so that he may hear the Word of God; and then escort him to where he can be secure. That is because they are without knowledge. (Qur'ān 9:6)

Martyrdom in Islam

The concept of warfare in Islam relates to the concept of martyrdom. Once there is war, the possibility of lives being lost is very high and as Erikson posits, "it is easy to kill and to be killed, what is hard is to make one's death count for life"[31]. This is called "martyrdom". According to Brown, the common denominator in all cases of martyrdom is that the martyr, in attesting to his/her faith, dies for a noble cause and that the martyr must feel that death is necessary to his/her cause which is a strong testimony of furthering the truth and righteousness of his/her belief.[32] Bowersock believes that martyrdom becomes the private, religiously internalised goal of the martyr, and then, through his/her sacrificial act, he/she makes public and advertises the goal to his fellow comrades.[33] He also believes that the public aspect of martyrdom serves both to intimidate the enemy, by demonstrating the fervour and commitment of the martyr, and to inspire and vitalise his fellow comrades, by serving as a role model.

In Islam, martyrdom is a great virtue with great rewards attached to it. Although, other forms of death from plague, stomach disease, drowning and falling from a tree or wall are also recognised as martyrdom and are equally rewarded with paradise in Islam,[34] martyrdom achieved through warfare in defence of Islam attracts greater comments and remarks in the Glorious Qur'ān. Qur'ān 22:58 for example promises them a lot of good things. It reads:

> Those who leave their homes in the cause of God, and are then slain or die, on them will God bestow verily a goodly provision.

Of the many good things promised them, Qur'ān 3:157 talks about forgiveness and mercy from God, saying those are better than worldly goods and materials:

> And if you are slain, or die in the way of God, forgiveness and mercies from God are far better than all they could amass.

Another verse says they will be taken to God:

> If a wound hath touched you, be sure a similar wound hath touched the others. Such days (of varying fortunes) We give to men by turns that We may know those that believe, and He may take to Himself from your rank, martyrs-witnesses to Truth.(Qur'ān 3:140)

Qur'ān 22:58&59 say they will be admitted into paradise:

> Those who leave their homes in the cause of God, and are then slain or die, on them will God bestow verily a goodly provision. Truly God is He Who bestows the best provision. Verily, He will admit them to a place with which they shall be pleased, for God is All-Knowing, Most-Forgiving. (see also Qur'ān 3:167-171)

Apart from these Qur'ānic passages, Prophet Muhammad also spoke gloriously about martyrdom and the martyrs of Islam. According to him, the martyr is forgiven at the first drop of his blood,[35] saved from the punishment of the grave,[36] as well as the great fear of the Day of Judgement.[37] It is also said that he will be dressed in the clothes of *Iman* (which is the decoration of belief) on the Day of Resurrection[38], wear the crown of honour on his head[39] and intercede on behalf of seventy members of his family on the Day of Judgement.[40] The Prophet also said he will secure a unique status in paradise[41] and also marry the virgins of paradise.[42] Taken together, these Qur'ānic passages and prophetic sayings convey the undeniable message that martyrdom occupies and attracts unique and unquantifiable rewards in Islam. This belief in the special qualities of the martyr in Islam perhaps accounts for why there has been a long list of martyrs which cuts across all developmental stages and generations in Islamic history. Mention can be made of Sumayyah and her husband, Yasir, who were the first and second martyrs in Islam respectively.[43] Others include Harith ibn Hala, the nephew and adopted son of Khadijah who was killed while defending the Prophet from the idolaters who mobbed him while reciting the Qur'ān in the precinct of the Ka'abah,[44] Khubayb who was captured on his way from Madinah where the Prophet had sent him for *da'wah* purposes[45] and Hamzah ibn Abdul Muttalib who lost his life in the battle of Hud.[46] The murder of Hussain, the grandson of Prophet Muhammad and seventy-one members of his family is also considered an act of martyrdom in Islamic history by some scholars.[47] All these teach and serve as examples for Muslims, including members of Boko Haram what awaits them in martyrdom in the cause of Allah.

An Analytical Study of the Activities of Boko Haram in the Light of the Islamic Concepts of *Da'wah, Jihād,* Warfare and Martyrdom

From the foregoing, one can see that members of Boko Haram can find bases for some of their activities in the teachings of Islam, particularly the Glorious Qur'ān. The formation of the Group, for example is an attempt by its members to form a group of Muslims "inviting to all that is good, enjoining what is right, and forbidding what is wrong" as contained in Qur'ān 3:104. It is an act of *da'wah* seriously enjoined on Muslims in a number of Qur'ānic verses as earlier quoted. Although people like Quadri have, on the basis of the nefarious activities of the Group disassociated it from Islam[48], and that is very reasonable and correct, there are proofs that it started like any other group formed by Muslims to advance the cause of Islam. It only became militarised as a result of the brutality of the security agencies in the country.

In a similar vein, members of the Group may take the condemnation of corruption through the condemnation of what they considered its remote cause (i.e. westernisation through western education) as a form of *Jihād* which is equally seriously enjoined on Muslims. In fact, for Boko Haram members, the armed struggle they are engaged in, too, is for the "weak, ill-treated (and oppressed) men, women, and children of the town (Nigeria) whose cry is: 'Our Lord, rescue us from this town, whose people are oppressors, and raise for us from Thee one who will protect, and raise for us from Thee one who will help' described in Qur'ān 4:75&76. This conclusion was reached having considered the impunity with which fraud and corruption are committed by the elite especially those in the corridors of power in Nigeria while several millions of the country's citizens are living in abject poverty.

Apart from world agencies' ratings of the country as (one of) the most corrupt nation of the world, which the country's leaders have always denied[49], daily occurrences in the country not only vindicate the positions of the world agencies but also substantiate them. For example, a judge of the Nigerian court recently imposed one year jail term or a fine of N750.000 on one John Yusuf, the chairman of the Police Pension Committee who confessed to conniving with others to defraud the Police Pension Office of the sum of N27.2bn[50]. The convict paid the fine and got his freedom and the trial took barely six months while the accused was on bail. Conversely, about the same time, one Austin Igadolor was sentenced to forty-five (45) years imprisonment *without* an option of fine for stealing the N50,000 worth of a phone of a serving governor[51]. These are aside other cases of corruption like that of James Ibori who was convicted by a London court for the same offences for which he was discharged and acquitted by a Nigerian court and that of Dieprieye Alamaisighiea who was granted state pardon in less than ten years of his conviction for looting state funds and money laundering offences. Such are the levels of corruption and the irrational exercise of judicial powers in the country that would give justification to Boko Haram members' understanding of such verses.

For the ordinary man on the streets and particularly Muslims who have religious instructions to fight oppression in whatever form it appears, this is unacceptable and must be resisted as a religious duty. Hence the Boko Haram crisis in the country. Members of the Group would, on the basis of this verse, see themselves as the ones that God has raised (i.e. the best of mankind described above and more clearly in Qur'ān 3:110)) to "rescue," "protect" and "help" the people (of Nigeria) from their leaders "who are oppressors". Consequently, whatever casuality they suffer in the course of this struggle will be endured by them in the hope that they would be rewarded with paradise as martyrs of Islam.

Conversely however, the Group erred by the indiscriminate killing of people including women, (school) children and the elderly especially through bombs and guns as this runs contrary to the position of Islam that those categories of people should not be killed even in war situations. It also erred by setting the villages of the defenseless people who have nothing to to do with governance in the country ablase. Thus, the inability of members of the Group to distinguish who an enemy is from a friend and considering all that fall within their target at a particular time as enemies is unjustifiable. Hence, Quadri believes and we share his opinion that although Islam recognises war as a lawful and justifiable course of self-defence and restoration of justice, freedom and peace, it also posits that no war should be waged indiscriminately in the name of religion[52]. Afterall, Islamic principle favours a lesser evil to a bigger one[53] and in this case, taking the lives of innocent people unjustly is a bigger evil compared to tolerating corruption.

It is also noteworthy that, in the light of Qur'ān 2: 193 quoted above which calls for the seizure of hostility upon peace move by the enemies, the Group erred by persistently rejecting both peace talks and amnesty being proposed by some people and being considered by Government. That is why even when peace talks were on and the committee to consider the possibility of amnesty for the Group was being set up, the Multi- National Joint Task Force set up by Government continued to fight members of the Group. That also explains why members of the Group continue to see value in Qur'ān 8: 15&16 which enjoin the Believers to employ strategies when they engage the Unbelievers in battle and even encourage them never to be afraid of being killed in the course of the battle as both sides in the battle are bound to suffer casualties of varying degrees. According to a Muslim *Jihādist* quoted by Timehin, "this method of martyrdom is the most successful way of inflicting damage against the opponents and the least costly to the *mujahidin* in terms of casualties".[54] This method is also said to be a modern war strategy as a soldier may also decide to fall upon a hand grenade in order to save the lives of his comrades[55]. While both acts assign meanings to death, transforming it into acts of choice and purpose that can be remembered, treasured, and possibly emulated by others in the struggle, the difference lies in that one is further rewarded with the best place in paradise.

The other perspective through which the activities of the Boko Haram group can also be assessed is on the basis of its ideologies and teachings. As noted earlier, the main teaching of the Group is that western education should be avoided by Muslims because, in the opinion of its founder, it encourages and perhaps permits corruption. This led a good number of its members to begin to disassociate themselves from western education. If this position is based on the teachings of Islam and specifically on the position of the Qur'ān on education, one would see that it will fall flat. This is because the Qur'ān places high premium on education without limiting the extent to which Muslims could go in acquiring it. Apart from Qur'ān 2: 30-32 which talk about the generality of knowledge God bestowed on Adam to prove that he and subsequently humankind are superior to the angels and Qur'ān 96: 1-6 which also speak of general knowledge at the beginning of revelation of the Glorious Qur'ān to Prophet Muhammad, other Qur'ānic verses on education include: "Are they equal, those who know and those who do not know" (Qur'ān 39: 9). Another one says: "God will raise up to suitable ranks and degree those of you who believe and have acquired knowledge" (Qur'ān 58: 11). None of these verses or any other one restricts the type of knowledge Muslims could acquire to either western or eastern.

Although a number of statements are credited to the Prophet Muhammad attaching greater value to Qur'ānic or theological form of knowledge, no known verse of the Qur'ān or statement of the Prophet restricts Muslims to such knowledge or any other one for that matter. It would therefore be wrong for the founder of the *Jama'atu Ahlus Sunnah li dDa'wah wal Jihād* to have condemned or forbidden western education for Muslims in its entirety. An intelligent approach would have been to identify areas where members of the Group have problems with and sensitise their members or the generality of Muslims about it or better still, establish their own schools where the grey areas would be taken care of. It therefore follows that the bases upon which the Group based its *da'wah, Jihād,* warfare and martyrdom or any other reason for its struggle are shaky and faulty and God alone knows if they merit the rewards attached to those Qur'ānic concepts and which probably they so much desire for embarking and sustaining the armed struggle.

Conclusion

The focus of this study is to give an objective analysis of the Boko Haram crisis in Nigeria in the light of the theological teachings of Islam as contained in the Holy Book of the religion with a view to contributing to ending it as well as forestalling similar occurrence in the future. After an indepth study of the reasons and circumstances surrounding the formation of the Group, four relevant Islamic concepts that help explain the perceptions, attitudes and actions of members of the Group were also studied in the light of the Qur'ān. The efforts have revealed that the Group, rather than being faceless as alleged by some commentators on the crisis, was born in the broad day light of events in the country. It was also found that reasons for the formation of the Group include but are not limited to the need to sensitise and make the Nigerian Muslims conscious of the perceived dangers of acquiring western education which, in the estimation of the founder of the Group is the basis of all the socio-political and economic injustices and imbalances in the country. It was also discovered that some of the actions of the Group are based on the Group's interpretation and understanding of certain portions of the Holy Book of Islam. For members of the Group also, they are fighting a just cause.

The challenge this study has thrown is whether or not Islam is a conflict-prone religion or its Holy Book (i.e. the Qur'ān) encourages war and violence. While it is true that the divine scripture provides guidance on all aspects of human life including *da'wah, Jihād*, warfare and martyrdom as a proof of its claim to being the Book of Guidance for mankind on all matters (Qur'ān 6: 38), it does not deserve being blamed for the wrong interpretation of its contents either by its adherents or its adversaries. As a divine book which has provided guidance for Muslims and indeed humanity since the seventh century, it remains inimitable and so it will be. One therefore conclude that the Qur'ān should not be seen as a conflict-prone book which instigates its adherents to violence but as one that liberates the human mind and makes people the architects of their own destiny. It renders inappropriate the common belief that "religion generally is the opium of the people".

Conclusively, one may note that the Boko Haram members might be wrong in their methodology or approach to the much-desired change in the way the country is being governed and might be silenced by force or persuaded to end violence which is the heart desire of every peace loving Nigeria including this writer, more Boko Haram– like groups and those which may not necessarily be of Muslim extractions would still arise in the country if all forms of socio-economic and political injustices that are manifested in wanton corruption and insensitivity to the plight of the poor do not stop. The existence of the Movement for the Emancipation of the Niger-Delta (MEND) and Movement for the Actualisation of the Sovereign State of Biafra (MASSOB) in the country, though ethnic based is indicative of this assumption. Those in the corridors of powers are therefore called upon to ensure equitable management and distribution of the resources of the country to the advantage of all. Members of the Group are also called upon to drop their arms and embrace dialogue, which is also recommended by Islam in situations like this.

Notes and References

1. *Da'wah* Coordination Council of Nigeria, *The Boko Haram tragedy, Da'wah* (Coordination Council of Nigeria, Minna, 2009), 1
2. *Da'wah* Coordination Council of Nigeria, 2
3. *Da'wah* Coordination Council of Nigeria, 1
4. *Da'wah* Coordination Council of Nigeria, 2

5. Abdur Rahman Doi, *Islam in Nigeria*, (London: Ta Ha Publications, 1984), 165.
6. Abdur Rahman Doi, *Islam in Nigeria*, 189
7. *Tajdid* means "renewal"
8. The above pieces of information were gathered at interactive sessions with a number of Northern Nigerian Muslims during the Ethical Reform Programme (EPR) jointly organised by Karimia Institute, Nottingham, United Kingdom and *Da'wah* Institute of Nigeria (DIN), Islamic Education Trust (IET), (Minna, Nigeria at IET, Minna, Nigeria between 28th February and 6th March, 2013).
9. *Tafsir* means "Qur'ānic exegesis"
10. As in no. 8 above.
11. Stories of *Boko Haram* make headlines of most Nigerian newspapers since the crisis started. For some of these stories, see *The Punch*, April 5th 2013, *The Punch*, April 23th 2013, *Tribune*, April 30th 2013 among others.
12. For example, see Y. A. Quadri, *All in the name of God*, the 133rd Inaugural Lecture, (University of Ilorin, Nigeria, 23rd May, 2013) ,34, 36 & 40.
13. A. F. Raji, *Da'wah: Between ideology and factionalism*, (Lagos: Al-Mustagfirun Research Institute, 2007), 2.
14. L. F. Oladimeji, *Da'wah* trends in Islam: a case study of the *Jama'atut- Tabliqh* in Nigeria, an unpublished Ph.D. thesis submitted to the Department of Religions, (University of Ilorin, 2005), 6
15. A. Afolabi, *Winning souls: a guide to effective communication for Islamic propagators*, (Lagos: Pioneer Publishing, 2008), 3.

16. B. Yusuf, "*Da'wah* and contemporary challenges facing Muslim women in secular states- a case study" in N. Alkali, A. Adamu, A. Yadudu & R. Motem (eds.) *Islam in Africa*, (Lagos: Spectrum Book Limited, 1993), 223
17. E. Racius, The multiple nature of Islamic *da'wah:* an academic dissertation, Faculty of Arts, Institute of Asian and African Studies, and Islamic Studies, (University of Helsniki, retrieved from http//:google.com.ng on 19th April, 2013).
18. A. A. Gulush, *Ad-da'watul-islamiyyah: usuuluha wawasailuha,* (Cairo: Egyptian Book House, 1987), 8
19. A. A. Gulush, *Ad-da'watul-islamiyyah: usuuluha wawasailuha.*
20. J. M Cowan (ed), *Arabic-English Dictionary*, (India: Modern Language Services), 142
21. *Da'wah* Institute of Nigeria, *Jihād and the spread of Islam*, (Minna: Islamic Education Trust, 2009), 7&8
22. *Da'wah* Institute of Nigeria.
23. Yusuf Ali, *The Glorious Qur'ān: texts, translation and commentary,* (London: The Islamic Foundation, 1975), 939
24. *Da'wah* Institute of Nigeria, p.8
25. Yusuf Ali, *The Glorious Qur'ān: texts, translation and commentary.*
26. Yusuf Ali, *The Glorious Qur'ān: texts, translation and commentary.*
27. Muhammad Husayn Haykal, *The Life of Muhammad,* (Lagos: Islamic Publications Bureau, 1982), 85
28. Muhammad Husayn Haykal, *The Life of Muhammad.*
29. Muhammad Husayn Haykal, *The Life of Muhammad.*
30. Mohammed al- Mustapha As-Subaaiy, *Min rawai'i hadaratina,* (Beirut: Darul- Qur'ān al- Kareem/IIFSO, 1980), 140.

31. E. Erikson, *Gandhi's truth on the origin of militant non-violence*, (New York, Norton Press, 1969), 6.
32. J. Brown, Gandhi, *prisoner of hope*, (New Haven: Yale University Press, 1989), 26.
33. G. W Bowersock, *Martyrdom and Rome*, (Cambridge: Cambridge University Press, 1995), 45
34. A. Z. A Al-Mundhiri, *Summarised Sahih Muslim*, Arabic-English, vols. 1&11, (Riyadh: Darus Salam Publishers & Distributors, 2000), 2493

35-41 M. M Khan, *Summarised Sahih al Bukhari*, Arabic-English, Riyadh: Darus Salam Publishers & Distributors, 1994, pp1087-1088. See also www impact-se.org/docs/reports/egypt.captereleven:Jihād and martyrdom (retrieved on 18th January, 2012)
42. A. S Najeebababi, *The history of Islam*,(vol. 2), Darus Salam Publishers & Distributors, 1994, p. 69. See also www.al-islam.org/restatement/10.html (retrieved 25th March, 2013).
43. www.al-islam.org/restatement/10.html (retrieved 25th March, 2013)
44. www.al-islam.org/restatement/10.html.
45. Najeebababi, *The history of Islam*, 69.
46. Najeebababi, *The history of Islam*.
47. Da'wah Institute of Nigeria, *Jihād and the spread of Islam*, , 6.
48. Y.A. Quadri, *All in the name of God*, 2013, 34, 36 & 40
49. *The Punch*, 23[rd]April, 2013, 8
50. *The Punch*, 23[rd]April, 2013, 18
51. *Nigerian Tribune*, 30[th]April, 2013, 1
52. Y.A. Quadri, *All in the name of God*, 2013, 38 & 39

53. Imran Ahsan Khan Nyazee, *Islamic Jurisprudence*, (Islamabad: International Institute of Islamic Thought and Islamic Research Institute, 2000), 310
54. S. O Timehin, *In search of truth*, (Lagos: Lantern Books, 2010), 15
55. H. Musirillo, *The acts of the Christian martyrs*, (London: Clarendon Press, 1972), 27

CHAPTER SIX

Peaceful Co-Existence in a Multi-Religious Society: An Islamic Perspective

Shittu, A. B.
Department of Philosophy & Religions,
Faculty of Arts, University of Abuja, Nigeria.
abshittu@yahoo.com
+2348072291640

Introduction

The escalation of religious related unrest around the world and Nigeria in particular has made the longing for peace and security to be intensified, especially in recent times. The spate at which confrontations between adherents of different faiths are taking the central stage is worrisome and thus suggests that a number of local and international treaties signed to declare violence illegal, seem to be active on paper and not in practical terms. Besides, such conventions have relatively failed to achieve the desired goal. It is therefore imperative to make a paradigm shift by using the religious dimension to address the situation in a more subtle way to appeal to the different parties involved that, violence, hatred and religious bigotry do no one any good. This contribution seeks to unveil forms of religious strife in Nigeria as well as some of the issues identified as the underlying factors responsible for the fracas. In the same vein, it uses practical examples as a platform to demonstrate that peaceful co-existence is the hallmark on which the Islamic faith was launched. Therefore, whoever professes the religion has no option but to build on the legacy of the early generation of adherents of the faith. Otherwise, such an individual may be acting contrary to the tenets of Islam. The author believes that peace and tranquillity could only reign in an atmosphere where there is tolerance and the spirit of give-and-take.

Types of Religious Unrest in Nigeria

The outward appearance of the chains of religious unrest in Nigeria, based on the nature, character and their sources, could be divided into three major categories, namely: intra-religious, inter-religious and ethnic/politically motivated unrest.[1] The categorisation is explained as follows:

Intra-Religious Unrest: This type of conflict, according to Akinwumi and Imam, normally erupts due to denominational differences within certain members of a particular religion. They argue that, in most cases, the crises emanate as a result of supremacy tussle between rivals, intolerance of a dominant sect or the refusal of an emergent revolutionary faction to accommodate the views, rights or practices of other denominations within the same faith. The age-old rifts between the *Sufi* Brotherhood and the "Reformers", popularly called *Izalah* on the one hand, as well as the crack between the *Sunni* and *Shi'ah* Muslims on the other are typical examples in this direction. Regrettably, such an "internal" conflict within a particular faith at a particular location gradually blows out of proportion and steadily engulfs the entire community, whose innocent members are usually affected in terms of loss of lives and property.

Inter-Religious Unrest: This type, typically begins in most cases as socio-ethnic unrest, but fought out under the idiom of inter-religious crises. It customarily involves members of two different religions, and habitually emanates as a result of intolerance on the part of one religious group to the other. Unfortunately, these conflicts at times escalate due to the complexity and diverse nature of the Nigerian society. At times, the causes may not even have anything to do with religion but religious groups are often drafted into it. This as well usually results in heavy casualties from both sides.[2]

Ethnically/Politically Motivated Unrest: The third category in the series, according to observers, is purely ethnic or political crises but misleadingly labelled religious due to the sensitivity of religion in the Nigerian society. Such unrest might have been sparked off by land or boarder dispute between two communities, or by a power tussle between two political rivals. Furthermore, misunderstanding that usually ensues between the Fulani herdsmen and the local farmers, is another irritating phenomenon. But since the majority of the people are adherents of the two major religions in the country, Islam and Christianity, in sensing a sign of defeat or marginalisation, each party normally seeks refuge under the canopy of its faith. In such a situation, the dispute is presented by each group as religious in order to quickly mobilise as many members as possible to its camp to sympathise and fight alongside with it.

Causes of Religious Unrest

It is asserted that the underlying factors for religious conflicts in Nigeria may be categorised into two: immediate and remote factors. This classification is the upshot of a critical scrutiny of some of the reasons that appear to have been responsible for the majority of the conflicts as discussed below:

Immediate Causes of Religious Unrest

Scholars and religious commentators believe that there are a number of factors directly responsible for the perennial religious unrest in the Nigerian society. In other words, these factors are regarded as prime movers of the strained relationship between Muslim and non-Muslim communities, which usually lead to religious disturbances. Some of those factors are:

Ignorance: Lack of adequate understanding of religion has been identified as a major factor militating against peaceful co-existence among adherents of different faiths in Nigeria.[3] This kind of ignorance is of two forms: first, ignorance of one's own religion, which usually makes an individual to behave contrary to the standard teachings of the religion he professes; second, ignorance about other peoples' religion, which may perhaps generate unnecessary hatred towards that religion and its followers. Similarly, such naivety customarily gives room for unsubstantiated allegations and irrational acceptance of all sorts of vilification about other people and their religion. In the same vein, some people that were born Muslims or Christians have little or no interest in seeking appropriate knowledge about their religion. They only capitalise on the fact that they are not converts, as such, they assume that everything about their faith is inborn. Such people often act irreligiously, and are usually ready to blindly follow the instructions of their leaders, irrespective of whether the latter are in conformity with the teachings of the faith or not.[4] According to a popular saying: "ignorance is not an excuse". Islam makes it mandatory on Muslims to seek adequate knowledge about their religion so as to avoid blind imitation.

Prophet Muhammad was commanded by the Almighty to read in the first set of revelation he received from Allah. He says:

> Read! In the name of your Lord, who has created (all that exist), has created man from a clot (a piece of thick coagulated blood). Read! And your Lord is the Most Generous, who has taught (the writing) by the pen, has taught man that which he knew not (Qur'ān 96:1-5).

Confrontational Preaching: Another factor directly militating against peaceful co-existence among adherents of different faiths in the country is confrontational preaching. The missionary nature of both Islam and Christianity in inviting people to belief and worship of the Almighty Allah is highly influential in guiding humankind to lead a spiritually structured life. This noble task is regarded as an obligatory duty in all monotheistic religions. In Islam, the invitation is called *Da'wah*, which is known as evangelism in Christianity.[5] But the way some preachers from both sides go about this noble duty usually creates serious problems in the society. In other words, some Muslim and Christian preachers are guilty of this "crime". Such a provocative act of preaching is usually carried out by "half-baked" religious personnel who do not weigh the gravity and consequences of their actions. This phenomenon is common to come by on public buses, bus and train stations and school campuses. Some preachers even go to the extent of name calling, which is against the teachings of religion. Provocative preaching is totally unacceptable in Islam and that is why it emphasises wisdom and fair preaching. Allah the Most High says:

> Invite (mankind, O Muhammad) to the way of your Lord (i.e. Islam) with wisdom and fair preaching, and argue with them in a way that is better. Truly, your Lord knows best who has gone astray from his path, and He is the best Aware of those who are guided (Qur'ān 16:125).

Religious Bigotry: Tolerance, which is defined as "willingness to accept or tolerate somebody or something especially opinions or behaviour that you may not agree with, or people who are not like you"[6] has a limit. This limitation is also acknowledged by Ahmad in the following words:

> First of all, it must be clearly understood that tolerance has its limits. Had tolerance been without any limits, intolerance too must have been tolerated without any scruple. But that is not the case. Tolerance is a culture of virtue; but it is not an absolute value.[7]

The high level of religious bigotry among adherents of religions in the Nigerian society accounts for some avoidable conflicts. In other words, lack of religious tolerance has led to religious unrest in which lives and property were destroyed. Followers of a dominant faith in a particular area decide that other minority groups should be subdued and denied any breathing space in the area. The minority group, on the other hand, also points fingers at the majority accusing it of marginalisation, double standard and oppression.[8] It is also worth mentioning that intolerance leads to fanaticism and ill feelings towards other people who do not share one's views and ideas, or see things the way one sees them. This kind of position usually metamorphoses into aggression and unwarranted hostility, not only towards people of other faiths, but also towards people of the same faith as earlier explained. As a way of encouraging Muslims to imbibe the culture of tolerance, Islam declares that no one should be forced against his will to accept Islam: "There is no compulsion in religion. Verily, the right path has become distinct from the wrong path." (Qur'ān 2:256). Allah the Most High also reiterates in another verse: "Then, if they turn away, your duty (O

Muhammad) is only to convey (the Message) in a clear way." (Qur'ān 16:82).

Unbalanced Media Reports: The role of the media in any society cannot be overemphasised, especially in maintaining peaceful co-existence among different religious groups in a multi-religious state like Nigeria. Regrettably, some section of Nigerian media cannot be exonerated from their complexity role in religious unrest. As a result of religious sentiment, some media houses report religious happenings according to their own bias to a certain religion, thus creating unnecessary tension, which at times leads to destruction of lives and property.[9] Being a powerful driving force behind virtually every event in today's world, the mass media reports are capable of making or marring relationship between states, communities as well as individuals. Bidmos summarises the influence of the mass media by writing:

> Experience has shown that the mass media reports, news analysis and features are capable of playing a positive or negative role in the relationship between Muslims and Christians depending on the intention and orientation of the journalist concerned. More often than not, reactions of the Muslim to Christian's actions or vice-versa are determined by the mass media reports.[10]

Kukah and Falola also explain the "complementary" role of the media to religious unrest in the following words:

> The media has helped in fanning and sustaining the embers of bigotry. The way it portrays religion places more premium on the altar of mammon than of the nation's well being.[11]

In order to substantiate the above claim, few examples on the complexity role of the media on the fragile relations between Muslims and Christians in Nigeria may not be an overstock. An unbalanced press report in 1981, which claimed that the Federal Government granted the Muslim community ten million Naira (N10,000,000.00) to put up a befitting Central Mosque for the Nigerian Muslims in Abuja, the new Federal Capital, had rocked Nigeria to its very foundation. However, the truth of the matter, as explained by a special adviser to the president on political affairs, was that both the Muslim and Christian leaders were given the same amount of money to build separate central places of worship for their congregations.[12]

In order to forestall breakdown of law and order, proper and meticulous use of all the faculties human beings were endowed with is highly canvassed by Islam.

> And follow not (O man) that of which you have no knowledge. Verily! The hearing, and the sight, and the heart, of each of those you will be questioned (by Allah) (Qur'ān 17:36).

Consequently, a believer is not allowed to say, write or be a witness to anything he has no adequate knowledge about, because he will be called for evidence and clarification on the Day of Resurrection.

Remote Causes of Religious Unrest

There are other factors identified as part of the causes that contribute to recurrent religious unrest in the country. These factors, according to observers, may not seem to be directly responsible for the conflicts, but however remote they may appear, they play a major role in igniting an already tense atmosphere between the two communities. Some of those factors are:

External Influence: Events in other parts of the world are also regarded to be indirectly responsible for religious unrest in different parts of Nigeria. Muslims and Christians alike take it upon themselves that whatever happens to their brethren in other places, either happiness or grief, should be shared, as a way of demonstrating their solidarity with their brothers and sisters in faith. However, the way and manner in which such solidarity is expressed sometimes results in bloodshed and destruction of public and private properties. One of such reactions was attacks on non-Muslims by some Muslims youth in some parts of Nigeria in reaction to blasphemous cartoons published by a Danish Newspaper in 2005. The Palestinian issue is another factor that strains relationship between Muslims and Christians. The same goes to the attempt by a Church in Florida, USA to burn copies of the Qur'ān on the ninth anniversary of September 11 attacks on the United States.

Another element of foreign influence is the loose nature of the Nigerian borders, which gives room for agents of religious fanaticism to sneak into the country and inject heretical beliefs in the minds of unsuspecting adherents of different religions, which have resulted in unruly behaviours among youngsters. A vivid example in this direction is the discovery by the Joint Task Force (JTF) in Borno State that majority of Boko Haram fighters are from neighbouring countries.

In as much as Islam encourages solidarity with one another in grief and happiness, such should not be taken to the extreme. In the same vein, innocent members of the public should not be harassed or intimidated on the account that their brethren have committed a crime somewhere; "... no person earns any (sin) except against himself (only), and no bearer of burdens shall bear the burden of another..." (Qur'ān 6:164). Allah also reiterates that Muslims should endeavour to have smooth relationship and cooperation with those who live in peace with them:

> Allah does not forbid you to deal justly and kindly with those who fought not against you on account of Religion and did not drive you out of your homes. Verily, Allah loves those who deal with equity (Qur'ān 60:8).

Poverty and Economic Disparity: Unemployment and enormous economic disparity among Nigerians have also been driving factors behind religious unrest. The dilapidated state of infrastructures and lack of lucrative jobs in the rural areas have left a bulk of rural dwellers with no options but to seek greener pastures in the cities. The influx of jobless able-bodied youth, who are desperate for acceptance into the "new-world" and ready to go to any length to achieve their goals, are mostly the recruits of the trouble makers. Some of this "economic migrants" may not even be devotees of a particular religion, but just see crisis situations as an avenue for them to earn a living by looting during riots.

Ensuring even distribution of the nation's wealth is the sole responsibility of the authority and this task must be carried out without prejudice. Islam sees leadership as a trust that must be executed with justice and fairness. This, according to Islam, is part of the trust man accepted from the Almighty Creator:

> Truly, we did offer *Al-Amānah* (trust) to the heavens and the earth, and the mountains, but they declined to bear it and were afraid of it (i.e. afraid of Allah's torment). But man bore it... (Qur'ān 33:72).

Ethnic Intolerance: Xenophobia is another indirect factor responsible for religious unrest in the country. Tribal bond, according to observers, plays a pivotal role in Nigeria in many aspects. It is even used on many occasions to determine who gets what and who takes what. Competence and quality, they argue, are thereby at times sacrificed on the altar of tribalism. Mancilla argues that the notion of indigenisation has deep social and political implications. She maintains that:

> …even if a person has lived in a particular place for most of his or her life, worked, married and had children there, he or she is still considered a 'non-indigene', a 'foreigner', a 'settler'. That person has to go or refer to his or her "state of origin" to claim citizenship rights.[13]

Islam discourages tribalism in all ramifications and encourages brotherhood based on trust and fair play. Allah the Most High says:

> O you who believe! Stand out firmly for Allah and be just witnesses and let not the enmity and hatred of others make you avoid justice. Be just: that is nearer to piety, and fear Allah. Verily, Allah is Well-Acquainted with what you do (Qur'ān 5:8).

Authority's Favouritism: The responsibility of every government is to provide basic amenities and protect its citizens. Every member of the society is entitled to be treated equally regardless of his social status, political and religious affiliations. However, in some quarters, the Nigerian authorities have been accused of partiality and favouritism that are said to have been instrumental in fuelling religious unrest. Findings revealed that the 1991 religious riots in Kano were triggered by government's refusal to grant entry visa to a renowned South African Muslim preacher, the late Sheikh Ahmad Deedat, to visit Kano, while a German Christian preacher, Rev. Reinhard Bonkie, was allowed to visit the same city. Hence, the Muslims felt a foul play and expressed their grievances and disapproval of the authority's double standard through demonstrations that had, however, gone out of control into bloody riots.[14]

Similarly, some security agents may not be exonerated from indirect involvement in religious crises. Findings revealed that when cautioned of a strange activity by a fanatic movement or group, instead of investigating the allegations and nip the trouble in the bud, if proved to be a security threat, they seem to have at times played down such reports or completely turned a blind eye at them. In addition, some security personnel have been accused of indiscriminately arresting innocent people for no justification. According to religious commentators, the matter becomes worst when their families and loved ones are unable to secure their release, though no evidence has been established against them. Another peoples' accusation of security agent's involvement in religious conflicts is extrajudicial killing. There are some reported instances where unarmed civilians were killed in front of their family members, which had arguably triggered civil disobedience.

Politics: Another factor identified as one of the causes of religious unrest in Nigeria is politics. The two major religions in the country, Islam and Christianity view politics and religion from different perspectives. In Islam, religion and politics are inseparable, while mainstream Christianity detaches religion from politics, and confines the former to private life.[15] Nevertheless, the problematic role of politics in religious conflicts in the Nigerian context does not rest squarely on separation of politics from religion *per se*, but is firmly rooted in the way politicians use religion as a pretext to achieve their selfish ends. As pointed out by Kukah, the two religions no longer plead for acceptance but are scrambling for domination:

These two religions are straddled across the Nigerian polity, each no longer knocking and pleading to be admitted but seeking to take over the architectural design and construction of the Nigerian polity.[16]

In order to rescue the nation from preventable bloodbath and destruction of public and private properties, which are being witnessed virtually on daily basis, in the "name of religion", politicians ought to play by the rules and should not smear religion with political disproportion.

Peaceful Co-existence in Islam

Contrary to the insinuations by some people with second-hand information about Islam that the religion is exclusive and intolerant of other religions and their followers, the religion of Islam could be regarded as the most tolerant faith on the surface of the earth. However, the overzealous actions of some Muslims, which sometimes contradict what the faith teaches, have left some non-Muslims with no option but to conclude that such people act according to the teachings of their faith. Badawi captures this scenario thus:

> As a religious faith, normative Islam is not identical with the actions of its 'followers'. Like other religions, followers or claimed followers are imperfect, fallible human beings. There are times when their actions conform, in various degrees, to the normative teachings of their faith. But there are also times when their actions are either independent of or even in violation of such normative teachings. Outsiders may see these offending acts as part of the practice of faith. Sometimes, these acts are committed, falsely, in the name of faith. These claims are made as a result of ignorance, 'sincere' misinterpretations, or even deliberate misrepresentations that are intended to provide sanction and authority for such acts.[17]

To evaluate whether a given act or argument conforms to the normative teachings of a given religion or not, Badawi argues that there must be some criteria for such evaluations, because, according to him, the history of various religious communities is replete with aberrations, even as it is replete also with successful implementation of the norms of their faiths. Human successes or failures are not always identical with ideal norms.[18] To identify these norms, Islam advises that its primary sources, the Qur'ān and the authentic *Sunnah* (sayings, deeds and silent approval of Prophet Muhammad) should be the preferred points of reference. Qur'ān 4:59 says:

> O you who believe! Obey Allah and obey the Messenger (Muhammad), and those of you who are in authority. If you differ in anything amongst yourselves, refer it to Allah and his Messenger, if you believe in Allah and in the Last Day. That is better and more suitable for final determination.

Therefore, in discussing peaceful co-existence from Islamic perspective, there may not be any better starting point than drawing inspiration from the precedents laid by Prophet Muhammad in the multi-religious city-state of al-Madinah. The Prophet migrated to the city of Yathrib (later named al-Madinah) as a Messenger of Allah and as a statesman to unite warring tribes, which had been torn apart by incessant civil wars. Having met another religious group, the Jewish community, in Yathrib, the Prophet sought their cooperation in moving the society forward and in defending it against internal oppression and external aggression. As a way of concretising this agreement, the Prophet proposed a constitution for the city-state with the Muslim community, which encompassed both the *Anṣār* and *Muhājirūn* (the hosts and immigrants) as the stakeholders on the one hand, and the

Jewish community on the other. The document served as the terms of reference for their accord. It acknowledged the Jewish citizenship and the legitimacy of their religion. It also spelt out the rights and duties of both parties in the society.[19] An extract from the constitution reads thus:

> In the name of God, the Compassionate, the Merciful. This is a covenant given by Muhammad to the believers and Muslims of Quraysh, Yathrib, and those who followed them, joined them, and fought with them. They constitute one *Ummah* (nation) to the exclusion of all men... Any Jew who follows us is entitled to assistance and the same rights as any one of us, without injustice or partisanship... The Jews of *Banu Aws* are an *Ummah* alongside the believers. The Jews have their religion and the Muslims theirs. Both enjoy the security of their own populace and clients except the unjust and the criminal among them... The Jews shall bear their public expenses and so will the Muslims. Each shall assist the other against any violator of this covenant... The town of Yathrib shall constitute a sanctuary for the parties of this covenant. Their neighbours shall be treated as themselves as long as they perpetuate no crime and commit no harm... The people of this covenant shall come to the assistance of one another against whoever attacks Yathrib... God grants His protection to whosoever acts in piety, charity and goodness.[20]

Motivated by the news of this accord, the Christian Arabs of Najran also visited the Prophet Muhammad to negotiate their own place in the emerging society. The Prophet invited them to Islam, some embraced, while the majority refused. This did not in any way prevent them from being granted autonomous status as their Jewish counterpart. After presenting them with some gifts, the Prophet directed that they should be escorted back to their place of abode by a Muslim bodyguard and a Muslim statesman, Mu'adh bin Jabal to serve their interest.[21] According to Muhibbu-Din, this constitution guaranteed the freedom of faith and opinion, the inviolability of the city, human life, property and prohibition of crime. Its application also paved the way for unprecedented development by first of all uniting the Arabs and according them a leading role in all facets of human endeavours. The Jewish community, however, later broke their promise to abide by the constitution and acted against the accord, which earned them expulsion from the city.[22]

The baton of tolerance and peaceful co-existence was also carried on by the second *Khalīfah* (successor) of the Prophet, 'Umar bin al-Khattab (581-644). This is shown in his treatment of the Jews and Christians of Byzantium after the fall of Jerusalem. The treaty of the surrender of the city, according to al-Faruqi, was written by Mu'awiyah (602-680) and signed by the *Khalīfah* and Sophronius (560-638), Patriarch of the city, on behalf of the Christians, which partly read thus:

> In the name of Allah, the Beneficent, the Merciful. This is the guarantee granted to the inhabitants of Aelia by 'Umar, Servant of God, and commander of the believers. He guarantees for them the safety of their persons, of their goods, of their churches and crosses – whether in good state of repair or otherwise – and generally of their religion. Their churches will not be changed into dwellings, nor destroyed. Neither they nor their other properties will suffer any damage whatsoever. In matters of religions, no coercion will be exercised against them; nor will any of them be hurt... The inhabitants of Aelia shall pay the *jizyah* (tax) like those of other cities. It will be their duty to eject the Byzantines (i.e., the troops of Byzantine Empire) and their clients from the city. Those that leave voluntarily will be granted safe passage. Those who choose to remain in the city may do so provided they pay the *jizyah* like the other inhabitants. The citizens of Aelia who wish to leave with the Byzantines may do so, and may carry with them their goods, properties and crosses. Safety is hereby granted to them as well... This treaty is given under the guarantee of God and the honour of the Prophet, of the *Khulafa'* and the believers on condition that the people of Aelia pay the *jizyah* due on them.

Witnesses: Khalid bin al-Walid, 'Amr bin al-'As, 'Abd al-Rahman bin 'Awf, Mu'awiyah bin Abi Sufyan who wrote it with his own hand in the year 15AH.[23]

Another remarkable event took place during the days of 'Umar bin al-Khattab. On his entry to Jerusalem, he found himself inside a Church at the time for one of the five daily prayers, when the patriarch, who was accompanying him, offered him to perform his prayers in the Church. The *Khalīfah* declined, and remarked: "If I do so, the Muslims may infringe upon your rights in a future age pretending to follow my example." Instead, 'Umar performed his prayers on the steps outside the Church.[24] As reported by al-Bukhari (810-870) in *Futuh al-Buldan*, which is also documented by Al-Faruqi, the same terms in the above treaty were granted by Khalid bin al-Walid to the inhabitants of the towns of Damascus, al-Hirah and 'Anat, as well as to other provinces brought under the sovereignty of Islam.[25] Commenting on these developments, Michael Nazir-Ali[26] argues that the tolerance exhibited by Muslims paved the way for the penetration of Islam to many Christian cities of the Middle East:

> Many of the leading cities of the Christian Middle East that capitulated to the Muslims in those days did so because they believed that Muslim rule would be more tolerable than the rule of Byzantium. So, the gates of Damascus were opened to the Muslim armies by the Christians of the town. Jerusalem capitulated without a fight, and a similar situation existed in Egypt. For Christians, it is a matter of repentance that the oppression by the Christians of the eastern Roman Empire against their fellow-Christians was of such intensity that people in Syria and Egypt thought that it was better to have Muslims as their rulers than their fellow-Christians.[27]

The interaction of the *crème de la crème* of Muslim generations with other religious communities in the city-state of al-Madinah and in other parts of the world speaks volumes about the tolerance demonstrated by the Prophet of Islam and his followers. This signifies the acceptance of plurality in human societies. In other words, forcing people to believe in God runs against His decree of free will, which includes the fact that some will reject Him. The ultimate reward or punishment for accepting or rejecting belief in God is deferred until the Day of Judgment. This value inculcates the attitude of being non-judgmental and accepting people as they are which was clearly stated in the Yathrib constitution, and practically implemented by the Prophet and his companions. However, acceptance of plurality, according to Badawi, does not mean accepting the plurality of ultimate truths, nor does it preclude sharing or compromising one's faith with others and even inviting them to it. Plurality means peaceful co-existence with those who hold differing beliefs and convictions.[28] Acceptance of plurality in human societies, which is an imperative platform for peaceful co-existence, is explicitly explained in the following verses of the Glorious Qur'ān:

> And if your Lord had so willed, He could surely have made mankind one *Ummah* [nation or community (following one religion only i.e. Islam)], but they will not cease to disagree. (Qur'ān 11:118)

> And had your Lord willed, those on earth would have believed, all of them together. So, will you then compel mankind, until they become believers. (Qur'ān 10:99)

The above verses and others in their ilk warn the believers not to go beyond presentation of the truth, or try to compel their audience to believe in what has been presented to them. In other words, they are forbidden from interfering with non-Muslims' decision of accepting or rejecting the Message. Similarly, an extension of being tolerant is to be humane to every member of one's society whether Muslims or non-Muslims. Prophet Muhammad was reported to have said in a Hadith narrated by ᶜAbdullah bin 'Umar: "(Angel) Jibril never ceased urging me repeatedly to be kind to my neighbour, until I thought he will make him one of my heirs."[29] He also says: "Anyone who believes in Allah and the Last Day let him be kind to his neighbour. Anyone who believes in Allah and the Last Day let him be hospitable to his guest."[30]

The above quotations underscore the importance Islam attaches to tolerance and peaceful co-existence with neighbours and other members of one's community. Likewise, these Qur'ānic and Hadith texts disqualify the notion of narrow partisanship that may lead to hatred or even violence against communities who perceive themselves as followers of other Prophets, as well as humanity as a whole. Due to unity and universality of the core teachings of all Prophets, Islam makes no distinction among the Prophets of Allah:

> The Messenger (Muhammad) believes in what has been sent down to him from his Lord, and (so do) the believers. Each one believes in Allah, His angels, His Books, and His Messengers. They say, "We make no distinction between one another of His Messengers" - and they say, "We hear, and we obey. (We seek) your forgiveness, our Lord, and to you is the return (of all)." (Qur'ān 2:285)

There are areas of disagreement between Muslims and non-Muslims, especially the Christians, on issues such as the trinity,[31] the alleged crucifixion of Prophet 'Isa (Jesus),[32] the original sin and the purported death of Jesus for mankind,[33] among others. Be that as it may, these issues in normal circumstances should not lead to religious fracas, which are prevalent in Nigeria and different parts of the world today. The Glorious Qur'ān gives various reasons why each human being must be honoured and dignified on account of being human and irrespective of his or her chosen beliefs. Such honour is symbolised by the way the Qur'ān describes Allah's creation of the human in the best of moulds and commanding the angels to bow down in respect to Adam. The Qur'ān also explains how the Almighty Creator honoured the children of Adam and raised them above other creatures (Qur'ān 17:70). Therefore, violating the sanctity of human life or dishonouring any human, with no justification, is tantamount to dishonouring what Allah Himself has honoured.

Rejection of belief in God will surely have consequences in the afterlife. However, it is up to Allah, the Almighty to determine these consequences. Such future determination has no bearing on the respect of the humanity of every person in this life. After all, the human beings are free agents, who are given choices to believe or disbelieve:

> And say: "The truth is from your Lord." Then whosoever wills, let him believe, and whosoever wills, let him disbelieve. Verily, we have prepared for the *Zālimūn* (polytheists and wrong-doers, etc.), a fire whose walls will be surrounding them (disbelievers in the Oneness of Allah)... (Qur'ān 18:29)

As such, each is individually responsible before God for his or her beliefs and moral choices. A person may be held accountable in this life only if such a moral choice infringes on the rights of individuals or society, such as the commission of crimes or acts of aggression. In other words, no human is entitled to dehumanise or punish another on the sole ground that the latter is following a particular religion. This value implies that peaceful co-existence among the followers of all religions and respecting their humanity is not only required, but also enjoined in the Qur'ān and Hadith, the primary sources of Islam.[34] Furthermore, Islam gives free choice in case of religion because, "sword can win territories but not hearts, and force can bend heads but not minds".[35]

Daʿwah and Free Will

Having attempted to explain Islam's recognition and respect for the free will bestowed on individuals to choose a religion or no religion,[36] and denunciation of forcing peoples to a belief, one may ask: Is calling people to accept another faith not a compulsion or infringement on their free will? Answer to this question has been provided in the following verses:

> Invite to the way of your Lord with wisdom and fair preaching, and argue with them in a way that is better. Truly, your Lord knows best who has gone astray from His path, and He is the best aware of those who are guided. (Qur'ān 16:125)

> Say: "Obey Allah and obey the Messenger", but if you turn away, he is only responsible for the duty placed on him and you for that placed on you. If you obey him, you shall be on the right guidance. The Messenger's duty is only to convey (the Message) in a clear way (Qur'ān 24:54).

It may be inferred from the above verses that sharing information about a religion or propagating one's faith, known in Islam as *Daʿwah*, is not the same as forcing it on others. Religions, so to say, may be regarded as goods or commodities in the market. The owner's efforts to persuade passersby to buy the goods by describing and eulogising his wares might not be tantamount to compelling them to purchase, as the final decision lies with the individuals. According to Badawi, the Qur'ān only makes it a duty on believers to communicate the message of Islam to fellow humans and to be witnesses to humankind. Being witnesses for Allah, he argues, includes both witnessing through righteous deeds and sharing what one believes is the truth, which is beneficial to humankind. The invitee has every right to accept or reject that 'invitation'. Conversely, compulsion, threats, bribery, deception, manipulation, and exploitation of the invitee's vulnerability (such as hunger, illness, disaster, etc) are inconsistent with the notion of invitation:

> And had your Lord willed, those on earth would have believed, all of them together. So, will you then compel mankind, until they become believers. (Qur'ān 10:99)

Therefore, whoever threatens or dehumanises a fellow man just because he/she is not a Muslim may be said to be doing so on his own accord, as Allah made it clear that it is He who guides, and no one, even the Prophet cannot singlehandedly guide anyone to the right path except by the permission of the Almighty. Qur'ān explains as follows:

> Verily! You guide not whom you like, but Allah guides whom He wills. And He knows best those who are the guided. (Qur'ān 28:56)

> Not upon you (O Muhammad) is their guidance, but Allah guides whom He wills. (Qur'ān 2:272).

Jihad and Peaceful Co-existence

The above discussion necessitates brief clarification on the misconception about *Jihad*, because some people think that by oppressing or maltreating non-Muslims, they are on the right cause of Allah and they will be rewarded for doing so. On the contrary, as argued above, Islam does not condone an iota of injustice from any quarters, and no matter who the oppressed are. At this juncture, looking at the meaning of *Jihad* and the context it is used in Islam could provide an insight into what *Jihad* is all about. According to Badawi, the Qur'ānic/Arabic term *Jihad* has been commonly mistranslated as "holy war". He argues that the Qur'ān was revealed in Arabic, not in English. The Arabic equivalent of the English expression "holy war", he explains, is *harbun muqaddasah,* an expression that is not found anywhere in the Qur'ān or in the authentic sayings of the Prophet.[37] Even when the Qur'ān speaks about defensive war, it never glorifies it or calls it "holy"; rather, it is described as something which is inherently hated (Qur'ān 2:216-217). However, as a last resort, it may be better than doing nothing in the face of aggression or oppression.[38]

Scholars assert that "*Jihad*" literally means "to strive" or "to exert efforts". Thus, in Islam, "to carry out *Jihad*" is "to show effort, or to struggle" in the path of Allah.[39] According to Abdul Majid, *Jihad* consists of two dimensions: the inner *Jihad* that seeks to curb negative and self-destructive forces within, and the external *Jihad*, which is a struggle against violence and tyranny by means of words and actions.[40] According to Badawi, *Jihad* is an Arabic term derived from the root J-H-D, which means, literally, "to strive or exert effort." It is the same root word from which the legal term *ijtihad* is derived, as *ijtihad* refers to the exertion of intellectual effort by scholars so as to come up with an informed religious opinion on contemporary issues or problems.[41] Prophet Muhammad once admonished his companions that "the greatest *Jihad* is the one a person carries out against his lower soul." "Lower soul" here means selfish desires and ambitions. On another occasion, the Prophet addressed his companions, saying: "We are now returning from the lesser *Jihad* to the greater *Jihad*."[42] When asked what the greater *Jihad* was, he replied, "It is the *Jihad* against your passionate souls." Abdul Majid maintains that this greater *Jihad* is therefore the inner battle to purify the souls of its imperfections, to empty the vessel of the soul of the pungent water of forgetfulness.[43] Apart from spiritual meanings, struggle in the physical sense is also considered as *"Jihad"* for which the exact word is *Qital* (fighting). However, Islam spells out the strict principles of *Qital*, among which are: in defence when one is attacked; to eradicate corruption from the earth; for the elimination of persecution, or for getting moral, religious and physical freedom for oppressed people. If for these purposes *Jihad* is waged, it could be regarded in the way of Allah, which is a just war for sacred cause. For achieving such noble cause, despite that, the Muslims are ordained to observe certain rules during the war.

When Islam forbids the old cruel and barbaric practices in war, it makes its own rules for the conduct of hostilities – if situation demands. Thus non-combatants are not to be made to suffer on account of war. Even against the combatants, one can use only that much force which is necessary to achieve the purpose of "just war" but not going beyond the limits. "Allah does not love those who go beyond the limits" (Qur'ān 2:190). Furthermore, if the enemy offers peace, one has no choice but to accept, and stop all hostilities. In the same vein, one cannot commit excesses or cruelties during the actual conduct of hostilities and war. In other words, acts of arson and pillage are prohibited. Destruction of property, plants and crops is also forbidden. Women, children, aged ones, and handicapped should also be spared. All the terms of treaties and other agreements have to be strictly adhered to, and places of worship are to be spared and protected.[44]Consequently, a situation where innocent school children are massacred, public and private properties are destroyed are totally against the teaching of Islam.

In a nutshell, the sole essence of the message of Islam and the mission of its Prophet as expatiated by the Qur'ān and the *Sunnah* is mercy to the entire mankind and other creatures of Allah, which include animals and plants. "And we have sent you not but as a mercy for all creatures (Qur'ān 21:107). This aim is however defeated, if anyone, in the name of Islam scares away, through his deeds and speeches the very people who are meant to receive mercy and thus making peaceful co-existence unattainable. Furthermore, al-Faruqi put this essence in a wider perspective:

> The essence of religious experience in Islam, we may say... is the realisation that life is not in vain; that it must serve a purpose, the nature of which cannot be identical with the natural flow of appetite to satisfaction to new appetite and new satisfaction.[45]

Therefore, an overzealous individual, who makes Islam distasteful to non-Muslims, may be presumed to be satisfying his own natural appetite, which is not identical with the teaching of the religion. Islam unequivocally prohibits acts of violence against any person, non-Muslims inclusive. Even during the period of war, Prophet Muhammad exclusively warned the Muslim armies not to destroy non-Muslim places of worship and directed his followers to save the crops and other vegetation in their fields.

Concluding Remarks

This study dwelled on peaceful co-existence through the Islamic lens. It based its arguments on the premises of various texts from the Glorious Qur'ān and traditions of the Prophet of Islam, practical live experiences and remarkable events. In order for these theories to materialise and transform into meaningful experience in today's world, all and sundry, especially Muslim faithful must abide by the teachings of Islam and strive to emulate the Messenger of Allah, the best example for mankind. By so doing, Nigeria, and indeed, our world will be safer and better for all to live in.

Notes and References

1. O. Akinwumi,*Crises and Conflicts in Nigeria Political History since 1960*, (Berlin:Lit Veralg Munster, 2004), 146. Also see: Y. O. Imam,*Religious Crises and Social Disruption in North Eastern Nigeria*,(Ibadan: Loud Books Publishers, 2004), 5.
2. S. Udoidem, "Religion in the Political Life of Nigeria: A Survey of Religious-Related Crises in Nigeria since Independence" in *New Strategies for Curbing Ethnic and Religious Conflicts in Nigeria*. F. U. Okafor (ed). (Enugu: Fourth Dimension Publishers, 1997), 165-181.
3. Y. O. Imam, *Religious Crises and Social Disruption in North Eastern Nigeria*, 10.
4. Y. O. Imam, *Religious Crises and Social Disruption in North Eastern Nigeria*, 10-11.
5. M. A. Bidmos, *Inter-religious dialogue: The Nigerian experience*, (Lagos: Islamic Education Bureau, 1993), 46.
6. A. S. Hornby, *Oxford Advanced Learner's Dictionary of Current English7th ed.*, (Oxford: Oxford University Press, 2005).
7. K. Ahmad, *Fanaticism, Intolerance and Islam*, (Lahore: Islamic Publications Limited, 1981), 5
8. Y. O. Imam, Y. O. Imam, *Religious Crises and Social Disruption in North Eastern Nigeria*, 10.
9. Y. O. Imam, *Religious Crises and Social Disruption in North Eastern Nigeria*, 6.

10. M. A. Bidmos, *Inter-religious dialogue*, 51-52.
11. M. H. Kukah, and T. Falola, *Religious Militancy and Self-assertion*, (Vermont: Ashgate Publishing Limited, 1996), 113.
12. M. A. Bidmos, *Inter-religious dialogue*, 52.
13. G. B. Mancilla, "Citizenship and Religion in Nigeria: Comparative perspectives of Islam and Christianity in Kaduna State", University of Sussex, <http://osun.org/isla/islam-in-kaduna-doc.html> (accessed 19 September, 2013).
14. S. Udoidem, "Religion in the Political Life of Nigeria", 177.
15. S. Udoidem, "Religion in the Political Life of Nigeria", 155.
16. M. H. Kukah, *Religion, Politics and Power in Northern Nigeria*, (Ibadan: Spectrum Books Ltd, 1993), ix.
17. Jamal Badawi, "Muslim and Non-Muslim Relations: Reflections on Some Qur'ānic Texts," <http://islamonline.net/english/Contemporary/2005/04/Article01.shtml> (accessed 21 May, 2011).
18. Jamal Badawi, "Muslim and Non-Muslim Relations".
19. M. A. Muhibbu-Din, *Ideal Moral and Spiritual Guidance in a Multi-Religious State (Nigeria): An Islamic Approach*, Birmingham: Centre for the Study of Islam and Christian-Muslim Relations, 1992), 4-5. Also see Ismail al-Faruqi, "Islam and other Faiths: The World's Need for Humane Universalism," in Altaf Gauhar (ed.), *The Challenge of Islam*, (London: Islamic Council of Europe, 1978), 131-150.
20. M. H. Haykal, *The Life of Muhammad*, translated by Ismail R. Al-Faruqi, (Lagos: 1982), 180-183. Also see Muhibbu-Din, 5-6.
21. M. H. Haykal, *The Life of Muhammad*, also see Islam and other Faiths, 147.
22. Muhibbu-Din, *Ideal Moral and Spiritual Guidance in a Multi-Religious State (Nigeria)*, 6.
23. Al-Tabari, ibn Jarir, *Tarikh ar-Rusul wa al-Muluk*, (Cairo: Dar al-Maᶜarif, 1979), vol. III, 609. Also quoted by al-Faruqi in his

book: *Islam and other Faiths*, Ataullah Siddiqui (ed.). (Leicester: The Islamic Foundation, 1998), 295-296.
24. Ishtiaq H. Qureshi, *The Religion of Peace*, (Karachi: Royal Book Company, 1989), 102.
25. al-Faruqi, *Islam and other Faiths*, 296.
26. Michael Nazir-Ali was born on 19th August, 1949 in Karachi, Pakistan to Christian parents, James and Patience Nazir-Ali. His father converted from Islam to Christianity. Michael Nazir-Ali was the 106th Bishop of Rochester in the Church of England and retired as diocesan bishop in September 2009. (Wikipedia).
27. M. N. Ali, *The Root of Islamic Tolerance: Origin and Development*, (Oxford: Oxford Project for Peace Studies, 1990), 3.
28. Badawi, "Muslim and Non-Muslim Relations: Reflections on Some Qur'ānic Texts".
29. Related by al-Bukhari and Muslim.
30. Related by al- Bukhari, Muslim, Ahmad and others.
31. "Surely, disbelievers are those who said: "Allah is the third of the three (in a Trinity)." but there is no *Ilah* (God) (none who has the right to be worshipped) but one *Ilah* (God -Allah). And if they cease not from what they say, verily, a painful torment will befall the disbelievers among them." (Qur'ān 5:73).
32. "And because of their saying (in boast), "We killed Messiah 'Isa (Jesus), son of Maryam (Mary), the Messenger of Allah," - but they killed him not, nor crucified him, but the resemblance of 'Isa (Jesus) was put over another man (and they killed that man), and those who differ therein are full of doubts. They have no (certain) knowledge, they follow nothing but conjecture. For surely; they killed him not [i.e. 'Isa (Jesus), son of Maryam (Mary)]: But Allah raised him ['Isa (Jesus)] up (with his body and soul) unto himself (and He is in the heavens). And Allah is ever All-Powerful, All-Wise." (Qur'ān 4:157-158).

33. And no bearer of burdens shall bear another's burden, and if one heavily laden calls another to (bear) his load, nothing of it will be lifted even though he is near of kin. You (O Muhammad SAW) can warn only those who fear their Lord unseen, and perform As-Salat (Iqamat-al-Salat). And he who purifies himself (from all kinds of sins), then he purifies only for the benefit of his ownself. And to Allah is the (Final) return (of all). (Qur'ān 35:18).
34. For more on peaceful co-existence, see: Jamal Badawi, "Muslim and Non-Muslim Relations: Reflections on Some Qur'ānic Texts."
35. Quoted by Abdul Majid in a paper titled: "Peaceful Co-existence of Various Cultures and Religions: An Islamic perspective with special reference to Spain", 8. <http://www.metanexus.nte/conference> (accessed 2 June, 2011).
36. "And say: "The Truth is from your Lord. "Then whosoever wills, let him believe, and whosoever wills, let him disbelieve." (Qur'ān 18:29).
37. Jamal Badawi, Muslim and Non-Muslim Relations: Reflections on Some Qur'ānic Texts.
38. Jamal Badawi, "Muslim and Non-Muslim Relations".
39. Abdul Majid. "Peaceful Co-existence of Various Cultures and Religions", 8.
40. Abdul Majid. "Peaceful Co-existence of Various Cultures and Religions", 8.
41. "Muslim and Non-Muslim Relations".
42. Quoted by Harun Yahya, *Islam Denounces Terrorism* (New York: Tehrike Tarsile Quran, Inc, 2002), 94-95; also available at: <www.islamdenouncesterrorism.com> (accessed 21 May, 2011).
43. Abdul Majid. "Peaceful Co-existence of Various Cultures and Religions", 8.

44. Abdul Rahman, *The Peace*, (Muscat Oman: Batna Printing Press, 1999), 128-129. Also quoted by Abdul Majid in "Peaceful Co-existence of Various Cultures and Religions," 9. All of the above points are explained in the various Qur'ānic verses and authentic Hadith of the Prophet (SAW). One would realise that although Islam permits *Jihad* but under strict conditions, and not for personal aggrandisement or for any worldly gain but for defence purposes and to eradicate corruption and persecution from the society and for the welfare of humanity. Therefore, *Jihad* should be understood in its true perspective and should not be confused with other wars of the world. Islam considers the killing of an innocent person tantamount to the killing of the whole humanity. "If anyone killed another person – unless it is in retaliation for someone else or for causing corruption in the earth – it is as if he had murdered all mankind. And if anyone saved a life, it is as if he saved the life of all mankind." (Qur'ān 5:32).
45. Al-Faruqi, R. I. *Islam and Other Faiths*, 17.

CHAPTER SEVEN

The Impact of Religion in Curbing Corruption in Nigeria

Ayoola, Adediran Amos
Department of Christian Religious Studies
Emmanuel Alayande College of Education
Oyo, Oyo State, Nigeria.
adediranayoola@yahoo.com
+2348062830185

Introduction

Corruption may be described as the non-performance of duties by a part of an organised system or as the performance of duties in a way that is detrimental to the system's original purpose. The common term that can be given to corruption and injustice is "unjust act" Adelowo (2009). Since 1960, when the country became independent, Nigerians have been trying hard by establishing various anti-corruption organisations like Economic and Financial Crime Commission (EFCC) and Independent Corrupt Practice and other related offences Commission (ICPC), but unsuccessfully to put an end to injustice and corruption in Nigeria. With many mosques and churches found in Nigeria, one expects that the level of morality would be high but the reverse is the case. However, the present situation in the country; where corruption can be felt at all tiers of government justifies the above assertion. Adelowo at a recent conference said, "Nigeria no doubt is experiencing a lot of unstable situations, inabilities of all sorts in the areas of economy, politics, education, behavioural patterns, cultural settings, religion and so on".[1]

The high rate of injustice and corruption in Nigeria is noticeable in all facets of human endeavour, even in the worship of God. President Obama of the United States of America captured the consequences of corruption in his address to the members of Parliament in Ghana, thus:

> No country is going to create wealth if its leaders exploit the economy to enrich themselves, or Police can be bought off by drug traffickers, no businessman wants to invest in a place where the government skims 20 percent off the top or the head of the port authority is corrupt..... No person wants to live in a society where the rule of law gives way to the rule of brutality and bribery.[2]

The above scenario explains the reason why the rate of development is low in Nigeria, despite the fact that she is endowed with natural resources. It is also obvious that the love of 'Money' is the root of injustice and corruption in Nigeria. The rate at which one acquires wealth determines the respect to be accorded one in the society. As a result of this, everybody wants to be respected, therefore all dubious means to acquire wealth are used.

In Nigeria, when one has the opportunity of getting a political appointment, people believe that such a person has crossed to a land of wealth, forgetting the fact that a call to political office is an avenue to serve the masses and not a short-cut to financial success. Bribery is the term of the day in both government and private parastatals in Nigeria i.e. people see collection of bribe as the term of the day and means of surviving the economic hardship.[3] The level of corruption is so high in Nigeria that, outside the country, such as United States of America, United Kingdom etc. accept the fact that Nigeria is a corrupt country[4].

Corruption has not only affected the social integrity of the nation but also the hopes of the people for development. Its manifestations include the inflation of government contracts in return for kickbacks; fraud and falsification of accounts in the public services; examination malpractices in our educational institutions; offering/acceptance of bribes; and perversion of justice. The business and industrial sectors of the economy collude with multinational companies by over-invoicing of goods, foreign exchange swindling, hoarding and smuggling of goods. Corruption also manifests in such forms as adulteration of market goods or the reduction of the quality and quantity of goods with the view to giving undue advantage to the sellers.[5]

To this effect, the government has devised various methods like the establishment of the Independent Corrupt Practices and Other Related Offences Commission (ICPC) and the Economic and Financial Crimes Commission (EFCC) to tackle corruption. However, the situation has not improved, for instance, before President Obasanjo came to power, Nigeria was occupying the 27th position on the corruption chart, but during his tenure, the country moved up to the first position as declared by Transparency International Organisation, which Obasanjo once chaired.[6] The aforementioned organisations have done a lot to curb corruption. However the problem has not been totally eradicated. It is on this note that we are looking at the role that religion can plays in reducing corruption in Nigeria.

Definition of Religion

There is no universally-accepted definition for the term religion. Some scholars of religion and philosophers have attempted to define religion from various perspectives. Some claim that religion is a feeling, an emotion, worship or fear of the Supreme Being i.e. the most high referred to as God. Some claim that it is an awareness and respect for metaphysical powers. Religion is part of man's culture and it is a means through which the metaphysical and Supreme Being i.e. unseen God has a close spiritual relationship with man.[7] However, a very meaningful definition of religion by *The Oxford Advanced Learner's Dictionary* says religion is the (organised) service and worship of a god, gods or the supernatural in other words a cause, principle or system of beliefs held with ardour and faith, considered to be of supreme importance.

The word 'religion' etymologically is derived from Latin. The meaning suggests a relationship, a bond, but also an obligation, a commitment, or a submission. In support of this view, Arowolo stated that religion, when explained in its simplest form is the relationship between God and man.[8] To him, it is a phenomenon that started at the time men began to respond to the goodness of God through worship. Immanuel Kant defined religion as the recognition of man's duties as divine commands. According to him religion is the belief, which sets what is essential in all adoration of God in human morality.[9] According to Martin Buber, religion is regarded as essentially the act of holding on to God.[10] Omidiwura opined that on the other hand, some scholars see religion as any system of thought and action shared by a group, which gives the individual a frame of orientation and an object of devotion. Julian Huxley defined religion as a way of life.[11]

Okponaviobo defined religion as "any phenomenon which seems to help the individual satisfy his or her spiritual thirst, as well as, prepare the way of the ultimate through the penultimate.[12] Ryle, an American philosopher argued that religion is loyalty to God or gods.[13] Religion may also be

---

Chapter Seven | Ayoola, Adediran Amos, in
Y.A. Quadri, R.W. Omotoye & R.I. Adebayo (Eds)
Religion in Contemporary Nigeria
London, Adonis & Abbey Publishers

defined as the awareness of the existence of a supernatural being behind all creation and the realization of the fact that all creatures are sustained by this Being; and therefore all are connected with and owe allegiance to this Being. Religion may also be seen as the pattern of beliefs and practices through which men communicate with, or hope to gain experience of that which lies behind the world of their ordinary experience. The aforementioned definitions reveal that the most basic element of religion is worship while moral conduct, right, belief and participation in religious institutions are constituent elements of the religious life as practised by believers and worshippers, and as commanded by religious sages and scriptures. Therefore, the definitions that regard religion as the way of life as arranged by the supernatural Being are essential aspects to be considered here.

Anatomy of Corruption in Nigeria

It is no more news that corruption has become a way of life among Nigerians. This is because it is found in almost all aspects of life as evident in the political setting, police force, judiciary, business world, among academics; even in religious institutions.[14] Benson Igboin rightly observed that corruption means to act contrary to a set of agreed, acceptable and shared norms.[15] This locates corruption within the framework of morality. However, hard facts about corruption are difficult to come by in Nigeria because corrupt officials always work hard to destroy evidence.

The main cause of corruption in Nigeria appears to be abject poverty. It is believed that the salaries of public officials compared to the economic situation in the country have led many people into corruption. Lack of purposeful leadership and sincere fellowship with fear of God are other reasons. There is also the desire to acquire material things by all means. Others include, greed, spirit of domination, lack of security in the social system, unemployment, retrenchment of workers, perverted moral order and illiteracy. The immunity against persecution granted certain public officials is said to be one of the determinant factors responsible for corruption in Nigeria.[16]

Many Nigerian leaders and top bureaucrats are setting bad examples of self-enrichment for the lower-level officials and members of the public. Hence, bribery and corruption are taken by many Nigerians as the norm even in the face of anti-corruption crusades intended to promote transparent governance.[17]

Corruption appears to be one of the major obstacles to the realization of Nigeria's developmental objectives. Various efforts have been made by successive governments to address the problem of corruption in Nigeria. These efforts include setting up programmes, such as, War Against Indiscipline; Mass Mobilization for Social Justice, Self Reliance and Economic Recovery; Poverty Alleviation Programme; Economic and Financial Crimes Commission (EFCC) and the Independent Corrupt Practices and Other Related Offences Commission (ICPC).[18] Some of the bodies have been commended; while at times villified by Nigerians. However, these bodies sometimes regard some corrupt important personalities as 'sacred cows', untouchable and persecute only those who have stepped on the toes of the people in power. However, it is argued that for a meaningful and effective anti-corruption crusade, government should look beyond mere programmes and legal structures. Therefore, the role of religion should not be overlooked since it develops people's minds and enables them to do right at all levels.[19] It is pertinent to point out that Salawu F.O. has enumerated some highly placed Nigerians who had been found guilty of curruption and sanctioned.[20]

The Impact of Religion in Curbing Corruption

Religion means different things to different people. In the first instance, it is seen by many in a narrow sense to refer to a particular group.[21] Some look at it from the point of view of the belief systems, moral norms values held by members of the society.[22] Some others see it as an integral part of the culture of a people and as such, this category of people opined that there should be an examination of the influence of society on religion and the effects which religion has on society.[23]

We define religion as "the means of communion and communication between the human and super human beings, between the sensible and the supersensible, between the finite and the infinite, between the visible and the invisible, in one word between man and God."[24] Religion is an intrinsic aspect of every human life and it forms the essential bed-rock upon which people's moral and social obligations are based. The question that has hitherto agitated the human mind is what is the relationship that exists between religion and morality? Or better still, what is the origin of morality? Scholars hold divergent views on this. In the first instance, some held the view that what we call morality has its origin in the society in as much as the society has inculcated in people the sense of right and wrong. Also, they contended that what we call "conscience" is inculcated in a person through the agency of the society. Another category of scholars opined that morality is a product of common sense. Experience, they say, is the best teacher, as it is the constant accumulation of this experience of over a long period of time that brought about the sense of right and wrong.[25]

Another group claims that morality is a product of Religion. It is God who puts in people the sense of what is right and what is wrong thereby bringing the sense of obligation. This was attested to by Alan Richardson when he stated that: "the sense of obligation to do that which is believed to be right is, infact, the pressure God put upon every human life..."[26] In the same vein, Emile Brunner corroborates this fact when he asserts interalia that "man is unable to construct an ethical system without recourse to the Deity..."[27] The same idea is expressed by Karl Barth, a theologian, when he said "ethical knowledge and achievement are only possible through God's revelation, especially His final revelation in Jesus Christ".[28] These imply that morality is indeed the idea of God who has imbued people with the consciousness of distinguishing right action from wrong ones. Therefore, we assert that morality and religion are two sides of the same coin and they cannot be detached from each other.

It is obvious from our discussion that the government has taken some measures to eradicate corruption, unfortunately, there are still some challenges in overcoming it. It is in the light of this that we want to recommend religion; as a catalyst. It is argued that we cannot have good morals without religion for the goal of religion is to ensure that the adherents are morally upright. Religion is a useful instrument for enforcing moral codes. Religion preaches brotherliness, rectitude and moral precepts, it is therefore regarded as the force that sanctifies and validates the customs and administrative institutions established for the maintenance of order and good government in human societies. Hence, for corruption to be minimised in our society, religion has a principal role to play. Apparently, some of the religious leaders in the Orthodox and Pentecostal Churches are not immune from corruption in Nigeria through the preaching of prosperity messages. Most of the church members who are not financially bouyant always look for means through which the Pastor's utterance will come to pass.

There are three main religions in Nigeria, namely; Traditional Religions, Islam and Christianity. All these religions have some common features, particularly, the worship of Supreme Being which is God. Each religion has its codes of ethics. In each of the religions, there are moral principles, which are meant to guide adherents in their behaviour. Arowolo stated that, in Christianity, there are moral principles based on the commandments inherited from Judaism while in Islam, it is the Sharia, which has been described as a way of life.[29] Nigerians appear to be highly religious as we can see in the establishment of many churches, mosques and shrines where they worship God as the Creator and Sustainer of the Universe. Since every Nigerian appears to be religious, it is expected of him/her to consider the following in his/her endeavours.

A religious man will find himself adopting those characteristic attitudes which are religious, and which in turn lead to a high norm or moral discipline. Similarly, a religious man will be reverent and this mood of reverence is a rich soil for moral idealism.

A religious man will be driven by the dynamics of his faith to a high sense of morality. In fact, every human life must be regarded as a form of divinity. Therefore, man has to strive to bring about social order that will ensure freedom to all men. As a matter of fact, all the three religions teach morals that enable man to be faithful to the rules and regulations of the society he finds himself.

Ethics and morality serve as the bases of all the three religions. From the Christian point of view, Biblical injunctions on ethics deals with the 'dos' and 'don'ts' of human conduct in relationship, first towards God, and secondly towards one's fellowmen. These moral concepts were divinely revealed. Morality, according to Bolaji Idowu is basically the "fruit of religion"[30] and each divinity punishes moral offences that are committed within its province.

Oludele stressed that moral education tries to develop in human beings the act of rational thinking and, in fact, a disposition to those things that would ensure the survival of the society. He further pointed out that moral education trains human conscience and teaches such values as honesty, faithfulness, love, dedication, diligence, respect, obedience, perseverance, patience and devotion. Consequently, moral education enables man to judge his actions and decide to do what is acceptable in the society. Many social ills that have eaten deep into the fabric of the society could have been avoided through moral education.[31]

Religion and religious bodies remain a potent solution that can encourage transparency in Nigeria's national life. Religion has been playing an important role in the education of the citizens both at the formal and informal levels since the colonial period. Many religious bodies in Nigeria have spent enormous resources on primary, secondary and tertiary education and have been able to help in building the moral and spiritual life of people. It has been aptly observed that character building is the cardinal role of religious instruction.[32] Although, the government is clamouring for science and technology, so as to meet up with the technological development of the western world.

In addition, Nigeria's national ethics encourages patriotism and transparency in national life. All these values are found in the Bible, Qur'an and other religious scriptures. Thus, the inculcation of religious values provides the needed opportunity for the attainment of these ethics which have the ultimate goal of reducing corruption and the encouragement of transparency and sustainable development.[33] In religious preaching, the citizenry receive exhortation against immorality, bribery, cheating, prostitution and lawlessness, which are impediments to sustainable development. In certain other traditional religious practices apart from the aforementioned, there are means of recovering stolen things – the accompanying punishment for culprits can also serve as deterrent to others. For example, Sango, one of the divinities in Yoruba land, is believed to be capable of killing the culprists through thunder.

In concrete steps, the religious bodies are expected to denounce corrupt practices. For instance, Catholic Bishops of Nigeria supported the anti-corruption law of the federal government with a prayer against bribery and corruption in Nigeria and a piece of advice to western financial institutions to stop co-operating with fraudulent public servants by not accepting stolen money for safekeeping in their banks.[34]

Finally, there is no doubt that religion as an institution is assisting in a sustainable development. It played dominant role in the growth of some developed countries before the separation of state and religion. For example, in USA and Germany. According to Ogunsi, protestant ethics assisted such countries.

Recommendations

1. Sound teachings of the tenets and doctrines of all religions should be encouraged in places of worship, schools and tertiary institutions. Religious studies curriculum in our schools and tertiary institutions should be reviewed;
2. There should be a strong fight to alleviate poverty and discrimination of all forms;
3. Corruption should be fought with all available resources rather than cultivating it;
4. The African value system should be protected from greed and avarice of the few Oligarchies that control the means of production and other basic instrument of life's ease.
5. Government shoud subsidise some basic human needs such as food, shelter, education, health services, good roads, and so on.

Conclusion

It has been revealed that corruption persists in the country because it has received inadequate attention from the Church, Mosque and shrine. Religion is a catalyst of change in the spiritual, political and social life of any society.

Every religion teaches its adherents to fear God. If there is fear of God in people, the act of corruption would be minimised. Therefore, all adherents of the three religions should do away with greed. This may result to the development of the physical, mental, psychological and spiritual potentials of men and can facilitate effective nation building. Most importantly, morality should be the watchword of every Nigerian. On this note, religion if adequately maintained is capable of eradicating corrupt practices in

Nigeria. This is because morality is a basic tenet of religion and through this the conduct of individuals is regulated.

Notes and References

1. E. Dada Adelowo, A Keynote Address in respect of 2009 NASRED Conference held at Osun State College of Education, Ilesa on 4th August, 2009. (Haytee Press and Publishing co., Ilorin), 2.
2. President Barrack Obama's Address to the House of Parliament in Ghana—*The Nation on Sunday*, 12th July, 2009, see *Saturday Punch*, (August 15, 2009), 2.
3. M. Peil, *Nigeria Politics, the people's view*, (London: Casewell, 1996), 64.
4. M. Peil, *Nigeria Politics, the people's view*, 75
5. S. Anyacho, *Corruption in the leadership Structure of Nigeria Polity*, (Jos: St. Paul Publications, 2002), 51
6. T. Oladimeji, "The Prophecy of Jeremiah in Jeremiah 38:1-13, Implications for Modern Day Prophets in a Corrupt Nigeria" in S. O. Abogunrin (ed) *Biblical Studies and Corruption in Africa.* (Ibadan: NABIS, 2007), 34.
7. E. A. Odumuyiwa, "Religion and Corruption in Nigeria: a dilemma of the Century". Being a paper presented at the 30th Annual Conference of the Nigerian Association for the Study of Religions. (EACOED Oyo, 2009), 4
8. O. Arowolo, "Religion and Moral Issues in Nigeria". NASRED, 2004, *Journal of Religion*, (Vol. VII Nos 1 &2), 1-2.
9. O. Arowolo, "Religion and Moral Issues in Nigeria", 2.
10. O. Arowolo, "Religion and Moral Issues in Nigeria", 3.

11. O. Arowolo, "Religion and Moral Issues in Nigeria", 4
12. F.E. Okponaviobo, *Understanding Philosophy of Religion*, (Ibadan: Fola-Murphy Printers and Company, 2000), 17-19.
13. F.E. Okponaviobo, *Understanding Philosophy of Religion*, 20.
14. B. G. Ogedegbe, "Prophet Amos' Message on Corruption: A Challenge to Christian Leaders in Nigeria" in S. O. Abogunrin (ed) *Biblical Studies and Corruption in Africa*, (Ibadan: NABIS, 2007), 198.
15. B. O. Igboin, "Gehazism: An Ethical Appraisal of Corruption in Religious and Political Situation in Nigeria" in S.O. Abogunrin (ed) *Biblical Studies and Corruption in Africa*, (Ibadan: NABIS, 2007), 632.
16. A.A. Adegbola, "Corruption and its Effects on National Politics" in M.A. Folorunsho et al (eds.), *Religion and Modernity, Nigeria*: (NASRED, 2007), 439.
17. A.A. Adegbola, "Corruption and its Effects on National Politics", 456
18. M. Peil, *Nigeria Politics: the People's View*, (London: Casewell, 1996), 62.
19. M. Peil, *Nigeria Politics: the People's View*, 75.
20. F. O. Salawu, "Effects of Corruption on Economic Growth and Development in Nigeria since Independence", *The Journal of Arts and Social Science*, (EACOED Oyo, vol. 4, No. 1, 2011), 30.
21. P. Bohana, *Social Anthropology*. (London: Holt Rinchart and Winston, 1969), 313.
22. K. Blibs, *The Future of Religion*, (London: Pelican Books, 1972), 5 ff.
23. P. Bohana, *Social Anthropology*, 313.
24. S. A. Adewale, "The Future of Religion," In *A Study of Religion and Culture*, Series 1, (A Publication of the

Department of Religious Studies, Ogun State University, Ago-Iwoye, 1997), 72.
25. E.B. Idowu, Olodumare: *God in Yoruba Belief* (London: Longman Press, 1962), 144.
26. A. Richardson, *Christian Apologetics*, (London: SCM Press, 1948), 12.
27. E. Brunner, *The Divine Imperative: A Study of Christian ethics*, Translated by Olive Wyon, (Philadelphia: Westminster Press, 1947), 53.
28. K. Barth, *The Knowledge of God and the service of God*, (London: Hodder and Stoughton, 1938), 146.
29. O. Arowolo, "Religion and Moral Issues in Nigeria", *NASRED, Journal of Religion*, (Vol. VII Nos 1 & 2, 2007), 1-2.
30. B. Idowu, *Introduction to the African Traditional Religion*, (Ibadan: John Archers Publisher, 2000), 16.
31. B. Ighorojeh, "Corruption and the need for a Religious Approach in the Anti-Corruption Crusade in the Nigerian State", in M. A. Folorunsho et al (eds.)*Religion and Democratic Governance in Nigeria*, (NASRED), 231-236.
32. J. A. Ogunji, "Religious Values as a Force in Shapping Development" in *International Review of Politics and Development*(IRPAD, Vol. 2, No. 1, 2004), 258.
33. J. A. Ogunji, "Religious Values as a Force in Shapping Development", 260.
34. A. A. Ajiberu, "Democracy and Corruption in Nigeria" in Ojo E. O. (ed) *Challenges of Sustainable Democracy in Nigeria*, (Ibadan: 1999, John Archers Publishers).

CHAPTER EIGHT

An Exegetical Study of Psalm 122 in the Nigerian Context

Ogunkunle, C. O.
*Department of Religions,
University of Ilorin, Ilorin, Nigeria*
calebogunkunle@unilorin.edu.ng
+234 803 581 4417

Introduction

In ancient Israel, going to the place of worship was always desirable and was a thing of joy for the worshippers. Psalm 122 demonstrates the mood of the people and the joy they derived in going to the place of worship. However, the level of insecurity in contemporary Nigerian society is a serious challenge which has made many Christians to think twice when it comes to going to Church. The activities of the *Jama'atu Ahlis Sunna Lidda'awati Wal-Jihad*, an Islamic sect known as Boko Haram, especially, in the northern part of the country have led to loss of several lives and properties. The level of insecurity has degenerated to the point that many congregations have devised various ways of screening people coming for Sunday services or other services during the week.[1] These measures are taken with the aim of preventing any possible attack on the church. The pertinent questions are: for how long will the church in Nigeria experience deadly attacks on innocent worshippers and church buildings? What is the motive behind the various attacks? For how long will innocent people of Nigeria live in fear and insecurity? Therefore, this study examines the level of fear and insecurity that is associated with religion, especially Christianity in Nigeria in comparison to what is found in Ancient Israel. It is an exegetical study of Psalm 122 in the Nigerian situation.

Conceptual and Theoretical Framework

The importance of peace in an individual's life, community, state or nation cannot be overemphasised. The individual needs peace for physical, spiritual and emotional growth while each state or nation needs peace for sustainable development. Incidentally, scholars in the area of peace study have come up with two types of peace, namely, negative peace and positive peace. Summarising the two categories of peace, I.O. Albert and I.O. Oloyede note:

> Negative peace is the absence of physical violence while positive peace is the absence of both structural and psychological violence. Negative peace is often imposed; it hardly results from an open revolution of the conflict. On the other hand, positive peace implies reconciliation and restoration through creative transformation of conflict. It is preferred to negative peace.[2]

The Longman Contemporary English Dictionary has a few definitions for peace: (a) a situation in which there is no war between countries or in a country; (b) an agreement that ends a war; (c) a feeling of calmness and lack of worry and problems; (d) a situation in which there is no quarrelling between people who live or work together.[3] The fact that peace is not just absence of war or conflict or civil disorder has been established by Bonnie Ayodele who says:

> It (peace) means something more fundamental and all-encompassing; it is the existence of harmony either in an individual or in the society, community, and nation or between nations. It is the absence of conflicts, belligerence, instability, strife, hostilities, negative propaganda and insecurity, to mention a few.[4]

Chapter Eight	Ogunkunle, C. O., in Y.A. Quadri, R.W. Omotoye & R.I. Adebayo (Eds) Religion in Contemporary Nigeria London, Adonis & Abbey Publishers

Olarinde examines the traditional belief and practices in the sustenance of peace with emphasis on the Yoruba culture. He identifies few Yoruba words that explain the concept of peace. These are *idera* (comfort), *itunu* (peace of mind), *itelorun* (contentment), *ifokanbale* (lack of worry or rest of mind) and *alaafia* (sound health or well-being).[5]

The Hebrew word for peace is *shalom* and it means completeness, soundness, welfare, peace. Specifically, it has six different meanings:

1. Completeness in number – Jer 13:19; Amos 1:6.
2. Safety, soundness in body – Psa 38:4; Isa 38:17; Job 5:24.
3. Welfare, health, prosperity – Gen 43:27; Exod 18:7; Judges 18:15.
4. Peace, quiet, tranquillity, contentment – Isa 32:17; Psa 4:9.
5. Peace, friendship – This can be in terms of human relations (Jer20:10; 38:22; Ob 7; Psa 41:10) or peace with God, especially in terms of covenant relation with Him (Isa 54:10; Num 25:12; Ezk 34:25).
6. Peace from war –Jos 9:15; Job 25:2; Lev 26:6.[6]

From the various definitions and concepts on peace, it is clear that peace is more than just the absence of war or conflict. The starting point of a lasting peace begins with individuals whose hearts or minds are free of unnecessary anxiety. In other words, every community or state or nation is made up of individuals and if the hearts of such individuals are troubled, certainly it will have a negative effect on the whole community. In the same vein, if the individuals in a community or nation have rest of mind, it will have a positive effect on the whole community.

It is assumed in this study that worshippers in Ancient Israel had rest of mind as reflected in the songs of ascents, that is, the songs sung on their way to the place of worship in Jerusalem. Psalm 122:6 specifically enjoined the worshippers to pray for the peace of Jerusalem. Certainly, the worshippers were deeply interested in the worship of Yahweh and they were willing to pray for the peace of Jerusalem as a result of the peace which each individual experienced.

It is also assumed in this study that the kind of peaceful environment that existed in Ancient Israel and which allowed the worshippers to worship God freely and to pray for the peace of Jerusalem is a mirage in contemporary Nigerian society. The recent activities of the *Jama'atu Ahlis Sunna Lidda'awati Wal-Jihad* (Boko Haram) especially, in the northern part of the country have made many worshippers to think twice before going to their places of worship.

Exegesis of Psalm 122

Psalm 122 belongs to the Pilgrim Psalms, that is, the 15 Psalms in the Psalter (Psalm 120-143) that are called the Psalms of degrees or ascents. The Hebrew word for ascent is *ma'eleh* which is a masculine noun which means to go up or ascending a stairway. Ten of the Psalms of Ascents are anonymous; four of them are attributed to David (Psalms 122, 124, 131 and 133); while Psalm 127 is attributed to Solomon. James L. Crenshaw notes a kind of progression in these 15 Psalms, from a cry of distress to a complete confidence in the LORD with Jerusalem occupying a central role in each of the three fold process of spiritual maturation (120-122, 123-128,

129-134).⁷ These Psalms are songs that worshippers sing on their way to the three annual feasts in Jerusalem namely, the Passover in spring, Pentecost in early summer, and Tabernacle in autumn. They are songs in which the worshippers expressed their joy in coming to the presence of the LORD. Each of the songs helped the people to focus their minds on what the LORD had done for their nation.⁸

Psalm 122 is rightly ascribed to David as it speaks of a united people and tribes going up to Jerusalem for annual religious festival. Warren notes that "the fact that King Jeroboam set up his own religion after the kingdom divided is evidence that the tribes must have been going to Jerusalem annually during the reigns of David and Solomon."⁹ Psalm 122 is closely related to Psalm 48 as the two Psalms describe the architectural features of Jerusalem. Anderson classifies Psalm 122 as one of the songs of Zion which was used at the Feast of Tabernacles.¹⁰

Structurally, Psalm 122 is divided into three stanzas namely verses 1-2 that speak of the joy of coming to Jerusalem; verses 3-5 that speak of the beauty of Jerusalem; and verses 6-9 that speak of prayer for the peace of Jerusalem. Clinton McCain notes the chiastic structure of the Psalm by observing the repetition of the word 'house'. He then has the following structure:

A vv. 1-2 the Psalmist and his companions and the house of the Lord
B vv. 3-4 Jerusalem
C v. 5 house of the Lord
B¹ vv. 6-7 Jerusalem
A¹ vv. 8-9 the Psalmist and his companions and the house of the Lord.¹¹

Psalm 122:1 is a declaration of joy of the Psalmist in going to the house of the LORD. He said: "I was glad when they said to me; let us go into the house of the LORD". The word *shamah'ti* which is the *qal* perfect first person singular is from the verb *shamah* and it means to rejoice or be glad. It is a spontaneous emotion or extreme happiness which is expressed in some visible or external manner. This emotion is associated with festivals such as circumcision, wedding, harvest, and triumph over one's enemies.[12] This emotion is accompanied by dancing, singing, and playing of musical instruments as in the case of David who was heralded by women of Jerusalem as he returned victoriously over the Philistines (1 Sam 18:6). Naturally, there are many other occasions that make a man cheerful in the Old Testament. These include wine (Psa 104:5; Judges 9:13; Eccl 10:19); ointment and perfume (Prov 27:9); a wise son (Prov 15:20; 10:1); and the Lord and His salvation (2 Chron 20:27).[13]

The Psalmist here was particularly glad when they said to him "Let us go into the house of the LORD". This house of the LORD was located in Jerusalem which occupied a unique position in Israel. It was the capital of Israel and afterwards, of the southern kingdom. It was the seat of central worship. It was first named as the city of the Canaanite (Joshua 1:10, 3, 5, 23). It was named in connection with David (2 Sam 5:6) and it became his royal seat (2 Sam 5:5, 13, 14; 8:7; 11:1) and it remained the capital until it was taken by Nebuchadnezzer in 588 BC (2 Kgs 25:1ff). It became the chief home of the returned exiles (Ezra 1:11; 2:11; Neh 2:11, 17). The point in this first stanza of Psalm 122 is that the Psalmist and other worshippers were glad to be in the house of God in Jerusalem.

Chapter Eight | Ogunkunle, C. O., in
Y.A. Quadri, R.W. Omotoye & R.I. Adebayo (Eds)
Religion in Contemporary Nigeria
London, Adonis & Abbey Publishers

Psalm 122:3-5 further describes the city of Jerusalem. The city was built and compacted together which speaks of unity and security of the city. In other words, as the stages of the walls and houses were bound firmly together, so the people were bound together in their worship of the LORD.[14] It is germane to note that just as Jerusalem was known as both "the city of God" and "the city of David" so also the place of worship in Jerusalem was known as "the house of the LORD" and "the house of David".[15] The twelve tribes of Israel were in Jerusalem to worship the LORD and to give thanks to Him.

Psalm 122:6-9, the third and final stanza of the Psalm is very crucial to our understanding of peace and security. It says:

> Pray for the peace of Jerusalem;
> May those who love you be secure
> May there be peace within your walls
> And security within your citadels
> For the sake of my brothers and friends,
> I will say, "Peace be within you."
> For the sake of the house of the LORD our God
> I will seek your prosperity.

The section begins with an imperative to pray for the peace of Jerusalem. The Hebrew word used for prayer here is *sha'al* which is a verb and it means to ask or inquire.[16] The verb is used about 176 times in the Old Testament, almost always in the *qal*. It signifies asking of a physical object from someone (Exod 3:22) or for information (Gen 32:17) or even demanding another person's death (Job 31:30).[17] *Sha'al* is also a kind of request that is frequently directed to God as in Psalm 122:6 which admonishes the people to pray for the peace of Jerusalem. It is of interest to note that the word *sha'al* is in the plural form. This is an indication that the call to pray was not given to an individual but to everybody in the community.

Also, the word *shalom* is important in the stanza. It occurs in verses 6-9. There is a strong alliteration in Psalm 122:6-9 which is mainly to emphasise the concept of peace desired by the Psalmist and the other worshippers. In other words, the words 'Jerusalem', 'peace', 'pray' and 'security' used in the section have the same root in Hebrew.[18]

The Nigerian Experience

Nigeria is generally regarded as "the giant of Africa and of the black world." It has a population of over 140 million, according to the 2006 census.[19] Although recently published figure by the National Bureau of Statistics estimated the population of Nigeria as 163 million.[20] The fact that Nigerians are very religious is established in the statistical figures derived from the recently conducted research on proliferation of churches, mosques and shrines in the nation by Ade Odumuyiwa. It was discovered that within the 774 Local Governments in Nigeria, there are at least one hundred (100) locations for religious activities in each Local Government Area.[21] He states further:

> By a conservative estimate, there are 77,400 places of worship for the Christians, Muslims and Traditionalists (i.e. churches, mosques and shrines). In our estimated figures, averagely every religious location, i.e. church, mosque or shrine has at least 1,500 people as worshippers in each of the 77,400 religious locations. In an estimated population of this country of about 110 million people, our conservative estimate of religious people in our society/country is about 106.1 million people. With this estimated figure, we can claim that almost every Nigerian is somehow a religious person.[22]

Again, the government of Nigeria in recent years has promoted and supported, consciously or unconsciously, religious activities in the nation.[23] The government gives maximum support to her Pilgrim Boards for both Muslims and Christians; this has made it possible for many people to go on pilgrimage to Mecca or Jerusalem annually. In addition, the Federal Government of Nigeria has enlarged the membership of the Nigeria Inter-Religious Council (NIREC) and its activities are being fully supported by the Government.

However, in spite of all the arrangements and opportunities to worship God in Nigeria, the level of insecurity of lives and properties in the nation is very high. The masses are exposed to all forms of dangers and challenges. The activities of the *Jama'atu Ahlis Sunna Lidda'awati Wal-Jihad* (Boko Haram) group in recent time, especially as touching the place of worship tend to make many people to be afraid of going for any form of service. Etymologically, Boko Haram comes from Hausa word "Boko" which means "Western or non-Islamic education" and the Arabic word "Haram" which means "forbidden". So 'Boko Haram' means Western or non-Islamic education is forbidden. Boko Haram is a controversial Nigerian militant group that seeks the imposition of Sharia law in the northern states of the country.[24]

The group was founded in 2002 in Maiduguri by Ustaz Muhammad Yusuf who was hostile to democracy and the secular educational system. In 2004, he moved to Kanamma, Yobe State where he set up a base called "Afghanistan". The membership of the group includes people from neighbouring Chad and they speak only Arabic. They refused to mix with the local people and they seem to have a grudge against other Muslims who do not belong to their group. By 2009, following the sectarian violence in Nigeria, the group became known internationally.[25]

Initially, the Boko Haram group started their attack on police outposts by killing police officers. On 7th September, 2010, the group broke into a prison in Bauchi State and set free over 700 inmates. In December, 2010, members of the group were blamed for a market bombing, following which 72 of its members were arrested by the combined military and police operation. The leader of the group, Muhammad Yusuf was also arrested during the operation. He was handed over to the police where he eventually died in their custody.[26] In January 2011, the group struck in Borno State, killing 4 people in Dala Alemderi ward in Maiduguri metropolis. On Friday, January 28th, 2011, Engr. Modu Fannami Gubio, the then gubernatorial candidate of the All Nigeria People's Party (ANPP) was assassinated along with five other people.[27]

The most disturbing part of their activities is the group's attack on worshippers and their places of worship. The worshippers that are mostly affected are the Christians and indeed the various attacks on them have brought discouragement to the people. Some of the several attacks on innocent worshippers include the blood carnage in Yola, the Adamawa State capital where about six gunmen unleashed terror on innocent worshippers at the Christ Apostolic Church in Demsawo area of Yola metropolis. Eleven people including a pastor were shot dead around 8.00pm during evening service.[28] Also, December 25th, 2011 was a bloody one for members of the Saint Theresa Catholic Church in Mandala, Abuja with the explosions that occurred in front of the church towards the end of the service. On that day alone, more than 25 people were killed, 13 cars burnt and 9 apartments shattered along with the church building that was badly damaged.[29] In another development, the Saint Finbarr Catholic Church Rayfield, Jos was attacked; the deadly bomb killed 11 people and 22 members were injured.[30] Unfortunately, the attack was taken to the university community at Bayero University, Kano, where Christians were attacked by gunmen at the places of worship and several people lost their lives including two professors.[31]

Another church service was brutally terminated in Yola, Adamawa State after suspected Boko Haram members marched into Christ Apostolic Church, Jimeta, spraying worshippers with bullets killing at least 16 worshippers. This came just 24 hours after members of the sect killed 8 and injured 19 in a similar fashion at the Deeper Life Bible Church, Gombe.[22] In addition, the fuel subsidy strike embarked upon by the Nigeria Labour Congress all over the nation in January 2012 turned out to have side effects on the Christians in Zamfara State. The youths between the ages of seven and seventeen stormed the gate of the Government House and attempted to gain entrance. They were protesting against their Governor's support of the removal of fuel subsidy. The protest was hijacked by hoodlums when they attacked and vandalised six churches in the state capital.[33]

James Bwala cites security threat as the reasons Christians are fleeing Damaturu and Potiskum. He quoted a resident of the community, Marcus Duniya who said that "many churches have closed as both indigenes and non-indigenes have fled to Nasarawa, Taraba, Jos and surrounding villages because they believed that they were no longer secured in Damaturu."[34] He says further:

> Look at the street, everywhere is empty. I know that over 200 people have fled Damaturu. In my church, the pastor left without even informing us, we learnt that he fled to Jos and he confirmed it. We are still communicating with him, and from what he is saying it is likely that he may not be coming back to the state.[35]

Speaking on insecurity and Boko Haram, President Jonathan in a church service was reported to have admitted that Boko Haram was everywhere including the three arms of government. He stated further:

> Some are also in the armed forces, the police and other security agencies. Some continue to dip their hands and eat with you and you won't even know who will point a gun at you or plant a bomb behind your house.[36]

Indeed, the current insecurity challenge in the nation is a serious concern to all well-meaning Nigerians. The poor masses are suffering. Unlike the nation of Israel in general and the city of Jerusalem in particular that experienced peace and conducive atmosphere for worship, the nation of Nigeria is currently going through a difficult time to which there must be an urgent solution. There is the need for the political leaders to look inward and do a thorough self-examination. The issue at hand is not how much money we budget or spent on security but how willing the leaders are to identify the issues and trash them out.

Solution/Way Forward

Several individuals have made various proposals as to how to deal with the Boko Haram group, so as to have lasting peace in the nation. Some people are of the opinion that military action is the way out. To a certain extent, the government has taken the option and this has led to the declaration of state of emergency on some local governments in some northern states where the Joint Military Force is in charge. Some other people are of the view that dialogue with the Boko Haram group is the best option.[37] Still, a large number of people believe that the best option and way out of our current predicament is prayer.[38] This is the option to which this writer subscribes. The challenge that is confronting the nation at this moment is complicated as it is both political and religious. Hence, it is on this note that this study recommends prayer among others, as the main weapon to fight the battle. This position is corroborated by the view of Apostle Paul who recognised the spiritual dimension of the battle confronting Christians (2 Cor 10:4-6; Eph 6:10-20). Also, the former Nigerian Head of State, General Yakubu Gowon was reported to have admitted that Nigeria was going through a difficult period. He believes that the effective weapon to stop Boko Haram sect's insurgence against Nigeria is prayer.[39]

The Psalmist says: "For the sake of the house of the LORD our God, I will seek your prosperity"(Psa 122:9). As Jerusalem, the house of the LORD needed peace because of its unique location, so also does Nigeria need peace as it is regarded as the giant of Africa. Therefore, it is imperative for all to pray for Nigeria and seek her prosperity and her good. This is because any major crisis in the nation will not only have negative effect on the nation but it will have a negative effect on the whole of the continent of Africa.

Conclusion

The research has demonstrated the difference between the worshippers in Ancient Israel and Christians in the contemporary Nigerian society. In Ancient Israel, as demonstrated in Psalm 122, people were glad to be in the house of the LORD; there was peace and security in the land; and generally, the atmosphere was conducive for worship. In contemporary Nigerian society, however, in spite of the so many places of worship, the various religious activities taking place, and the so much support that the government is giving to various religious groups, worshippers' morale has been dampened as a result of insecurity. The threat to lives and properties in the nation especially, the places of worship in the northern part of the country, has robbed many innocent worshippers of the joy of going to the house of the Lord. Therefore, the study submits that all political leaders must come together to iron out issues so as to give peace a chance in the nation. Also, everyone, both the leadership and followership must look inward and take time to pray for the peace of the nation. Prayer is the main weapon to fight every spiritual battle.

Notes and References

1. Recently, the administration of the University of Ilorin made an arrangement for the anti-bomb squad to be available during Church and Mosque services on Sunday and Friday respectively. Since then cars have not been allowed around the building during services and members are screened as they go in for worship.
2. I.O. Albert and I.O. Oloyede, (eds.) "Beyond Adversarial Conflict Management" in *Dynamics of Peace Process*, (Ilorin: Centre for Peace and Strategic Studies, 2010), 2.
3. "Peace" in *Longman Dictionary of Contemporary English*, (Essex, England: Pearson Educational Limited, 2003), 1041.
4. Bonnie Ayodele, "Curriculumnising Peace Education as a strategy for Conflict Management in Africa" in I.O. Albert and I.O. Oloyede (eds.) *Dynamics of Peace Process*, 79.

5. Nurudeen Olarinde, "Traditional Beliefs and Practices in the Sustenance of Peace" in I.O. Albert and I.O. Oloyede (eds.) *Dynamics of Peace Process*, 302.
6. F. Brown; S.R. Driver and C. A. Briggs, *The New Brown-Driver-Briggs-Genesius Hebrew and English Lexicon with an Appendix containing the Biblical Aramaic* (Peabody, Massachusetts: Hendrickson Publishers, 1979), 1022-3. [Henceforth called BDB].
7. James L. Crenshaw, *The Psalms: An Introduction,* (Grand Rapids: Wm B. Eerdmans Publishing Co. 2001), 22.
8. Warren W. Wiersbe, *Be Exultant: Praising God for His Mighty Works,* (Colorado Springs: Cook International, 2008), 142.
9. Warren W. Wiersbe, *Be Exultant: Praising God for His Mighty Works,* 149.
10. A. A. Anderson, *The New Century Bible Commentary: Psalms 73-150* (Grand Rapids: Wm B. Eerdmans Publishing Co. 1983), 854.
11. J. Clinton McCann, *A Theological Introduction to the Book of Psalms: The Psalms as Torah* (Nashville: Abingdon Press, 1993), 153.
12. Merrill F. Unger & William White, *Nelson's Expository Dictionary of the Old Testament* (Nashville: Thomas Nelson Publishers, 1970), 321.
13. Bruce K. Waltke, "*Shamah*"in *Theological Wordbook of the Old Testament Two Volumes.* R. Laird Harris; Gleanson L. Archer; and Bruce K. Waltke (eds.), (Chicago: Moody Press, 1980), 2:879.
14. Warren W. Wiersbe, *Be Exultant,* 151.
15. J. Clinton McCann, *A Theological Introduction to the Book of Psalms,* 153.

16. BDB, 981.
17. Gary G. Goshen, "*Sha'ah*" in *Theological Wordbook of the Old Testament Two Volumes*, 2:891.
18. Ordinarily, one wonders why the word *sha'al* is used in this Psalm for prayer instead of *phalal* which is the common verb in Hebrew for prayer. It means to pray, meditate or intervene. Obviously, the uncommon word is used so as to give weight to the use of alliteration in the Psalm.
19. For detailed information on land and resources, people, arts, economy, government, and history of Nigeria, see Microsoft Encarta Premium (2006) and S.S. Lawal, *The Unmerited Favour* (Abuja: Midianett Ltd. 2011), 97.
20. Ifeanyi Onuba, "112.5 million Nigerians live in Poverty" n. p. [cited 12 May 2012]. Online: http://www.punchng.com/business/business-economy/112-5-million-nigerians-live-in-poverty-nbs
21. E. Ade Odumuyiwa, "A Religious but Criminal Society–Any Remedy?" 19th Inaugural Lecture, (Olabisi Onabanjo University, Ago-Iwoye. Tuesday, 27th February, 2001), 7.
22. E. Ade Odumuyiwa, "A Religious but Criminal Society–Any Remedy?", 8.
23. Perhaps the reason for this may be connected with Karl Marx's theory of religion who sees religion as the opium of the masses. In other words, the political class is probably promoting religious activities so as to take advantage of the poor masses. See, C.O. Ogunkunle, "Humankind's Wickedness and God's Goodness: A Theological Study of the Oppressed in the Psalter in the Nigerian Context." A paper presented at the

Departmental Seminar in the Department of Religions, University of Ilorin on 9th May, 2012, pp. 1-18.
24. http://en.wikipedia.org/wiki/boko_haram. (Accessed on 12th March 2013).
25. http://en.wikipedia.org/wiki/boko_haram.
26. Oluokun Ayorinde, "Tragic Peace Mission" *The News.* Volume 37, No.37 (03 October, 2011), 14-17.
27. See, Ben Adaji, "Blood-Thirsty Boko Haram" *The News.* Volume 36, No 66 (14 February, 2011), p. 19; C.O. Ogunkunle "An Exegetical Study of Genesis 34 within the context of Religion and Violence in Nigeria" in R. A. Akanmidu (ed.),*Thoughts in the Humanities.* (Keffi: Department of Religious Studies, Nasarawa State University, 2011), 393; and *The Nation,* January 8th, 2012, 19.
28. Wale Akintunde, "Again Gunmen kill 11 in Adamawa" *Sunday Tribune* (8th January 2012), 4.
29. Yusuf Alli; Yomi Odunuga; Augustine Ehikioya; & Dele Anofi "Bloody Xmas Day" *The Nation* (26th December, 2011), 1ff.
30. Yusufu Aminu Idegu and Marie-Therese Peter, "11 dead in Jos as suicide bombers attack church". *The Nation* (12th March 2012), 1ff.
31. *See:* "Terrorists attack Bayero University: Two Professors, 13 others shot dead" *The Punch* (30th April 2012), 1 & 8.
32. Yusuf Alli, "Boko Haram kills 16 in Yola" *The Nation* (8th January 2012), 1ff.
33. Muhammad Sabiu, "Other sides of Zamfara strike action" *Sunday Tribune* (15th January 2012), 48-9.

34. James Bwala, "Boko Haram: Why Christians are fleeing Damaturu, Potiskum" *Sunday Tribune* (29th January 2012), 32.
35. James Bwala, "Boko Haram".
36. Olawale Rasheed, "Boko Haram: Enemies within and without" *Sunday Tribune* (22nd January 2012), 15.
37. One Apostle of Peace who believes in dialogue is Archbishop Ignatius Kaigama. See, Ignatius Ayau Kaigama, *Peace, not war. A Decade of Intervention in the Plateau State Crises (2001-2011)* (Jos: Hamtul Press, 2012), 1-244.
38. Ignatius Ayau Kaigama, Peace, not war, 190-194. The President, CAN declared Thursday 14/06/2012 as a national day of prayer by all Christians against Boko Haram activities in the nation.
39. Idowu Adelusi, "Only prayer can stop Boko Haram threat- Gowon" *Sunday Tribune* (6th May, 2012), 6.

CHAPTER NINE

The Growth and Expansion of Pentecostal Churches in Ilorin, Kwara State, Nigeria

Omotoye, Rotimi Williams
*Department of Religions,
University of Ilorin, Ilorin, Nigeria.
graquarters@gmail.com
+2348033933033*

Introduction

This work is on Charisma as a determinant in the growth of Pentecostal Churches in Ilorin metropolis of Kwara State, Nigeria. Ilorin is the capital of Kwara state and an acclaimed Islamic centre since the 19th century. Kwara state was created in 1967 by the military government led by General Yakubu Gowon. It is located in the North-central zone of the country. The first un-successful attempt to introduce Christianity to the community was made in 1855 by Rev T.J. Bowen of the Baptist Mission. Bishop Samuel Ajayi Crowther also made an attempt in 1857 which also failed because he was not permitted to establish a church. Christianity became a permanent institution in the town in the first decade of the 20th century. It was introduced by the Mainline Christian Missionaries, such as, the Church Missionary Society, Baptist, Catholic, Sudan Interior Mission (SIM) later known as Evangelical Church of West Africa and now called Evangelical Church Winning All.

Another effort was made to evangelize the community of Ilorin with the emergence of African Independent Churches

(AIC) in the second decade of the twentieth century. The AIC (*Aladura*) Churches are Cherubim and Seraphim, Christ Apostolic Church, Church of the Lord (*Aladura*) and Celestial Church of Christ. Most of the above mentioned Churches were introduced to the community by itinerant traders and some pastors.

There was a dramatic change in the history and establishment of Churches with the emergence of Pentecostal Churches in the 1970's. Our focus in this study are the Pentecostal Churches whose founders and headquarters of Churches are based in Ilorin. The phenomenal growth of the Churches is examined based on Charisma displayed by the founders of such Churches.

Apart from the term "Pentecostal Church", H.W. Turner also coined the term "New Religious Movements" to describe the wide variety of religious independence[2]. Scholars in tertiary institutions, especially in Universities, have devoted much attention to them because of the phenomenal growth of the Churches. According to Essien, "due to the global spread of the New Religious Movements, presently, special International Research Documentation Centers have been created for the study of New Religious Movements at Lima, Peru, by Kenneth Scott; at Durban, South Africa by G.C. Oosthuizen, at Birmingham, England, by Harold Turner. The Melanesian Institute is giving the research of New Religious Movements a high priority on its broader agenda.[3] Of recent, Danny McCain a Lecturer in the Department of Religious Studies, University of Jos, Nigeria also established a Centre of Research for the Study of Pentecostal Churches.[4]

There are three major religions in Nigeria which are practised in Ilorin community namely: African traditional religion, Islam and Christianity. African traditional religion was the indigenous religion of the people. The concept of God was found amongst the people before the introduction of Islam and Christianity. Idowu posited that "the real keynote of the life of the Yoruba is neither in their noble ancestry nor in the past deeds of their heroes. The keynote of their life is their religion. In all things they are religious."[5] The two foreign religions came to convert the indigenous people to either of the two religions. Christian Missionaries in particular succeeded in converting people to Christianity through some strategies of western education and improved medical facilities.

Ojo highlighted the different Pentecostal churches in Nigeria as the Foreign Pentecostal churches which emerged in 1931, while indigenous Pentecostal churches emerged in 1950's. The Charismatic movements constitute the newest[6]. In this study, we shall not make any distinction between the Pentecostal and Charismatic churches because they all share some common features.

According to Ojo the churches share common phenomena through literature, crusades, camp meetings, Fire or Holy Ghost or Power crusades, open air evangelism etc.[7] Richard Burgess also defined Pentecostalism as a movement that stresses the experience of the spirit and the practice of spiritual gifts[8]. In other words, the churches have some common features which are points of attraction to the people. The methodologies adopted in this study are historical, phenomenological and comparative[9]. As an historical method, the analysis and interpretation of data were based on the principles of historical method[10]. This involves an attempt to interpret past trends for the purpose of understanding the present conditions and predicting what conditions are likely to be met in future. The phenomenological approach seeks to unfold the archaeological realities of the objects, beliefs and practices under study without presuppositions. This made us to take active part in the observation of the activities of the churches. Daramola viewed it as a process whereby individuals or a group of people are commissioned to watch and record the happenings or events, or even study behavioural patterns in settings of interest[11]. This method was considered necessary because a research work such as this requires eyewitness accounts. In view of this, an attempt was made to attend the various services and programmes of the churches under study. Coupled with the above was the Comparative methodology. The reality or otherwise of the people's views are critically examined and compared to the relevance of the objects or practices in relation to contemporary views, especially as they relate to dynamics of social change.

Danmole submitted that Ilorin emirate represents the most southerly of the emirates within the Sokoto Caliphate that was established after the successful jihad in Hausaland during the early 19th century[12]. By its location in the transitional belt between the open savanna to the north and forest zone to the south, Ilorin was advantageously located to attract settlers from both the north and the south. Danmole went further to say that "The movement of population to Ilorin before the jihad can be accounted for through the activities in the town of three major figures in the period towards the jihad. These were the Afonja, al-Salih and Solagberu"[13]

There is no doubt that the community was dominated by Muslims before the imposition of British colonial authority on the emirate in 1900. The Emirs however tried to protect Islam jealously from incursion of the Christian missionaries. However, the colonial laws gave the Christians the opportunity of spreading the gospel in the community. Hence, the influx of Christians to the area. This was not without the challenges posed by the Muslims to the Christians.

However, Ilorin community has witnessed an influx of Christians from the Southern part of the country. For instance, the Ijesa textile dealers known as *Osomalo* were found in Igbominaland and Ilorin at the beginning of the 20th century. Many of them were Christians before they left home as itinerant traders. The construction of railway lines from the Southern states to the Northern states also contributed to the expansion of Christianity to Ilorin[14]. Some of the railway workers were from the Southern states of the country and had been converted to Christianity before they took up the job. These Christians used to meet in a fellowship and thereby propagate the gospel in an Islamic community. Revd Jefferson Bowen of the Baptist mission and Bishop Samuel Ajayi Crowther of the Church Missionary Society (CMS) visited Ilorin in 1855 and 1857 respectively[15]. The Emir on the throne, then Shitta welcomed the clerics but did not allow them to establish churches. His action was to protect Islam from incursion and influence of Christianity.

The Christians in Ilorin were persistent in their appeal and request for a place of worship from another Emir, Shehu Suleiman. He eventually granted them a piece of land outside the town[16]. From our investigations, majority of the early Christians in Ilorin were attending the CMS (Anglican) church. This eventually led to the establishment of St Barnabas Anglican Church, Sabo-Oke. Other Christian denominations, such as the Baptist, Methodist, and Catholic followed suit.

Chapter Nine | Omotoye, Rotimi Williams., in Y.A. Quadri, R.W. Omotoye & R.I. Adebayo (Eds) Religion in Contemporary Nigeria London, Adonis & Abbey Publishers

Later the African church was established and it was followed by the emergence of *Aladura* churches.

The relaxed political atmosphere in Ilorin also brought about the establishment of the following Pentecostal churches : The Rhema Church, New Testament Christian Mission, Jesus is Life Outreach Ministry, King's Vine, Be of the Same Mind Evangelical Ministry, Shield of Faith Ministry, Potter's Household, Canaan Ministries, Trinity Household of Faith, and Christ Assembly. Others are, Christ Proclaimer's Ministries, Jesus Revolution Revival Mission, Endtime Over Comers Mission, Dominion Life International Church, Elevation Christian Centre, Potter's Porch, Search the Scriptures Gospel Ministry, and the Word Commission Ministry. These churches were founded and established in Ilorin metropolis by some educated individuals who are professionals, academics and civil servants.

In fact, some of the church founders are full-time/part-time pastors in their churches. Many of them were former members of the Mainline or *Aladura* Churches. It is observed that these churches survive in Ilorin because of the charisma being displayed by the founders of the churches. Ordinarily, the leadership of the earlier churches sees the leaders of Pentecostal churches as "sheep stealers" from the Mainline and *Aladura* Churches.

As Ojo opined Pentecostal churches "are led by the educated elite, which though small in number, exert considerable influence in the society"[17]. Many of them are graduates from Universities and incidentally lecturers in Universities, Polytechnics and Colleges of Education. For instance, Rev. (Dr.) Steve Metiboba of Shield of Faith Ministry is presently a Professor and Deputy Vice-Chancellor at Kogi

State University, Ayingba, Kogi State; Pastor George Adegboye of Rhema Church and Pastor Emmanuel Oset of the Champions Church were former Lecturers at the Kwara State Polytechnic, Ilorin; Professor Timothy Opoola, the founder of Strong Tower Ministry is a Professor of Mathematics at the University of Ilorin; Rev. (Dr) J.O.Adeoti, the founder of Joint Heirs Church, is a Senior Lecturer in the Department of Business Administration of the University of Ilorin and Rev Idowu Olawuyi of Trinity of Household of Faith, holds a Master's degree in Fishery management and is a senior civil servant at a Federal ministry in Ilorin.

Another peculiarity noted was that some of the founders of the Pentecostal Churches in Ilorin were Muslims before they were converted to Christianity. For instance, Pastor Mohammed Alli, the Pastor in charge of Christ Assembly and Pastor Rahman Moses Popoola, the General Overseer of New Testament Christian Church were Muslims by birth though they are non-indigenes of Ilorin. Their understanding of the Qur'an and the Hadith is reflected in their comparative teachings of the gospel.

Pentecostal Churches whose founders do not have the headquarters of their churches in Ilorin are outside the scope of this study. However, many of them have branches in the town. Examples are Sword of Spirit Ministries, Redeemed Christian Church of God, Deeper Life Christian Church, Living Faith Church, and Latter Rain Assembly, Fire and Miracle Ministries, Christ Embassy, etc. The headquarters of these churches are based in cities, such as Ibadan, Lagos and Abeokuta in South-western part of Nigeria.

It is necessary to mention that some of our earlier studies and researches on Pentecostal churches are on churches located in these urban and relatively peaceful and economically booming areas of the country. In fact some of the Church founders started their Churches in Ilorin or some parts of the Northern states but quickly relocated to the Southern area probably because of religious intolerance being witnessed in the Northern states or in order to be associated with the economic boom and prosperity of the area. There are many successful business men and women in the South-west who are seeking protection and prayers of church founders, notwithstanding the sources of their wealth.

The church founders also feel more protected in the South-western states of Nigeria because the area is relatively peaceful and without regular religious violence and conflicts as being witnessed in the Northern states. The Living Faith for instance started in Ilorin in 1981, moved to Kaduna and later relocated the headquarters of the church to Otta, Ogun State[18]

Pentecostal Churches in Ilorin

The emergence of Pentecostal churches is a new development globally, especially at the beginning of the 20th C. in Europe. It became a major issue in Nigeria after the Nigerian civil war in the 1970's. It reflected the religious, social and economic insecurity and political instability in the country. According to Ojo "by the 1990's, the movements had become a major factor in Nigerian public life as they sought to give religious visibility to the middle class that had already been decimated by harsh economic realities".[19] The African people are religious; religion forms the bedrock of their lives from time immemorial. Everything in Africa was done religiously from birth to the time of death. Pentecostalism is inherent in the religion of the people. Ojo's position is germane when he said that "Charismatic movements in Nigeria have indigenous roots, and are sustained because of their affirmation of African cosmology of spiritual powers"[20]

The introduction of Pentecostal churches into Nigeria was led by the late Arch-Bishop Benson Idahosa the founder of the Church of God Mission based in Benin City, Edo State[21]. This was followed by the emergence of the following churches: The Living Faith Church (Winners Chapel), Deeper Life Christian Church, Latter Rain Assembly, Redeemed Christian Church, Christ Embassy, Sword of the Spirits, and Fire and Miracles Ministries. They all enjoy the activities of the vibrant media that are located in Ibadan and Lagos. In an earlier work, Omotoye said that "Human society is a dynamic organization. If the society is to be progressive, humane and visionary, there is a need for purposeful, dedicated, courageous, honest and determined leaders".[22] Coupled with these attributes, a leader who is to be highly respected in the religious circle must be charismatic. This will serve as a motivator to his or her followership.

The qualities of the founders of the Pentecostal churches have contributed to the growth and development of Pentecostal churches in Ilorin. The following are some of the available Pentecostal churches and their founders in the town.

1. The Ever Increasing Ministries (Rhema Chapel) (Pastor George Olawale Adegboye).
2. End time Overcomers Mission (Revd S.O. Olayinka)
3. Jesus Revolution Revival Mission (Pastor Johnson O. Kusina)
4. Potter's Household (Pastor Victor Philip Ibitoye)

5. New Testament Christian Church (Rev. Moses Rahman Popoola)
6. The Shield of Faith Assembly (Rev (Dr) Steve Metiboba)
7. Trinity Household of Faith (Rev. Idowu Olawuyi)
8. Word Commission Ministries (Evangelist Isaac Omolehin)
9. King's Vine Church (Rev. Sam Abejide)
10. Jesus is Life Outreach Ministries (Bishop (Dr) David Bakare)
11. Be of the Same Mind Evangelical Ministry (Pastor Evangelist David Akano)
12. Search the Scripture Gospel of Christ Ministry (Strong Tower) (Evangelist Professor Timothy Opoola)
13. Christ Proclaimer's Church (Pastor J.T.Opatola)
14. Elevation Christian Centre (Pastor Tope Ajetunmobi)
15. Dominion Life International Church (Rev. Barrister Bode Amoo)
16. Canaan Ministries (Champions' Church) (Rev.Emmanuel Oset)
17. Potter's Porch International Church (Pastor J.T. Aboyeji)
18. Christ Assembly (Rev.Joseph Mohammed Alli)[23]
19. Joint Heirs Church (Rev. (Dr) J.O.Adeoti
20. Powerful Prayer Church (Rev.Noah Adeosun)

We shall examine some of the churches above in order to have some information about the founders of the churches and the qualities that constitute the charisma they possess. The word Charisma has been defined by *the Longman Dictionary of Contemporary English* as "a natural ability to attract and interest other people and make them admire you". The above mentioned church founders have demonstrated some leadership qualities which are attractive to some christians and non-christians alike in course of their preachings and teachings in Ilorin and using radio and television stations.In fact,many of them have published some christian literature which have made them to be acceptable by the educated elite in Nigeria.

The Ever Increasing Ministries (Rhema Chapel)

The Church was founded by Pastor George Adegboye. He was born on 7th December, 1958 in Offa, Kwara State into a polygamous and Baptist family. Polygamy in Africa is seen as a social and not a religious matter[24]. In fact in the olden days, one's status was determined by the number of wives and children one man had in the society. Though, he was born in a mission church, George left his father's church by establishing a Pentecostal church which is opposed to polygamy as an institution of marriage.

According to Ojo the church has about 50,000 members[25].The quoted figure of membership of the Church was as of 2007 when Ojo presented his Inaugural Lecture at the Obafemi Awolowo University,Ile-Ife.There is the propability of an increase as of date.The teaching and presentation of sermon of the founder is attractive to many people.He quotes the Bible off-hand from Genesis to Revelation with easy and modesty.In fact,he is often referred to as "mobile or moving Bible" in some circles. The International headquarters of the church has a beautiful architectural design. The majority of the pioneer members of the church are youths, especially students in tertiary institutions in Ilorin. George Adegboye used to be a lecturer at the Kwara State Polytechnic, Ilorin before he went into full time ministry. The church has a bible training institute and a nursery and primary school. A printing press was established to handle the printing of tracts and other related church books.

In propagating the gospel, the Pastor is always on the Nigerian Television Authority, Ilorin every Monday at 7.30-8.00 pm.He is assisted by his wife Rev Mrs. Oloruntoyin Adegboye. In other words, women are given the opportunity to serve as leaders in the church. The church is located along the University of Ilorin main campus road in Tanke.

The Church is noted for religious tolerance and understanding with the Ahmadiyya Islamic group. The mosque is directly opposite the Church. The Muslims often benefit from the free medical facilities occasionally provided by the Church. It is also observed that there is an understanding between the church and mosque worshippers to park at any available park in the premises of any of the two institutions. Olademo corroborated this position in her work thus As construction works progressed at the Rhema chapel,Reverend Adegboye noticed that some construction was ongoing at the Ahmadiyya mosque also and directed that some cement bags be taken there to assist in the construction.The Ahmadiyya were surprised and delighted and this further cemented the love between the two groups"[26],The two different religious groups have shown religious understanding and peaceful co-existence which is needed in a multi-religious society like Nigeria in general and llorin in particular. The Church is also making its luxurious bus available to assist in conveying students of the University of Ilorin to and from the campus whenever there is a need to do so. This gesture appears to be a strategy of winning and attracting students to the church.

New Testament Christian Church

The New Testament Christian Church was established by a Muslim convert called Pastor Rahman Moses Popoola an indigene of Omu-Aran, a town in Irepodun Local Government of Kwara state. He is a Geologist by profession and graduated from Ahmadu Bello University, Zaria. He started the ministry in 1980's. The branches of the church are found in many towns of the Federation, such as, Lagos, Lokoja, Ibadan Port-Harcourt, Kaduna and Federal Capital Territory Abuja. He preaches on the Nigerian Television Authority, Ilorin every Sunday at 7.30pm. Rev.Popoola is a prolific writer. He has published the following books to his credit: *Dynamic Spiritual Growth, New Life School Manual, Freedom from Evil,* and *Believers Shut Out of Heaven*. The church has a regular attendance of about 5,000 worshippers every Sunday. The focus of his preaching is sanctification and holiness. The church has eight centres of worship in Ilorin metropolis. These are located in Amilegbe, Ayetoro, Akerebiata, Ero-Omo, Fate, Gaa-Akanbi, Kulende and Tanke. The headquarters of the church is on Salvation road, off Stadium road, Ilorin. Rev.Popoola's ministry has become attractive to some people because of his teaching on holiness and divine healing.

The Shield of Faith Assembly

The church was established by Rev. Professor Steve Metiboba. He is from Iyara in Ijumu area of Kogi State. The church was founded in 1996. He was a lecturer in the Department of Sociology, University of Ilorin some years ago.He later transferred his service to Kogi State University, Ayingba, Kogi State,where he is a Professor of Sociology and Deputy Vice-Chancellor as of 2014. The Church is located at Flamingo close, off Stadium road, Ilorin. There is a focus on prophecy and vision in the church. As a result of this people from different denominations worship in the church. The son of the founder, Prophet Sanmi Metiboba, a graduate of the University of Ilorin and a full time Priest is now in charge of the church. There are weekly and monthly healing programmes that attract people to the church.A visit to the church in course of our research has shown that majority of the worshippers are youths and emphasis is laid on vision and miracles.

Trinity Household of Faith Church

Rev.Idowu Olawuyi is the founder of the church. He is a native of Imeri, a town in Ondo state. He was a former Rev Canon in the Anglican Diocese of Kwara before he established the Trinity Household of Faith Church. He holds a Masters degree in Fishery Management from the University of Ibadan, Ibadan, Oyo State. He is a senior officer in a Federal parastatal in Ilorin. He was the Chaplain in charge of the Anglican Youth chapel of the Cathedral Church of Saint Barnabas before his exit from the Church. He left the church because of irreconcilable disagreement with Bishop Olusegun Adeyemi of Kwara Anglican Diocese in 1996.

Rev.Idowu Olawuyi started the Trinity Household of Faith in September, 2006 at Salem house, Amilegbe, Ilorin. The church has moved to a permanent place Graceland, at Tanke,

Ilorin. The founder started the church with almost 90% of the Youths chapel of St Barnabas Anglican Church, Sabo Oke. The Church organises Bible school for children annually during vacation and has established a viable Nursery/Primary/Secondary schools named Hill Top Schools. The wife is also a Pastor in the church. She is addressed as Pastor Dr (Mrs.) Bolanle Olawuyi and is an Associate Professor in the Faculty of Education, University of Ilorin. The church has more than twenty house fellowship centres in the city. Rev. Olawuyi always appears on both Kwara State Radio and Nigerian Television Authority, Ilorin to preach the gospel. The church has become more acceptable in Ilorin because of the monthly early prayers offered for some days at the beginning of every month. It is observed that many christians and non-christians are attracted to the programme.

Word Commission Ministry

The Word Commission Ministry was founded by Evangelist Isaac Omolehin. The church is located on an expansive land at 15, Ajase-Ipo road, Ilorin. The founder of the church was born in 1955 at Iluke, Kogi State. He obtained a degree in Animal Science from the University of Port-Harcourt in 1983. He started a Joint Christian ministry in 1984 known as Christ United Mission but due to a misunderstanding, he left the Joint Ministry to start the Word Commission in 1996. The popular annual programme titled Shiloh always attracts people of different traditions. He starts each year with fasting and prayer that would last for about one hundred and twenty days with a title: "Let thy Kingdom come." Pastor Omolehin preaches at 7.30 am every Sunday on Kwara State radio. There are twenty-one branches of the church in Ilorin. Branches are also found outside the town in Lokoja, Aiyetoro Gbede, Isanlu and Kaduna. The church has a nursery/ primary school and a college as part of her contributions to the development of education in Ilorin. Recently, the wife of Pastor Omolehin started an orphanage at Idofian, some kilometers to Ilorin. This is seen as an act of social welfare of the church for the society.The centre provides free water supply to the community and a Bible College has been established in Idofian,so as to prepare the Ministers of God for the teaching of the gospel.

Search the Scripture Gospel of Christ Ministry (Strong Tower)

The church was founded by Evangelist Professor Timothy Opoola. He is a lecturer in the Department of Mathematics, University of Ilorin, Ilorin. He was born in Ijagbo, a town in Kwara state. The church was established in 1994. It is located along the University of Ilorin road. Professor Opoola is the President of the Pentecostal Fellowship of Nigeria, Ilorin city and also elected as the President of Christian Association of Nigeria,Kwara State in 2013.His educational status and position as a Christian leader has been a point of attraction to the church by students of the University of Ilorin. He is assisted by his wife Mrs. Elizabeth Omolara Opoola, a PhD student in the Department of Religions, University of Ilorin. She is presently a senior teacher at the Cherubim and Seraphim Secondary school, Sabo-Oke, Ilorin. It is observed that majority of the members of the church are students of the University of Ilorin. Evangelist Opoola preaches on the Nigerian Television Authority.

Canaan Ministries (Champion's Church)

Rev. Emmanuel Oset was born in Kabba, Kogi state. He read History and International Studies at the University of Ibadan, Ibadan, Oyo State. He was a lecturer at the Kwara State College of Technology, now known as Kwara State Polytechnic before he went into full time ministry. It is interesting to note that he was one of the pioneering Pastors of the Living Faith Church established by Pastor David Oyedepo in Ilorin in 1981 before the latter moved to Kaduna. Rev Oset is married to Mrs. Grace Oset and blessed with children. The twentieth year of existence of the church was celebrated in 2011. The church has a nursery and primary school within the church premises in Sango, Ilorin. This is an indication of the commitment of the church to the development of education in Ilorin metropolis. The regular ministration of the Pastor on the Nigerian Television Authority every Sunday is a point of interest to many people and admirers.

Elevation Christian Centre

The Church was founded by (Surveyor) Tope Ajetunmobi. He was born in 1972 in Ilesa, Osun State. He holds a Higher National Diploma in Engineering from the Kwara State Polytechnic, Ilorin. He was trained by Pastor Mike Bamidele of Victory Life Christian Church, Ilesa, Osun State. He is married to Mrs. Pamilerin Ajetunmobi and blessed with children. The Church started in 2006 and is located along Police barrack "F" division, Tanke, Ilorin. It is on record that the church has contributed significantly to the sponsorship of some students at the University of Ilorin with the hope of supporting the church in future.

Dominion Life International Church

The founder of the Dominion Church is Rev Barrister Bode Amoo. He was born in 1960 at Omupo an Igbomina town in Irepodun Local Government area of Kwara state. He attended the University of Lagos for a degree in Law. He was a lecturer for some years at the Kwara State Polytechnic, Ilorin before he went into full-time ministry. He is happily married with children. The Dominion Life Church was started in 1995 and the headquarters of the church is located at Gaa Akanbi, Ilorin. The church has succeeded in winning a significant number of youths in her evangelism and spiritual development. However, there is a need to improve on her contribution to the socio-economic growth of the community. There are about two hundred and fifty regular worshippers in the church every Sunday. The church is still focusing her attention on the consolidation of the headquarters of the church even though there are fellowship centres of the church in Ilorin metropolis.

Be of the Same Mind Evangelical Ministry (Seed of Harmony Bible Church)

The Church was established by Pastor David Akano at Tanke, Oke-Odo, Ilorin. He started his ministerial work at Deeper Life Christian Church, Ilorin. According to him, he decided to establish his own church because of his religious experience and directive from God. The founder of the church has shown his commitment in the preaching of the gospel and he has been seen as a counsellor to many students in the community. Mrs. Florence Nike Akano, the wife of the Pastor is an assistant pastor in the church and is blessed with children. Her position has shown that women are permitted to lead in the Pentecostal churches. It is observed that majority of the membership of the church are students of the University of Ilorin, Ilorin. It is high time the church established at least a Nursery/Primary school, so as to improve the educational growth of the community.

King's Vine Church

The church was founded by Rev Segun Samuel Abejide who attended University of Ilorin where he read Performing Arts. He taught for four years at the Cherubim and Seraphim Secondary School, Sabo-Oke, Ilorin. He served as a Pastor in the Rhema Church before establishing his King's Vine Church in the year 2006. In our investigation he was described as one of the younger generation of pastors who believe that christians should take the front burner in the political leadership of the country. He also believes that religious freedom and liberty should be guaranteed in ilorin. He preaches on Radio Kwara every morning, so as to encourage christians and in obedience to the command of Jesus Christ in Matthew 28:19. The church is at a rented house which is located at Oro road, Ilorin. The worshippers in the church are about two hundred on any Sunday. There is a need to find a more spacious location for the church, so as to avoid traffic hold-ups on Oro road during Sunday worship hours. The emphasis of the founder of the church on healing and miracles have been point of attraction to many people.

Characteristics of Pentecostal Churches in Ilorin.

The phenomenal growth of Pentecostal churches is noticeable in their presence in the nooks and crannies of the town. The factors that are responsible for the growth are:

Healing

The Pentecostal churches lay much emphasis on healing of the sick in their churches. It is believed that with God all things are possible. Faith, as required in Hebrews 11:1, is expected from those seeking healing in the churches. The founders of these churches are believed to have spiritual gifts of healing which manifest when they pray for sick people. As a result of this, different sicknesses are brought to them. This phenomenon has drawn many people from other denominations to the Pentecostal churches. In the course of our investigation, different testimonies were heard in the churches on divine healing.

In all the Churches visited, parallels were drawn from the different miracles that were performed by Jesus Christ and his apostles in the bible to assure their members of the power of miracle. Ojo has identified four major areas of healing. These are physical healing, deliverance, success and prosperity, and healing activities over the political and socio-economic conditions of a nation.[27] Many big signboards are placed on streets while advertisements are announced on radios and televisions to draw people to these churches. Healings of different kinds are announced and testifiers are brought to authenticate "the goodness of God". However, it may be necessary to ask: Are all the claims true and authentic? Some people who claimed to have been healed of some sicknesses are later seen with the problems.

Prayer

This is the pivot of the Pentecostal churches. The members are encouraged to commit every situation of life to the hand of God. In our investigation, we observed that many of the people in the churches are also members of the mainline churches. They came to attend different programmes in the Pentecostal churches in order to pray and seek solution to their problems. Recently, a new Pentecostal church known as "Powerful Christian Church" was established at Sabo-Oke by Pastor and Pastor Mrs. Noah Adeosun. The church has a special programme for women every Wednesday of the week starting at about 8.00am. It is observed that the programme has recorded a success because of the number of women from different denominations and non-Christians in attendance. Many workers and civil servants desert their offices while traders close their shops to attend the prayer sessions. Heavy traffic is witnessed whenever the programme is on-going in Sabo-Oke, Ilorin.

Aylward Shorter opined that prayer in the mission churches is stereotyped, memorized or read, fitting all circumstances[28]. Emotions and feelings are very important elements in prayer as it is understood by the African and they determine the depth, the sincerity, even the worth of the prayer, not to talk of the wording and the mood. Such a prayer can only be spontaneous. African prayer is what may be termed "charismatic improvisation" prompted by the need of the moment. Such prayers are long and at times accompanied with fasting. In some of the churches members are encouraged to bring bottles of water or oil for prayers. Psalms in the bible are read and the water or oil are blessed and sanctified for healing. Night vigils and prayer meetings are organized, so as to pray for protection and find solution to some problems.

Prophecy

The concept of prophecy is found in the Pentecostal churches as a way of divine guidance. In Africa, it is believed that there is no smoke without fire. There is a cause for every misfortune and disaster. In other to avoid such calamity, the prophets are visited, so as to predict what the future has for them. According to Omoyajowo:

> It is however true that people in distress flock into them in search of solution to their spiritual problems, for the cure of their diseases, for protection from both their physical and spiritual enemies and for the fulfillment of their ambitions and hopes.[29]

At the beginning of a new month, a programme called "begin the month with the Lord" has been introduced in almost all the churches. The Pastors are expected to declare the mind of God to the people. This kind of prophecy is also expected at the beginning of every year.

Evangelism

The Pentecostal churches are seen as committed to the command of Jesus on evangelism as recorded in the Gospel of Matthew 28:19. "Go ye therefore to all nations..." Many strategies and methods have been adopted to proclaim the gospel in Ilorin which is traditionally an Islamic community.

Many of the churches occasionally embark on street evangelism and revivals. However, such efforts are not permitted in some parts of the town like Oja Oba, Okelele, Balogun Fulani and other core areas where the indigenes of Ilorin are residing.

The use of tracts, radio and television has been successful in the propagation of the gospel in the community. Many of the Pentecostal churches are involved in this exercise. Although it is expensive and exorbitant to pay the television and radio stations. Some evangelists and pastors like Evangelist Isaac Omolehin, Pastor George Adegboye, Emmanuel Oset, Professor Timothy Opoola, Professor Alfred Adegoke, M.R. Popoola, etc. feature on the Nigerian Television Station, Radio Kwara and FM Radio. These churches are working and cooperating in the field of evangelism. They are all under the umbrella of the Pentecostal Fellowship of Nigeria and Christian Association of Nigeria. International and National Evangelists and Pastors are invited for crusades and revivals in the community. For instance, the German Evangelist, Reinhard Bonnke, Pastor William Kumuyi, David Oyedepo and the late Timothy Obadare, etc are always hosted by the organisations. Such open revivals and crusades have assisted in winning souls for Jesus Christ.

Upholding of Family Ethics

The teachings of Pentecostal churches are contrary to that of the *Aladura* churches that practise polygamy as an African way of marriage. The Pentecostal churches encourage only monogamous marriage and discourage divorce, fornication and adultery. Every Christian home is expected to hold morning family worship, read the bible and attend fellowships. It is emphasised that man is the head of the home as outlined in the bible. Husbands are expected to love their wives and wives are expected to be submissive to their husbands while children are to obey their parents. The fathers are expected to provide for the family. In other words, there is no room for extra-marital affairs and visit to beer parlours and hotels that harbour prostitutes. Ojo quoted Ogbu Kalu that the conversion experience creates "the backdrop for accessing charisma as the power freely given to achieve self discipline, sobriety, holiness and righteousness, and this experience is further consolidated in new ethics as part of the new Christian identity"[30]. This brings about discipline, orderliness and peace into every family that accepts the teachings of the church wholeheartedly.

Women in Pentecostal Churches

Women in the Pentecostal churches are recognised and valued. In fact they play complementary roles to their husbands. In many of the churches studied, they are called Pastor Mrs. and are next to their husbands in the pyramids of authority. They are allowed to officiate during worships and recognised as leaders in the churches. Some of them are seen in hand bills, posters and signposts erected along the roads advertising their churches and some of them appear with their husbands on television programmes. For instance, Mrs. Oset of Canaan ministry appears on the television along with other members of the choir of the church before the ministration of her husband and plays the guitar with melodious songs after the completion of sermons by her husband. She is also in charge of the Nursery and Primary schools established by the church.

In the course of our investigation, we observed that women are also founders of some Pentecostal churches. For instance, Pastor Mrs. Amila is the founder of Christ the Messiah Church located at Unity road, Ilorin. This is a different tradition from the activities of the mainline churches that are reluctant to ordain women as priests. Women's spirituality and talents are recognised and encouraged in the Pentecostal churches.

Music and Dancing

These features are part of worship in the Pentecostal churches in Ilorin. Instruments of different kinds are used in worship. Guitars, piano, organs, drums and, of recent, African drums have been incorporated into worship. Since many of the worshippers in these churches are youths, dancing is a prominent aspect of worship. It is believed that worship in the mainline churches is boring and not so interesting; with the new mode of worship in Pentecostal churches, the youths are captured.

Challenges of Pentecostal churches in Ilorin

A major challenge being witnessed in Ilorin town is religious rivalry between Christians and Muslims. Muslims are aware of the phenomenal growth of the Pentecostal churches in Ilorin and its implications on the spread of Christianity. At times, land is not sold to Christians to build churches. In fact some areas are seen as no "go area" for the churches. In the month of April, 2012, a Living Faith church building under construction was demolished by some "unknown people" in Sango area of Ilorin. The two religious centres were located too close to each other.This led to religious disturbance and mis-understanding in the area.In 2013,a Living Faith Church was burnt along Airport/Eyenkorin/Ogbomoso road. The Living Faith Church alleged that the church was burnt by the muslims who claimed that the land had been sold to them earlier by the land owners.

Exorbitant prices being charged by television and radio stations is another challenge. The government is encouraging privatization of parastatals and companies for effective and profit management of such agencies in the country. The parastatals are encouraged to generate adequate and enough funds to maintain such organizations. This has necessitated a hike in the fees being paid by the churches to purchase air time on these stations. In fact some churches had to stop airing their programmes as a result of the increase in charges.

Contest for space and location. Jesus Christ mandated His disciples to go and proclaim the gospel to the whole world (Matt.28:19).Many Pentecostal churches are seen contesting for location amongst themselves. It is observed that two or three churches hold services in the same building. This has brought about un-healthy rivalry, condemnation and disturbance of church programmes.

Conclusion

Pentecostal churches are multiplying steadily in Ilorin in spite of the fact that the community is traditionally regarded as an Islamic community. Some of them are contributing significantly to the religious, political and socio-economic development of the community.The founders of the various Pentecostal churches in Ilorin have been able to make use of their education,status and commitment to the course of the christian gospel to propagate christianity in Ilorin. It is therefore observed that the charisma of the founders of such churches is a major factor in the growth of the churches in Ilorin. Many of them are seen to be intellectuals, educated elite, professionals and civil servants. These are demonstrated in the strategies and methods being employed in the propagation of the gospel. The challenges notwithstanding, the churches are growing and they are attracting other Christians in African Indigenous churches, mainline churches and other religions into the fold. It is necessary to note that there is a need for further research on the claim of the churches on the authenticity of divine healing especially as this is a point of attraction to such churches.

Notes and References

1. Adam Gadsby (eds), *Longman Dictionary of Contemporary English,* (Essex: Pearson Education Limited, 2007), 248.
2. Antonia Essien, quoted H.W. Turner in an article titled "Dynamics of New Religious Movements in Nigeria" *Journal of Religious Studies*, Department of Religious Studies, University of Uyo, (Vol. No 1 1998, 93)
3. Antonia Essien, quoted H.W. Turner in an article titled "Dynamics of New Religious Movements in Nigeria", 94
4. The first Centre for the Study of Pentecostal Churches in Nigeria was established by Danny McCain at the University of Jos, Jos, Nigeria.
5. Bolaji Idowu, *Olodumare God in Yoruba Belief,* (Lagos: Longman, 1996 new edition), 5.

6. Matthews A. Ojo, Inaugural lecture series 227 titled: *Of Saints and Sinners: Pentecostalism and the Paradox of Social Transformation in Modern Nigeria*, (Obafemi Awolowo University Press Limited, 2009), 4.
7. Matthews A. Ojo, Inaugural lecture series 227 titled: *Of Saints and Sinners*.
8. Richard Burgess, *Nigeria's Christian Revolution: The Civil War Revival and its Pentecostal Progeny (1967-2006)*, (India: Richard Burgess, 2008), 5.
9. Michael P. Adogbo and Crowder E.Ojo. *Research Methods in the Humanities*, (Lagos: Malthouse Press Limited, 2003), 13-18.
10. Michael P. Adogbo and Crowder E.Ojo. *Research Methods in the Humanities*.
11. Ayodele A. Ajayi, quoted Daramola in his work titled "Dynamics of Growth in Mountain of Fire and Miracles Ministries in Yorubaland, 1989-2006. (Unpublished PhD Thesis submitted to the University of Ibadan, Ibadan, 2008), 12
12. Hakeem O. Danmole, "Emirate of the 'Yarba' Ilorin in the Nineteenth Century" in H. Babbayi and A.M.Yakubu (eds). *The Sokoto Caliphate History and Legacies, 1804-2004* (Volume One, Kaduna, Baraka Press, 2006), 21
13. Hakeem O. Danmole, "Emirate of the 'Yarba' Ilorin in the Nineteenth Century".
14. Rotimi Omotoye, "Christianity and Educational Development in Ilorin metropolis (1855-1995)" *Journal of Religious Studies*, Department of Religious Studies, University of Uyo, (Vol. No 1,1998), 107
15. Rotimi Omotoye, "Christianity and Educational Development in Ilorin metropolis (1855-1995)".

16. Rotimi Omotoye, "Christianity and Educational Development in Ilorin metropolis (1855-1995)"
17. Matthews A.Ojo, Inaugural lecture series 227 titled: *Of Saints and Sinners*.
18. Rotimi Omotoye and E.O. Opoola (2012) "The Church and National Development: A Case Study of the Living Faith Church(Winner Chapel) in Nigeria" in Centre for the Study of New Religions www.Cesnur.org, 5
19. Rotimi Omotoye and E.O. Opoola (2012) "The Church and National Development".
20. M.A. Ojo, "*Of Saints and Sinners*, 26.
21. Don Akhilomen "Televangelism and the Development of the Nigerian Child" in Onah A.Odey (eds) et.al *Religion, Ethics and Population Development*. A Publication of the Nigerian Association for the Study of Religions (NASR, 2007) 32-33
22. Rotimi Omotoye, "Charisma and Leadership Crisis: An Examination of the Christ Apostolic Church in Nigeria" in Ade P. Dopamu(eds.) et.al *Religion, Leadership and Society: Focus on Nigeria*, A publication of the Nigerian Association for the Study of Religions (NASR, 2004), 37-45
23. Oral interview conducted with the Pentecostal Church Founders in Ilorin by Rotimi Omotoye and some 400 level RCS students in 2010 at different dates and venues.
24. Rotimi Omotoye "Christianity and Cultural Development: An Examination of the Aladura Churches in Yorubaland" in Ade P.Dopamu et.al (eds) *Dialogue Issues in ContemporaryDiscussion*, (Akute: Big Small Books, 2007) 336.
25. Matthews Ojo, Inaugural lecture series 227 titled: *Of Saints and Sinners*: 41.

26. Oyeronke Olademo, A paper titled: "Religious Tolerance in Ilorin: A case study of Rhema Church and Hamadiyyah Mosque, Tanke, Ilorin". The paper was presented at a Conference in Abuja 2013. It was organized by Afe Adogame, University of Edinburgh on *Religious Terorrisim in Africa*,
27. Matthews Ojo, Inaugural lecture series 227 titled: *Of Saints and Sinners:* 41.
28. Shorter Aylward, *African Christian Spirituality*, (London, Geoffrey Champion), 109.
29. J.A. Omoyajowo, *Bishop I.O.S, Okusanya, A Biography*, (Abeokuta, Gbemi Sodipo Press, 1992), 3.
30. Ogbu Kalu quoted by M.A.Ojo

CHAPTER TEN

Prospects and Challenges of Arabic and Islamic Studies in Nigeria with Particular Reference to Yoruba Land

Tajudeen Adebayo
Chief Producer,
Voice of Nigeria, Lagos, Nigeria.
ibnadebayo2002@gmail.com
+2348033938927

Introduction

Article 1 of the World Declaration on Education for All (1990) described goals of education as follows: To survive, to develop full capacities of an individual, to live and work in dignity, to participate fully in development, to improve the quality of his life, to make informed decisions and to continue learning[1]. To achieve these goals, one must acquire competences in one's chosen field. Competence is defined as the ability to meet a complex demand. Each competence corresponds to a combination of interrelated cognitive and practical skills, knowledge and personal qualities such as motivation, values and ethics, attitudes and emotions.[2] Key competences are individually based competences considered necessary or desirable for effective participation in democratic societies and for coping with global demands, particularly those related to the so-called knowledge economy or information society[3].

The philosophers Canto-Sperber and Dupuy drew on their expertise in moral and social-philosophy and the philosophy of mind not only to address the question of key competences but also to consider what constitutes 'the good life'[4]. Haste emphasised from her socio-psychological viewpoint the need to look at individuals in a cultural, social and linguistic context[5]. For Perrenoud, a sociologist, the central question to be addressed was what competences are needed by everyone to freely exercise his or her autonomy in multiple social fields. He associated a successful life with not being abused, alienated, dominated or exploited[6]. Levy and Murnane[7], as well as Goody[8] used an empirical approach to the issue of competence. Levy and Murnane used relevant economic theories and empirical results to address the question of the competences workers need to succeed in the labour market. Goody, the anthropologist, rejected engaging in a de-contextualised discussion of key competences on the grounds that theory must always be considered in relation to practice.

Competence could be summarised under three sub-headings; acting autonomously, using tools interactively, and interacting in social heterogeneous groups. Acting autonomously entails the development of personal identity and the exercise of relative autonomy in the sense of deciding, choosing and acting in different social fields. Using tools interactively is meant in its broadest sense of the term to include language, information and knowledge in addition to physical tools which include the ability to use the technology interactively. Interacting in socially heterogeneous group focuses on the interaction with others who have different views of life. Human beings are dependent on ties to others for material and psychological survival, for a sense of self identity and social meaning.[9]

This chapter seeks to apply these competence tests on graduates of Arabic and Islamic Studies currently serving in the public service with particular reference to Yorubaland. Selected fields include Security services, Media, Electoral body and Banks. Competences of the randomly selected individuals are assessed based on three criteria: ability to act autonomously, use tools interactively, and interact in socially heterogeneous groups.

Islam and Arabic Language in Africa: a historical overview

Arabic had had a reasonable contact with Africa prior to the advent of Islam. More than slavery, it was the African gold, for its quality and quantity that attracted foreign explorers to Africa, first from the Carthaginians and then the Arabs[10]. With the advent of Islam and, soon to follow, the adoption of Arabic as the lingua franca of the Muslim nations, the currency, diffusion and status of Arabic became enhanced in the whole of North Africa.[11].

The Arabic language has a long interaction with Nigeria. The history of writing in Arabic extends over a period close to 800 years in the Nigerian region[12]. It covers the era before the colonial era, the colonial and the post-colonial periods. Before the advent of Islam in Africa, there had been trade relations between the Arabs and the Africans. Trading, as we know, requires conversation between the seller and buyer. The Arabic language, which was more advanced than local languages, was adopted for the purpose. It was this trade relation that sowed the seed of the Arabic language in Africa, though, its scope was limited to commercial centres and names of items that were not known to Africans.[13]

The main factor responsible for the spread of Arabic to areas outside the Arabian Peninsula was Islam. Being the language of the *Qur'ān* and Islamic branches of knowledge, Arabic has inevitably been interwoven with Islam.[14] In all the communities that have embraced Islam, the history of Arabic is traceable to the advent of Islam in such communities[15]. Nigeria is not an exception. This is because Muslims must learn and commit some chapters of the *Qur'ān* to memory for observing their daily *Salāt* and other religious duties and the fact that Islam encourages learning. While describing this, Ogunbiyi said:

> In response to this religious inclination, one finds all over the country, especially in the Northern and South-western parts, traditional Qur'ānic schools known as Ile-Kewu in the Yoruba-speaking areas of Nigeria, in virtually every quarter of urban centres, in villages and hamlets where there is a large concentration of Muslims for the propagation of the knowledge of Arabic among the young and the old.[16]

With the advent of the popular Sokoto Jihad, the Arabic language became the *lingua franca* of the state. It was often the only means of communication between the communities of Tuareg, Kanuri, Hausa, Fulani, Nupe or Yoruba.[17] It played a vital role in politics, economy, social and judicial sectors. This was evident in the numerous works left by the Sokoto scholars before the invasion of the colonialists.

Influence of Arabic on some other languages.

The Arabic language has great influence on languages of the Muslims all over the world. In Asia, Persian, Turkish, Urdu and Malay are amongst the languages that have been tremendously influenced by Arabic.[18] Even the English language had benefited from the generosity of the Arabic language considering the information made available on line and is quoted below:

> Arabic has contributed many words to the English language, many of them beginning with the Arabic definite article al-. These include *algebra, alcohol, alchemy, alkali, alcove, alfalfa,* and *albatross.* Others are

mosque, minaret, sultan, elixir, harem, giraffe, gazelle, cotton, amber, sofa, mattress, tariff, magazine, arsenal, syrup, sherbet, and *artichoke. Coffee* is also an Arabic word, which entered English by way of Turkish and Italian. The word *assassin* comes from a similar Arabic word meaning "hashish addicts."[19]

In Africa too, Somali, Swahili, Madinka, Wolof, Hausa, Fulfulde, Kanuri and Yoruba have acquired loans from Arabic words and expressions[20]. Thus, Arabic has enriched these languages with thousands of religious, political, legal and commercial words and expressions[21]. Scholars have written so much about the Arabic loan words in Hausa, Fulfulde, Yoruba, Swahili and other languages. In an article entitled "Arabic loan words in Hausa" Goerner, Salman and Armitage we have this:

> Many of the words in the Hausa language have Arabic origins. If any one doubts the importance of these words, he would find it interesting to venture into a Hausa speaking Community with an Arabic speaker. Using only Arabic, such a speaker has been found to establish a far degree of communication with the people. Some would attribute this understanding of Arabic to the omnipresence of the Koranic Schools. However, experience has shown that a Hausa speaker untrained in Koranic Arabic understands conversational Arabic as well as the average Koranic Student. They recognize the Arabic loan words without knowing their derivation and grasp the meaning expressed. [22]

Abubakar cited about 1,500 frequently used words of Arabic origin in Hausa language[23]. He also identified other aspects of borrowing besides the lexical/semantic level such as pronominal suffixes for first and second persons for both masculine and feminie[24]. It is interesting to note that some Arabic words have common meaning in many African languages. That is an indication that the Arabic language can serve as a unifying factor in Africa. At times the equivalence of such Arabic words had sometimes become unknown in the borrowing languages.

An overview of the curriculum of Arabic and Islamic Studies in Nigeria

The overview presented in this study of the courses leading to the award of bachelor's degree and Master of Arts in Arabic and Islamic Studies is based on what obtains in the Department of Arabic and Islamic Studies in the University of Ibadan, Department of Arabic; and Department of Religions in the University of Ilorin.

The Arabic curriculum contains courses in Arabic Conversation, Composition, Reader, Grammar, Morphology, Literature of the Pre-Islamic era, Early Islamic and Umayyad period, Abbasid period, Modern Arabic literature, Arabic literature of the Spain and the Literature of the Mahjar. Other areas covered include Arabic Rhetoric, Syntax, Literary criticism, Translation, Phonetics, Arabic calligraphy, Theatre in Arabic, Lexicography, Arabic prosody, and Arabic novel among others.

The Islamic Studies curriculum cover area such as: Islamic fundamentals, Early history of Islam and *Jahiliyyah*, *Sīrah*, Textual study of the *Qur'ān* and *Hadīth*, Islamic Thought and civilisation, Islamic Philosophy, Ethics, Islamic law, Sufism, Theology, Islamic economic system, Islamic politics, Islam in Africa, *Tafsīr* among others.

Based on the above mentioned courses, a graduate of Arabic and Islamic Studies has been prepared to work in various quarters in the public and international spheres for the reasons to be mentioned. The issue of survival as enumerated in the World Declaration on Education for all is the ability of a course of study to prepare its graduates with basic skills and exposure required to either secure a job or become self-employed. With translation skills, one can secure a job in international and regional bodies such as African Union and United Nations. One could also establish a translation firm facilitating International trade and businesses. As a corollary to that, translation and interpretation is relevant in broadcasting[25], advertising[26], international conferences, judiciary[27] and state security to mention but a few.

The literature in any given language exposes a student to culture and ways of life of the owner of the language. The Arabic literature from pre-Islamic era to the modern time is considered to be one of the richest. It has attracted attention of many orientalists[28] who have written several works on various era of Arabic literature. With lessons in Arabic literature of different era and rhetoric, the graduate is prepared to take up challenging jobs in security services such as State Security, Nigerian Army, and Navy among others.

Arabic Grammar and morphology are rich areas for students of Arabic to make name and career. In the course of their study, students would have come across several household names in Arabic grammar[29], linguistics, philology and lexicography[30]. Interestingly, non Arabs especially of Nigerian origin[31] and non Muslims[32] have contributed immensely to the development of Arabic lexicography.

The Arabic calligraphy is an important aspect of Islamic art which remains unexplored. Muslim artists have organised Islamic Art Exhibition featuring some of these fantastic artworks[33]. Theatre, drama in Arabic and Arabic short stories and novels contain high potentials for graduates of Arabic. These areas remain virgin land except for few Nigerian Arabic scholars who have written drama and short stories in the Arabic language[34]. Such books are often recommended for school children.

The above enumerated areas are areas of potential development for graduates of Arabic. They can live with dignity as translators, authors, litterateurs, grammarians, novel and short story writers of international repute. They can thrive in an array of profession through which they can contribute their quotas to the development of the society. Through these professions, graduates of Arabic could sustain themselves and improve their standards of living in the society. Having gone through these trainings, such graduates can make informed decisions as members of a given community. They have the opportunity to develop themselves in their chosen careers through on-the-job trainings and they can as well pursue second and doctoral degrees in Arabic Studies or any other related field.

Islamic Studies is another area in the Nigerian tertiary system through which its graduates, depending on their versatility, can make career in certain professions. For instance, one could work in a bank especially now that Nigeria's apex bank has given approval, in principle, for the first Islamic bank in the country[35]. Even the conventional banking sector in Nigeria hardly discriminates against any field of learning because regardless of one's specialisation, one would still have to be trained in banking. All that is required of one to get and sustain a job in the sector is one's trainability. Even though, public administration is not singled out as a course of study, graduates of Islamic Studies can pick that from the Islamic administrative systems of various Islamic states. The Islamic law is a discipline on its own. A student of

Islamic Studies could specialise in *Sharī'ah* Law or combine it with Common Law to become a lawyer.

The Islamic thought has become a specialisation in Islamic Studies. The establishment of the Nigerian office of International Institute of Islamic Thought (IIIT) [36] in Kano, Nigeria, has given a boost to efforts towards Islamisation of knowledge[37]. This effort, which emanated from the United States, has opened wide opportunities for graduates of Islamic Studies, humanities and social sciences as a whole. Even though, the Islamic politics faces vehement opposition like any other Islamic system, its evolution has already started with the aborted regime of Muhammad Mursi in Egyptian politics. Musri was elected as a President on the platform of Freedom and Justice Party which was formed by the Muslim Brotherhood. In the nearest future, services of specialists in Islamic politics will definitely be required. Even in the current political dispensations, a graduate of Islamic Studies in politics should make a difference in his ways of doing things. A course in Islamic history could lead an interested student in history to make a career in history[38]. Scholars of Arabic and Islamic Studies have rendered an unprecedented service towards the preservation of African history[39].

Despite all these potentials and opportunities embedded in Arabic and Islamic Studies, there has been a dearth of students across the tertiary institutions that offer both courses in the South Western Nigeria. Lawal Manzoor A. presented a statistics in his paper titled: "The State of Islamic Education in South-Western Nigeria" that the total number of students of both courses in all tertiary institutions in the South Western part of the country with the exclusion of Lagos State University and University of Lagos, Akoka was less than 1,500.

The said statistics covered the period between 2005/2006 to 2008/2009 academic sessions of all the tertiary institutions in the region[40]

A review of selected individuals

A sizeable number of Nigerian graduates of Arabic and Islamic Studies are currently making waves in the State Security Service of Nigeria. The service needs, as applicable in any country, an array of disciplines to discharge its duty effectively. Nigeria is blessed with more than 500 languages[41] and culture with a dialect of Arabic known as Shuwa Arabic in Borno State as one of them. In this case, multi-linguists are needed to aid the service.

Some graduates of Arabic and Islamic Studies, whose identities will not be declared for security reasons[42] are currently serving in the State Security Service. They serve in various capacities such as areas of intelligence acquisition, planning and execution of protective security for public office holders. They assist in making analysis and estimates regarding national security threats. They have participated in several trainings both home and abroad that enabled them to use the tools of the job interactively. These tools include intelligence, conversation and ammunitions as the situation may demand. They have served in different commands in different parts of the country and some of them, for their versatility and usefulness, have been commended and acknowledged several times in their field.

Despite their Arabic and Islamic backgrounds, these graduates have demonstrated high sense of responsibility in discharging their duties. Security issue in Nigeria, in view of strange bombings in some parts of the country, has become very important. Language competence is required to differentiate between the fake and real threat in a situation whereby every one that wears a beard has become a potential security threat. The ability of these graduates to interact in social heterogeneous groups is obvious in their participation in delivering lectures to various cadres in the service, as well as their ability to serve in various commands of the country.

However, with the permission of officers concerned after going through my write up about them, I will mention few names. Captain Wasiu Yekeen (b. 1982) had his preliminary Arabic trainings in Madrasatu Bushra, Adjame, Abidjan, Ivory Coast and Assanusiyyah Comprehensive High School, Odeomu, Osun State.[43] He graduated from NDA as a 2nd Lieutenant with B.A. (Hons) Arabic in 2006 and is currently a Major in the Nigerian Army. Another military personnel worthy of mentioning is Lieutenant Luqman Kayode Badmos (b.1977) who is currently serving in the Education Corps of Nigerian Army. He read Linguistics but took minor courses in Arabic from the University of Ilorin from where he graduated in 2006.

Also making waves in a security related field is another graduate of Education and Islamic Studies, University of Ilorin (1997) Abdul Azeez Rasheed. He started his career in security operations from Bemil Nigeria Limited, Ojodu, Lagos in 2002. He was a contract employee attached to the US Consulate General, Lagos where he later secured his current job.

Security operations and management is a broad sector that emphasises professionalism. These include: facility and executive protection using private guards, crime prevention and investigation, mobile and static patrol, crowd control, ceremonies security protocol, fire prevention and safety, private investigation and specialized security operation, sales, services and installation of security/safety equipments and other security consulting services.

The area of private security is becoming more relevant in Nigeria in view of rising crime, terrorism, corrupt state security organizations, conflicts in the oil-rich Niger Delta and more recently Boko Haram in Northern Nigeria. It is in this context that Nigeria's private security industry has experienced rapid growth. Hence, establishing a private security company opens doors of success.

Among the selected fields where graduates of Arabic and Islamic Studies have flourished and are still flourishing is the media. Ustadh Naj'mdeen Adegbite Binuyo, was the 3rd Head of the Arabic unit of Voice of Nigeria. He joined the Arabic service of the then External Service of Nigerian Broadcasting Corporation (NBC) in 1967 when he left Sudan where he was working as a translator in the Nigerian Embassy. Prof. Asif F. Ahmad, of the National Open University of Nigeria was the producer of 'Africa This Week' on Voice of Nigeria before he became a lecturer at the Department of Arabic and Islamic Studies of University of Ibadan. Professor Murtada Bidmos, one-time Dean of Education, University of Lagos, Akoka had also worked in the Arabic Service of VON before he joined the academia.

Among those who had served in the media was Abdul-Lateef Oyebisi (b. 1953), who holds a B.A. (Arabic Literature and Islamic Studies) of the University of Ibadan (1988). He retired in 2013 as an Assistant Director in charge of Voice of Nigeria, South-West Bureau Office in Osogbo, Osun State. The competence of Abdul-Lateef Oyebisi in the area of language was evident. He was formally of the Arabic service of VON, later of the Yoruba Service before he became the administrative head of a whole zonal office. His creativity, dynamism and ability to use language effectively were apparent in his career development. His movement from one section to another has given an added opportunity for an all-round experience and is also an indication to his administrative competence. To represent Voice of Nigeria at zonal level is an indication that he could interact easily at top management level of the corporation.

Tajudeen Adebayo (b.1972) is an International award winning broadcaster, who holds a PhD in Arabic Studies. He earned his Bachelor's degree from the University of Ilorin (1997), Master's degree (2000) and Ph.D (2009) from the University of Ibadan. He is currently the head of Arabic Service of VON.

Serving in the electoral body is Abdulwahid Adedoyin (b.1979) who hails from Oyun local Government of Kwara State. He had his preliminary Arabic Studies at the Arabic Institute of Nigeria, Elekuro, Ibadan and later graduated from Bayero University, Kano in 2003 where he read Arabic Studies. He gained employment with Independent National Electoral Commission (INEC) in 2007 as an administrative electoral officer in charge of collating the Commission's policy statements.

Another personality to be discussed is Olabisi Waheed Oyedele (b. 1974) who hails from Ijagbo in Kwara State. He had his preliminary studies at Ansar-ud-Deen Primary and Secondary schools before he gained admission to study Islamic Studies at the University of Ilorin. Olabisi is currently a banker with Sterling Bank Plc. His banking career started during his National Youth Service year at Trans International Bank Plc in 1998/1999. Thereafter he worked with Magnum Trust Bank before the merger of the bank with other banks to form a mega-bank now known as Sterling Bank Plc. Currently, he works with Skye Bank Plc. Olabisi Waheed has demonstrated his versatility in a field different from his course of study. His movement is also an indication that he can interact socially in social heterogeneous groups ranging from his co-workers as well as the customers. Also as the head of operation at a point in time, he must have acquired administrative skills.

In the field of Library Science, Dr. T.M. Salisu, a graduate of Arabic and Islamic Studies, University of Ibadan, 1972 has distinguished himself. After his graduation, he obtained a Masters degree in Library Science in 1974 before he joined University of Lagos as a Librarian also in 1974. He was the first University Librarian of the University of Agriculture, Abeokuta (UNAAB) from February 1991 till February 2001 and a former Director of Institute for Human Resources Development (INHURD). In recognition of his capability to give quality leadership and make positive contributions to the overall development of the University, Dr Salisu was appointed the Pioneer Head of the newly-created Office of Advancement (OFA) of UNAAB in January 2013. The appointment is for a period of one year.

In the Nigeria Customs Service, Afolabi Dokun Lamidi, a graduate of Arabic and Islamic Studies, University of Ibadan, 1973 rose to the rank of the Customs Area Comptroller before retiring. He is currently a chief in his hometown, Ede, Osun State.

Ambassador AbdulKabir Assayuty, another product of Arabic served in Nigerian Ministry of Foreign Affairs in various capacities in different countries before he was appointed the Nigerian ambassador to Mali and Kuwait.

Hon. Justice Muttalib Ahmad Ambali, another product of Department of Arabic and Islamic Studies, University of Ibadan was a seasoned Administrator before he joined the Shariah Department of Kwara State Judiciary. He joined mainstream civil service between 1971 and 1979 where he served in various capacities. In 1980, he became a foundation member of the Sharia Court of Appeal of Kwara State by taking appointment as the pioneer Chief Registrar of the Court. A year later, he was appointed a Kadi of the Court, where he waited patiently for 18 years before he rose to the position of Grand Kadi in 2000. He headed the Court for 8 years before he retired in 2008 at the age of 65.

Alhaji Ahmad Olayiwola Kamal, a native of Ilorin, Kwara State is another graduate of Arabic, who served in various capacities in several Kwara State Ministries such as Education and Health. He was a Chief Education Officer, a Permanent Secretary and later became a Commissioner.

Challenges facing Graduates of Arabic and Islamic Studies in the Public Sector

In the course of this study, some selected interviewees highlighted some of the challenges they face in public service. Most of these graduates found themselves in the fields different from the courses they were taught in the University. This took them some time before they could adapt properly.

Another challenge was inferiority complex especially in the multinational organisations. Some graduates of Arabic and Islamic Studies feel inferior to graduates of other courses, a feeling that has led some to limit their job opportunities. In addition to that is the challenge of how to maintain neutrality in the course of discharging their duties amidst threats and intimidations. Sustaining Islamic teachings in the presence of hundreds of people who do not share the same ideology could be daunting. This is because the concepts of Islamic history, especially during the era of *Khulafā 'ur-Rāshidūn*, and the faith, which they were taught are mostly at variance with a society bedeviled with moral decadence and indecency. The challenge is how to reflect such moral standard in this period of incessant ethno-religious conflicts in some parts of the country and the issue of global terrorism as a whole. It is, without a doubt, a challenge to the entire Muslims as every Muslim is considered a suspect of terrorism and a member of Boko Haram.

Every job has its own hazard but some professions are more hazardous than others. Security jobs and electoral-related jobs can be more hazardous and life threatening. Inter departmental transfer in some of the public services can destabilise the public servants in their quest to maintain a family.

Limited or lack of adequate exposure to Arabic dialects and culture can be a disadvantage for the Nigerian graduate of Arabic who finds himself among the native speakers of the language for the first time. This is because most native speakers of the language prefer to use their dialects rather than classical Arabic which is taught in Nigerian institutions.

Some interviewees expressed the fear that they may forget their primary course of study which is Arabic and Islamic Studies as a result of lack of use or limited usage as the case may be.

Some organisations provide equal opportunities, fair-play and equitable treatment in employment to all people without regard to race, colour, religion, sex, national origin, age, disability, political affiliation, marital status, or sexual orientation. But, perhaps, due to lack of information of these opportunities, Muslims are not many in such organisations.

Suggested Solutions

Arabic and Islamic Studies in our institutions need to be broadened to include courses in administration, management, psychology and information technology.

There is a need for more active partcipation of students of Arabic and Islamic Studies in extracurricular activities such as campus politics and sporting events. This will bring them in contact with students of other courses who might not share the same faith with them. Such steps will prepare them for when they get to the larger world without losing their identities as Muslims. We have seen in the past some students of Arabic and Islamic Studies who had occupied positions in campus politics and that did not have any negative impacts on neither on thier faith nor academic performaces.

Choice of job should be based on personal interest and passion for the job and not solely because of the monetary incentive attached to it. Graduates of Arabic and Islamic Studies should endeavour to share information among themselves, especially information on job opportunities. There is a need for building confidence, competence and dynamism so that they can be relevant in any sector. It suffices to know that a multi-linguist with relevant skills stands a better chance in the job market.

Conclusion

Arabic and Islamic Studies as courses of study in tertiary institutions in Nigeria are faced with low patronage by students partly because of the economic viability of the courses and also because of lack of adequate exposure of their potentials. This current study explored the opportunities available for graduates of Arabic and Islamic Studies. It assessed the challenges faced by selected graduates of Arabic and Islamic Studies of Yoruba origin. The criteria used were their ability to act autonomously, use tools interactively, and interact in social heterogeneous groups.

Both courses are economically viable depending on individual versatility and dynamism. Selected graduates mentioned in this study passed the acid tests set therein. They all excelled in their professions. However, there is a need to broaden Arabic and Islamic Studies curricular to include administration, management, psychology and information technology. Such step will attract more students and make graduates of Arabic and Islamic Studies more marketable.

Notes and References

1. The World Bank. *Lifelong learning in the global knowledge economy: challenges for developing countries.* 2002. Retrieved on 8th June 2011 from the website:http://www1.worldbank.org/education/pdf/Lifelong%20 Learning_GKE.pdf [cited 6.6.2003].
2. Dominique Simone Rychen: An overarching conceptual framework for assessing key competences in an international context lessons from an interdisciplinary and policy-oriented approach. Retrieved

from:http://www.cedefop.europa.eu/EN/Files/BgR1_Rychen.pdf on wed- 8-6-2011
3. Dominique, Simone Rychen: An overarching conceptual framework.
4. M. Canto-Sperber, J.P. Dupuy, Competencies for the good life and the good society. In: Rychen, D. S.; Salganik, L. H. (eds) *Defining andselecting key competencies: theoretical andconceptual foundations.* (Göttingen: Hogrefe and Huber, 2001), 67–92.
5. H. Haste, Ambiguity, autonomy and agency: psychological challenges to new competence. In: Rychen, D. S.; Salganik, L. H. (eds) *Definingand selecting key competencies: theoreticaland conceptual foundations.* (Göttingen: Hogrefe and Huber, 2001), 93–120.
6. P. Perrenoud, The key to social fields: competencies of an autonomous actor. In: Rychen, D. S.; Salganik, L. H. (eds) *Defining and selecting keycompetencies: theoretical and conceptualfoundations.* (Göttingen: Hogrefe and Huber, 2001), 121–150.
7. F. Levy, R.J. Murnane, Key competencies critical to economic success. In: Rychen, D. S.; Salganik, L. H. (eds) *Defining and selecting keycompetencies: theoretical and conceptualfoundations.* (Göttingen: Hogrefe and Huber, 2001), 151–174.
8. J. Goody, Competencies and education: contextual diversity. In: Rychen, D. S.; Salganik, L. H. (eds) *Defining and selecting key competencies: theoretical and conceptual foundations*, (Göttingen: Hogrefe and Huber, 2001), 175–190.
9. C. Ridgeway, Joining and functioning in groups, self-concept and emotion management. In: Rychen, D. S.; Salganik, L. H. (eds) *Defining andselecting key competencies: theoretical and conceptual foundations*, (Göttingen: Hogrefe and Huber, 2001), 205–211.

10. E. W. Bovil, *The Golden Trade of the Moors*, (OUP,London 1970), 21-23 as quoted in R.D. Abubakre's inaugural lecture: Survival of Arabic in difficult terrain. University of Ilorin, 2002.
11. J. S. Moon, *Sweetman's Islam and Christian Theology*, (Centre for the Study of Islam and Christian Muslim Relations. Selly Oaks, Birmanghan, n.d.), 49-50 as quoted in R.D. Abubakre's inaugural lecture.
12. J. Hunwick, The Arabic literary tradition in Nigeria. *Research in African literature*, (Retrieved Mar 04, 2008 from http://www.jstor.org, 1997), 210.
13. See S.A.S. Galadanci. *Harakat al-Lughat al-Arabiyyah WaAdabiha fi Naijiriyah*. 2nd ed. (Riyadh. 1993), 17
14. S.H.A. Malik. *Arabic, The Muslim Prayers and beyond*. Inaugural lecture. Dept. of Arabic & Islamic Studies, University of Ibadan. (Ibadan University Press. 1999), 3.
15. S.H.A. Malik. *Arabic, The Muslim Prayers and beyond*,10.
16. I.A. Ogunbiyi. *Of Non-Muslim Cultivators and Propagators of Arabic Language*. Inaugural lecture. Foreign Languages Department, (Lagos State University. 1987), 9-10
17. S.H.A. Malik, *Arabic, The Muslim*, 23
18. Arabic Language. (Retrieved March 18, 2005 from www.worldlanguage.com/Arabic.htm)
19. S.H.A. Malik. *Arabic, The Muslim*, 23.
20. S.H.A. Malik. *Arabic, The Muslim*, 23.
21. I.A. Ogunbiyi. *Of Non-Muslim*, 12. Quoting M. Goerner, Y. Salman, & P. Armitage, Two essays on Arabic Loan Words in Hausa. Occasional paper. No 7. Department of English. (Ahmadu Bello University, Zaria).
22. I.A. Ogunbiyi. *Of Non-Muslim*, 12
23. I.A. Ogunbiyi. *Of Non-Muslim*, 13

24. S.H.A. Malik. *Arabic, The Muslim...* Making reference to Ogunbiyi, I.A. Arabic loan Words the Yoruba Language, (Arab Journal of language Studies. 3. 1), 161-180
25. Translation is an integral part of modern day broadcasting because the world has become a global village. Language is no longer a barrier to gathering materials for news and programmes. For more information on relevance of translation to Nigerian Arabic broadcasting see my PhD thesis titled: *Investigation of Arabic Broadcasting in Nigeria, 1970-2006* submitted to the Department of Arabic and Islamic Studies, (University of Ibadan February 2009), 59- 63.
26. In International trade, advertisers now employ services of translators to render information on packages of advertised products in several languages including Arabic. The writer was once a consultant in translation from English to Arabic for FCB Redline, a Public Relations & Promotions Practitioners located in Lagos. This is also applicable in electronic broadcast such as Radio, Television and Internet.
27. In court cases involving the Arabic language such as libel or defamation, the judiciary often require the service of graduates of Arabic to act as witness to such cases or as interpreter.
28. Prominent among the orientalists who contributed immensely to the Arabic literature are A.J. Arberry, 1965. *Arabic Poetry for students*, R.A. Nicholson, 1921. *Studies in Islamic Poetry*, H.A.R. Gibb & Harold Bowen, 1963. *Islamic Society and the West*, Philip K. Hitti, 1958. *History of the Arabs*, Jaroslav Stetkevyeh, 1970, (The Modern Arabic Literary Language, Chicago and Robert Irwin, 1983), *The Arabian night*.

29. For concise biography of popular Arabic grammarians and linguistics, see Abdul Bāqi bn 'Abdul Majīd al-yamāni, 1986. *Ishāratut ta'yīn fī tarājumi n-nuhāt wa l-lughawiyyīn*, Saudi Arabia.
30. The German orientalists contributed a lot to the development of Arabic lexicography. I will mention just few of them and their popular publications for the purpose of this paper: Hans Wehr, *Arabisches Wörterbuch für die Schriftsparche der Gegenwart*, 1952 translated to English by David Cowan, *Léon Berche, Lexique arabe-françois*, 1938. J.B. Belot, *Vocabulaire arabe-françois*, G.S. Colin, *Pour lire la presse arabe*, 1937. among others.
31. Professor Z.I. Oseni, Department of Arabic, University of Ilorin was the pioneer in the area of Arabic drama in Nigeria with his book *al-'amīd al-mubajjal, Auchi 1994*. Thereafter he also authored other books such as: *al-Ṭabaqat al-'ulya (*the Upper Class) Auchi, 2006. *Al-Tājir wa ṣāḥib al-Maṭ'am*, Auchi, 2005 and *Qiṣaṣ khaṭṭ al-istiwā'* (Equatorial line stories) Auchi, 2004. Other scholars are Dr. Barihi Adetunji, 2005. *Fuhūṣ-ul- afāhiṣ fī funūn-il-'aqāṣiṣ* (searching for hollow nests in story telling) Ibadan, and Imam Moshood Abdul-Ganeey Adebayo Al-Oyowy, 2001. *Ustādhun ragma anfihi'* (A teacher in defiance of him) Sagamu.
32. Prominent among non-Muslim cultivators of Arabic in Nigeria are Professor Isaac Ogunbiyi and Dr. Kole Omotosho.
33. Forum for Islamic Education and Welfare in collaboration with Halal Art Gallerieo organized 3rd Islamic Art Exhibition titled: "Extract from the Master Artist" in 2006. It featured Islamic artworks by Muslim artists such as Ridwan Adk-Oshinowo, Musliu Adeola Balogun among others.

34. Professor Z.I. Oseni, Department of Arabic, University of Ilorin was the pioneer in the area of Arabic drama in Nigeria with his book *'al-'amīd 'al-mubajjal, Auchi 1994*. Thereafter he also authored other books such as: *'al-Ṭabaqat 'al-'ulya* (the Upper Class) Auchi, 2006. *'Al-Tājir wa ṣāhib 'al-Maṭ'am*, Auchi, 2005 and *Qiṣaṣ khaṭṭ 'al-istiwā'* (Equatorial line stories) Auchi, 2004. Other scholars are Dr. Barihi Adetunji, 2005. *Fuhūṣ-ul- 'afāhiṣ fī funūn-il-'aqāṣiṣ* (searching for hollow nests in story telling) Ibadan, and Imam Moshood Abdul-Ganeey Adebayo Al-Oyowy, 2001. *Ustādhun ragma 'anfihi'* (A teacher in defiance of him) Sagamu.

35. Islamic banking is a form of non-interest banking which does not invest in gambling, alcohol, nudity and some other unethical businesses. It is very vibrant in a number of Western countries. According to Wasim Ahmad in his dissertation titled: *'Islamic Banking in the UK: opportunities and challenges'* submitted to Kingston Business School, London, dated 6th October 2008, A big movement of Islamic Banking started in the Western countries especially United Kingdom, Australia and United State (Shanmugam, Perumal and Ridzwa, 2004). In the UK, two main high street banks are providing Islamic financial services on competitive basis and Islamic Bank of Britain is fully Shariah compliant. There are 21 conventional institutes in the UK which provide Islamic financial services according to Sha'riah law to 1.8 million Muslim people (Imeson, 2007). Its introduction in Nigeria started during the period when Prof. Charles Soludo was the Governor of the Central Bank of Nigeria (CBN) but became popularized during the era of Sanusi Lamido Sanusi as the Governor of the CBN in 2011.

Chapter Ten	Tajudeen Adebayo, in Y.A. Quadri, R.W. Omotoye & R.I. Adebayo (Eds) Religion in Contemporary Nigeria London, Adonis & Abbey Publishers

36. The International Institute of Islamic Though (IIIT) is a cultural and intellectual institution established and registered in the United States of America at the beginning of the 15th Hijrah Century (1401/1981) with the following objectives: to provide a comprehensive Islamic outlook through elucidating the principles of Islam and relating them to relevant issues of contemporary thought, to regain the intellectual cultural and civilization identity of the Ummah through the Islamization of the humanity and social sciences and to rectify the methodology of contemporary Islamic thought. The Nigerian office of IIIT is one of its overseas offices spread all over the world. For more information on its activities, refer to *al-Ijtihad, the Journal of Islamization of knowledge and Contemporary Issues* published by IIIT, Nigerian Office, Kano.
37. Islamization of knowledge is defined by Sulaiman, 2000 as *an attempt through which aspects of the body and purpose of knowledge and of the process and methodologies of discovering, validating, imparting and applying it, which oppose Islam, are identified and made subservient to the Islamic worldview.* As quoted by R.I. Adebayo,2008, Islamization of Knowledge, Global developments, Individuals efforts and Institutional contributions, (IIIT, Nigeria Office, Kano),13.
38. Prof. H.O. Danmole is a professor of history. (He holds B.A. Arabic & Islamic Studies, Ibadan, 1974), His PhD is on history of Ilorin Emirate.
39. See Ogunbiyi, I.A., 1987. *Of non-Muslim cultivators and propagators of the Arabic language,* inaugural lecture, Foreign languages department, Lagos State University, 23. See also Malik, S.H.A., 1999. *Arabic, the Muslim prayers and beyond,* inaugural lecture, Department of Arabic & Islamic Studies, University of Ibadan, quoting Hunwick, J.O. 1965. (Report

on a seminar on the teaching of Arabic in Nigeria, Ibadan and Kano), 3.
40. Lawal Manzoor A. 2011. The state of Islamic Education in South-Western Nigeria in *al-ijtihad, the Journal of the Islamization of Knowledge and contemporary issues*, IIIT, Nigeria office, Vol.9. No 1, January 2011/Muharram, 1432. P.106. The statistics covered University of Ibadan, Al-Hikmah University, Ilorin, Unilorin, Olabisi Onabanjo University, Osun State College of Education in Ilesa, Kwara State College of Education, Ilorin, Tai Solarin College of Education, Omu-Ijebu, Ogun State, Tai Solarin University of Education, Ijebu-Ode, Ogun State, MOCPED, Naforija, Epe, Lagos State and Emmanuel Alayande College of Education, Oyo.
41. Nigerian languages downloaded on Monday 19th Nov. 2012 from http://www.onlinenigeria.com/languages/languages.asp
42. Some close friends of the writer who are currently serving in the state security service pleaded anonymity in view of the sensitivity and confidentiality condition attached to the job.
43. The writer was privileged to interact closely with Captain Wasiu Yekeen as one of his students during his National Youth Service year at Assanusiyah Comprehensive High School Odeomu, Osun State where Captain Wasiu had his secondary education. Since then, the Captain distinguished himself as an intelligent and obedient student with bright future. His giant achievements at this tender age are not any way surprising to the writer in view of his antecedents.

CHAPTER ELEVEN

Inhibiting Factors Against Education of Muslim Children in Nigeria

Bidmos M. A.
Department of Arts and Social Sciences Education
University of Lagos, Akoka, Yaba, Nigeria.
bmurtala@yahoo.ca
+2348023255158

Introduction

The establishment of private Muslim schools and universities in Nigeria in recent times is a pointer to the impulse felt by Muslims concerning the educational plight of the Muslim child. There is a noticeable deep concern among Muslims regarding the plight of the Muslim child who, by omission or commission, suffers deprivation in terms of access to education. As a complement to government public schools, Muslims have put in their widow's mite as manifested in the existing Muslim primary, secondary and tertiary institutions either through individual or corporate efforts. The crux of the matter is that despite the efforts of government and Muslims, a teeming population of Muslim children is out of school. For example, according to the former Minister of Education, Dr. O. Egwu who said that out of 34.92 million children expected in school, only 24.42 million are[1]: hence a shortfall of 10.5. The intriguing question is, how many of these 10.5 million children are Muslims? The figure will certainly be staggering given the population of Muslim children working as bus conductors, vulcanizers, mechanic apprentices, house helps, hawkers, touts, etc. Against this background, this study aims at achieving two objectives, namely to identify factors that make education inaccessible to the Muslim children; and to plan strategies that can effectively take care of the educational needs of the Muslim children. Meanwhile, as a prelude to the above, it is expedient to briefly examine the attitude of Islam to education.

Education in Islam

It is quite instructive to note that the first revelation given to Muhammad, the prophet of Islam, revolves around education, creation and instructional materials (such as pen);[2] and that learned people are accorded the position of honour and respect[3]. Also, the Qur'ān emphasises the importance of science-based subjects such as Biology, Anatomy, Medicine, Geography, Agriculture, Technology, Geology, Pharmacy, etc[4]. In the same vein, the Hadith makes education compulsory for every Muslim.

It is also noteworthy that Islamic education flourished in the medieval period: a period referred to in Europe as Dark Age which was a period of illumination, learning and civilisation in the Muslim domains by virtue of the establishment of universities and teaching hospitals where advanced researches in all branches of knowledge were conducted as attested to by both Fafunwa[5] and Hitti[6].

Thus, it is clear from the above, that Islam and learning are intricately interwoven. To that extent, it is incontrovertible to affirm that the understanding of Islam and application of its tenets are possible only on the strength of education. It is a known fact that Islam is made of five pillars which are divinely designed and prescribed for man to enable him to live in comfort, peace and bliss. But it is the learned, the educated who can appreciate the purpose of the pillars of Islam. So, education to Islam is the foundation of Islam. To that extent, the Muslim community's unseriousness with education, would have grave consequences. If, so far, Muslims have not properly understood, accurately practised and effectively propagated Islam, it is because they have been pursuing all of these without recourse to education. Given the position of education in Islam therefore, why does the Muslim child suffer deprivation?

The Inhibiting Factors

Apparently, it seems Muslims are now poised to address the case of deprivation suffered by the Muslim child. But at the onset, it is necessary to identify the factors that have so far conspired to deprive the Muslim child access to education. The same factors, if not checked, are capable of thwarting whatever strategies that may be put in place to address the issue. The factors include:

(a) Government's Attitude

What is the attitude of government to education? Is education a priority programme in the government agenda? There are indices that give us an idea about the government's attitude to education. First, is the seemingly endless reforms in education which started in 1969 with the National Curriculum Conference, the resolutions of which culminated in the National Policy on Education 1977. This was revised in 1981, 1998 and 2004. The reform continued with the 10-Year Strategic Plan in 2007, Roadmap for the Nigerian Education Sector, 2009 and the Presidential Task Force Team on

Education, 2011. If the reform of 1969 continued till 2011, when do we expect the final product? And when do we start its implementation?

Secondly, asides the aggressive initiative of the defunct Western Regional civilian government, the present day politicians pay lip service to education. They are rather more concerned with 'building' democracy now and the nation later. The amount of money being spent on democracy bears a testimony to the truism that it is 'democracy now and nation building later'. Only recently, a political party stated its intention to build a national secretariat in Abuja at the cost of N200bn. How much will be needed to maintain a N200 billion structure? How much will be needed to pay the salaries and allowances of the staff in the structure? What is the worth of the services to be carried out in the structure, at least in relation to nation building and the quality of life of the citizenry?

Third, whatever little money government puts in education, the biggest chunk goes on the managerial aspect of education while only the crumbles reach the classroom and the teacher. For instance, it is a common feature to establish agencies that often duplicate each other such as the Department of Higher Education in the Federal Ministry of Education, National Universities Commission, Nigerian Educational Research and Development Council (NERDC), the Curriculum Unit in the Ministry, Primary Education Board (SPEB), Education Districts, School Management Board (SMB), School Management Committee (SMC), etc. The duplication of functions in these agencies can be illustrated with the functions of NUC and those of Higher Education Department in the ministry. Aside the overlapping of functions, the fact remains that the funds allocated to these agencies are at the expense of provision of standard instructional materials and teachers' welfare. Another related issue is the redeployment of many well-trained and highly experienced teachers from the classrooms to the multiple administrative establishments whose main duties seem to be to attend meetings and write memos, rather than provide quality service. Consider this lamentation by an ex-Kwara State Commissioner for education Mr. Bolaji Abdullahi:

> Two of my schools received a notification from NECO that they had no results for the 2009 examination, after the students had seen online versions of the same result that NECO claimed the school does not have. Still about NECO, a school received in a particular year three version of NECO results [7].

These revelations were made in reaction to the news that only six percent of 234,682 candidates passed exams in a recently released results.

(b) Muslims' Attitude to Marriage

The institution of marriage is given its due attention in the Qur'ān. Characteristically, the Qur'ān will pride itself with leaving no stone unturned in all human affairs (Q 6:38). Chapter four (*Suratun-Nisā'*) of the Qur'ān provides an elaborate narration on marriage institution. The purpose of marriage is explicitly stated in the Qur'ān 30: 21 while the details are stated in chapter four. Polygamy is the aspect of marriage that is relevant to our immediate discourse. Muslims are given the privilege of marrying up to four wives (Q.4:3). To appreciate the rationale behind the Islamic provision on polygamy, the following analysis suffices:

(i) Islam pegged polygamy at four wives by way of sanitising the unwieldy marital culture preceding Islam. The cases of prophets David and Solomon[8] remain fresh in human experience. In the African setting, even to date, there is no limit to how many wives an African man can marry. In 1978, Fela Anikulapo Kuti married 27 wives in one day in Lagos, Nigeria.

(ii) The Qur'ānic legal provision on polygamy came immediately after the battle of Uhud which resulted in so many orphans and widows whose welfare was made mandatory on Muslims through institution of polygamy[9], among other measures.

(iii) To enjoy this provision, Islam attaches some responsibilities which must be strictly observed by any Muslim desirous of polygamous life. These include treating the wives with equity, sticking to one wife in case of inability to maintain equity, and taking a house maid whose lifestyle is moderate rather than a glamorous lady with a very high taste. It should be noted that in this part of the Muslim world, those who practise polygamy do so without any consideration for the divine responsibilities attached to it. This has resulted in the production of children they cannot educate.

It may be argued that in present-day Nigeria, we have a situation akin to that of the post-Uhud situation; why can't we apply polygamy to cater for the single ladies among us? As logical as that argument may sound, there is no sense in using a measure to solve a problem which in the final analysis creates another problem of a more serious consequence. A conservative estimate of 90% of the children who are out of school comes from polygamous homes. The rest are as a result of poverty, broken homes and loss of parents. This view is underscored by remarks made by the Governor of Kano State, Rabiu Kwankwaso, at the Children's Day celebration on May 27, 2013, that 'parents in the North give birth to 20-30 children, choose only two of them and send the rest away'[10] .Therefore, providing schools for such children from polygamous homes may be misconstrued by the polygamists, as a license to continue to have more children because, according to their naïve thinking, God has raised some philanthropists who are kind enough to take care of their children.

(c) Muslims' Attitude to *Hajj*[11]

The details of *Hajj* are elaborately explained in the Qur'ān and *Sunnah*[12]. Prophet Muhammad as a role model in all spheres of life, performed *Hajj* only once in his 23 years of prophethood. It is quite instructive to note that he passed on about 81 days after his pilgrimage which is tagged in Islamic history as the farewell pilgrimage[13]. This suggests that *Hajj* is the last of the obligatory acts of worship a Muslim performs.

In Nigeria, what is known as Nigerian character which is a special way of doing things in a negative way has permeated the performance of *Hajj*. It is unimaginable that some people could dare to modify an act of worship prescribed by Allah which is the reason why the Qur'ān asks rhetorically, whether man want to teach Allah the religion? (Q.49:19). The early generations of Nigerian Muslims used to perform *Hajj* at an advanced age and by road for lack of modern day transport facilities. As from 1960s, the enthusiasm of Nigerian Muslims was heightened due to, among other factors, the availability of modern transport facilities. Subsequently, organised trips to Makkah twice a year, one for *Umrah* and another for *Hajj* commenced. This amounts to undertaking the trip twice a year as a result of which a Nigerian Muslim could boast of having been to the holy lands 30 times in 15 years.

It is estimated that about 80,000 Nigerians have been performing *Hajj* every year in the last 10 years. If an average of one million naira is needed to perform Umrah in Ramadan (it is now a vogue to witness the last 10 days of Ramadan in Makkah) and the same amount is needed to perform *Hajj* three months later by the same estimated population, it means that 80,000 Nigerians would spend every year N160bn. If the cost of sponsoring the Federal and State government contingents, is added to the cost of maintaining the federal/state governments pilgrims Boards, we shall need another N160bn. This means that what we need to prosecute *Hajj* and *Umrah* every year is N320bn.

Another worrisome (if not sinful) aspect of *Hajj* operations in Nigeria is to allow some unqualified persons to embark on *Hajj* trips. These include the aged who are too weak to face the rigour of *Hajj* rites. It means that those who indulge in this practice have refused to take the advantage of a prophetic tradition which allows a child to perform *Hajj* on behalf of his aged parents. Others are pregnant women, minors who should be in school, non-Muslims who join under various guises, thugs that are sponsored as a form of political gratification, the professional Alhajis/Alhajas who perform *Hajj* every year either for fun or for business[14], and the Almajiris who are recruited by business tycoons with a view to using the

Almajiris' Basic Traveling Allowances (BTA) to pursue their (the sponsors') businesses. When the eight categories listed above are deducted from the estimated 80,000 pilgrims, we would be left with about 20,000 legitimate pilgrims from Nigeria.

Another form of wastage is perpetrated by the Pilgrim Welfare Boards/Commissions that recruit non-experienced welfare officers whose duty it is to attend to the religious and social needs of the pilgrims. But how can such welfare officers who lack basic knowledge and practical experience of *Hajj* and lack proficiency in Arabic guide the pilgrims? To navigate conveniently in Saudi Arabia during the *Hajj* period and attend to the needs of the pilgrims, a welfare officer must be conversant with the *Hajj* rites in theory and practice. He must be proficient in spoken Arabic. The Nigerian students in Saudi Arabian universities meet those criteria. The recruitment and remuneration of such students as welfare officers would be easier for about $1/5$ of the cost of airlifting and paying the allowances of the non-experienced welfare officers from Nigeria.

The practice of sending contingents under *Amirul Hajj* (Head of the contingent) by both Federal and State governments to *Hajj* every year, also constitutes wastage. The relevance of these contingents to the pilgrims is questionable, more so as there are no such contingents from other Muslim countries.

Furthermore, some well-to-do Muslims are in the habit of sponsoring people on pilgrimage. On point of the Islamic jurisprudence, the practice is questionable because the ability to afford the expenses of *Hajj* is one of the conditions to be fulfilled by an intending pilgrim. This suggests that *Hajj* is not compulsory for those who lack the means. But then, we must find out whether a Muslim who solicits for *Hajj* sponsorship has children of school age? Are the children in or out of school? If children from such homes are out of school, sponsorship of this type is absolutely unnecessary. Both the sponsor and the beneficiaries should respect the Qur'ānic injunctions on Education and *Hajj* by making the child's education a top priority. The experience and data utilised in this segment are gathered from personal involvement of the writer in *Hajj* operations in 1973, 1990 and 2004[15].

It is expected that Nigerians would mirror the positive impacts of these frequent performance of Hajj. The expected impacts should reflect in their religious and social lives.

The impressive mosque maitenance culture and the deployment of professionally trained imams should be replicated back home in Nigeria where the maintenance of the mosque needs much to be desired and Imams are not professionally trained many of whom are self appointed.

Strategic Plan of Action

An enduring solution to the problem facing the education of Muslim children requires a pragmatic approach, part of which is the identification of the three factors listed above. To the extent that two of the factors are related to Muslims' attitude and practices, it is appropriate to start sourcing the solution from within.

(a)   Marriage

The interpretation of verse three of *Sūratun-Nisā'* (Q.4:3) is central to the habit of the reckless bearing of children who lack adequate parental care and by implication, are out of school creating the menace of millions of Muslim children roaming the streets in various forms and shapes. Those who practise polygamy partially interpret the verse. They dishonestly stopped at *(wa rubaa')* four wives. The pragmatic approach, therefore, is to seek the assistance of the Chief Imams and the *mufassirūn* (exegetes) of the central mosques through Muslim Ummah of South-West of Nigeria (MUSWEN) that the verse in question should be, henceforth, completely and sincerely interpreted. It is the chief Imams and the *Mufassirūn* alone, if they are convinced with the proposal, who can prevail on the imam Ratibis to start giving the verse in question its correct and sincere interpretation.

The segment of the verse that has been so concealed is as follows:

1. But if you fear that you shall not be able to deal justly (with them), then stick to only one.
2. Or opt for that which your right hands possess (that again is in case your financial standing cannot cope with a free, sophisticated woman).
3. 1-2 above constitute a suitable path of honour to prevent you from doing injustice.
4. A Muslim in all this should admit the fact that monogamy is a rule while polygamy is an exception, observed only as a corrective measure.

This complete and correct interpretation of the verse should become the theme of sermons on Fridays in central mosques. It should also become a topic of discussion on radio and television and at various Islamic occasions. The point of emphasis in all this is the implication of partial interpretation of the verse which is the reckless bearing of children that cannot be provided for. They are so denied because there is no consideration for their up-bringing at the stage of planning for multiple wives. Added to this is the critical analysis of the *Ahādith* of the Prophet Muhammad which revolves around the obligation of children's education. Relevant are such *Ahādith* as 'seek knowledge even up to China', and 'to seek knowledge is obligatory on every Muslim male or female'.

(b) Government's Role

As feasible as the above proposal may sound, its successful implementation is predicated on the political will of the government. For example, government should:

1. mandate the Nigerian Inter-Religious Council (NIREC) to sanitise pilgrimage operations in Nigeria in line with the above proposal;
2. task NIREC to visit Senegal, Ghana, Malaysia and one Arab country to ascertain the extent of government's involvement in *Hajj* operations;
3. empower NIREC to enforce regulations limiting the number of the intending pilgrims by preventing unqualified persons that hitherto constitute about 3/4 of the pilgrims population from Nigeria[16];
4. stop sending official contingents under an Amir to Saudi during Hajj;
5. discontinue with the practice of providing grants to pilgrim Boards or Commissions;
6. hand over *Hajj* operations to private organisations in line with the practice in other Muslim communities around the world;

7. provide the private bodies with guidelines under the supervision of NIREC and the relevant ministries such as the ministries of External Affairs, and Internal Affairs;
8. Regarding polygamy and its menace, government can rely on the principal Muslim organisations in Nigeria such as Supreme Council for Islamic Affairs, Jama'atu Nasrul Islam, MUSWEN, Ansarul Islam, NASFAT, NAJOMO and Ansar-Ud-Deen to enforce the strategies proposed earlier;
9. task the organisations to persuade their members to appreciate the need to have the number of children they can conveniently cater for; and
10. mandate the organizations to explain to their members that polygamy as it is practised now is tantamount to violation of the tenets of Islam.

Conclusion

According to this study, three factors affect the education of the Muslim child. The factors are the government's attitude to education, Muslims' attitude to the marriage institution and *Hajj* institution. Arising from these factors are the reckless production of children that some parents cannot cater for and shortage of funds to finance education. To rescue the Muslim child from the current state of deprivation, the study recommends a paradigm shift as postulated in the measures highlighted above. It is emphasised that the proposed measures are not novel, after all, but a return to the basis in terms of strict compliance with the divine injunctions on Education, Marriage Institution and *Hajj* operation. This simply means sanitisation of *Hajj* operations and normalisation of marriage institution through:

a. correct interpretation of relevant Islamic literature on both *Hajj* and marriage;
b. persuasion of Muslims to have children only in accordance with their resources;
c. limitation of government's intervention in *Hajj* operations to setting rules/regulations to private bodies that would be charged with managing pilgrimage trips;
d. strict application of Shari'ah guidelines on the qualification of intending pilgrims and the frequency of performing *Hajj* by any individual;
e. discontinuation of sponsorship of *Hajj* contingents under an Amir by government;
f. substantial review of the mushroom administrative units in the education sector; and
g. discontinuation of incessant education policies that are rarely implemented.

The study opines that a – g above will result in a manageable population of children as well as conservation of funds from regularised *Hajj* operations; these funds can be channeled to financing education. It concludes that to maintain the status quo will be tantamount to a partial belief in the message of the Qur'ān (Q2 : 85) to which a sincere Muslim will not venture.

Notes and References

1. Sam, O.Egwu, *Roadmap for Nigerian Education Sector*, (Federal Ministry of Education, 2009), 20
2. Qur'ān 96:1-5

3. Qur'ān 35:28
4. Qur'ān 22:5, 23:13-14,35:28,58:11,7:185,50:20
5. A.B. Fafunwa, *History of Education in Nigeria*, (London. George Allen and Unwin, 1974), 42 & 53
6. P.K. Hitti, *History of the Arabs*, (London: Macmillan, 2002),557ᶠ
7. *The Sunday Punch* (April 4, 2010). Back page
8. 2 Samuel 3:2-5; 1 Chronicles 14:3; 1 Kings 11:3
9. Muhammad Haykal. *The Life of Muhammad*, (London, Shoruk International. 1983), 271.
10. *Sunday Punch* Editorial (Neglect of Nigerian children) June 2, 2013, 16
11. *Hajj* is the fifth pillar of Islam, that is, a mandatory act of worship, to be performed once in a life time by those Muslims who have the means. Its features include *Ihrām, tawāf* round the Kaᶜabah, *Sa'y* between Safa and Marwa, prayer at the station of Prophet Ibrahim, an assembly on mount 'Arafat on the 9th day of *Dhul Hajj*, to remember Allah in the days described as *ayyamut tashriq*, etc.
12. Qur'ān 3:96-7,2:158,22:27-9
13. Muhammad Haykal, *The Life of Muhammad*, 483
14. It should be remarked that it is permissible to go to Saudi Arabia on business outside the pilgrimage period which should not be pursued under the guise of Hajj.
15. This writer was appointed by the Nigeria Pilgrim Board to serve as a preacher during the 1990 *Hajj* operations.
16. This is in line with an appeal which was sent out by the Saudi authorities during the Umrah period of 2013 Ramadan to the Muslim communities all over the world that Muslims should henceforth reduce the number of the intending pilgrims with a view to minimising the congestion experienced around Kaᶜabah and other holy places.

CHAPTER TWELVE

Dividends of International Islamic Organisations in Nigeria

Adebayo, R. Ibrahim
Department of Religions,
University of Ilorin, Ilorin, Nigeria.
rafiu@unilorin.edu.com; adrafhope@yahoo.com
+2347035467292

Introduction

The daily reports of ethno-religious crises in Nigeria have created serious fear in the minds of the world that religion is only out to be used in the hand of a few individuals to achieve their selfish end. The hope that religion would serve as a saving ground for the hues and cries of the populace has now been dashed, as religion itself is being used as an instrument of hatred, polarisation, division and controversy. With particular reference to Nigeria, the wound of the 1981 Maitasine riot of Kano and its suburbs has not yet healed when the Boko Haram uprisings engulfed the nation creating fear and unrest with the loss of many lives and the destruction of property. This development has made many to lose faith in religion as an instrument of progress, development and as an institution from which many people seek succour.

Consequently, many conferences are being organised to address the challenges of religion in contemporary Nigeria. What attracts much attention in such conferences is the challenge of terrorism. It is our contention that there is the need to appraise the services rendered Nigeria by some Islamic organisations. Among other purposes, this study aims at correcting the impression of those who think that the only way to preach Islam is through violence in the guise of *jihād* or that the nation can develop only through terrorist activities. It will also shed light on how *da'wah* ought to be by citing practical examples and not necessarily through mere preaching. The ultimate aim of this study is to stress that rather than throwing the baby with the bath water, religion has been, and is still being used as a veritable weapon to combat illiteracy, poverty and all manner of social ills in the society.

One is aware of the fact that there are some home-based Islamic organisations that are faring well internationally. These include the Ansarud-Deen Society, the Muslim Students Society of Nigeria (MSSN), the Federation of Muslim Women Associations in Nigeria (FOMWAN) and the Nasrullahil Fathi Society (NASFAT). These societies and many others have made significant contributions to the education, economic and social well being of the people. Other Muslim organisations delving into alleviating poverty within the *ummah* by using the *zakat* institution include the Zakah and Sadaqah Foundation, Forum for Islamic Education and Welfare and the Muslim Welfare Fund. That notwithstanding, our focus in this study is to consider such international societies not indigenous to Nigeria, that have impacted positively in Nigeria. This step is taken to erase the notion that such organisations are harbouring and promoting acts of terrorism in their host countries.

The Organisation of Islamic Conference (OIC)

The first conference of this organisation could be said to have taken place in Rabat, Morocco between 22nd and 25th September, 1969, while subsequent meetings held between 23rd and 25th March, 1970 at Jeddah and December 1970 at Karachi actually gave birth to the OIC. The Charter of the

Organisation was however approved at a meeting held in Jeddah between 29th February and 4th March 1972. The Charter of the Organisation spells out her objectives among which are:

1. To enhance and consolidate the bonds of fraternity and solidarity among the Member States;
2. To safeguard and protect the common interests and support the legitimate causes of the Member States and coordinate and unify the efforts of the Member States in view of the challenges faced by the Islamic world in particular and the international community in general;
3. To respect the right of self-determination and non-interference in the domestic affairs and to respect sovereignty, independence and territorial integrity of each Member State;
4. To support the restoration of complete sovereignty and territorial integrity of any Member State under occupation, as a result of aggression, on the basis of international law and cooperation with the relevant international and regional organisations;
5. To ensure active participation of the Member States in the global political, economic and social decision-making processes to secure their common interests;
6. To promote inter-state relations based on justice, mutual respect and good neighbourliness to ensure global peace, security and harmony;
7. To reaffirm its support for the rights of peoples as stipulated in the UN Charter and international law;
8. To support and empower the Palestinian people to exercise their right to selfdetermination and establish their sovereign State with Al-Quds Al-Sharif as its

capital, while safeguarding its historic and Islamic character as well as the Holy places therein;
9. To strengthen intra-Islamic economic and trade cooperation; in order to achieve economic integration leading to the establishment of an Islamic Common Market;
10. To exert efforts to achieve sustainable and comprehensive human development and economic well-being in Member States;
11. To disseminate, promote and preserve the Islamic teachings and values based on moderation and tolerance, promote Islamic culture and safeguard Islamic heritage;
12. To protect and defend the true image of Islam, to combat defamation of Islam and encourage dialogue among civilisations and religions;
13. To enhance and develop science and technology and encourage research and cooperation among Member States in these fields;
14. To promote and to protect human rights and fundamental freedoms including the rights of women, children, youth, elderly and people with special needs as well as the preservation of Islamic family values.[1]

Ever before the creation of the OIC, there had been interaction between Nigeria and Arab nations. The United Arab Republic (UAR) for instance sent a delegation to Nigeria in November 1960 and it donated £2,000 to the reconstruction of the Sultan Bello Mosque. It also donated £10,000 towards the Sokoto Mosque appeal fund in April 1961.[2] In addition, the UAR awarded scholarship to twelve Nigerians at Al-Azhar University, while the Sardauna was given the honour of "Grand Cordon of the Order of the Nile" in July 1961, and an honorary doctorate by Al-Azhar University in July 1962.[3] This cordial interaction culminated in the visitation of the then Chief Imam of Madinah, Sheikh Abdul Aziz to Nigeria in 1964 to open the £100,000 Sultan Bello Mosque in Sokoto while Prince Faisal equally donated a sum of £60,000 to the Sardauna to aid his Islamic programmes and £40,000 for the construction of the Lagos Central Mosque.[4] It can therefore be said that there had been interaction of the then Premier of the Northern Region of Nigeria, Sir Ahmadu Bello with the League of Arab Nations. The romance of the Premier with the Arab nations which could have led to the creation of an international Islamic organisation was however truncated by the 1966 military coup in Nigeria wherein the Premier was assasinated. However, Nigeria could be said to have been present at the summit conference of Islamic leaders in Morocco in 1969 where the idea of the OIC was mooted. This is because a Nigerian Muslim delegation led by Sheikh Abubakar Mahmud Gumi was in attendance at the conference. This is in spite of the fact that the then Head of State, General Yakubu Gowon informed the Summit conference not to give the Nigerian delegates any official recognition, as those who attended the conference did so on their personal and private capacity, because Nigeria did not intend to join any religious organisation.[5]

With the formal inauguration of the OIC in 1972, the government of Nigeria allowed Nigeria to be an observer in the organisation. Efforts to make the nation a full-fledged member of the OIC were not successful due to the multi-religious nature of the nation. In fact, the General Muhammadu Buhari's administration ordered the Ministry of External Affairs then under Ibrahim Gambari to advise it on the subject. The response was not in favour of Nigeria's full membership of the Organisation. Soon after the administration of Buhari, Nigeria however, became the 46th member of the OIC through a delegation to Fez led by Rilwan Lukman on the 18th January, 1986.[6]

The longevity of Nigeria in an observer status, together with her failure to fulfil her financial obligation to the Organisation, has denied her many opportunities accrueable to members of the organisation. For instance, General Buhari's administration was said to have requested for a loan of $2 billion from the OIC in 1984. The request was however not granted on the excuse that Nigeria was an ordinary observer and not yet a full member of the Organisation. Furthermore, the failure of the country to offset her arrears of membership dues of about 15 years during which she was an observer, denied her the opportunity of accessing the OIC loan facilities of the IDB. In addition, at a meeting between Nigeria and the OIC in Lagos in 1989, the Imo State Government was billed to benefit from the Organisation's grant facility of $70 million to tackle erosion and ecological disaster in the State. This was however frustrated by non-release of the counterpart funding by Imo State government.[7]

Islamic Development Bank

The Islamic Development Bank (IDB) was established with the following objectives:

a. to meet the need to foster the well-being of the people of Muslim countries and to achieve a harmonious and balanced development in those countries on the basis of Islamic principles and ideals;

b. to meet the need for mutual financial and economic co-operation among the Muslim states in economic, social and other fields;
c. to meet the need to mobilize financial and other resources both from within and outside the member countries, and to promote domestic savings and investments and a greater flow of development funds into member countries.[8]

For it to achieve the above set objectives, the IDB established the Islamic Research and Training Institute (IRTI), which according to Nejatullah Siddiqi, "conducts in-house research, sponsors external research, publishes a research journal, conducts training courses, organises seminars and conferences, and maintains a database on the economies of Islamic countries."[9] In addition to this, the IDB interacts with all regional and international financial institutions, like the International Monetary Fund, the World Bank and the Asian Development Bank.[10]

In Nigeria, the report of Jaiz International Plc, the first full-fledged interest-free bank in the country, reveals that the Islamic Development Bank was ready to assist in providing management and technical support to Jaiz, while also recommending that the Islamic Bank of Bangladesh Limited (IBBL) should assist in providing managerial and technical support to the proposed bank.[11] In addition to this, the Islamic Research and Training Insitute (IRTI), an organ of the IDB, has collaborated with some institutions in Nigeria to organise conferences and workshops. For instance, the First University of Ilorin International Conference on Islamic Banking and Finance which was held between 6th and 8th October, 2009, was organised in collaboration with the Institute. The Institute also involves Nigeria in its training programmes. A clue to this is its invitation of Nigeria to participate in the 2014, 2015 and 2016 Training Work Programmes and suggest lists of courses for the programme or propose new alternative training courses relevant to the level of economic and social development of the country.It even requested the nation to provide IRTI with the names and contact details of the national institutions in the country that would cooperate with it in organising the training courses.

Furthermore, the Islamic Education Trust, (IET) in Minna, Niger State, has an office in its Administrative Block for the Islamic Development Bank scholarship. The scholarships are meant for Muslim students in universities undertaking first degrees in Science, Engineering, Medicine, Pharmacy and Architecture. More than four hundred and fifty candidates have benefitted and are still benefiting, from this laudable programme in various universities in Nigeria. In addition to this, some Nigerian postgraduate students have been assisted materially by the IDB to enhance their researches in Islamic economic-related subjects.[12]

In her Special Programme for the Development of Africa (SPDA), President of the Islamic Development Bank, Dr. Ahmad Mohammed Ali at a programme in Abuja revealed that the IDB has earmarked N310 billion to support the implementation of Nigeria's transformation agenda for a two-year period, between 2012 and 2014. This was confirmed by the nation's Vice President Namadi Sambo, at a special meeting of African Governors' Forum on the Special Programme for the Development of Africa held at Khartoum, Sudan.[13] In addition to the above, the IDB President offered to assist the Federal Government of Nigeria in the rehabilitation of the Lagos-Ibadan Express road.The bank also approved

$98m for Almajiri education in the northern part of the country.[14]

Al-Haramain Islamic Foundation (HIF)

The move by some Muslim philanthropists to assist the less privileged ones throughout the world culminated in the establishment of the Haramain Islamic Foundation in 1412H (1992). These philanthropists, most of whom were natives of Saudi Arabia, therefore decided to carry out their charitable services by feeding the poor and taking care of the orphans, widows, distressed and the sick. Prominent among them were Abdul-Rahman as-Sadiq, Muhammad ibn Malik, Muhammad ibn Ammar and Shaikh Bilal Ussein al-Badawiyy. The body has its headquarters in Riyadh, Saudi Arabia and has comprehensive aims which cut across all facets of life. They include:

a. Provision of shelter, food and medicine to refugees and the distressed as well as assisting in repatriating them to their various countries at the end of the crisis.
b. Construction of schools and other educational institutions; sponsoring teachers and students; provision of syllabus and organisation of in-service courses; and printing and distribution of beneficial books;
c. Lodging of stray children and taking care of orphans and the poor, widows and handicapped; and
d. Building of hospitals and clinics and the provision of instruments and essential apparatus and the distribution of medicine; and combating of epidemics and fatal diseases and organisation of medical campaigns.[15]

An assessment of the activities of this body in areas outside Nigeria, reveals that it has met some of its aims, especially in the sphere of education. The organisation has published quite a good number of books which are distributed freely to institutions and places of worship. Confirming this, Soliman al-Buthi, one of the Directors of the Oregon Islamic charity, Al-Haramain Islamic Foundation, Inc. says:

> We distributed our materials to anyone who requested them, and a vast spectrum of organisations, from U.S. federal and state governments, to military and law enforcement bodies, as well as schools, libraries, temples, churches, missionaries, and synagogues sent us written thank-you letters for the materials and presentations provided. Over time the requests for our resources became enormous and we had to struggle to meet the enormous demand.[16]

The Nigerian branch of the HIF was officially commissioned on 25th December, 1997, with its office in Ibadan, the capital city of Oyo State. The course of establishing the branch in Oyo State was championed by two alumni of Islamic University in Madina, Alhaji Taofik Abdul-Ganiyy, a native of Iwo in Osun State, and Alhaji Abdur-Rauf, a native of Ibadan. The Nigeria office became functional in July, 1998 when Shaykh Bilal Ussein al-Badawiyy was deployed to Nigeria as the Director of the Body. The body initially focused its attention on *daʿwah*. One of the dividends of this body in Nigeria is that it provided job opportunities for many people. For instance, the office employed more than sixty Nigerians into its different departments. Twenty people were deployed to the Daʿwah department, ten are in charge of the educational programme in the education department; ten in charge of project execution and the remaining ten in accounting department.[17]

The Daʿwah activities of the body have actually impacted the lives of Muslims religiously, spiritually, socially and economically. The body sponsored quite a good number of Islamic programmes on radio and television. The huge amount paid for dissemination of Islamic messages through the media no doubt brought financial benefits to the media houses concerned, particularly the Broadcasting Corporation of Oyo State (BCOS) and the Osun State Broadcasting Corporation, (OSBC). In addition, no one can doubt the fact that the huge amount being spent on the execution of different projects of the body has direct economic benefits for Nigerians, such as sellers of building materials. Also, the patronage of dealers of food items, sheep and cows during the month of Ramadan when the body organises *iftar* at different mosques has had positive economic impact on the people of the affected areas.

In the field of poverty alleviation, the Haramain Islamic Foundation has made positive impacts on the lives of the people. The body encouraged and provided opportunities for Muslim women to learn different professional and vocational jobs through a vocational centre established in Bashorun area of Ibadan. At the centre, many women, particularly orphans and widows, learnt tailoring, weaving, soap-making and other vocations. The body also bought products like soaps and clothes and other materials produced from the training centre for distribution to students, poor and needy Muslims, and others.

Apart from establishing mosques in towns and villages in Yorubaland, particularly Ibadan, Oyo, Iwo, Ogbomoso and others, the HIF went to the extent of establishing clinics in towns like Ibadan and Ogbomoso. In addition to this, the body was devoted to payment of hospital bills for patients who could not afford payment, while visiting hospitals, orphanage centres and rehabilitation centres for the purpose of preaching, praying and donating to the patients there.[18]

In the field of education, the HIF made meaningful impact as the body established many schools in some towns in Yorubaland. For instance, it established the Ibn Malik College at Jegede in Ibadan, while it had some Qur'an memorisation centres spread across Yorubaland. Moreover, it enriched the libraries of some primary and secondary schools such as the Shariah College of Alhaji Abdur-Rasheed Hadiyatullah of Iwo by donating books and other educational materials.[19]

However, this prosperous organisation gradually witnessed its waterloo in the wave of the September 11 attack on the U.S.A which consequently made every Muslim organisation a potential sponsor of terrorist activities, while some even appeared in the America's list of terrorist suspects.

The International Islamic Relief Organisation (IIRO)

The IIRO is an affiliate of the Muslim World League. According to Wikipedia, the body is a member of the International Islamic Council for Daʿwa and Relief (IICDR), and has observer status at OIC, consultative status at the United Nations Economic and Social Council (ECOSOC) and links to Islamic Educational, Scientific and Cultural Organisation (ISESCO) among many others.[20] Her programmes are well-spread, covering various departments such as social, welfare, engineering, society development and seasonal projects, emergency relief, health care, educational care and Qur'anic memorisation. It also collaborates with the World Health Organisation (WHO), United Nations International Children's Emergency Fund (UNICEF), United Nations High Commission for Refugees (UNHCR) and the World Food Program. The body is also said to have provided a number of relief packages for the 2004 tsunami and earthquake victims in Indonesia, Sri Lanka, Maldives and

Thailand. In the same vein, it assisted the victims of the 2005 earthquake in some parts of Pakistan.[21] According to Wikipedia, the Organisation spent approximately US$36 million on about 2258 projects in 81 countries in 2003/2004. Out of this amount, about US$13 million was spent on social welfare, US$2 million on educational care, US$2 million on health care and US$4 million on emergency relief.[22]

The regional office of the IIRO in Nigeria is located in Kaduna, the capital city of Kaduna State. The activities of the organisation cut across most of the states in Nigeria. Apart from the fact that it has programmes for orphans in form of providing clothing for them, it also pays stipends as medical and school fees for orphans who are registered with them. This project which was so popular in cities like Ibadan, Kaduna, Ilorin and Osogbo in the 1980s is gradually becoming unpopular probably because of lack of sponsorship from the IIRO headquarters.[23]

Apart from this, the body established a clinic in Jalingo, Taraba State. It has also organised series of public enlightenment programmes on HIV prevention amongst youth in the State.[24] It is important to note that many Muslims have been gainfully employed by the IIRO in Nigeria. This is true of many Nigerian graduates from Saudi Arabian Universities who are employed to oversee the various programmes of the organisation. While some are employed for *da'wah* purpose, others are employed as teachers in Arabic and Islamic schools in Nigeria. The organisation also distributed motorcycles to those it employed as *Du'āt* for them to move from village to village in their missionary activities. The organisation also published Islamic books which are distributed free to schools and individuals. The publication of these books was beneficial to the nation, as it improved the economic status of publishers and increased the knowledge of their readers.

One of the annual programmes of the IIRO in Nigeria under the headship of Alhaji Ismail Hausawi is the breaking of fast *(Iftār)* programme for Muslims during Ramadan. The programme is helpful to Muslims who could not afford the means to break their fasts during the month. The programme is handled in Ibadan by Alhaji Ahmad Tiamy. In the same vein, the body organises special *Ileya('Idul-Adhā)* programmes at Ibadan, Kaduna and Ilorin, where cows are slaughtered and distributed to Muslims who could not afford the sacrificial offering.[25]

Furthermore, the organisation constructed mosques in some towns in the country. In Yorubaland for instance, it has a mosque in Ifon and Ibadan. Some Arabic schools were also constructed by the organisation in Ibadan, Ilorin and Kaduna. In addition, wells were sunk in some places in Lagos, Ibadan, and Ilorin to ease the problem of shortage of drinkable water.[26]

The International Institute of Islamic Thought (IIIT)

The First International Conference on the Islamization of Knowledge held in Lugano, Switzerland in 1977 culminated in the establishment of the International Institute of Islamic Thought in the United States of America in 1981. The Institute, which is purely academic, was established with the aim of providing a comprehensive Islamic outlook by elucidating on the principles of Islam and relating them to relevant contemporary thought; regaining the intellectual, cultural and civilizational identity of the *ummah* through the Islamization of the humanities and the sciences; and rectifying the methodology of contemporary Islamic thought in order to enable it to resume its contribution to the progress of human civilization and give it meaning and direction in line with the values and objectives of Islam.[27] To achieve these objectives, the Institute gives out grants to Islamic scholars with the understanding that they will carry out research on certain Islamic subjects or problems and then present their findings. It has organised seminars, conferences, lectures and workshops and has published and made important scholarly works accessible in Arabic, English and other major languages of the world. The popular American Journal of Islamic Social Sciences (AJISS) is published by the Institute and serves as an outlet for scholars to publish their research findings and other academic papers.[28]

In addition to the above, the Institute promotes researches by disbursing annually three awards valued at 500 dollars each, to candidates whose researches contribute to Islamic thought.[29] The Institute has quite a number of overseas offices in countries like Sudan, Lebanon, India, Bangladesh, Saudi Arabia, Nigeria, Cyprus, Belgium, Morocco, Turkey, Pakistan and many other countries. It has also entered into joint academic agreements with several universities for the realisation of its objectives.[30]

In line with the objectives of the headquarters of the IIIT, the Nigeria office of the Institute embarks on similar intellectual activities. It organises outreach programmes in form of staff and students' seminars. It has also single-handedly organised international conferences as well as collaborating with some universities and other similar bodies in this area. For instance, it organised an international conference on Muslim Educational Reforms in the Muslim World with the Faculty of Education, Bayero University, Kano in 2002. In January 2003, the Institute also organised an

International Workshop on Qur'anic Schools for West and Central African Countries with the Islamic Educational, Scientific and Cultural Organisation (ISESCO), Morocco, the International Islamic Charitable Organisation (IICO), and Faculty of Arts and Islamic Studies, Bayero University, Kano.[31] In 2010, an International Conference on Islamic Universities was organised by the Institute. It was held at Mambaya House, Kano. The Nigeria office of the Institute has a Directorate of Publications which provides opportunities for the exchange of ideas and the dissemination of research findings and as well creating avenue to have access to invaluable academic works and legacies.

The Nigerian office of the IIIT has awarded not less than seventy research grants to postgraduate and undergraduate students whose topics of research are in close association with the objectives of the Islamization of knowledge programme. The opportunity to publish academic research works has also been created by the IIIT through the floating of a journal titled *Al-Ijtihad: The Journal of Islamization of Knowledge and Contemporary Issues* and the publication of books. The Research Directorate has also commissioned people to write papers on areas of interest to the Islamization of knowledge programme. Books have also been donated to many institutions of learning to ease the problem of the dearth of reference materials in the field of Islamization of knowledge and other disciplines. In addition to this, the Nigeria office at Kano has a library "with a reasonable number of assorted books, dissertations and journals."[32] A mini library is also established at the University of Ilorin where scholars have access to materials related to the Islamization of knowledge programme.

The World Assembly of Muslim Youth (WAMY)

The World Assembly of Muslim Youth (WAMY) with its headquarters in Riyadh, Saudi Arabia, was founded by Late King Faisal Bin Abdul-Aziz in1392H (1972CE).[33] The aims of the organisation are:

1. Serving the true Islamic ideology based on *Tawhid*;
2. Consolidating the factors of ideological unity and strengthening the Islamic fraternal relationship among the Muslim Youth;
3. Crystallizing and supporting the constructive role of youth and students in developing an Islamic society; and
4. Assisting Islamic youth organisations all over the globe through effecting a co-ordination in their activities and helping them to implement their projects.[34]

WAMY is the first international Islamic organisation that specifically deals with youth affairs and it serves as an umbrella body for over 450 Islamic youth organisations in the five continents. It organises an international conference every three years for the purpose of deliberating on important international issues that have direct bearing to youth development. Most of these conferences were held at the headquarters of the body in Riyadh. It also organises local and regional youth camps which are held in different parts of the world all year round.

The Daʿwah Committee of the WAMY has published many books and pamphlets which are widely distributed to various countries, Nigeria inclusive. It published more than 10,000 copies of the *Comparative Study of Islam and Christianity* for use of the Riyadh-based Cooperative Office for Call and

Guidance. Also, 10,000 copies of Abul A'la Maududi's *Toward Understanding of Islam* was published. At its headquarters in Riyadh, WAMY has a library which hosts thousands of books on different Islamic subjects and many periodicals in different languages.[35]

It needs to be mentioned that Nigeria has hosted the regional office of the WAMY, and it has organised numerous programmes for Muslim youth in the country. The body has published quite a good number of books which are distributed free to people for the purpose of disseminating Islamic message to the grassroots.

In 2011, the World Assembly of Muslim Youth (WAMY) provided meals for 1,000 Muslims in Lagos to break their fast. The event, *Iftar Sahim* (Breaking of fast for those who fast) was held at The Muslim Congress (TMC) Dawah Centre, Ijeshatedo, Lagos.[36]

Nigeria is one of the beneficiaries of the WAMY's SR 3.8 million scholarships to 725 students of various nationalities to enable them complete their studies and obtain master and doctoral degrees in various disciplines. The number of Nigerians and their institutions are however not mentioned. Other countries slated to benefit from the scholarship as mentioned by Dr. Khalid Al-Ahmadi, Director of Administration of Educational Affairs at WAMY, are Burkina Faso, Somalia, Bangladesh, Palestine, Syria, Yemen, Pakistan, Tunisia, Burundi, Togo, Mauritania, Chad, Afghanistan, Iraq, Jordan, Eritrea, Ethiopia, Ivory Coast, the Philippines, Ghana, Senegal, Djibouti and Thailand.[37]

The body has equally featured prominently in the establishment of the Al-Hikmah University in Ilorin, Nigeria. It also assists in subsidising the school fees of candidates who are admitted to read Arabic and Islamic Studies. It has also donated reading materials to the University's library.

The Cog in the Wheel of International Islamic Organisations' Achievements in Nigeria

The September 11 2001 attack on the World Trade Centre in New York has a serious consequence on Islam and Muslims generally. The suspicion that Muslims are terrorists became more pronounced with that incident. Most of the Islamic organisations championing the cause of Islamic projects were labelled and stigmatised as sponsors of terror. For instance, several employees of the IIRO were imprisoned and accused of supporting or participating in terrorist movements in some countries. In 2006, the United States forced the Indonesian branch of the IIRO to close down because the regional head of the NGO, Abdul Al-Hamid Sulaiman Al-Mujil, was accused of being a member of *al-Qaeda* and a local terrorist group, the *Jemaah Islamiyah*.[38] In Oregon, the activities of the Haramain Islamic Foundation was brought to a halt, as the United States government impounded and froze the Charity's assets in February 2004 upon the allegation that it had links to terrorism. According to Soliman al-Buthi, Article II of Al-Haramain's 1998 Articles of Incorporation states: "[The] Al Haramain Islamic Foundation, Inc., stands against terrorism, injustice, or subversive activities in any form, and shall oppose any statement or acts of terrorism. Al Haramain Islamic Foundation, Inc., believes such conduct is contrary to Islamic principles."[39] In spite of this, this Muslim organisation was accused of sponsoring terrorism. Haramain was listed in Nigeria to have been among the Islamic organisations that were harbouring terrorists. This made the Oyo State government to order the closure of the foundation. The case was taken to court and the organisation was found innocent. However, it was too late for the organisation to continue operations as the Saudi government was said to have ordered the closure of the Foundation.[40]

The International Islamic Relief Organisation (IIRO) equally suffered the same fate as the activities of the body were brought to a halt consequent upon the allegation, from some quarters, that the body was a major radical Islamic organisation "responsible for fuelling Islamic militancy around the world" as submitted by Steven Emerson at the National Commission on Terrorist Attacks upon the United States. The Organisation is busy battling with how to delist its name from the list of terrorist groups as maintained by the United Nations Council Committee.[41] In the same vein, the IIIT headquarters in the United States was attacked soon after the September 11 attack on the US. This affected the programmes of the Institute for some years. The Nigeria office of the IIIT also experienced some setbacks, as it could not get the normal subventions from the headquarters to execute some of her programmes. In some cases, it had to apply for loans to pay her workers.[42]

Apart from the global suspicion of the organisations by the so-called world powers, most of these organisations in Nigeria face internal challenges, as Christians are suspicious of them and are not favourably disposed to their activities. The Nigerian membership of OIC has been seriously criticised by Christians as an attempt to Islamise the country; this is in spite of the fact that the constitution has declared that: "The Government of the Federation, or a state shall not adopt any religion as state Religion." This fear was expressed by Umejesi to the effect that with the membership of Nigeria in the OIC, Nigeria has been slated for total Islamisation which shall be declared a Federal Islamic Sultanate, with the Sultan of Sokoto as the Supreme Sovereign of Nigeria.[43] However, Oloyede considers the fear that Nigeria by joining the OIC, would become an Islamic state as baseless and cites some of the advantages of being a member of the organisation thus:

> In the same vein the issue of Nigeria's membership of Organisation of Islamic Conference (OIC) has its economic significance but which has not been judiciously tapped by the government possibly for fear of being accused of one-sidedness and possible condemnation by non-Muslims. Whatever the case may be, if countries like Gabon, Cameroon, Benin, Sierra Leone and other African countries are members of the Organisation without becoming Muslim or Islamic countries, one wonders the wild cacophony which surrounded the membership of Nigeria on this body. Indeed, the awareness on the part of the London and Paris Clubs of creditors that Nigeria as a member of the OIC could borrow money from the Islamic Development Bank in Jeddah, Kingdom of Saudi Arabia without interest influenced their decision to cancel parts of the accumulated debt of Nigeria from their extortionate interest.[44]

Ever since Nigeria's membership of the OIC, numerous unfounded allegations have been levelled against the nation's leadership, ranging from Nigeria's donation of US \$21billion to the Islamic Development Fund of the OIC, to the Islamisation of the country, to the extent that Umejesi erroneously attached the construction of 'government buildings' in Abuja in the shape of a mosque as part of the implementation of the OIC agenda to make Abuja the headquarters of Islam in Africa.[45]

The spate of religious crises in the northern part of the country can also be a stumbling block against Nigeria maximising the benefits of international Islamic organisations in the country. The Boko Haram has been seen as being sponsored by some religious bodies, and in such a case, the charity organisations may not be willing to come to the aid of the Muslims, for fear of being accused of sponsoring acts of terrorism.

In addition to the above, some Muslim leaders who have access to foreign assistance from different charity organisations are not sincere in rendering the expected charitable assignment given to them. There have been instances where some were said to have collected money for the purpose of constructing mosques from a particular organisation, only to send fake pictures of already completed mosques to the sponsors abroad, giving false impression that they had actually carried out the assignment. In addition, some collected money for projects they never executed. In other words, the spirit of materialism has driven them to set aside their spiritual conscience, as they have forgotten their accountability to man and to God, their Creator.

Conclusion

We have discussed the spirit of internationalisation demonstrated by a few Islamic organisations in extending their hands of charity to different parts of the world, not minding their race, tribe and nationality. From this, we can conclude that religion is a vehicle of progress, growth and development, if allowed to be used positively.

Apart from the above, we have taken a look at some factors hampering maximal utilisation of the opportunities offered by the international organisations in the country. It is on the basis of this that we offer the following suggestions:

- Home based Islamic organisations should learn a lesson from the international Islamic organisations in Nigeria by taking up the responsibility of improving the lot of the less privileged in the society. They should look inwards in the generation of revenue to carry out these responsibilities. Most of the international organisations depend on collection of Zakat and other poverty

alleviation institutions like *waqf*, and *hibah*. Such must be encouraged among Muslims in Nigeria.
- Adherents of other religions should learn how to tolerate others, especially when their programmes have direct bearing to human development. Unnecessary fabrications and unhealthy rivalry should be avoided for religion generally to regain its expected role of human, physical and spiritual development.
- The so-called world powers should not, for reasons of security, deal unjustly with innocent Muslim organisations. They should have facts and figures before labelling an organisation a terrorist group in order for the world not to accuse them of giving a dog a bad name just to hang it.
- The international Muslim organisations should be transparent in their modes of operation to avoid being stigmatised. They should not allow unscrupulous elements to intervene in their mode of *jihad*, or hide behind them to perpetrate any act of terrorism, as this goes against the spirit of Islam which calls for dissemination of Allah's message with wisdom and good admonition.
- The organisations should remain steadfast in their activities not minding those who are out to label them with all sorts of bad names, if actually there is no skeleton in their cupboards.

Notes and References

1. Charter of the Organisation of Islamic Cooperation retrieved from OIC charter-new-en-pdf in www.oic-oci.org (accessed on 11/03/2014).

2. J.N. Paden, *Ahmadu Bello Sardauna of Sokoto: Values and Leadership in Nigeria;* (Zaria, Hudahuda Publishing Company, 1986), 533-543.
3. J.N. Paden, *Ahmadu Bello Sardauna of Sokoto*.
4. J.N. Paden, *Ahmadu Bello Sardauna of Sokoto*,543.
5. See "Nigeria Rejoins OIC" in Elombah.com – A Nigerian Perspective on World Affairs in http://www.elombah.com/index.php?option=com_content& view (accessed on 11/03/2014).
6. C.J. Korieh, "Islam and Politics in Nigeria: Historical Perspectives", in C.J. Korieh & G.U. Nwokeji (eds), *Religion, History and Politics in Nigeria; Essays in Honour of Ogbu U. Kalu.* (Maryland, University Press of America Inc. 2005), 115-117.
7. Raji Shittu, "The Impacts of the Organisation of Islamic Conference (OIC) on Nigeria"; *Journal of University Scholars in Religion (JUSREL),* (vol. 1, 2011), 131-132.
8. Faud al-Omar & Mohammed Abdel-Haq, *Islamic Banking: Theory, Practice and Challenges;* (Karachi, Oxford University Press, 1988), 88-89.
9. Mohammad Nejatullah Siddiqi, *Islamic Banking and Finance* (A series of three lectures delivered at UCLA in a Fall 2001 seminar for the business community, 2001), 12.
10. Mohammad Nejatullah Siddiqi, *Islamic Banking and Finance*
11. Jaiz International Plc, *Private Placement of 10.500,000.000 Ordinary Shares of N 1.00 at N1.oo Per Share;* (2006), 14.
12. R.I. Adebayo, "The Islamic Education Trust: An Educational Experiment in Nigeria"; *The Muslim World League Journal,* (Vol. 33, Nos 5 & 6, 2005), 44-45.
13. Islamic Development Bank Doles Out N310bn For Nigeria's Transformation, in the "Leadership" April 25th 2012, inhttp://www.leadership.ng/nga/articles/21027/2012/04/03 . (accessed on 25/4.2012).
14. Islamic Development Bank Doles Out N310bn For Nigeria's Transformation, in the "Leadership" April 25th 2012,

inhttp://www.leadership.ng/nga/articles/21027/2012/04/03 (accessed on 25/4/2012).
15. Haramain Charitable Foundation Journal (Worldwide Humanitarian Service, June, 2003), 1ff.
16. http://www.islamdaily.org/en/charities/5346.al-haramain-islamic-foundation-inc-director-solima.htm (Accessed on 5th December 2012).
17. M.M. Salaudeen, "Activities of Haramain Islamic Foundation (HIF) in Oyo State". A Long Essay of the Department of Religions, (University of Ilorin, 2006), 56-76.
18. M.M. Salaudeen, "Activities of Haramain Islamic Foundation (HIF) in Oyo State"
19. M.M. Salaudeen, "Activities of Haramain Islamic Foundation (HIF) in Oyo State".
20. http://en.wikipedia.org/wiki/International_Islamic_Relief_Organisation. (accessed on 10/6/2012)
21. http://en.wikipedia.org/wiki/International_Islamic_Relief_Organisation.
22. From Wikipedia, the free encyclopaedia retrieved on 5th December 2012.
23. Oral interview conducted with Alhaji Abdur-Razaq Raji, a one-time worker with the IIRO in Osun State. (Interviewed on 18th August, 2012).
24. Taraba State, Nigeria, Report of Rapid Assessment in Selected LGAs; Family Health International, Dec. 2000.
25. An oral interview conducted with Alhaji Shaykh Abdul-Hameed Salahudeen, the Chief Imam of Ila-Orangun, and a one time member of the Organisation in Osun State. (Interviewed on 10th June, 2012).
26. Interview with Alhaji Abdur-Razaq Raji.
27. The objectives of the IIIT are contained in every inner back page of *the American Journal of Islamic Social Sciences (AJISS)* (Published by the IIIT and AMSS).
28. R.I. Adebayo, *Islamization of Knowledge: Global Developments, Individual Efforts, & Institutional Contributions;* (Kano,

International Institute of Islamic Thought, Nigeria Office. 2008), 100.
29. R.I. Adebayo, *Islamization of Knowledge*.
30. R.I. Adebayo, *Islamization of Knowledge*.
31. R.I. Adebayo, *Islamization of Knowledge*, 102.
32. S. Sulaiman, "An Appraisal of the Islamization of Knowledge Programme in Nigeria", *Al-Ijtihad: The Journal of Islamization of Knowledge*, (vol. 2, No. 1, 2001), 20.
33. Islamic Future, (vol. XI No. 48, June/July 1995), 7.
34. The objectives of WAMY are contained in the inner page of all publications of the Association.
35. Islamic Future, (vol. X – No. 47, May, 1995), 13.
36. WAMY feeds 1,000 Muslims SEKINAH LAWAL 15/08/2011 02:29:00In the National Mirror in http://nationalmirroronline.net/features/18531.html. (Accessed on 17/5/2012)
37. Saudi Gazette.com.sa http://www.saudigazette.com.sa/index.cfm?method=home.regcon&contentID=2008100618513).
38. http://www.observatoire-humanitaire.org/fusion.php?l=GB&id=81 (accessed on 10/6/2012.)
39. http://www.islamdaily.org/en/charities/5346.al-haramain-islamic-foundation-inc-director-solima.htm (Accessed on 5th December 2012).
40. M.M. Salaudeen, "Activities of Haramain Islamic Foundation (HIF) in Oyo State", 89.
41. http://en.wikipedia.org/wiki/International_Islamic_Relief_Organisation. (Accessed on 5th December 2012).
42. Interview conducted with Mallam Muhammad Bima, a one time Deputy Director, Administration, (IIIT office Kano, on July 2010).
43. I.O. Umejesi, "Religion and Politics in Africa: The OIC Membership and Implications for Member States – Nigeria as a Case Study"; in C.O. Isiramen, I.O. Umejesi, P.O.O. Ottuh

and E.A. Falaiye, *Issues in Religious Studies and Philosophy*, (Ibadan, En-Joy Press & Books, 2010), 333.
44. I.O. Oloyede, "Religious Experiences in a Multi-Religious State: The Nigeria Example." A Keynote address delivered at the 1st National Conference of the Department of Religious Studies, Kwara State University, Malete, (On 19th October, 2010), 9.
45. I.O. Umejesi, "Religion and Politics in Africa", 336.

CHAPTER THIRTEEN

Ethno-Religious Crisis and its Implication for National Security and Development

Odudele, Rotimi
Department of Christian Religious Studies
College of Education, Ikere-Ekiti, Nigeria
rotiodu@yahoo.com
+2348033663188 or +2348051693675

Introduction

For the past few decades, Nigeria as a nation has witnessed different kinds of crises, ranging from religious, communal, political as well as economic stress. It is a fact that the multiplicity of religions in Nigeria provides the premise for inter-religious crisis. This is manifested in religious intolerance, religious bigotry and religious particularism. Religious crisis becomes a common thing in nearly every section of Nigeria. It has occurred in Kano, Bauchi, Kastina, Borno, Jos, Zaria, Kaduna, Yola, Sokoto, Maiduguri, Ilorin, Owerri and Lagos to mention just a few. All these crises have resulted in the loss of lives, destruction of valuable property, enmity among citizenry and socio-political instability. This study aims at proffering solutions that will have a lasting grip on the Nigerian society. It was discovered that nearly all the past attempts to bring these religious crises under control did not last long. The writing gives room for dialogue, tolerance, mutual understanding, peaceful co-existence and recognition of both human and moral values. It concludes on the note that it is from a peaceful atmosphere devoid of religious crisis that national security can be maintained and guaranteed. Thus, religion is capable of solving the contemporary problem of ethno-religious crisis that is threatening peaceful co-existence of Nigerians, if properly utilised.

Ethno-religious crisis is gradually becoming a permanent feature of Nigerian communities. Consequently, peace is becoming elusive and a mirage. Political opponents see themselves as somebody to be dead than being alive while people of different ethnic groups kill one another over insignificant differences. The police and other security forces cannot, alone, handle these various kinds of crises that lead to breach of peace and security.

According to Olayinka, every human society irrespective of its nature, structure and background strives toward achieving certain goals and objectives either short or long term.[1] The major objective is to build a progressive society which is called nation building. However, in the pursuit of these goals and objectives, peace and security are of paramount importance. To realise the peace and security in question, the efficacy of religion cannot be over-emphasised.

Conceptual Framework

To give this study a fair treatment and to facilitate good understanding of the work, it is crucial that the following basic concepts are given proper theoretical examination: religion, ethno-religious crisis and national security.

The concept of Religion

It is very difficult to come by a generally acceptable definition of religion. The obvious reason for this is that religion unlike other subjects or disciplines cannot be pinned down to only one definition. Thus, religion has no satisfactory description or single or universally acceptable definition. That is why everybody defines religion in the way they look at it. Hence, the understanding of the concept of religion is worth noting.

Etymologically, the term religion is a Latin word *relegere* meaning join or bind together. That is to say, certain people that are joined together by principles, values or covenant towards the ultimate reality. Comte cited in Dzurgba sees religion as an expression of an immature thought and powerful emotion. He went further to describe religion as a collective delusion, a symbolic thinking or an understandable behaviour. He therefore considers religion to be illusion and meaningless as it was unable to comprehend external realities. This description is unacceptable for it only examined religion from negative point of view without considering the positive aspects.[2] Emile Durkheim cited by Lawal defines religion as a unified system of beliefs and practices which are related to separate things which are things that are set apart and forbidden. He maintains that religion contributes to the establishment and maintenance of order in the society by creating condition for social well being, self discipline, social solidarity, social cohesion and continuity of culture and knowledge[3]. Thus, he sees religion from functional point of view.

The Concept of Ethno-religious Crisis

As observed by Fadahunsi, ethno-religious crisis remains the unfortunate political, economic and social legacies of military dictatorship in Nigeria. He opined that during the military interregnums, the usurpers of political power overturned the true Federal Constitution negotiated by the founding fathers of modern Nigeria; which had now been substituted by a militarised unitary constitution with the concentration of powers at the centre at the expense of the component units that made up the polity[4]. This anomaly and many others are the basis of ethno-religious crises in the country. However, it should be noted that ethno-religious crisis is not limited to military era alone. For the purpose of this work, ethno-religious crisis implies the breakdown of understanding between people of different cultural and religious background which results into physical and psychological unrest within a country.

The Concept of National Security

According to Martin, national security is the concept of safety for the territory and population of a state and by extension the policies adopted for its preservation[5]. Security is sometimes conceived as the assurance of future welfare. From this broad context, national security could be regarded as the whole range of measures affecting the economic and social welfare of a population as well as provision against aggression from abroad or subversion from within. However, the term is usually invoked either when the safety of a given country is threatened by armed forces or when military action offers a possible answer to other dangers, such as a wave of illegal immigration. *The New Encyclopedia Britannica* says "security and protection system guard persons and property against a range of hazards, including crime; fire and attendant risks, such as explosion; accidents; disasters; sabotage; subversion; civil disturbances; bombings (both actual and threatened); and in some systems, attacks by external enemies"[6].

Ethno-Religious Crisis in Nigeria

According to Dzurgba as cited by Odudele, he argued that aggressiveness, hostility and brutality have mostly marked men's religious behaviour[7]. It is a fact that the church tortured and even killed some of her own adherents who were condemned for heresy or apostasy in the 15th and 16th centuries. The persecuting exercise was regarded as an inquisition. The holy wars conducted by Christians against Muslims, during the middle ages, are best known to us as crusades. The propagation of Islamic religion has been allegedly done occasionally through religious wars called Jihads. It is of paramount importance to say at this point in time that contemporary society has witnessed and is still witnessing a lot of religious crises, especially in the Northern part of Nigeria. In Nigeria, Kano witnessed Maitasine disturbance in 1980 and 1982. The Kaduna religious riots in 1987 and 2000, the current Boko Haram crisis in various Northern states, are great threats to peace in Nigeria.

Besides, we had communal crisis in Warri, Delta State between May 30 – June 9, 1999; ethno-religious crisis of Oodua Peoples Congress Yoruba versus Hausa traders in July 18, 1999 in Sagamu; the Hausa/Fulani Muslims versus Oro cult members in Shagamu November 9, 1999; Itsekiri versus Urhobo in November11, 1999; Ilorin Hausa/Fulani Muslims versus Christians in December 19, 1999; Ibadan Hausa/Fulani versus Yoruba in January 5, 2000. Other crises are: Edo communal clash in Etsako Central Local Government in January 30, 2000; Kaduna religious riot over the introduction of Sharia in February 21, 2000; Aba religious riot in February 28, 2000; Communal clash between Elewu versus Okrika communities in March 18-19, 2000; Demboa religious riots between Hausa/Fulani Muslims and others in March 28, 2000; Saki Hausa/Fulani Muslims versus Christians in April 24, 2006; Ethnic violence between Jukun and Tiv in October 12, 2001; Osogbo religious crisis between Muslims and Christians in November 29, 2001; Communal clash between Itsekiri and Urhobo in January, 2002 and many other ethno-religious crises in recent times[8].

A number of factors can be identified to be responsible for the incessant ethno-religious crisis in the country. Such factors include lack of tolerance, boundary dispute, unfavourable government policies and programmes, indigene- settlers problem, superiority complex, distribution or sharing of resources, economic factor etc. Thus, a number of consequences often trailed or occurred as aftermath of ethno-religious crisis. Even though one cannot mention categorically all the consequences but some of them are well pronounced and regular reoccurrence anytime there is crisis in the country. There is destruction of lives and properties, displacement, economic loss, negative image for the country, breeding ground for criminals etc.

Efficacy of Religion in Contemporary Ethno-Religious Crisis

Religion permeates every aspects of man's existence in the universe, be it political, social, cultural or economic life of the people. No religion preaches violence. The three main religions in Nigeria, namely, Christianity, Islam and African Traditional Religion all advocate and preach peace and peaceful co-existence of all citizens[9]. It has been used as the most important instrument in the social control of man and the society. Thus, the efficacy of religion in contemporary ethno-religious crisis cannot be over emphasised.

Religion Ensures the Continuous Existence and Survival of the Society: Odiba identifies the positive role of religion as holding society together as a form of "social glue"[10]. Thus, there should be peaceful co-existence and recognition of both human and moral values because religion serves as a social bond that holds the society together. It strengthens the basic beliefs and values of the society. Religion maintains social cohesion of all its members to live in unity and peace. Religious ceremonies are performed to remind people that they have a common history and identity thereby ensuring the continuity and survival of the existence of the society.

Religion Helps to Bring About Radical Social Change: A radical change takes place in religion as a social phenomenon. In Nigeria, religion helps to bring about radical social change. Religion gives room for tolerance and dialogue when necessary. Here, a social change is the alteration in the patterns of social action and interactions. Thus, religion introduces new ideas and information about education, medicine, literature, agriculture, sports, markets, organization and administration. Religion establishes new form of education, dressing, marriage, law courts, and languages in Nigeria.

Cultural Transformation: The relevance of religion could be seen in cultural development. Religion helps in transforming the society by introducing new cultural elements. Religious doctrines, laws, organisations, modes of dressing, dogma, buildings, patterns of marriages, training of children, burying the dead and many other items of culture are influenced through religion. Morality is used to give meaning and purpose to the cultural behaviour. Wherein the culture deviates from the real religious meaning, then it has to be checked, so that there is a balanced relationship between the cultural elements and religious ideology.

Religion Reforms and Resettles Deviants: A deviant is a person who is deficient in moral and social standards from what is normal and accepted. Religion can be used to call the out-law persons or sinners back to repentance, and makes them become socially integrated into the society. Religion struggles with the ultimate problems of human life that deprive man from behaving in the morally and socially accepted ways. It gives a sense of direction and makes people to act and behave in a specifically desired ways. It moves people away from despair and restores confidence in them. Those who are religious tend to be more obedient, conforming and less deviant. This is because religion as an instrument of social control provides an integrative ideology[11].

Self-adjustment and Solace: Religion is a very useful element or tool for self-adjustment and solace especially when man is faced with the problems of life and neuroses. It is a mechanism for adjustment and of solving problems. It is in this context that religion provides a patterned and familiar way of over coming life and environmental crisis and of the preparation and hope for a comfortable future. Religious believers are better adjusted on measures of psychiatric impairment, and religious activity is positively related to adjustment in old age. Hence, religious individuals may be able to face better life crisis and less likely to commit suicide.

Religion Stimulates Social Habits and Checks Anti-Social Behaviour: Odiba opines that religion is "an efficient means of social control, stimulates social habits and checks anti-social tendencies".[12] Religion aids morality and shapes the ethical life of the people. It embodies ethical norms in religious laws. Morality originated from religion and without morality no society can survive. Religion introduced taboos in order to promote harmony, ethical standard and peaceful co-existence in the society. Some religious laws have forbidden the mechanism of birth control, the sale of alcoholic beverages, abortion, conducting business on sacred days, adultery, stealing, murder, lying, unhealthy, rivalry competitions, crisis etc.

Religion Fosters Social Solidarity and Friendships: Religion serves as a powerful means for the solidarity among its members, and nearly all the great social institutions have been born in religion. Religion enhances cohesion, orderliness, stability, unity, harmony, co-operation, security consensus, cordiality and peaceful co-existence. Thus, religion serves as a pivot of togetherness in its eradication of loneliness and isolation.

However, it should be noted here that religion (if not well used) could also be a source of conflict. Experience has shown that religion is a source of conflict; and conflict produces lawlessness, disorder, insecurity and instability in the society. It is felt that the insistence by a given religion that its members have exclusive possession of truth, knowledge, goodness and salvation is fanaticism. Fanaticism thrives on opposition, because one religion needs another one with which it can define its membership. The tendency is to create religious intolerance and militancy which have caused a lot of crises worldwide.

Implication of Ethno-religious Crisis on National Security

The implication of ethno-religious crisis on national security is tremendous and cannot be over emphasised in any way. Firstly, ethno-religious crisis will lead to exposure of the country's security strength[13]. The inability of the security forces to nip in the bud these ethno-religious crises before they escalate to the level of wanton destruction and killing exposes the quality (in terms of knowledge, readiness, expertise and equipment) of the country's security forces. More often than not, the security agencies are usually caught napping and by the time they put their acts together, several lives would have been lost.

Secondly, as a result of ethno-religious crisis, there is destruction of lives and properties. More often than not, precious lives and properties running into several millions of naira are usually destroyed as a consequence of ethno-religious crises in different parts of the country.

Third, ethno-religious crises do breed ground for criminals. The incessant natures of crisis in the country also has the implication of breeding social miscreant and criminals who by their access to weapons of war (which are usually sophisticated) become terrors to both their immediate community and the larger society. After the crisis, it is always difficult if not impossible to retrieve such weapons back from the people in question.

Fourth, incessant ethno-religious crisis has continued to give the country negative image in the international community[14]. This bad image portrays the country as unpeaceful and underdeveloped. Besides, this has continued to scare away foreign investors who might have helped to develop the economy. No serious investor will invest his money in a country where crisis can erupt at any time and be made to forfeit all his investments.

As a result of ethno-religious crisis, there is a displacement of people. Those who are lucky to escape death are made to become refugees elsewhere for survival. Such people loose contact with their families, loved ones and businesses which could be means of survival and sustenance.

Observation and Recommendations

Religion as a resource for peace has potential to solve ethno-religious crisis and to build peaceful co-existence in contemporary Nigeria. The three major religions in Nigeria, Islam, Christianity and African Tradition Religion share certain common beliefs, which serve as basis for common actions for peaceful approach to crisis situations. Each of these religions has a belief in a Supreme Being, Creator of the universe and father of all mankind. God has established some moral order in the universe, which if followed will make peace in human relationships. The re-interpretation of these religious leaders.

According to Christian teachings, a person is not to take revenge for any wrong done to him/her, but to leave things to God who is the avenger. And according to Muslims, the word "Islam" means peace and submission to Allah. It implies that Muslims, should be lovers of peace. If the adherents of both Christianity and Islam would practise what the two religions teach, Nigeria would be a more peaceful country than it is today[15].

For the fact that God in His infinite wisdom has seen it wise to put together Christians and Muslims to live in one country, it implies that He has good reasons for doing so. In living together, Christians need Muslims and Muslims need Christians. In order to ensure peace and peaceful co-existence in the nation, the following recommendations are suggested.

- The religious leaders should concentrate on teaching those things that unite us and not on what divides us. Religious leaders should stop preaching on what may provoke one religious group against the other. Each religious group should only preach its own doctrines and not misinterpret the doctrines of other religions. Seminars and symposia should always be organised by different religious groups and there should be inter-religious dialogue for mutual understanding of each other.
- At the university level, Comparative Religion can be taught to enable students to compare and contrast with emphasis laid on areas of agreement, tolerance and security of people's lives and properties. The government of the nation owes it a duty to re-introduce the teaching and learning of religion/moral education in schools and make it compulsory for all students. Religious bigotry should be stamped out and proper tenets of religion should be taught and practised. This helps to eradicate ignorance.
- At home, parents and siblings are to encourage folk stories that stressed tolerance, endurance, justice and peaceful co-existence. Fatherhood of God for everybody and mutuality should be emphasised.
- Finally, the state must protect the rights of every citizen to freedom of conscience as enshrined in the constitution[16]. It must also take steps to address socio-

economic and political inequalities, which are catalyst for ethno-religious crises.

Notes and References

1. E. O. Olayinka, Christian Religion and Development in Nigeria in the 21st Century, in Nwanyanwu, O. J. (ed). *Issues and Problems of Development in Nigeria in the 21st Century*, (Abeokuta: Visual Resources 1999).
2. A. Dzurgba, *God and Caesar: A Study in the Sociology of Religion*, (Ibadan: John Archers Publishers Limited 2002).
3. B.O. Lawal, *Teaching Religions in Colleges and Universities*, (Ibadan: Stirling-Horden Publishers, 2003).
4. A. Fadahunsi, Ethnic and Religious Conflicts in Nigeria: Implications for the Economy in Babawale T. (ed). Urban Violence, Ethnic Militias and the Challenges of Democratic Consolidation in Nigeria, (Lagos: Malthouse Press Limited, 2003).
5. L. Martin, "National Security" Microsoft at Encarta at Encyclopedia, (Microsoft Corporation U. S. A. 2005).
6. *The New Encyclopedia Britannica* – (Macropaedia knowledge depth 15th Edition, Vol.32, 1980), 465.
7. R. Odudele, *Religion and Moral Instructions in Schools*, (Akure: Al-Hafiz Publishers, 2006), 12
8. *TELL Newspaper*, (September 24, 2001 and February 18, 2002).
9. C. Ayuba and Z.T. Alex, The Role of Religion in Promoting Peace and Security.
    National Development in Nigeria. In A. A. Adeniji Lateef, S.A. Adeyemo and B.R. Adeniji (eds). *Peace, Security and National Development*, National Association for

the promotion of studies in Religions, Education, Languages and General Studies, (Ibadan: Remo Ind. Printers. 2007).
10. I. Odiba, "Positive Function of Religion." *Nigerian Newsday*, (December 30, 2002).
11. V. Ukiwo, *Politics, Ethno-Religious conflicts and Democratic Consolidation in Nigeria*, (London: Cambridge University Press, 2003).
12. 12. I. Odiba, "Positive Function of Religion." *Nigerian Newsday*, (December 30, 2002).
13. I. A. Adebimpe, and A. O. Ogunsola, Ethno-religious Violence in a plural society: A Case Study of Nigeria. In M. A. Folorunsho, et al (eds), 2007.
14. Sunny Isu, "The Virtues of Forgiveness", *Nigeria Newsday*, (December, 30, 2002), 7.
15. O. Adeniji, *Essays on Nigerian Foreign Policy's Governance and International Security*, (Ibadan: Doctung publishing 2000).
16. 16. R. Odudele, *Religion and Moral Instructions in Schools*, (Akure: Al-Hafiz Publishers, 2006), 12

CHAPTER FOURTEEN

A Comparison of Polygamy as a Concept in African Religion and Christianity

Opoola, Elizabeth Omolara
*Department of Religions,
University of Ilorin, Ilorin, Nigeria.
opoolaelizabeth@yahoo.com
+2348033578627*

Introduction

Marriage is a union between a man and a woman. They become united as one body. The stronger the bond of unity the more successful the marriage is; the weaker the bond, the less successful it is.[1] Marriage is sacred and complex. In Christianity it is not a human invention but of God's. 'Then the Lord God said, it is not good that man should be alone; I will make him a helper fit for him' (Gen.2:18). It is an intimate relationship usually formalised in the form of a wedding ceremony. Christopher opines that marriage is a contract between two families and two individuals.[2] Also, Igenoza, from his exegetical study of marriage gathered various opinions and interpretations about the word 'one flesh'. Beeston, interpreted one flesh to mean 'kinship or clan'. That is, the two families in a traditional set up are brought together. Renner also opines that, it is not more than a sexual intercourse, why Delitzsch according to Igenoza sees the idea of one flesh as 'spiritual unity'.[3]

In the Old Testament, marrying many wives was permitted: (Deut. 21: 15-17; Exo. 21:10) ' If a man has two wives, the one loved and the other disliked and they have borne him children, both the loved and disliked, …' If he takes another wife to himself, he shall not diminish her food, her clothing, or her marital right'. It is observed that this type of marriage was common among the Israelites because of their association with 'pagan' culture.

G.Y. Wenham summarises that, 'one flesh' does not mean sexual union, procreation, or spiritual and emotional relation, but something that has to do with blood.[4] Also, Wenham has this to say:

> ... the lives of two individuals of the opposite sex from different backgrounds become intricately bound together that they now have a common destiny, looking in the same direction, sharing their problems, harmonizing and living with their differences.[5]

Igenoza concludes that marriage from the beginning as planned by God, was to be an intimate form of human relation between two equal complements of the opposite sex, created in the image of God.[6] Therefore, this type of intimate relationship was designed to be monogamous.

Mbiti understands marriage to be the focus of existence, a drama in which every one becomes an actor or actress, not just a spectator. He further stressed that everyone must be interested in it.[7] This assumption could be controversial. We want to submit that marriage should be optional and a matter of interest. Paul in I Cor. 7:28 says: "whoever is married has not committed any sin, nevertheless, such people shall have trouble in this life". From Paul's statement marriage is a thing of choice. On the other hand, African culture does not allow a man or a woman of marriageable age to remain unmarried.

Polygamy in African Religion

The African people were polygamous in marriage from the beginning. Marrying multiple wives at the same time, were common in African societies and this did not affect their religion. It fitted well into the social structure of traditional life, serving many useful purposes.[8] Mavumilusa and Alana opine that polygamy has to do with women because marriage is tied to the status attributed to women by the society because of the place they occupy in the minds and hearts of men.[9] Clignet's view about this type of marriage is that it is an instrument for the merciless domination of women by men.[10] This domination of women by men is again confirmed in Mbiti's statement that a man with many children is "reborn" in the multitude of his descendants and will be remembered by many after his death.[11] A woman would also be remembered in the multitude of her descendants.

Nevertheless, it is unfortunate that women are given little or no recognition. On this note, African mentality that the bigger the family, the more respect one receives in the community according to Mbiti is not always true.[12] Polygamy as we can see is an integral part of African Religion, customs and tradition. This form of marriage in the opinion of J.L. Gibbs is acceptable and tolerated by 78% of different anthropological groups.[13] Although, the percentage may be lower due to various reasons; such as exposure, western education, economic factor etc. Africans should not however, be condemned for what they are and believe in. No culture is to be regarded as better or worse, higher or lower, less human, more primitive or advanced, more savage or civilized than others. Those who became attached to Western civilization adopted a negative attitude towards African religious ideas, beliefs, idioms, festivals, rituals and institutions.[14] Hillman attributed this attitude to an excessive measure of Western cultural arrogance. She says:

Western culture is not only superior totally and cumulatively to other cultures, but that it is also more human and, thus, the only appropriate instrument for the communication and incarnation of Christianity.[15]

This Western mentality is what Hilaire Belloc termed "Europe is the faith; the faith is Europe".[16] In a situation whereby people think that their own customs and conceptions are the best, is simply having a lack of respect for other cultures and tradition. Before the advent of Christianity, there were basic patterns and structures in every society. African tradition should therefore, not be seen as primitive and something to be abandoned because of the influence of a new religion.

Polygamy in Christianity

Polygamy in ancient Israel was tolerated under the law in the Old Testament. Although, it was contrary to the commands of God, these marital customs were not forbidden in later Israelite legislation.[17] (Exo. 21:10; Deut. 21:15-17) For example, marrying one's half sister as Abraham did and two sisters marrying the same man as in the case of Jacob.[18] Biblical heroes married many wives; some of them are Abraham, Isaac, Samson, Boaz, Elkanah, David, Solomon, Ahasuerus, Rehoboam, Belshazzar, Abijah and Jehoram. This type of marriage found among the Jewish tradition was acceptable perhaps, to keep the family unit strong and to reduce ungodly religious influences to the barest minimum.

Plurality of marriage was common in Judaism because of cultural background of 'pagan' kings the Israelites came in contact with.[19] The marital practices found among the patriarchs were the customs of ancient Babylonia and Assyria of the second millennium from where the patriarchs migrated.[20] Solomon's choice of multiple wives was for a purpose. He wanted to excel in everyway, in wealth, wisdom and power, which was a sign of royal greatness in his time.[21] In an attempt to do this, he followed the customs and practices of "pagans" in defiance of God's commands.[22] He married Moabites, Ammonites, Edomites, Sidonians, Egyptians and Hittites. These marriages however, had political undertone. Mavumilusa opines that polygamy at the time of the patriarchs, was men's failure to grasp the Lord's promise to Eve on the subject of her descendants and the birth of the one who would crush the serpents head (Gen. 3:15).[23] Some patriarchs thought that the one who would crush the serpents head would be born directly to them. Therefore, it was absolutely imperative for them to have many children.

Christopher argued that, a practice may be regulated to ameliorate its worst effects without that practice being fundamentally approved.[24] We have said that polygamy was tolerated in the Old Testament but it gradually faded away to give way to monogamy. Genesis account makes us to understand that from the beginning, God made them male and female. This is a pointer to monogamy. Eugene Hillman, notes that, New Testament conclusion about marriage is a clear confirmation of the monogamy hypothesis.[25] He believes that as far as Christianity is concerned, polygamy was abolished by Jesus Christ.

Arguments in Favour of Polygamy

There are several arguments put forward in support of polygamy. Having multiple wives in Africa is a sign of wealth and influence. Polygamy was a product of economic, social and political circumstances of the indigenous society.[26] In an agrarian society, having many wives and children is a great advantage, because the children help on the farm and in cattle rearing. With a high infant mortality rate there was the need for many wives in other to have a large number of children which brings about high productivity to the family.[27] A man struggles to have many children because when he dies he would receive a befitting burial. Parents buried in this way would occupy a high status in the world beyond.[28]

Polygamy helps to remove the shame of barrenness. If the first wife has no child, to reduce anxiety and shame the man takes another wife. It is un-African to die childless because children are regarded as the greatest human achievements. In case of death or sickness, other wives and children assist in doing other jobs in the family. Another reason given was that many African women do not have sexual relations after childbirth for about two years. This prompted most men to have many wives. Also, the man's wealth is greatly increased if he has female children, through bride-price during wedding.

Ididi supports multiple wives because of the population of women which he believes has outnumbered men. He estimated it to be ratio 3:1. Ididi's feeling is that many young women might remain unmarried if they do not participate in polygamy. However, his estimate is not correct. According to the United Nations estimates, Winkler said that, based on demographic data for every 103 boys born there are 100 girls which put the ratio of boys to girls at 1.03:1.[29] Some men, marry widows left by their late brothers because of tradition. These widows are sometimes imposed on them by family tradition.[30] Any woman who refuses this idea of marriage is victimized and sent out of the family. Some men whose job require them to be transferred frequently from one station to another may also decide to take a second wife; instead of having a concubine in their new place of work. Most often they leave the first wife and the children in their former station.[31]

Arguments against Polygamy

We believe that whatever argument that is given in support of polygamy in Africa, we must not deny the fact that there are some challenges that are associated with it. Eric observes that one of the problems of African men is selfishness characterized by laziness and a high sexual *libido*.[32] They indulge in polygamy to satisfy their sexual demands. In pursuit of selfishness, they destroy harmony in society, which often leads to diseases, delinquent children, death, orphanages, prostitution, domestic violence, infidelity and lawlessness in the society.[33] Children from polygamous homes may sometimes possess questionable character and use abusive words. Polygamy with all its advantages does not really limit prostitution and adultery.

Most traditional reasons in support of this type of marriage are no longer valid. Problems of barrenness, divorce, political and socio-economic benefits attached to polygamy are not without solution in the modern age. Some of the reasons mentioned above for adopting polygamy are no longer acceptable today. For example, adoption of children could be an alternative to the problem of barrenness, most couples are separated instead of divorcing one another, while education, exposure, economic meltdown are being taken into consideration before embarking on a polygamous type of marriage.

Implications of Polygamy

Polygamy causes material and financial difficulties and fosters social injustice and scenes of suffering. Plurality of wives brings satisfaction to the man while it may not be so with the women. No true love is expressed in this type of marriage. There is a low development rate for women in the sense that, the chances of higher education, entry into desired professions or political responsibilities are low. Most homes of this nature end up in chaos.

With the coming of Christianity to Nigeria in 1842,[34] the missionaries preached against polygamy as it was seen as being against the moral teachings of Jesus Christ. Many converts accepted this and embraced the Christian form of marriage.[35] It is believed by the Christian missionaries that in the beginning marriage was monogamous:

> ... and God blessed them and God said unto them, be fruitful and multiply and replenish the earth and subdue it; and have dominion over the fish of the sea, and over every living thing that moveth upon the earth. (Gen. 1:26-28; 2: 7-25)

In a marriage, a man and woman make a public vow to live together in a sexual and social union until death parts them. To this agreement God stands as a witness. God's presence in a marriage confession means that each party is responsible to Him for keeping their vows. Jesus Christ expressed the moral obligation to faithfulness when He speaks of marriage as a union in which God is not merely the witness but also the one who makes the bond. "... the two shall become one flesh therefore what God has joined together, let not man put asunder." (Matt. 19:6) Harvey Anthony argues that, the above biblical expression or quotation may be interpreted to mean that there should be no divorce in marriage. [36]

Although, Christians are found in different cultures, they must not be governed by the cultural standards of this world.[37] Robinson says that believers are not of this world but of the kingdom of God where Christ is seated at the right hand of God.[38]

In the New Testament, it is evident that monogamy is the ideal marriage. Christ emphasised on a monogamous union instituted by God since the creation of man and woman. The teaching of the New Testament does not encourage polygamy. Paul in Eph.5:22-23 explains the responsibilities of the husband and wife to each other. It is true that the scriptures emphasise the blessings of having many children as stated in Psalm 127: 4-5; however, this is not to emphasise the need for many wives:

> Like arrows in the hands of a warrior are sons born in one's youth.Blessed is the man whose quiver is full of them. They will not be put to shame when they contend with their enemies in the gate.

It must be noted that blessings do not come to those who disobey God's commands in marriage. In the passage, God is talking about the importance and strength of children. Culture and tradition do not justify polygamous practice in Christian religion. The marital life of some heroes in the Bible is not an excuse for similar practice in the 21st century. Although, it appears polygamy is not the plan of God for man, yet we can say that plurality of wives is not an act of rebellion against God. It must be noted that great men of God in the Bible married many wives.

There is no where in the Bible that says polygamy contravenes the divine injunction. When one of the wives of Abraham, the maid of Sarah, Hagai ran away, God instructed her to go back to her mistress and submit to her. This did not show any act of rebellion rather the custom and tradition on which the Israelites operated permitted multiple wives just as it is being practised in some African churches. However, those who have gone into polygamous marriages before their conversion into Christianity should be accommodated by the church. They should not be persuaded to seek divorce which is worse than polygamy.

At the Lambeth conference of 1888 [39] there was a decision to admit polygamous converts into the Baptism and the Lord's Supper. But such people cannot become elders, deacons or leaders in the church. This is supported by I Tim. 3:1-12. The Overseer must be husband of one wife who is able to manage his children and his household well. A Christian who chooses to have a second wife for no other reason than death, must be disciplined by the church and be refused the position of an elder.

Although, the teaching of Jesus Christ on divorce and re-marriage among the Pharisees in Matt. 19: 4-5 established the position of Jesus Christ on this subject. "...He which made them at the beginning made them male and female." (Mk. 10: 1-8; I Tim. 3:2; 12; Tit.1:6). All the cited passages above show that polygamy is not encouraged in the New Testament. It seems that people who choose to be polygamous do so for personal interest. However, our focus is from the Christian perspective, nevertheless, polygamy could not be condemned out rightly.

Conclusion

Polygamy is practised in African traditional religion because of the socio- economic and political benefits attached to it. In as much as polygamy was an acceptable practice among the Israelites, it should not be seen as contravening to divine ordinances. The adoption of it by the African Churches should not be condemned either.

Similarly, polygamy is a cultural heritage among the African traditionalists. The practice therefore is as old as the religion itself. However, the adherents of Christianity who are against polygamy should allow the system to operate because it should be a matter of "live and let live". Polygamy is a traditional heritage from the forefathers of the present generation. This is not to say that polygamy is good in its entirety.

A Christian man is encouraged to marry one wife, and to maintain domestic harmony and stability. This is necessary for effective Christian witness in the world. It will also help to minimize misunderstanding, hatred and chaos among women.

Notes and References

1. W.H.R. Rivers, Polygamy in Ancient Israel in J. Hastings (ed) *Encyclopedia of Religious Ethics*, vol.8 (Edinburgh: T & T Clarks, 1918), 27
2. Christopher Ash, *Marriage, sex in the service of God*, (England: Intervarsity Press, 2005), 341
3. M.O. Igenoza, *Polygamy and African churches: a Biblical Appraisal of an African Marriage System.* (Ibadan: The African Association for the study of Religion 2003), 4
4. G.J. Wenham, *Genesis 1-15* (Waco, Texas: Word Books, 1987). P.71

5. Wenham *Genesis 1-15,* 71
6. Igenoza, *Polygamy and African churches,* 83
7. J.S. Mbiti, *African Religion and Philosophy,* (London:Heinemann Education Books Ltd. 1967), 142
8. Mbiti, *African Religion and Philosophy,* 142
9. Mavumilusa Makanzu, *Can the Church Accept Polygamy?* (Accra: Asempa Publishers, 1972). p.9 also E.O. Alana, *"Christianity and Polygamy"* in *JARS,* (Vol. 7 Ilorin: Department of Religions 1990), 17-25.
10. Remi Clignet, *Many Wives, Many Powers.* (Evanston: Northwestern University Press, 1970), 4
11. Mbiti, *African Religion and Philosophy,* 142
12. Mbiti *African Religion and Philosophy,* 142
13. J.L Giibs (ed.) *Peoples of Africa* (New York: Rine hart and Winston, 1965). pp.28-32 also wiki.answers.com/9/how_much_population2009 Tobanairaland.com/791027
14. J.F. Ade Ajayi and E.A. Ayandele, *Writing African Church History, in church crossing frontiers:* Essays on the Nature of Mission in Honour of Bengt Sundkler. (Uppsala, Sweden, Boktryyekeri; Aktiebolag, 1969) 93-94.
15. Eugene Hillman, *Polygamy reconsidered: African Plural Marriage and the Christian Church,* (Nairobi: Trans Africa Publishers Ltd. 1975),140
16. Hilaire Belloc, *Europe and the Faith,* (London: Freedom Publishers, 1920), 331
17. Igenoza, *Polygamy and African churches,* 107
18. Igenoza, *Polygamy and African churches,* 107
19. D. Russell, *Communicator's Commentary 1&2 Kings* (Waco, Texas: Word Inc. 1987) pp.129-135
20. Igenoza, Igenoza, *Polygamy and African churches,*107
21. Christopher, *Marriage, sex in the service of God,* 249
22. B.W. Anderson, *Understanding the Old Testament* (New Jessey: Prentice Hall Inc: 1975), p.158

23. Mavumilusa Makanzu, *Can the Church Accept Polygamy?* 60
24. Christopher, *Marriage, sex in the service of God*, 251
25. Hillman, *Polygamy reconsidered: African Plural Marriage and the Christian Church*,140.
26. E.A. Ayandele, *The Missionary Impact on Modern Nigeria. 1842-1914: A Political and Social Analysis* (London: Longman Group Ltd. 1991), 335
27. E.A. Ayandele, *The Missionary Impact on Modern Nigeria*, 335
28. E.A. Ayandele, *The Missionary Impact on Modern Nigeria*, 335
29. Muhamad Ididi, The New Vision Discussion Board. Wwwv152.securesites.net/bdetail.php2010
30. Mavumilusa, *Can the Church Accept Polygamy?* 45
31. Igenoza, *Polygamy and African churches*, 672-673
32. Eric, The New Vision Discussion Board. wwwnewvis2.securesites.net/bdetailphy2010
33. Eric, The New Vision Discussion Board. wwwnewvis2.securesites.net/bdetailphy2010
34. O. Kalu (ed), Christianity in West Africa, (London: Longman Ltd 1980), 12
35. E.A. Ayandele, *The Missionary Impact on Modern Nigeria*, 337
36. Igenoza, *Polygamy and African churches*, 288
37. Igenoza, *Polygamy and African churches*,228
38. D.W.B. Robinson in J.D. Douglas (ed.) *The New Bible Dictionary* (London: I.V.P. 1975). p.229.
39. Igenoza, Igenoza, *Polygamy and African churches*, 287.

CHAPTER FIFTEEN

The Obsession of Nigerians with Miracles in the Islamic and Christian Religions

Musa, Yusuf Owoyemi
Department of General Studies
University of Utara Malaysia
Sintok, Kedah Darul Aman, Malaysia
owoyemi2@yahoo.com

Introduction

Looking at the current religious situation in the Nigerian society today, a keen observer of the phenomenon will notice an unusual obsession of Nigerians with miracles.[1] It is as if to be religious is to have the power to do unimaginable things. Religion is now equated with miracle and a man of God must not only be able to perform wonders, he must also have the power to cure all kinds of illness and solve all kinds of problems miraculously – either by hook or by crook, as long as the 'job' is done nothing matters, to Nigerians, it is all miracles! Not only is the importance and purpose of religion being eroded by this misconceived belief and obsession for miracles, the religious psyche of Nigerians has been so destroyed that, to preach without the claim of having the power to perform what is beyond human capability, is to waste one's time, as nobody is ready to listen to talks of piety and living a righteous life and humility, which is the essence of all religions.[2]

To gain the attention of Nigerians, a religious preacher in any religion must not only claim to be very close to God, he must have the ability to convince Nigerians that he is now the chosen of God, to perform all kinds of miracles and must demonstrate this, even if it is by arranging people to claim being cured of their diseases and financial or economic problems after he/she had prayed for them.[3] In other words, in Nigeria today, religion means miracles and to be religious is to have the power to perform miracles. Thus, this misconception and misuse of religion calls for a thorough investigation of the purpose and role of miracle in religions generally. The questions are; does miracle necessarily equate religion? Does being religious mean having the power to perform miracles? What is the role of miracles in religion? Why and what is responsible for the present obsession of Nigerians for miracles? In answering these questions, this study will look at the role and purpose of miracles in the two revealed religions in Nigeria – that is, Islam and Christianity – since it is their activities in the nation that have led to this misconception and misunderstanding.

In carrying out this task, the definition of miracle will be the first to be looked at before exploring the role and purpose of miracles in Islam and Christianity. It is hoped that this exploration will answer the questions raised above and also provide answers to the last question raised – that is, why, and what is responsible for, the present obsession by Nigerians for miracles?

What is miracle?

The general understanding of miracle is that it is an extraordinary event beyond human capacity and capability. It refers to an event happening, or which has happened, and is beyond the comprehension and explanation of human reasoning. Sometimes, in religious parlance, it is seen as the intervention of a divine power in human affairs or, furthermore, the intervention of a foreign power in human matter which is up and above ordinary day-to-day activities of human being.

However, in order to have a clear understanding of miracle, we need to look into the dictionary meanings of the word so as to be precise and concise in answering the question, what is miracle?

According to *The Brill Dictionary of Religion*, "miracles are basically ambivalent elements of religion, as they are both expected to occur, or be believed in, as part of religious life and are also liable to arouse criticism and scepticism. Miracles occur outside the course of everyday existence, provoking both belief and unbelief."[4] The *Webster's New World Dictionary of American English*, on the other hand, defines miracle as follows: (1) an event or action that apparently contradicts known scientific laws and is, hence, thought to be due to supernatural causes, especially, to an act of God. (2) a remarkable event or thing; marvel. (3) a wonderful example [a miracle of tact].[5] Furthermore, the *Dictionary of Philosophy and Religion* defines miracle as that act or event "which causes wonder. It is ordinarily taken to apply to an event which cannot be understood as part of the natural order."[6]

From the definitions above, it is clear that miracle means something that is extraordinary, supernatural and beyond the natural law of nature and human explanation. It is usually something out of the blues, and may involve divine intervention, as in an act of God. Thus, for a miracle to take place or for a person to perform a miracle, in the case of religion, that person must possess a kind of power that is supernatural or divine in nature and which is not common among all human beings.

An Overview of the concept of Miracle

Miracle has a significant role in religion, even though it is not the essence of religion itself. It nonetheless, plays a very important role in the authentication of religion, especially in the Abrahamic religions (Judaism, Christianity and Islam). However, as significant as miracle is, it is meant to only help in convincing the adherents of the truth of their religion and act as a further proof of the presence of divine power above what man knows in the physical world. Miracle helps to authenticate the fact that there is a power above man to which he must bow and direct his worship and that as much as there are physical phenomena which follow a particular law – generally called nature – there are other phenomena which are not physical and which could be more powerful than what man knows. Furthermore, in the religions which uphold the concept of God as the overall Supreme Being, miracle helps to authenticate His power and control over ordinary and well known phenomenon and the fact that His power can override the known natural law of things, which are His creations and all come under His control and will.

Moreover, even in the religions where the concept of God is not that explicit and where what happens to one is believed to be the result of what he/she has done in the life before the present one, there is also the belief that a holy man or saint can intervene for one and remove all the evils of bad things that may happen to one. Thus, this is a form of divine intervention even if it is not explicitly called miracle.[7] Likewise, in some religions, the word 'miracle' is seldom used and what is common is the 'intervention of the gods' which could also be interpreted or seen as a form of miracle in that religion, since it involves the intervention of a divine being.

Having said the above, it should, however, be noted that miracle does happen too outside religion, as strange and supernatural phenomena are not limited to the field of religion alone. But, even if such a thing happens, it is still viewed as the working of a divine being and a divine intervention, thus, in the end it is returned to the sphere of religion, since it is only in religion that such a phenomenon is believed in and upheld as an authentic presence of God or the power of a divine being at work, as the case may be.

In the light of the above, we now turn to examine the role that miracle is meant to play in Islam and Christianity and to see, through their holy books, if performing miracles make what one is doing to be truly religious or if miracle can take the place of the essence of religion as people are being made to believe now in Nigeria.

Miracle from the Qur'anic Narrative

Islam, as a religion, does not lay much emphasis on miracle, as it is merely seen as a vehicle of authenticating the mission of the prophets of God and to convince the people that they are truly God-sent.[8] The prophets, through the performance of miracles, convinced the people of the existence of one true God and that He deserves their obedience and worship. In Islam, miracle is meant to help the people understand that before God, they are helpless, as He can do whatever He wills with them if they refuse to obey and worship Him. What Islam, as a religion, emphasises is the worship of one supreme God, Allah, obeying His commands, living a righteous and pious life, which will lead to the salvation of man in the next world where he would have to give account of all that he did in his present life. This will in turn, earn him paradise or hellfire depending on what he did while on earth. As such, Islam rarely regards miracle or gives it any special place in the scheme of thing as it is the good deeds, righteous and pious life of man that are important. In order to further highlight this assertion, we would look at some of the miracles that the prophets performed in the Qur'an, the circumstances and conditions that warranted them and what they were meant to prove to those who were witnesses to those miracles.

First, it should be kept in mind that the prophets themselves always make the people to understand that they can of themselves perform no miracle except it is granted by God Himself or with His permission. The following Qur'anic verses are quite instructive in this direction:

> Has not the story reached you (O people!) of those who (went) before you? of the people of Noah and `Ad and Thamud? and of those who (came) after them? None knows them but Allah. To them came apostles with Clear (Signs); but they put their hands up to their mouths and said: "We do deny (the mission) on which ye have been sent and we are really in suspicious (disquieting) doubt as to that to which ye invite us." Their apostles said: "Is there a doubt about Allah the Creator of the heavens and the earth? It is He Who invites you in order that He may forgive you your sins and give you respite for a term appointed!" They said: "Ah! ye are no more than human like ourselves! Ye wish to turn us away from the (gods) our fathers used to worship: **then bring us some clear authority**." Their apostles said to them: "True we are human like yourselves but Allah doth grant His grace to such of His servants as He pleases. **It is not for us to bring you an authority except as Allah permits**. And on Allah let all men of faith put their trust." (Q 14:9 – 11)[9]

From the above quoted verses of the Qur'an, one can easily understand the fact that the message that the prophets came to preach was more important than demonstrating miracles; and even if miracles were to happen, it would be with the permission of God and not their own making. Moreover, the prophets did not just perform miracles at their whims and caprices; it was the people who usually requested for it in order to be sure of the truth of what they were being called to believe in or due to their arrogance and disbelief, in case of the disbelievers. The following example of Prophet Isa (Jesus) and his disciples amply justify this assertion.

> Behold! the disciples said: "O Jesus the son of Mary! can thy Lord send down to us a table set (with viands) from heaven?" **Said Jesus: "Fear Allah if ye have faith. They said: "We only wish to eat thereof and satisfy our hearts and to know that thou hast indeed told us the truth; and that we ourselves may be witnesses to the miracle.** Said Jesus the son of Mary: "O Allah our Lord! send us from heaven a table set (with viands) that there may be for us for the first and the last of us a solemn festival and a sign from Thee; and provide for our sustenance for Thou art the best Sustainer (of our needs). Allah said: "I will send it down unto you: but if any of you after that resisteth faith I will punish him with a penalty such as I have not inflicted on anyone among all the peoples. (Q5:112-115) [Emphases mine]

Likewise, the story of Pharaoh and Prophet Musa is another example in this direction. Prophet Musa was forced to perform miracle and show Pharaoh that he was indeed sent by God when Pharaoh threatened to imprison him. "(Pharaoh) said: "If thou dost put forward any god other than me I will certainly put thee in prison!" (Moses) said: "Even if I showed you something clear (and) convincing?" (Pharaoh) said: "Show it then if thou tellest the truth!" So (Moses) threw his rod and behold it was a serpent plain (for all to see)! And he drew out his hand and behold it was white to all beholders!"[10] (Q26: 32– 33)

In addition, when these miracles happen, the prophets made it known that it was the making of God and not by their own power, as in the case of Jesus Christ:

"And (appoint him [Jesus]) an Apostle to the Children of Israel (with this message): I have come to you with a sign from your Lord in that I make for you out of clay as it were the figure of a bird and breathe into it and it becomes a bird **by Allah's leave**; and I heal those born blind and the lepers and I quicken the dead **by Allah's leave**; and I declare to you what ye eat and what ye store in your houses. Surely therein is a Sign for you if ye did believe. (Q3:49.) [Emphases mine].

Likewise, Prophet Muhammad, when he was asked by the unbelievers to punish them with the punishment of God as he had been preaching, he replied thus:

Say: "For me I (work) on a clear Sign from my Lord but ye reject Him. **What ye would see hastened is not in my power.** The Command rests with none but Allah: He declares the truth and He is the best of Judges." Say: "**If what ye would see hastened were in my power the matter would be settled at once between you and me.** But Allah knoweth best those who do wrong." (Q6:57 – 58) [Emphasis mine]

All the examples above show that the prophets were not calling people to come and receive miracles, neither were they preaching the curing of all kinds of diseases for a person who believes in God. Rather, their call centres on worshipping the one true God, obeying His commands and living a righteous and pious life as commanded by God. The prophets neither called themselves angels nor claimed to have special powers, knowledge of the unseen, nor have a special treasure of mercy or wealth, they were simply humble servants of God calling for people to believe in God, do good deeds and live a pious life. The miracles that they performed were either asked for by the unbelievers or came as a punishment for the unbelievers or asked for by the believers in order to increase their faith. Thus, miracle was not the focal point of the messages of the prophets of God; it only serves as an accessory and an avenue for the authentication of their message and mission. This, therefore, explains why miracle is not given much attention and priority in Islam.

Miracle from the Biblical Narrative

Although Jesus performed many miracles, it is also from his words that these miracles were meant to show the people that he was sent by God and that what he was telling them was nothing but the truth. The central message of his mission was to alert the people to the fact that the strict following of the legal injunctions of God as brought by Moses without love and kindness to one's fellow human being meant nothing in the sight of God.[11] Likewise, living according to these injunctions without a firm belief in God and total submission to Him does not guarantee entering paradise for the people. Thus, it will be observed that he was critical of the Pharisees and the Scribes who all claimed to be pious representatives of God but whose actions and beliefs were contaminated with extravagances, show and arrogance. It is, therefore, all these evils that Jesus came to correct and the miracles that he performed were meant to authenticate this message and to let people know that he was truly a messenger of God.[12]

When Jesus performed a miracle, what is clear from his words is that he intended to breed faith in the people through it and this faith in God was his major concern. The following incidents reported in Matthew chapter 9 verses 18 to 30 are pointers to this fact.[13]

> As He was speaking these things to them, behold, a ruler came and worshipped Him, saying, My daughter has just died, but come and lay Your hand on her, and she will live. And Jesus rose and followed him, and so did His disciples. And behold, a woman who had been suffering from a hemorrhage for twelve years approached from behind and touched the fringe of His garment, For she said within herself, if only I

touch His garment, I will be healed. And Jesus, turning and seeing her, said, **Take courage, daughter; your faith has healed you.** And the woman was healed from that hour. And when Jesus came to the ruler's house and saw the flute players and the crowd making a commotion.

He said, Depart, for the girl has not died but is sleeping. **And they laughed scornfully at Him.** But when the crowd had been put out, He entered and took hold of her hand, and the girl rose up. And this report went out into all that land. And as Jesus passed on from there, two blind men followed Him, crying out and saying, Have mercy on us, Son of David! And when He came into the house, the blind men came to Him; and Jesus said to them, Do you believe that I am able to do this? They said to Him, Yes, Lord.

Then He touched their eyes, saying, **According to your faith, let it be done to you.** And their eyes were opened. And Jesus sternly charged them saying, See that no one knows! (All emphases are mine).

Those who 'laughed scornfully at Him' have no faith and the miracle was meant to elicit that in them. This is also the case when Jesus woke Lazarus from the dead. Here there were people who also mocked and challenged him to raise Lazarus from the dead since he had made the blind from birth, see. However, in doing this miracle, he explicitly said it was done so that the people around him may believe that he was sent by God. This incident was reported in John 11 verses 1 to 45. However, the relevant portions here are as follows:

And He said, where have you put him? They said to Him, Lord, come and see. Jesus wept. The Jews then said, Behold how He loved him! **But some of them said, Could not He who opened the eyes of the blind man also have caused that this man would not die?** Jesus therefore, moved with indignation again in Himself, came to the tomb. Now it was a cave, and a stone was lying against it. Jesus said, Take away the stone. Martha, the sister of him who was deceased, said to Him, Lord, by now he smells, for it is the fourth day that he is there. Jesus said to her, **Did I not tell you that if you believe you will see the glory of God?** Then they took the stone away. And Jesus lifted up His eyes and said, **Father, I thank You that You have heard Me.**

> And I knew that You always hear Me; but because of the crowd standing around, I said it, that they may believe that You have sent Me. And when He had said these things, He cried out with a loud voice, Lazarus, come out! And he who had died came out, bound hand and foot with clothes, and his face was bound about with a handkerchief. Jesus said to them, Loose him and let him go. (verses 32 – 44) (All emphasises are mine)

However, after having done many miracles and yet many in the cities where these miracles were done still did not believe in him, Jesus cursed the cities to show that the essence of message was not fulfilled in the cities – which is the repentance of the people from their sins and faith in God and His prophet. Matthew chapter 11 verses 20 to 24 records this as follows:

> Then He began to reproach the cities in which most of His works of power took place, because they did not repent: Woe to you, Chorazin! Woe to you, Bethsaida! For if the works of power which took in you had taken place in Tyre and Sidon, they would have repented long ago in sackcloth and ashes. But I say to you, It will be more tolerable for Tyre and Sidon in the day of judgment than for you. And you, Capernaum, who have been exalted to heaven, to Hades you will be brought down. For if the works of power which took place in you had taken place in Sodom, it would have remained until today. But I say to you that it will be more tolerable for the land of Sodom in the day of judgment than for you.

Finally, pulling the rug off the feet of miracles as nothing compared to a pious life and faith in God, Jesus said the following as recorded in Matthew chapter 7 verses 21 to 23.

> Not everyone who says to Me, Lord, Lord, will enter into the kingdom of heavens, but he who does the will of My Father who is in the heavens. Many will say to Me in that day, Lord, Lord, was it not in Your name that we prophesised, and in Your name cast out demons, and in Your name did many works of power? And

then I will declare to them: I never knew you. Depart from Me, you workers of lawlessness [iniquities]. [Emphasis mine]

All the discussion above points to the fact that miracle does not mean being religious. A religious person, as Christ said is "he who does the will of My Father", that is, the will of God. Thus, this is why Jesus Christ himself said to a young man who asked him "Teacher what good thing shall I do that I may have eternal life?"[14] (That is, enter into paradise.) Jesus replied by saying "...if you want to enter into life keep the commandments."[15] In other words, keeping the law of God and living a pious life is the only ticket to paradise and not performing miracles as this has no value in the scheme of things before God. In concluding this section, it is important to quote Williams L. Reese who says:

> miracles have gathered around all of the great religious leaders, and yet most of them – including Confucius, Lao-Tzu, Buddha, Mohammed, and Christ in some of his sayings – protested against miracles and refused, at least at times, to give their followers a sign.[16]

The reason for their refusal, as we have explained before, is not far fetched. It is simply to guard against the danger of the people becoming obsessed with miracles and in the process forget the central message of their mission – which is loftier than miracles and all the 'wonders' that may come with them.

Reasons for the abuse and obsession of Nigerians with Miracles

Having explained the roles of miracle in the two popular religions in the nation and come to realise that it is just a helping mate in these religions and not their essence as it is held by the majority of the practitioners of these religions in

Nigeria now, it is pertinent at this juncture to identify and explain the reasons why there is abuse and obsession for miracles among the Nigerian masses.

It is important to note that this development is a very recent one in the Nigerian religious sphere. The obsession for miracles in Nigeria started in the late eighties to early nineties consequent upon the economic meltdown and the problem of ineffective governance which facilitated the institutionalisation of corruption. The breakdown of social and basic amenities which the people, hitherto, enjoyed but which was put beyond their reach as a result of the degeneration in the system of governance could also be advanced as reasons for the popularization of miracles among adherents of different religions in Nigeria.

Having noted the above, it is also pertinent to point out that the list for the reasons why there is an obsession for miracles in Nigeria could be endless. It all depends on how one views the situation and from which angle one is looking at the current situation of the nation. However, in this study, four major reasons are identified as being responsible for the current religious situation in the country: 1, Failure of Government, 2. Modernity, 3. Lack of Religious Knowledge and 4. Lack of a Standard Religious Regulatory Body.

1. Failure of Government,:- The failure of successive governments to make life better for the people has resulted in the people becoming frustrated. The loss of confidence in government coupled with the degeneration of government institutions and facilities has made many people to turn to religion as the last hope of a place where they could find solace and solve their problems. Although Nigerians like all Africans are religious people, that does not take away the fact

that their frustration with those in government has driven them into religion, either as a place of succour from poverty and lack of access to essential facilities or as a full time paid job.[17]

Corruption has made poverty to become entrenched in the polity, as people are denied suitable jobs and social amenities which are basically their rights.[18] Poverty has driven many to the point of doing the unimaginable.[19] Some, in the course of seeking a solution to their poverty resorted to devilish habits such as ritual killings for money, using their wives, children or even parents for ritual purposes or in exchange for money from evil spirits.[20] The situation is so bad that some even use parts of their body in exchange for money. Others build shrines, mosques or churches for the purpose of duping people or living on their little contributions or tithes. Some others have resorted to selling their children or agreeing to bear children for others all in the effort to survive.[21]

Second, many government institutions are no longer functioning. Although money is being budgeted every year for these institutions. The money is either misappropriated or embezzled. As a result people's welfare is neglected and dubious religious people capitalise on this situation to draw people into their nets with promises to help them through miracles.

Likewise, the failure of government to provide social amenities has made the people to be gullible. Many sicknesses that could easily be treated in the hospitals are now subjects of miracles as the hospitals are either poorly equipped or the masses cannot afford to pay the bills demanded. Thus, the roving Pastors and *Alfas* capitalise on this by promising to heal the people of these sicknesses and by organising prayer sessions of healing where people who they claimed to have healed come to give testimonies. This is to convince others to come to the pastor or imam. This has led to many people losing huge sums of money and property, as they are made to make a pledge of money or property to the preacher after the person is cured. All these are due to the fact that the necessary facilities and welfare programmes which the government ought to put in place are not there.[22]

2. Modernity:- Like all contemporary societies, the Nigerian society is not immune from the luxury brought by modernity. The former traditional way of life in which the people adhere to has been or is being eroded by the onslaught of modern life.[23] The craze to own luxurious things ranging from cars to mansions, to extravagant clothing, shoes and jewellery, has made people to forgo traditional values in which modesty and humility in material possession are treasured. Nigerians, in their bid to out do one another in material possession have resorted to all kinds of means in getting wealth. This, in turn, has given the fake men of God the leverage to preach about having the power to change the fortunes of people.

In the mad rush for wealth, those who are not able to compete with those in power where corruption thrives, have resorted to floating churches, mosques and shrines as their own way of amassing wealth. While they promise the people deliverance from their problems, both financial and others, they dupe the people of their hard-earned money by asking them to contribute to the 'house of God' or pledge their property to the 'Lord' so as to earn abundant reward and be blessed immensely. As the gullible fall for this, the pastors and imams ride exotic cars in convoys and fly from one part of the country to another, in private or chartered jets. The congregation who donates and gives this money live in poverty with the hope that through the prayer of the pastor or imam, they will one day live better lives too!

The breakdown of the traditional value system means people now worship those with wealth irrespective of how they get it.[24] Unlike the traditional value system where people question and reject those whose source of wealth is suspected, the modern Nigerian society warmly welcomes such people, giving them endless traditional titles and awards. Thus, one now sees traditional rulers associating with criminals and corrupt government officers.[25] The fear of God no longer checks the people, as they now see material things as the ultimate thing to live and die for. It is this same situation which leads some pastors and *alfas* to admonish any of their members who is in government to take advantage of the situation by stealing as much as possible from the government coffer because, according to them, 'this is his own chance to take his share of the national cake'! In addition to this, they assure the adherent that they have the power of prayer to protect him/her from detection and that whatever sins he/she commits will be forgiven by God through their special and miraculous intervention, as long as he/she continues to be their member and donates generously to the 'house of God'.[26] However, as is apparent to any serious and discerning religious practitioner, this assertion by these imams and pastors is nothing but a lie. In the Islamic religion, for example, the concept of *Halal* and *Haram* (lawful and unlawful) is very important when it comes to earning the means of livelihood. Islam is against any money or material which is not lawfully earned by its adherents. In line with this, when the concept of *Halal* and *Haram* is discussed in Islamic teachings, it is not related to what Muslims eat and drink alone, but includes how Muslims earn their means of livelihood and property. The following Qur'anic verses forbid Muslims from eating that which is not lawfully earned and trying to unlawfully take over other people's property through bribery, deceit and cheating:

> And do not consume one another's wealth unjustly or send it [in bribery] to the rulers in order that [they might aid] you [to] consume a portion of the wealth of the people in sin, while you know [it is unlawful]. (2:188)
> O you who have believed, eat from the good things which We have provided for you and be grateful to Allah if it is [indeed] Him that you worship. (2:172)
> [Allah said], "O messengers, eat from the good foods and work righteousness. Indeed, I, of what you do, am Knowing. (23:51)
> Indeed, those who devour the property of orphans unjustly are only consuming into their bellies fire. And they will be burned in a Blaze. (4:10) [27]

Likewise, according to the Prophet, just as Allah has commanded all the prophets to eat and spend only *Halal* things, He has also commanded the believers to follow suit and not to eat and spend things which are *Haram*.

> On the authority of Abu Huraira (may Allah be pleased with him), who said: The Messenger of Allah said: "Allah the Almighty is good and accepts only that which is good. Allah has commanded the Faithful to do that which He commanded the Messengers, and the Almighty has said: "O ye Messengers! Eat of the good things, and do right.." (Quran 23:51). And Allah the Almighty has said: "O ye who believe! Eat of the good things wherewith We have provided you.." (2:172). Then he mentioned [the case of] a man who, having journeyed far, is dishevelled and dusty and who spreads out his hands to the sky [saying]: O Lord! O Lord!-while his food is unlawful, his drink is unlawful, his clothing unlawful, and he is nourished unlawfully, so how can he be answered!" (Muslim).

In addition to the above, the following *hadith* quotations talk about the consequences that will befall a person, both in this world and in the hereafter, whose means of livelihood is *Haram*:

> Anas (may Allah be pleased with him) said to the prophet (peace and blessing be upon him) 'O Messenger of Allah! Supplicate to Allah for me to make my Du'a' acceptable.' The Messenger (pbuh) replied, "O Anas! To have an acceptable Du'a', you should eat only the Halal (Lawful) since a person may be deprived of his Dua' being answered for forty days because of eating a mouthful of Haram food." (Al-Asfahani in Al-Targhib)
> The Prophet (pbuh) said, "...Assuredly, no one earns Haram money but what he spends, gives as charity or leaves behind will be his fuel in Hell-fire. Verily Allah does not obliterate evil by means of evil, but He obliterates evil by means of good." (Ahmad)
> The Prophet (pbuh) said, "When the pilgrim, who journeys to Hajj, by Haram money, says. 'Here I am! At your service." Our Lord, here I am! At your service. Allah will say to him, "your calling is rejected and your Hajj is valueless." (lbn Hajar)
> He [The Prophet] (pbuh) also said, "Whoever purchases a garment by ten dirhams which contain a Haram dirham, Allah never accepts his prayer as long as he wears this garment." (Ahmad)
> The Messenger of Allah (pbuh) said, "On the Day of Judgment, there will come some people with righteous deeds which are as huge as the Mount of Tuhamah. These righteous deeds would be soon scattered and invalidated. Consequently, those people would be thrown into Hell-fire." The Companions (may Allah be pleased with them) wondered, "O Messenger of Allah! How would this happen!" He (pbuh) replied, "Those people used to perform Prayer, fast, give Zakah and offer Hajj, but they used to consume Haram so Allah invalidated their righteous deeds." (Tabarani) [28]

Thus, from all this, it is apparent that the imams (and pastors) lie when they promise their adherents deliverance from sin in a miraculous way when they steal government money or earn their means of livelihood illegally. The only solution to earning illegally is to return what has been taken back to whoever it belongs to because even if one gives it in charity, it is not accepted as a good deed because of the illegal way in which it was acquired in the first place – although some scholars hold that if by giving it away in charity the giver does not hope for a reward, he/she will be absolved of the sin of eating or spending haram.[29]

> Ibn Mas'ood (ra) narrates that The Prophet (pbuh) said, "A slave of Allah who acquires haram wealth and gives charity from it, it is not accepted from him. If he spends from it, he does not have any blessing (barakah) in it. If he leaves it behind him (i. e. he dies) it will be a means of taking him to the fire (of Hell). Verily, Allah does not wipe out evil deed with evil deed; instead, He wipes out evil deed with good deed. Indeed, the repulsive does not wipe out the repulsive." (Musnad Ahmad, Sharh Assunnah; Mishkaatul Masaabih, pg. 242)

3. Lack of Religious Knowledge: -Many Nigerians lack the basic knowledge of the religion they practise. They depend on hear-say about their religion instead of reading and studying about it themselves. Many will quote their pastors and imams endlessly without referring to their holy books or traditions. They place so much trust on these men of God to the extent that they accept whatever they hear from them as the divine words of God without question, even if these are against common sense and the teachings of the religion itself. They seem to forget that these men are human and fallible in their understanding and interpretation of the holy texts and that by reading and studying these messages themselves, they, the congregation, could gain insights into their religion and be better guided.

Some pastors and imams know little about the religion. Most of them became religious leaders because of the economic situation as a way out of poverty and not because they are qualified to lead. The little they know is the basic knowledge; but because the people themselves know nothing, they become leaders with this little knowledge. This is why many of them engage in activities that are contrary to the teachings of their religion.

Since their focus is on miracles, some preachers prefer to learn devilish and diabolic occult practices with which they deceive and hypnotise the people rather than taking their time to learn about the religion. Thus, lack of the basic religious knowledge of the people has contributed in a big way to their seeking miracles which these dubious preachers make them believe is the essence of religion.

4. Lack of a Standard Regulatory Body for Religions:- Although there are some bodies that see to the affairs of religions like the Christian Association of Nigeria (CAN) for Christianity, the Nigerian Supreme Council for Islamic Affairs (NSCIA) and others for Islam and some other Traditional Religion Associations for the Traditional religions, all these bodies are mere associations with no constitutional powers to sanction and prosecute any offending person or groups.

The knowledge that one could get away with whatever he/she does in his/her religion has given some of these dubious pastors and imams the audacity to say and preach anything. This is why some of them have the boldness to come out and say that they hold regular meetings with God and His angels. Some even declared themselves the anointed or chosen one of God sent to the people in the present time. Some others have even claimed to be god incarnate. There is the need for a regulatory body in each of the religions which can check these excessive and illogical claims, and if necessary prosecute and ban the perpetrators. Thus, until there is a regulatory body or bodies for religion, the activities of these fake men of God may not be curbed and the obsession for miracle by Nigerians will not diminish.

Conclusion

It is clear from the discussion above that miracles are not the essence of Islam and Christianity and that they are merely accessories which are done to validate the message of a prophet when he is challenged by the unbelievers or when they are requested for by the believers in order to strengthen their faith. Thus, the notion that miracles can be equated to Godliness is a misconception and a way employed by dubious and irreligious people to dupe and swindle people of their money and property.

It is also clear that being religious and living a pious life is a different thing entirely from having the power to perform miracles and that the former is more commendable than the latter in all ways imaginable, as miracles could be done even through the power of the devil and other occult means which are all against the teachings of religion.

It was also established that the present obsession for miracles by Nigerians is a recent development brought about by four major factors which resulted from changes in the social structure of the nation brought about by the failure of government to give the people the basic necessities of life due to corruption, erosion of traditional values by modernity, lack of religious knowledge and the absence of a religious regulatory body which could effectively check the excesses and false claims of dubious men in religious garb.

Notes and References

1. For some of the news items on this and videos go to "miracles in Nigeria" in www.google.com; also specifically see these websites www.youtube.com/watch?v=7CIHPor_haA www.youtube.com/watch?v=FR4NMs09H6Q, (accessed on March 7, 2014).
2. See www.christianpost.com/Missions/General/2007/09/nigerian-pentecostalism-thriving-on-miracles-prosperity-promises-16/index.html, (accessed on March 7, 2014).
3. See these news items on the following websites for confirmation of this assertion http://www.globalnewsnig.com/end-time-pastor-chris-oyakhilome-sells-his-miracle-clothes-for-multi-million-naira-%E2%80%A6-his-fake-miracles/; http://www.omg.com.ng/2013/08/winners-chapel-others-shut-down-in-cameroon-over-fake-miracles/; http://www.osundefender.org/?p=135941 (accessed March 7, 2014).
4. Kocku von Stuckrad, ed., *The Brill Dictionary of Religion*, Vol. III, (Leiden; Boston: Brill Publishers, 2007), 1230.
5. Victoria Neufeldt and David B. Guralnik (eds.), *Webster's New World Dictionary of American English*, third college edition, (15 Columbus Circle, New York: Prentice Hall, 1994).
6. William L. Reese, *Dictionary of Philosophy and Religion*, New and Enlarged edn., (New Jersey: Humanities Press International Inc., 1996), 485.
7. This is applicable particularly to Buddhism.
8. See Muhammad Salim, *Miracles in Islam*, (Kuala Lumpur, Malaysia: Pustaka Antara, 1991).
9. All the Qur'anic references in this section are taken from Muhammad Yusuf Ali's English Translation of the Holy Qur'an in *The Alim (computer file): the world's most useful Islamic software*, by Shahid N. Shah, (Houston, Texas: ISL Software Corporation, 1996).

10. See Qur'an 26: 15 – 33) for the full story of this event. Also see the story of Prophet Noah and his people concerning this issue in Qur'an (11: 25 – 44).
11. See Ismail Raji Al-Faruqi, *Christian Ethics: A Historical and Systematic Analysis of its Dominant Ideas*, (Kuala Lumpur, Malaysia: A. S. Noordin, 1999).
12. See the Holy Bible in Matthew chapters 5 to 7 for the teachings of Jesus on these assertions.
13. All the Bible quotations used in this paper are taken from *The New Testament: Recovery Version*, (Anaheim, California: Living Stream Ministry, 1991).
14. The Holy Bible, Matthew Chapter 19 verse 16.
15. The Holy Bible, Matthew Chapter 19 verse 17.
16. William L. Reese, *Dictionary of Philosophy and Religion*, 485.
17. See Toyin Falola & Mathew M. Heaton, *A History of Nigeria*, (Cambridge, U. K.: Cambridge University Press, 2008); Peter Lewis, "From Prebendalism to Predator: The Political Economy of Decline in Nigeria" in *Corruption in the Developing World*, Robert Williams & Robin Theobald, eds., (Cheltenham, U. K.: Edward Elgar Publishing Limited, 2000); also some of these articles on these websites give an insight to the level of corruption in Nigeria www.africaeconomicanalysis.org/articles/gen/corruptiondikehtm.html ; www.boston.com/news/world/africa/articles/2004/12/17/corruption_costs_nigeria_40_percent_of_oil_wealth_official_says/; http://www.hrw.org/en/news/2007/01/30/nigeria-corruption-and-misuse-rob-nigerians-rights (accessed March 7, 2014).
18. See www.hrw.org/en/news/2007/01/30/nigeria-corruption-and-misuse-rob-nigerians-rights (accessed on March 8, 2014).
19. See this article on poverty in Nigeria http://aderinola.wordpress.com/2007/06/09/mass-poverty-in-nigeria/ (accessed on March 8, 2014).

20. See http://www.csicop.org/sb/show/ritual_killing_and_pseudoscience_in_nigeria/ (accessed on March 8, 2014).
21. See http://news2.onlinenigeria.com/news/top-stories/169757-ijeoma-okafor-lagos-mother-sells-her-children-to-survive.html ; http://www.bbc.com/news/world-africa-22484318 ; http://allafrica.com/stories/201401310108.html ; (accessed on March 8, 2014).
22. See Chimobi Ucha, Poverty in Nigeria: Some Dimensions and Contributing Factors, Global Majority E-Journal, Vol. 1, No. 1 (June 2010), 46-56 http://www.american.edu/cas/economics/ejournal/upload/Global_Majority_e_Journal_1-1_Ucha.pdf ; http://www.irinnews.org/report/71787/nigeria-basic-services-a-challenge-to-nigeria-s-new-leaders ; (accessed on March 8, 2014).
23. See Dare Arowolo, The Effects of Western Civilisation and Culture on Africa, Afro Asian Journal of Social Sciences Volume 1, No. 1 Quarter IV 2010 http://www.onlineresearchjournals.com/aajoss/art/53.pdf ; Mwalimu George Ngwane, The Erosion of Traditional Values in Our Christian Homes http://www.gngwane.com/2012/03/the-erosion-of-traditional-values-in-our-christian-homes.html (accessed on March 8, 2014).
24. See Brian-Vincent Ikejiaku, Political Corruption, Critical Governance Problem Facing the Nigerian State: Comparative Assessment of Various Regimes, *The Journal of African Policy Studies Volume 16 No. 2, 2013*. http://www.academia.edu/1555571/Political_Corruption_Critical_Governance_Problem_Facing_the_Nigerian_State_comparative_assessment_of_various_regimes (accessed on March 9, 2014); Faloore O.O., Political Corruption And Poverty In Nigeria *African Journal for the Psychological Study of Social Issues Volume 12 No. 1-2, 2009*

25. "While you are stealing and taking the people for a ride, remember to have four sets of insurance: the backing of your traditional ruler; the backing of your pastor or imam and those of *marabouts* or *babalawos*; payments to *timbers* and *calibers*; and also, look for a pool of journalists to either write in your favour or have enough clout to kill the story." Quoted from www.nigeriansinamerica.com/articles/2773/1/Akin-Oshuntokun-and-Nigerias-History-of-Corruption/Page1.html (accessed on March 9, 2014); also see http://www.nigeriavillagesquare.com/articles/uche-nworah/the-role-of-traditional-rulers-in-an-emerging-democratic-nigeria.html (accessed on March 9, 2014); http://allafrica.com/stories/200710180133.html; Ashara Dennis Uche, Strengthening and Building Partnership in the Fight against Corruption: The Role of the Family and Traditional Institutions At the 3-Day International Conference on Corruption, Governance and Development in Nigeria by the Aminu Kano Center for Democratic Research and Training, Mambayya House, Bayero University – Kano in Conjunction with UNECA and UNDP, December 6 – 8, 2011. http://www.academia.edu/3596760/Strengthening_And_Building_Partnership_In_The_Fight_Against_Corruption_The_Role_of_the_Family_and_Traditional_Institutions (accessed on March 10, 2014).

26. See http://www.sundaynews.co.zw/index.php?option=com_content&view=article&id=37557:miracles-or-money-calls&catid=43:entertainment&Itemid=135#.Ux76TD-SzGA; https://www.ministrymagazine.org/archive/2010/04/miracles-in-nigeria; http://www.theatlantic.com/international/archive/2013/12/in-nigeria-miracles-compete-with-modern-medicine/282517/ (accessed on March 10, 2014).

27. All the Qur'anic quotations in this section are taken from Saheeh International, *The Quran (Arabic Text with Corresponding English Meaning)*, (Saheeh International Publisher, 1997).
28. All the Hadith quotations in this section are taken from *The Alim (computer file): the world's most useful Islamic software*, by Shahid N. Shah, (Houston, Texas: ISL Software Corporation, 1996).
29. See Effect of Haram Food and Haram Earnings, http://as-sahabah.org/index.php/islamic-library/54-haram-food-and-haram-earnings (accessed March 10th, 2014.)

CHAPTER SIXTEEN

Traditional Religion and Ethical System of the People of Isiala-Mbano Local Government Area of Imo State, Nigeria

Patricia Ebere Nwazonobi
Department of Philosophy and Religion,
Faculty of Social Sciences and Humanities,
Ebonyi State University, Abakaliki-Nigeria.
patricianwazonobi@gmail.com
+2348037760765, +2348079759085.

Introduction

This work investigates what the people of Isiala-Mbano Local Government Area of Imo state cherish as values and what they hold in contempt in their religion and ethical system. In Isiala-Mbano tradition, there is no clear cut demarcation between religion and ethics because they are closely interwoven. The connection is hard to grasp because morality is both inside and outside religion.[1] Religion exerts a force and makes a contribution in creating new standards, morals and ethics suitable for any changing society.

The major characteristic of Isiala-Mbano religious life is its variety, communality and utility which exists in the number of gods/deities, shrines, places where they are sited, worshipped and the method and manner of worship. Notably, the evil or sin is not committed against the deities alone but against all the inhabitants of the land. For instance, the punishment for the sin of one man could be visited on the kinsmen, sometimes on everybody. Also, the blessings of the gods are shared by all. When closely observed in any worship is for benefits or pleading for atonement for sins committed individually or communally. "Even when the authority of a deity has been established through evidence of sorts, someone may ask: what if I refuse to obey the order of a god?"[2] Religion has an answer to that: the god may intervene directly and deal with a disobedient man by subjecting him to misfortune, illness and death. Deviant behaviours which were shunned and discriminated against to discourage people from engaging in them became an accepted way of life both to the Christians and traditional society. It is disheartening watching everyday as Western religion superimposes itself on cherished cultural values of the people of Isiala-Mbano as if it has a better moral and ethical principles.

The people of Isiala-Mbano seem to be attracted to Christian religion because of its ostentatious nature which shields deviant behaviours of its adherents and condemns traditional religious and ethical system as evil and barbaric. Threat of boycott of the burials of Christians who compromise with traditional systems compels the people to succumb to the pressure of Christianity irrespective of the discomfort and alienation from one's culture. The desire for dignitaries and crowd during burials gave Christianity domino effect to override traditional values since it has manipulated and depopulated traditional practitioners. Ethics or morality has traditionally been perceived in purely religious form.[3] It is important to document the religious ethical system of the people of Isiala-Mbano to save it from extinction and encourage the people to be proud of their traditional religion and ethics and avoid self-defeating syndrome which has sidelined the rich and cherished culture.

Traditional Religion and Ethical System in Discourse

The view in this academic discourse is what religion and ethics are in the traditional African society as perceive by some scholars of religion and ethics. Actually, African traditional society like any other traditional society is shrouded with several religious sentiments and that inform certain practices that seem mystifying. The sentiments and practices have their overt manifestations in their understanding and definitions of life and death. Both have religious and mystic significances and as such have overt effect on the development of African religious thinking, which run contrary to western Christian thoughts. The consequence therefore is that African people of Isiala-Mbano found themselves at religio-spiritual and cultural cross-road without knowing where to go, since their cultural foundations have been eroded by modern development of western Christianity. This position undermines the autonomy of religious culture and ethical values of the people. It was Smart[4] that affirms nature of this ethical autonomy of every religious culture when he avers that 'every religion has as a set of social and ethical norms or ethical dimension'. He sees religion as a representation of feelings and answers to living questions implicit in life. In expressing the 'implicit' side of the questions and answers stressed the connection between religion, meaning and values, here Smart spelt out the logical relationship between religion and morality and intimate relationship between ideologies, religion and politics. In solving the puzzle, Smart asked, "How does a religious morality differ from a secular or common-sense one? He explains that a religious morality perceives morality from itself as being not just morality, but also something religious.

In the same vein, Amadi[5] became concerned with the effects of religion and how people have used religion positively and negatively to achieve their goals in life. He maintained that, "Religion has played a particularly important role in the ethical philosophy all down the ages because it has been a useful instrument for enforcing moral codes". Consequently, Geisler[6] evaluates ethics in terms of morals and mores in terms of ethnicity. What is morally right is what the community says is right. Community demands are the ethical commands. Each society creates its own ethics. Whatever similarity may happen to exist between moral codes in different social groups is simply due to common needs and aspirations, not to any universal moral prescriptions.

Against this backdrop, Stott[7] approached religion and ethics from the perspectives of social and moral dilemma dating from the wanton torture of animals for sport, the bestial drunkenness of the populace, and the inhuman traffic of Africa Negroes, the kidnapping of fellow countrymen for exportation as slaves. The morality of parish children, the universal gambling obsession, the savagery of the prison system and penal code, the welter of immorality, the prostitution of the theatre, the growing prevalence of lawlessness, superstition and indecency, the political bribery and corruption are religious and moral issues. Stott further points at the ecclesiastical arrogance and truculence, the shallow pretensions of Deism, the insincerity and debasement rampant in Church and State such manifestations suggest that British people were then perhaps as deeply degraded and debauched as any people in Christendom. Stott's observation is not far from the problem facing Nigeria particularly, Isiala-Mbano Local government Area of Imo state, Nigeria.

Indigenous Religion of the People of Isiala-Mbano Local Government Area of Imo State

Isiala-Mbano does not have a central clan deity rather, practises decentralised religion, which is the worship of God through inanimate objects. Each community operates, based on what it considers sacred in its environment but the deities of *Iyiafo, Duruemezuru, Amadioha, Ikenga*, the earth goddess (*Ala* or *Ahiajoku*), ancestral worship (*Ndiichie*), *Umune* (Ancestral link) and *Ofo* (Staff of justice) which control other deities exist in every community in Isiala-Mbano. *Ala, Ogu* (the guide to all ethical judgments) and *Umune* play both religious and ethical roles and would be better discussed as ethical concepts. Smart and Horder[8] in their edited work add that every religion has a set of social and ethical norms (ethical dimension) that anchors on doctrines, myths and values relating directly to belief.

Each village has its own deity (*Agbara*), groove and sacred forest (*Uhu-ala*). Also, every village has sacred trees like *Egbu, Ogwu, Akwu, Ogirishi, Aboshi, Ngwu* and so on. There were (and still are) family shrines, where members of the family gather to worship and minister to their dead ancestors with libations and incantations. The worship usually takes place at *ibari/obi* whether family, kindred and village squares. Individual shrines *uhu- chi* existed for individual worship which was sited according to the specification of a diviner (*dibia-afa*). *Iyiafo* is a female deity of irascible and rash decision that acts at the least provocation in any matter on merely mentioning its name. On this note, *Iyiafo* was invoked to avenge in any injustice done against the weakling especially women. Its shrine is situated either in the market or village square. It sometimes even serves as family deity according to the need and myth of its origin in its enthronement in the environment.

The *Amadioha* deity had its prophets called *Ndi- ubu*, Seers and Diviners.[9] *Ndi-ubu* could forecast an event before it happened though most of these Seers worshipped *Amadioha*, the god of thunder and dreaded for their spiritual prowess. They used to operate at midnight when everybody was asleep. They would start by making incantations around their environment and after obtaining permission from *ala* (earth goddess) would then walk out to the open. One peculiar thing about *Ndi- ubu* is that they would never walk past the *Ojukwu* palm tree unless permission is granted to them by the spirit through incantations.[10] It is *ndi-ubu* that is invited to cut down anyone who commits suicide by hanging, perform the necessary rituals before the corpse is buried. The symbol of *Amadioha* is a white tusk known as *Odu-Amaioha*.

There was also the worship of *Ikenga*, the god of wealth, affluence and bounty, whose symbol is the right thumb signifying strength, wealth and endurance. If a man's *Ikenga* is not strong enough, he would be considered to be destined to be poor all his life. In addition, there was and still is the *Agwuishi* deity, which is the cult of traditional doctors; is blamed for insanity, hard- luck, poverty, lack of direction and so on. Whenever anyone goes out of his or her usual behaviour, the person would be asked if *Agwuishi* is in control of such actions. In case of insanity, it would be proved beyond reasonable doubt that *Agwuishi* is not responsible through divination before exorcism or medication would commence.

In addition, children are perceived as guarantee for retirement benefits, security against external aggression, continuity of the lineage, tools for befitting burial to parents and to inherit whatever is left of the parents at death.[11] If on the contrary, a man dies without a son to inherit him the first son in the family buries him and inherit his belongings including his wife, daughters, *Ofo* and title. This type of inheritance is called "*Irimkpe onye nwushiri ebo*". It is based on this reason that every Isiala- Mbano and Igbo man struggles to have male offspring, to inherit his property and name at death. Primogeniture is strictly practised and there is a great value for male sex.[12] The type of paragraph practised in Isiala- Mbano is hereditary (*Opara-mpunala*). The exact meaning of this is that when an *Opara* dies his *Opara* takes over and acquires the position of the father and dominates every member of the family including his father's siblings irrespective of his age. There is no exception to the rule even to titled men and their thrones. The *Opara* inherits a lion's share of the father's assets and in most cases because of their greedy nature would confiscate all and leave others with nothing. This act of greed forces other members of the family to wander far and wide for greener pastures.[13] In Osu and Ugiri Clans, the last son inherits the mother but in Mbama clan the first son dominates all. Any *opara* that dies before the father loses out of inheritance no matter the number of sons he has. Therefore, a recognised first son (*opara*) is the one who is alive to bury his father.

If within one year of the death of an *Ozo* title holder, his first son gives a goat and performs the ceremony of inheritance and offers other prescribed items to the *Ozo* title holders in his zone, in redemption of his father's title, then he is considered to be qualified to hold onto his father's title for life. He occupies the same position as his father and will take the father's share for life. "The inherited *Ozo* title is almost at the same level with a full-fledged *Ozo* title that was conferred, although the holder of the inherited *Ozo* is not given the '16' commandments of the confraternity, not urinated for, and no water would be poured for him".[14] He simply inherits what the father had.

Traditional Ethical System of the People of Isiala-Mbano Local Government Area of Imo State

In Isiala-Mbano tradition, there is no clear cut demarcation between religion and ethics because they are closely interwoven. But for the sake of our discourse which anchors on ethics, it becomes necessary to extract ethics as much as we can from religion. In order to have orderly social life, there is need for agreements, understandings, principles, or rules of procedure to ascertain the rightness and wrongness of actions in any given community. The family takes precedence over other social structures in Isiala-Mbano therefore; marriage is accorded a great respect as the foundation of the family system. The true values of human life as perceived in Isiala-Mbano include respect for elders; 'community fellow-feeling, as reflected in communal land tenure and ownership; a live and let live' philosophy; altruism (including medical and economic variants of it), and hospitality. Hence, honour is given to elders and it is in this regard that their advice is likened to the power of an oracle. At the same time, chastity, truthfulness, the virtue of contentment and other related values play indisputable roles in the moral assessment of individuals, community, nation and the larger society. Therefore, logical degree of contentment stimulates good neighbourhood. Greed is shunned while moderation is esteemed as a virtue. Extended family system encourages communalism; therefore, individual members assist one another to achieve their goals in life.

Reincarnation (*Ilo-uwa*) plays a vital role in the traditional ethical system of Isiala-Mbano. There is a strong belief that an individual's personality and character traits revolve around the individual's incarnate. Therefore, it is common to hear someone vow that she/he would not reincarnate with a certain trait again in his/her next life. Usually, when someone is too zealous about any issue, people around would always wonder if she/he pursues that same course and failed in his/her last reincarnation. If a person portrays any negative or positive personality or character trait, the cause of the trait is quickly attributed to the person's previous incarnate.

The earth goddess, *Ala,* assumes an enviable and important position in Igbo religion which Isiala- Mbano is a part of. The moral breaches and transgressions against *Ala* attract mystical sanctions. In addition, expiatory sacrifices are performed whenever there is any breach of any moral order to appease the earth goddess. The shedding of blood of a kinsman or any other evil against a kinsman is considered to be *ochu* and *aru,* respectively against *Umune* and the earth goddess. There are taboos or ritual avoidances which custom prescribes for holding specific offices or positions.

Umune is the mythical origin of a family or kindred. It is a spiritual bond of oneness of the family or kindred. *Umune* is the eternal link of brotherhood in Isiala-Mbano; the arbiter in intra family or intra kindred disputes. Nobody would dare transgress *Umune* or the offender could die or experience series of horrendous incidents. It is the shrine of justice and truth. The symbol is kept in the family or kindred *Ishi- obi.* An accused may be required to swear by *Umune*, then a year after the oath and no evil befalls him, his innocence is accepted but if any bad incident happens to the accused within one year of swearing the oath, he would be considered to be guilty and might be penalised according to the crime committed. An offence against *Umune* is regarded as the highest moral evil. Again, if the offence committed is murder (*ochu*) or manslaughter (*oghom*), a living human sacrifice was required to expiate the evil consequences on the land.[15] Anyone used in such expiation invariably became an *osu-umune*.

Each ancestral link (*Umune*) has an *Obi* which is an institution that unifies *Umune*. It is a taboo for one to betray a kinsman or commit evil of any kind against a member of the ancestral link. Nwokoro, Ezekwem & Ugboaja[16] express that *Obi* is the institution of ancestral authority of the patriarchal maximum lineage whose central authority in the family, kindred and village organogram is known as *Ishi-obi*. The *Opara* is the head of *Umunna* and represents the ancestors. His symbol of office is the "*Ofoukwu*" (the *big* staff of justice). The *Oparaishi-obi*'s *Ofo* is called *Ofoukwu* because it controls individual *Ofo* and the *Umune*. *Ofo* is the symbol of power and strength and a nexus to the spirit of the departed. With *Ofo*, an *Nze* or intending *Ozo* title aspirant would be able to communicate with the gods and ancestors, and place curses on those who offend him and bless those who are in favour with him. *Ofo* is administered to detect source of crime and culprits in communities. The *Ofo* is seen only when there is need to appease the spirit of the ancestors, or to invoke justice. Moreover, any member of the family who dies without an issue is buried by the *Ishi-obi* and the dead member's property would be returned to *Ishi-obi*. In this regard, *Ogu* is the incantation of the eldest *Ofo* holder. Before the administration of the *Ofo* oath, *Ogu* will precede it because the person(s) taking the *Ofo* oath will state his or her claim to the land in dispute thus:

I/we state here before the *Ofo* that the land is mine/ours and if I am lying, may the ofo kill me/us, and the *Ofo* holders will hit the *Ofo* hard on the ground and say, "*had*" four times representing the market days of *Eke, Orie, Afor* and *Nkwo*.[17]

Ofo holders therefore, were revered and held in high esteem. On regular basis live animal is sacrificed and the blood sprinkled with care on the *Ofo*. The *Ofo* looks very black with stains of blood, bits of kola nuts, alligator pepper, and other items that may have been placed on it over the years to appease the gods and ancestors. If one's father had an *Ofo*, the tradition is that the eldest son inherits the *Ofo*, which may have passed from generation to generation. In circumstances of where those whose fathers had an *Ofo* may not seek for a second *Ofo*. Though for purposes of personal identity, one whose father had an *Ofo*, will be called *Ofonta* while his father's, grand fathers' or great grand fathers would be called *Ofoukwu*. "A man may have many sons who may also aspire to have an *Ofo* or the *Ozo* title, each of them will certainly go through the process of 'putting a mouth' on their father, by performing the aforesaid ceremony of having his own *Ofo* and *chi*".[18]

Ogu is regarded as a moral guide that ascertains the rightness and wrongness of one's action. *Ogu* is the moral force, that potent spur of righteousness, which drives the innocent against his aggressor. *Ogu* also functions as warning, advice, judgement, prayer, defence and so on. The symbol of *Ogu* is represented with stick but the generally accepted stick is *Ogirishi*. This stick could be fresh (*Ogu-ndu*) or dry (*Ogu-okpoo*) depending on the purpose to which it is issued. All individuals are advised to hold *Ogu* firmly in every aspect of life for peaceful coexistence. When there is any misunderstanding among people, the aggrieved person(s) could issue *Ogu* to the offender through a friend or relative to express his/her anger against the offender. If it is a fresh *Ogu* that is issued, then it means that the aggrieved does not want the incident to repeat itself. But if it is a dry one it means that the offence is severe. In other words, the offender is advised to retrace his steps and keep away from the aggrieved person.

There is a general consensus that any act of sorcery against another without justification (*Oguziri-ezi*) will neither harm nor kill the victim. In the face of conspiracy, injustice, oppression and humiliation the assailant is always advised to operate on the right *Ogu* in order to avoid the wrath from the supernatural. Similarly, the victim is advised to hold *Ogu* for the assailant to attract vengeance from the supernatural. *Ogu* in this regard comes in terms of, prayer/invocation, pouring of libation (*Itummai/owurummai*) by men while the women nod their clenched fist on the ground (*Igo aka-ala*) as they pour out their grievances. This last mentioned type of *Ogu* has claimed the lives of many and wrecked havoc in many homes. When this judgement is observed, it is assumed that *Ogu* is against the assailant (*Oguamanaya*). *Oguamanam* (*Ogu* should not be against me), *Ogundu* (literarily means fresh *Ogu* but actually depicts that long life anchors on uprightness), *Oguzie* (Right *Ogu*). In order to check some excesses an *Ogu* must be issued which depicts warning. *Ogu* is an anchor to which ethics operates in Isiala-Mbano. Therefore, the people of Isiala-Mbano should be issued an *Ogu* (*Gbajiige ogu*) for relegating their religious and ethical system to the background.

In Isiala- Mbano, capital crimes and development issues are discussed at clan level. Hence, morality from the point of views of Ikenga- Metuh, Ahunanya, Uzoigwe & Iheakanwa[19] are 'clan and community centred' rather than universal morality. The child is taught to shun cruelty, betrayal, injustice, humiliation but embrace acts of dignity, nobility and self contentment.

Marriages within villages, communities and clans of Isiala-Mbano were approved while the ones outside were highly discouraged for fear of adulteration of religion and culture and corruption of good manners. It is easier to investigate the background of intending couples within an environment than elsewhere. Those who were involved in distant marriages were taunted and humiliated with a derogatory name "*O purun'uzoburumkpara*" meaning someone who picked fiddlestick on the way. Today such discrimination rarely exists because of westernisation. Besides, it has become a trend in marriage.

The Rape of Religious-Ethical System of the People of Isiala-Mbano since August 27, 1985

Besides the humiliation Christianity and Westernisation subjected African Traditional Religion which is the pillar of the religion and ethics of the people of Isiala-Mbano, suffered much rape and humiliation since August 27, 1985. Wealth and riches were not appreciated or celebrated by communities unless the source of it is ascertained to be through hardworking. Titles and leadership positions were given to people of virtues, honour, proven integrity and dignity to foster good moral behaviours among the people. The Ibrahim Badamosi Babangida's military regime from August 27, 1985 to August 27, 1993 ushered in moral bankruptcy, fraud (419) that swept away what was left by Christianity in our religious and ethical system in Nigeria, Igboland inclusive.

The era of fraud "419" Obtaining By Tricks (OBT) which had its boom between 1987-1996 and enthroned "robbery" as a means of livelihood not only in Isiala-Mbano but to the entire Nigerian nation. The pioneers of "419" were extravagant enough to attract recognition and admiration of a greater population of the people. As a result, the lucrativeness of fraud attracted more apprentices than any other business. Those apprentices whose luck have not clicked before the General Sani Abacha Military Government introduced Decree "419" to nab fraudsters were trapped in confusion and frustration. The climax was the "Otokoto" saga of 1996 which brought a hot chase to all illegal transactions in Imo state. This was the era of kidnap of corpses that belong to prominent personalities from the mortuaries and demand for ransom before the corpses would be released to their families for burial. Little Anthony Ikechukwu Okonkwo, a groundnut hawker was beheaded by Innocent Ekeanyanwu a gardener at Otokoto Hotel Amakohia Owerri. Ekeanyanwu in his confession implicated wealthy businessmen and politicians which led to revolutions, trials and judgements on the head-hunters fraudsters and so on with Otokoto and Leonard Unaogu as key players.[20] Notably, there was a paradigm shift from skills/trades particularly, the type of apprenticeship that the boss establishes the former after an agreed number of years of service due to the abuse of the terms of agreement to "419"apprenticeship.

There is a paradigm shift from education and the honour accorded to it since the introduction of "419" in 1985. Nwazonobi[21] observes that graduates were given undefendable blow as dropouts who are fraudsters and traffickers acquired the wealth the graduates could not acquire in spite of their education. The most degrading aspect of it is that many graduates are unemployed and still depend on their relatives financially and in some cases have gone to these fraudsters and people from other spheres of life for financial assistance. This has discouraged parents from training their children in tertiary institutions. The youth on the other hand, have become demoralised in their academic pursuit and have resorted to vile means of making money. Therefore, education is gradually becoming a top show for the female sex in Igboland but predominantly in Isiala- Mbano Local Government Area. Educated women attract more suitors than uneducated ones. Even, roadside mechanics in the neighbourhood want to marry educated women to supplement what is lacking in them. While some educated men prefer to marry the wives they would educate in tertiary institutions. Days are gone when the girl child is given out in marriage to sponsor the boy-child's education or establishment.

The Destruction of Religious and Ethical System of the People of Isiala-Mbano by the Church

Is it right for a visitor to take over a-master's bedroom while the host takes over the guest room? This is demonstrated in the religious activities of Christianity and African Traditional religion in the neighbourhood. The communities in Isiala-Mbano have the norms, values and standards of living which determine the religious, ethical and moral behaviours of the people which stipulate sanctions and punishment for offenders. Religious leaders do not directly make policies but do exercise a great deal of cultural power in society.

The Church interferes and destroys the administration, norms and standards of the people of Isiala-Mbano thereby stripping members of the community and leaders of the power and authority. For instance, the church places sanctions on any member who participates in traditional festivals, masquerades, last bridal wealth of a dead married woman before her burial; discussing circumstances that led to a deceased and subsequent punishment which deter people in the community from being brutes to one another. A deceased family and the community have no right again to decide when to bury their decease relations rather the Church decides when and how it would be else they would not be part of the burial. This incident is worst practised in the Anglican denomination. As if that is not enough, a specified quantity of raw food is taken to the Anglican clergymen of the parish the deceased belonged to before they would come for the burial of their member. Is this not a likely sin committed by the two sons of Eli in 1Samuel 2:12 that earned the name, "Worthless men". Ilogu[22] observes that,

> Therefore the Church in Igboland grew up, as it were, divided away from the cultural roots of Igboland to wear an additional toga of foreignness other than the foreignness that belongs intrinsically to the gospel itself as a "colony of heaven" on earth.

Is the Christianity practised in Nigeria different from that of Ghana? In Kenyasi No. 1, Asutiffi North in Brong/Ahafo region of Ghana the church does not run the affairs of the community. At death the family affected reports to the traditional ruler who in turn alert the Church the decease belonged to and fix time. The Church neither fixes time nor decides text of the burial. They live their religious and ethical lives without the interference of the Church. This is visibly seen in the way the Ghanaians wear their traditional attires at ceremonies as the culture stipulates for each whether in the Church or civil gathering.

The Isiala-Mbano traditional religious and ethical life was there before the advent of Christianity and its westernisation.

But Christianity with its ethnocentric behaviour seems to have domino effects on the people as it attracts more crowds at burial than African Traditional Religion. It is considered a great honour crowd at burials. Why would people be bared for associating with their kinsmen in the name of religion thereby alienating them from their cultural environment? Again, it seems there is a misrepresentation of the 'gathering of the brethrens' as instructed in the Bible by the church leaders in Igboland. Does it mean that if you are a member of a church you no longer belong to your community? It is necessary to ascertain the reasons behind these sanctions and alienation from identifying with their fellow citizens. In other words, if members of the Church attend cultural dances and the likes, the Church would be empty and lose the money that would be realised as Tithes and offerings.

The threats of denial of burial rites by the Church make the people vulnerable especially to those who are advanced in age. When those who are advanced in age consider all they have committed in the Church they find it difficult to lose their life investment in the Church and have no choice than to be a slave so as to pull crowd at burial. Religion, Marx held, was a significant hindrance to reason, inherently masking the truth and misguiding followers as is seen here that Christian religion is a hindrance to self-realisation and self-actualisation to the people of Isiala-Mbano. Every religion is the product of a particular culture within which it grew.[23] Its doctrine reflects the worldview of that culture, its understanding of reality, and its way of looking at things, at that particular time. In order to have orderly social life, there is need for agreements, understandings, principles, or rules of procedure to ascertain the rightness and wrongness of actions in any given community. However,

> Religious suffering is, at the same time, the expression of real suffering and a protest against real suffering. Religion is the sigh of the oppressed creature, the heart of a heartless world, and the soul of soulless conditions. It is the opium of the people (Karl Marx: 1818-1883).[24]

As it stands today, parents cannot give names to their children without the consent of a clergyman of the Church they belong else the child will not be baptised with the name. Usually parents give name to their children based on their life circumstances or situations that led to the birth of the child which is in compliance to the religion and ethics of the people of Isiala-Mbano. Authentic human development acknowledges the human and the rights of that person as essential to human life.[25] Clergymen award titles indiscriminately to people with questionable characters as far as they could afford the cost. Men of virtues and fear of God without money are sidelined in favour of the rich.

The Consequences of Self-Defeating Syndrome of Traditional Rulers in Isiala-Mbano Local Government Area of Imo State

The traditional rulers and priests are supposed to be the custodians of whatever their people hold sacred, moral and ethical principles that foster virtues and good moral behaviours. Would it be an exaggeration to say that traditional rulers and priests in Isiala-Mbano are stripped of their duties and obligations by the government and Church thereby relegating them to mere ceremonial heads? In Nigerian traditional religion, the priests of *Ifa*, *Amadioha*, *Chukwu* and other gods still act as intermediaries between men and gods and interpret their commands, which often contain patterns of behaviour.[26] Leadership without authority and power is like wearing a tie on bare body. Are the communities supposed to be under traditional rulers or the Church? Why an alien religion would be so domineering that it swept away all the moral codes and disciplinary measures used in curbing deviant behaviours? Is it not right for the traditional rulers to give Church leaders the codes of conduct for operating in their territory? Jehovah witness has faced banned in Cuba, the United States, Canada, Singapore, and Nazi Germany because of their religion's doctrine of political neutrality (Persecution of Jehovah's witnesses).[27]

Traditional rulers and Church leaders are competing for who would give the highest title. Titles are no longer for heroes, virtues, morally upright individuals but for whomever that could afford it financially irrespective of the source of the money. Traditional leadership used to be hereditary. The emergence of fraud (419), Obtaining by tricks (OBT) brought about politics in traditional leadership. Some people who made money through vile means usurped power from poor traditional rulers in compliance with political elites undauntedly making their leadership unpopular.

Effects of Devaluation of Traditional Religious and Ethical System on National Development

The practice of any religion without commitment to the moral way of life is an abomination before the supernatural. The adherents of African traditional religion (*Ndi o ji ofo*) as practised in Isiala-Mbano Local government Area genuinely committed to their religion without considering the religious economy. Besides, judging from antecedents of moral uprightness, traditional believers are morally upright than their Christian counterparts. Omoregbe[28] adds that, "Those who corruptly enriched themselves through immoral means are greatly Christians and Muslims who throw their religion and morality to the wind as soon as they see money. Where religions and government fail in the welfare of the people due to corruption and mismanagement of resources the people are subjected to untold hardships.[29] It is noteworthy that an immoral way of life is a foolish and self-destructive way of life, and it can never lead to happiness or self-fulfillment especially when one is detached from one's root.

The people of Isiala-Mbano are like a fish doped out of the sea and so are their Igbo counterparts that are completely rooted out of their moral culture which horizontally shuns corruption, dishonesty, fraud, selfishness, embezzlement of public funds and other infamous acts. The superimposition of alien religion (Christianity) which is vertical in approach did not specify any punitive action but rather, preaches repentance and forgiveness. From the antecedents of ethical principles, moral code and moral guide by both Christianity and African Traditional religion, it seems the later welds more power to the people than their Christian counterparts in case of moral behaviours, peace and unity. This gave leverage to all manner of evil not only in the place of discourse but in Nigeria as a nation. It is only religion that is truly sensitive to the fullness of man's dignity, nature and potentialities; man cannot live by politics and science alone.[30] If *Ofo* and *Ogu* are to be applied in our daily activities there would not be cases of stealing, embezzlement of public funds, and all kinds of vices because as it applies in one locality another group enforces their own moral code then, public office holders would shun corruption.

Recommendations

It is important to document the religious ethical system of the people of Isiala-Mbano to save it from extinction. There is need to revitalise communalistic ethics in which the main criterion of goodness is the welfare or well-being of the community. Such ethics will create the enabling environment conducive to an alternative development; supporting a truly human development.

The people of Isiala-Mbano should stop idealising a befitting burial or attach much importance to mammoth crowd that participate in one's burial ceremony because the Church have seen how much they idealise crowd in burial and decide to use it to control their religious and social lives.

Any Christian denomination operating in Isiala-Mbano Local Government Area should allow the people (the members) to participate in communal life of the people which anchors the religious and ethical system because it is difficult and disheartening to separate humans from their shadow. Any denomination which refuses to comply or respect the moral code of the people of Isiala-Mbano should be banned from operating in the environment.

The Church leaders should allow parents to give their children names according to their heart desires and life experiences especially Igbo names. A name depicts the Igbo cultural values, philosophy and worldview hence, must not be linked to *Chi* or *Chukwu* (God) or, a Biblical name which depicts Jewish culture and philosophy before it must be accepted. The Anglican Communion in Imo State should reverse the rule of taking their food at burials raw. They deserve preferential treatment but not in this regard. They can be served cooked food and drinks in an inner room but not compelling bereaved families to bring specified quantities of drinks and raw food to their parsonage before they would officiate in any burial ceremony.

It is time to revert back to moral etiquettes as observed in the traditional religion and ethics of the people of Isiala-Mbano because it has a powerful hold on the moral life of the people than the imposed Christian ethics which allows evil to triumph indefinitely until judgement day.

Conclusion

The major characteristic of Isiala-Mbano religious life is its variety, communality and utility which exists in the number of gods/deities, shrines, places where they are sited, worshipped the method and manner of worship. Religion exerts a force and makes a contribution in creating new standards, morals and ethics suitable for our changing society. The Christian religious actors in Isiala-Mbano have turned Christianity to an association instead of track to salvation and moral building. Its doctrine reflects the worldview of that culture, its understanding of reality, and its way of looking at things, at that particular time. Religion has played a particularly important role in ethical philosophy all down the ages because it has been a useful instrument for enforcing moral codes.[31] While man formulates the moral code, he enlists the influence of religion for its enforcement. In other words, in Isiala-Mbano ethics, man proposes, god enforces *"onye kwe, chi ya ekwe."*

The people of Isiala-Mbano Local Government Area should not sit back and watch an alien religion to sweep off their cherished values. The conversion of souls is not the problem but destroying shrines, grooves, sacred trees, objects and functions is unacceptable. Relegating things like *Ofo-na-ogu*, reincarnation, ritual of umbilical cord, ancestors, and so on to the background is a disservice to the people. The Europeans and other parts of the world today come to Africa to buy symbols of deities and masquerade because they ignorantly destroyed those things in the past and now have realised their mistakes by buying from African nations to replace what they lost. Also, they come to Nigeria in the disguise of tourism to watch masquerades and other traditional dances and functions, then why do we want to abandon our own to embrace the solitary life of the whites which they are tired of ? The Christian religious actors are actually doing a disservice to our traditional religion and ethics for self aggrandisement and enrichment not really for salvation of souls.

Presently, most individuals in African nations are divided by self-interest; in other words assume that the common good would take care of itself. As a result, communal decision-making and participatory development are conveniently ignored thereby making mockery of democracy. If authentic human development is to take place, an alternative development is required that takes the people's rights be it religious, civil or communal rights seriously.[32] In other words, Isiala-Mbano should not be lured to be like Northern Nigeria where Islamic religion has stepped down their indigenous religion to the background.

Chapter Sixteen | Patricia Ebere Nwazonobi, in
Y.A. Quadri, R.W. Omotoye & R.I. Adebayo (Eds)
Religion in Contemporary Nigeria
London, Adonis & Abbey Publishers

Notes and References

1. John Stott, *Issues Facing Christians Today: New Perspectives on Social and Moral Dilemmas.* (London. Marshall Pickering 1990),145.
2. Elechi Amadi, *Ethics in Nigerian Culture.* (Nigeria. Heinemann Educational Books Ltd 1982), 4.
3. Gerard A. Bennaars, *Ethics, Education and Development: An Introductory Text for Students in African Colleges and Universities.* (Nairobi. East African Educational Publishers. 1993), 14.
4. Ninian Smart, "What is Religion" in *New Movements in Religious Education.* Smart, N. & Horder, D. Ed. (London. Maurice Temple Smith Ltd 1975), 13-22.
5. Elechi Amadi, *Ethics in Nigerian Culture,* 6.
6. Norman L. Geisler, *Christian Ethics: Options and Issues.* (Britain. Apollos 1995),18
7. John Stott, *Issues Facing Christians Today: New Perspectives on Social and Moral Dilemmas,* 38
8. Ninian Smart, "What is Religion" 24.
9. Edwin Ugboaja, *The Story of the Last Five Centuries 1500 -2000.* (Enugu. Okoro K. C. International Press 2002).28; Tasie, J. C., Uzowuru, M. I. & Ohuabunwa, C. C., 54, 59, 61 years, (Personal interview at Umuelemai, Isiala- Mbano Local Government Area of Imo State on April 14, 2013).
10. Edwin Ugboaja, *The Story of the Last Five Centuries 1500 -2000,* 29.
11. Patricia E. Nwazonobi, "Polygamy in Dialogue with Ethics: A Case Study of Isiala-Mbano Local Government Area of Imo State, Nigeria" in *Ilorin Journal of Religious Studies.* Vol.3, No.2. (Ilorin. Department of Religions, University of Ilorin 2013), 117-131.
12. Edwin Ugboaja, *The Story of the Last Five Centuries 1500 -2000,* 30.

13. Samuel O. Nwazonobi, 60 years (Personal communication at Okwelle- Amauzari, Isiala-Mbano Local Government of Imo State on December 28, 1991).
14. Ahunanya Ekwem, *Amauzari Proper*. (Port Harcourt. CANECC Nigeria Limited 2006), 218.
15. Samuel O. Nwazonobi, Sunday Ibeawuchi, 58 & 68 years (Personal communication at Okwelle- Amauzari, Isiala-Mbano Local Government of Imo State on December 30, 1989 & July 6, 2013)
16. Erastus Ezekwem, 70 & Ambrose Nwokoro, 64 years (Personal interview at Mbama Clan, Isiala-Mbano Local Government Area, Imo State on April 14, 2013).
17. Ahunanya Ekwem, *Amauzari Proper*, 218.
18. Ahunanya Ekwem, *Amauzari Proper*, 218.
19. E. Ikenga- Metuh, *Comparative Studies of African Traditional Religions*. (Onitsha. IMICO Publishers 1987,8 & Ahunanya, P. I., Uzoigwe, L. C. & Iheakanwa T. T., 45, 48, 50 years, (Personal interview at Ugiri Clan Isiala-Mbano Local Government Area of Imo State on April 16, 2013).
20. Mimi Ubini *A Must Read: The Otokoto Ritual Killings of 1996* Retrieved on January 9, 2016 from www.mimiubini.com/2015/07/a-must-read-otokoto-ritual-killings-of.html
21. Patricia E. Nwazonobi, *Women Liberation: A Case Study of Amauzari Indegenous Society in Isiala-Mbano Local Government Area of Imo State*. A Project Submitted to University of Port Harcourt, Faculty of Humanities, Department of Philosophy and Religion 2000),6.
22. Edmund Ilogu, *Christianity and Igbo Culture*. (New York: London. NokPublishers, Ltd 1974),230
23. Joseph Omoregbe, *Ethics: A Systematic and Historical Study*. Nigeria. (Joja Educational Research and Publishers 1993), Xiii.
24. Karl Marx (1818-1883) *Karl Marx on Religion: How Religion Affects Social Inequality*. Retrieve on July 16, 2015 from

http://study.com/academy/lesson/karl-marx-on-religion-how-religion-affects-social-inequality.html

25. Gerard A. Bennaars, *Ethics, Education and Development: An Introductory Text for Students in African Colleges and Universities.* 8.
26. Elechi Amadi, *Ethics in Nigerian Culture*, 6
27. "Persecution of Jehovah's witnesses" (2015). Retrieved on February 15, 2015 from http://en.wikipedia.org/wiki/Persecution_of_Jehovah%27s_Witnesses
28. Joseph Omoregbe, *Ethics: A Systematic and Historical Study*, Xiii.
29. Patricia E. Nwazonobi, P. E. (2015). "Humanism, Religion and Terrorism" in Contemporary Journal of Inter-Disciplinary Studies (65-76). Vol. 2 No. 2. Netherlands. Academic Network Publishing.
30. John Mbiti, *African Religions and Philosophy*. (London. Heinemann 1969), 274.
31. Elechi Amadi, *Ethics in Nigerian Culture*, 5.& Ibeawuchi: T. K. 72 years (Personal Interview at Anara, Osu Clan in Isiala-Mbano Local Government Area of Imo State on April 14, 2013)
32. Gerard A. Bennaars, *Ethics, Education and Development: An Introductory Text for Students in African Colleges and Universities*, 8.

CHAPTER SEVENTEEN

The Trends of Application of Islamic Legal System in Yorubaland of Nigeria

H.A. Abdulsalam
Department of Religions,
University of Ilorin, Nigeria.
abulsalam2619@gmail.com
+2348035749228

Introduction

The *Sharī'ah* as a path to be followed encompasses the whole life of a Muslim as it librates him from the servitude to other than Allah.[1] It will be recalled that prior to the establishment of the British rule in Nigeria particularly in both Northern and Western part of Southern protectorates (Yorubaland), Islam had been in existence. Muslims were in large number in the Northern areas which were largely under the rule of the Sokoto caliphate. Uthman b. Fudi and his lieutenants had ruled the North before the advent of the British conquerors[2]. On a similar note, Islam had been established firmly in Yorubaland some centuries before the British. Though there was no formal Islamic government in Yorubaland as obtained in the North.[3]

With the advent of the British rule, three interacting systems of law were identified in Yorubaland. These were customary law, a general term for the legal tradition of the Yoruba people; *Sharī'ah* (Islamic law) which applies to the Yoruba Muslims by virtue of their religious beliefs; and general (British) law which was received from the British conquerors.[4] The implication of the above submission is that before the establishment of British institution in Nigeria customary law governed the aspects of matrimonial relationship in Yorubaland[5]. This is not, however to suggest that the *Sharī'ah* law was never applied in the area, particularly where the rulers were Muslims.[6] The practice of the *Sharī'ah* law was well established among some Yoruba Muslim communities. The *Sharī'ah* thus became a part of culture within the circle of some Yoruba royal families before the British rule.

The name Nigeria (Niger-area) has its origin in the river Niger which traverses the country from North-West to South[7]. A cross road of Africa since ancient times; this area constituted of many republics and princely states which formed part of what was known as the belt of the great-Empires of the Western Sudan[8]. Nigeria is regarded as the most populous African country with diverse ethnic and cultural mix of almost 160 million people, some 250 ethnic groups, and about 500 languages, occupying an area of 923,768 square kilometers (356,699 square miles).[9] Today the principal groups in the country- Nigeria are in the North, Fulani, Hausa, Kanuri, Nupe and Tiv; in the South are Annang, Edo, Ibibio, Igbo, Izon, Itsekiri, Urhobo and in the West, Yoruba the focus of this paper.

The Yoruba

In ancient times, just as today, west of lower Niger lay the home of the Yoruba.[10] The Yoruba have several traditions about how their people began life. One of such traditions explains that it was at Ile-Ife, which Yoruba regard as the cradle of their nation that mankind was first created[11]. Another tradition tells the story of a great ancestor and hero, Oduduwa. He is said to have come from far in the east and settled at Ile-Ife and it was from there that his descendants went out to rule the various branches of the Yoruba.[12] One of his sons, for example is said to have become the first Alafin of Oyo, one of the leading Yoruba towns that first experienced *Sharī'ah* practice before the advent of British colonization during the reign of Alafin Oba Lawani Agogoja (1905) the first Muslim Alafin as well as the father of first Oba (King) of the second dynasty of Benin.[13]

Whatever the historical antecedent to the emergence of Yoruba ethnic group, the group is the biggest of the ethnic groups that live in the South of River Niger, and Yoruba is the convenient descriptive terminology that is applied to this ethnic group. The term Yoruba is also used for their language with its variety of dialects. The dialects include Ekiti in Ekiti State, Ijebu and Egba in Ogun State, Ijesa, Igbomina and Ife in Osun State.[14] The area now known as Oyo, Osun, Ondo, Ogun, Ekiti and Lagos States will herein be referred to as Yorubaland.

Sharī'ah practice before the advent of colonization

Islam had a long history in Yorubaland, having penetrated unplanned and unannounced long before the political disintegration of the Old Oyo Empire.[15] This accounts for the fact that today, Muslims form a reasonable percentage of the population in the area. Yoruba people had their earliest contact with Islam through Hausa states and some West African countries in about the 15th century.[16] It is difficult to be precise about the date of entry of Islam into Yorubaland because it was adopted in private capacity of the individuals. What is certain is that in the 17th century, mention was made of Muslims in Yorubaland. This is to say that Islam had reached southern Nigeria long before the *Jihad* of Uthman bn

Fūdī in 1804.[17] This assertion is very close to the view that Islam came to Yorubaland towards the close of the 18th century.[18]

An eminent Yoruba Muslim scholar, Shaykh Adam Abdullah al-Ilori opined that Islam had been known in Yorubaland particularly in the place known as Oyo-Ile since the 13th century C.E. during the reign of Mansa Musa, the king of Mali.[19] By 1830, some Muslims had penetrated the interior of Yorubaland from the Northern Nigeria through Ilorin.[20] Notable among these scholars were Ahmad Qifu and 'Uthman bn Abi Bakri who came to Ibadan during the reigns of Oluyedun and Bashorun Oluyole respectively.[21]

Uthman bn Abi Bakri was a learned scholar who hailed from Katsina, a seat of Islamic learning at that time. He had earlier settled down in Borno and later moved to teach and preach Islam in the south in places like Ijebu-Ode, Abeokuta and Ibadan.[22] He was made the Imam of Ibadan Muslim community on his arrival there.[23] Evidently, Islam was established before 1840 in Ardra-Badagry, Igboho, Ijaiye, Ikoyi, Iseyin, Ketu, Lagos and Oyo.[24] It thus showed that by 1840, there was a considerable degree of Islamization in Yorubaland. In many of the large towns, there were some sprinklings of Muslims. Owu contained many Muslims before the distruction in 1825.[25] Badagry also had some Muslim communities whose colourful celebrations of *'idul-fitr* was watched? by Lander on 27th March 1830.[26] It could therefore be understood from the above historical records that Islam was not new in many towns and villages of Yorubaland before the advent of British rule in Nigeria.

Before the establishment of British institutions in Nigeria in 1914, customary law governed all aspects of judicial administration including matters relating to matrimony.[27]

Inspite of this, *Shari'ah* law was applied to the Muslims particularly where the rulers happened to be Muslims. With this position, the Muslims were conscious of the fact that law that had to do with their religion should be applied to them. Thus, *Shari'ah* became a part of their culture within the circle of some Yoruba Royal families before the British rule as earlier inferred. For example, in Iwo, a prominent town in Yorubaland, Oba Momodu (as spelt by the Yoruba people) Lamuye (d.1906) appointed a *Qadi* in his court to adjudicate in cases affecting his predominant Muslim subjects in accordance with the provision of the *Shari'ah* law.[28] By inference, it could be understood that the *Shari'ah* practice had been in operation before the advent of colonial rules which amalgamated Nigeria in 1914 and introduced different institutions on Nigeria soil.

In addition, two students named Lawani and Muhammad served consecutively as *Qadis* (judges) in the same town (Iwo) and decided cases relating to matrimonial issues of the Muslims.[29] At Ikirun, Late Oba Aliyu Oyewole, the 7th Akinrun of Ikirun (d.1912) appointed a *Qadi* in 1910 to adjudicate on matters relating to Islamic cases.[30]

Although, *Shari'ah* was not an official law operating in Yorubaland, before the advent of the colonization, the fact remains that *Shari'ah* was in practice in some notable towns in the area as discussed above. It could then be understood that North was governed by the *Shari'ah* as against the South which was governed by the customary law. The difference between the two protectorates could therefore be attributed to the existence of the caliphate through the *jihad* of 'Uthman b. Fudi and his lieutenants. One of the main reasons why *Shari'ah* was not fully entrenched in South-West was due to the fact that there were intra ethic wars in the area between the 18th and the

19th centuries which surely had adverse effects on the application of Islamic law.[31]

From the above submission, it can be understood that the *Sharī'ah* practice, among the Yoruba Muslims before the advent of the colonial masters and the amalgamation of the two protectorates, (North and South) was restricted to communities where their rulers were Muslims. Few notable towns had been mentioned in this respect. This was the situation before the arrival of the British colonialists. The implication of this situation was that majority of the rulers in the area were non-Muslims and this led to non- co-ordination of their socio-religious and legal activities. While, non-Muslim rulers held tenaciously to their religious beliefs and took to customary practices in matters relating to legal issues, the few Muslim rulers adhered strictly to Islamic legal practices particularly on the issues relating to matrimony.

As briefly mentioned above, the intra-ethnic wars contributed in no small measure to the application of Islamic law in the area,[32] and this largely, as submitted by Ajetunmobi affected the Muslims in their bid to establish *Qadi* courts, inspite of the fact that by 1894 Islam had gained ground in the entire Yoruba land and the general pattern of life of the Muslim community was conducted in conformity with the *Sharī'ah*. In this regard, Ajetunmobi agreed that:

> In the period 1861-1894, a most striking feature of the development of Islam was the further entrenchment of Muslim in the political set up of many of these (Yoruba) towns and the corollary movement towards the establishment of an Islamic state.[33]

The above quotation summarises the ability and efforts of the Yoruba Muslims before the colonization to come together as a body asking for the entrenchment of *Sharī'ah* into their body politic and as a constitutional rights. They were able to do this through the patronage of societies with Islamic bias, having realized the fact that they were not as formidable as their counterparts in the Northern protectorate where majority of the rulers were Muslims and *Sharī'ah* was easily established. This submission is corroborated with Ajetunmobi's statement that:

> Muslim rulers of Kanem-Borno and Hausa Fulani Empires did not only enforce the application of the Maliki doctrines of Islamic law like their counterparts all over West Africa but they complementarily attempted to re-organize the fiscal system of empires to conform with the *Sharī'ah*.[34]

The above statement is no doubt a testimony to the fact that *Sharī'ah* practice was more pronounced, even before the colonialists, with North than what was obtainable with southern protectorate regarding the application of law. Thus, efforts would now be made to look at the status of the Sharī'ah after the colonization of the territory called Nigeria.

The status of the *Sharī'ah* after the colonization in Yorubaland

When the British colonialists arrived Nigeria, *Sharī'ah* was neither the official legal system nor was Islam the state religion among the Yoruba Muslims of the South as was the case in the North except Ilorin. The *Sharī'ah* practices in some notable towns mentioned earlier on were disbanded by the colonialists in 1918.[35] The abolition was due to the understanding of the contents and effects of the *Sharī'ah* in the Sudan and British protectorate. To the British government, the criminal aspect of *Sharī'ah* otherwise known as *hudud* (crime and punishment) in which Allah directs that offenders should be punished was too harsh. One of such directives has to do with theft where Allah declares "And as for the male thief and the female thief cut off (from the wrist joint) their right hands as a recompense for that which they committed" (Qur'an 5:38). This directive to them (colonialists) is considered too harsh and inhuman, repugnant to natural justice whereas the purpose is to serve as deterrent to others.

The colonialists alleged that the *Sharī'ah* administration was not only too harsh as earlier said but against humanity. With the abolition of these courts, the cases hitherto adjudged in the courts were taken to the Mosques by the Muslims for consideration. Thus, the influence of *Sharī'ah* legal system was prevented from further growth in Yorubaland. This means, in effect, that aspects of the law that regulate the day-to-day life of Muslims were not totally prevented but they were not incorporated into the body of their law. The implication of this is that the Islamic legal practice had been technically or indirectly schemed out of the legal policy of the government.

In 1900, the statute of General Application was imposed by the British on the people of Nigeria. This further caused the eclipse of *Sharī'ah* applications in Southern Nigeria. Hitherto, there were customary courts in all the states of the study area. For example, in Lagos the customary courts had and still have civil jurisdictions only while in other states, i.e. Oyo, Ogun, Osun, Ondo and Ekiti, the courts exercise both civil and criminal jurisdiction on a number of cases.[36] The adoption of legal pluralism (combination of British legal system and Nigerian customary/*Sharī'ah* law) for the area by the British colonizers had been caused by variety of factors, ranging from ethnic heterogeneity, adaptation of Islamic law and subjugation to foreign (British) rule.[37]

Despite this legal harmony, Muslims in the area were allowed to contract marriage in accordance with the dictates of the *Sharī'ah* law, but the resolution of disputes which may arise there from have to be settled in accordance with the customary law as against the law used in the contract of the marriage. Muslims frowned at this development because proper administration of legal procedure will never be obtained in such a customary court. It must be placed on record that in the customary courts, an Islamic aspect was integrated in which a Muslim with or without much Islamic studies background would be appointed to administer justice with *Sharī'ah* dispensation. This is as a result of the influence of Islamic practices that permeated the area. In those courts Muslims are being considered for appointment as Presidents or members of the customary courts as against the practice some years back. From the available record, Muslims are in majority in most of the courts in Osun, Oyo and Lagos states.[38]

Meanwhile, the effect of the appointment of these Muslims could not be felt seriously because the appointed members were handicapped in the discharge of their responsibilities. This is because they could not adjudicate on cases with the *Sharī'ah* since they have to base their decisions on customary laws whose features are not necessarily that of the *Sharī'ah*. In addition, the members were not originally learned in the *Sharī'ah* law. As such, they could not adjudicate in line with the principles of Islam. However, the appointment of the Muslims personnel either as President or members of the customary courts is an indication that, to a certain extent, all forces or agents of discrimination against Muslims have been reduced but not totally eliminated.

Agitation of *Sharī'ah* Courts in Yorubaland

Agitation for the establishment of *Sharī'ah* court in Yorubaland is not new. It is as old as the religion itself in their respective domains. Buttressing this position, Ajetunmobi submits that:

> It is of note that Muslim Akus in Fourah Bay, Freetown, were given "the priviledge of having their own *Qadis* courts for a while". On their return to Lagos late in the nineteenth century, Lagos Muslims petitioned Governor Carter to allow them disperse justice with the *Sharī'ah* like their fellow Muslims in India.[39]

As can be deduced from the above statement, Muslims in Lagos then were forced to forward in 1894 the petition by the unsatisfactory nature of British legal system to their environment. However, there was no favourable response to the petition despite the fact that the petition was very well articulated by the signatories who were prominent and enlightened Muslims in the town. They were Muhammad Shitta Bay, Yusuf Shitta, Al-Imam Ibrahim, Ahmad Tijani, Othman Animashaun and many others.[40] In Oyo State, it is on record that in 1938, the Ibadan Muslim community requested from the colonial masters that they should be allowed to apply *Sharī'ah*.[41] If a petition had been written at such a time, it can be concluded that Muslims in Yorubaland, like their counterparts in other parts of the Muslim world were conscious of the role Islam should play on them by advocating the dispensation of justice with the *Sharī'ah*.

In 1976, the National Joint Muslim Organization (NAJOMO) also sphere-headed a petition to the Constitution Drafting Committee set up by the then Military Government demanding the establishment of Sharī'ah courts in Ogun, Oyo and Ondo States.[42] In the early eighties during the second republic in Nigeria, National Council of Muslim Youth Organization (NACOMYO) renewed the agitation by forwarding a powerful petition to the administration of Governor Bola Ige for the implementation of *Sharī'ah* provision at the state Assembly as provided by Nigerian Constitition.[43] To the dismay of the Muslims in Oyo State then, the petitions were turned down which nearly set the state ablaze as demonstration was organized by the body (NACOMYO) to arouse the feelings of the Muslims in the state.[44]

These petitions bear eloquent testimony to the fact that the Yoruba Muslims are not only conscious of their religion – Islam, they are conscious of their needs and rights. It is amazing to note at this juncture that from our research,[45] it is observed that the law governing the dissolution of Christian marriages despite the fact that, they were conducted in the court Registry in line with the Christian doctrines and principles, had been removed from the aegis of the Yoruba customary courts to the High Court. It is considered pertinent that Muslims marriage dissolutions should equally be removed from the customary courts to give both religious practitioners (Muslims and Christians) equal right in all states requesting for it. Thus similar jurisdiction could be established to cater for the Muslims. In view of this, one subscribes to the view that:

> In the same token, if Muslim courts cannot be established to try Muslim marriage dissolution, customary courts must be re-organized to dissolve such in the law with which it was contracted.[46]

If this quotation is adopted, the plight currently being faced by the Yoruba Muslims in particular and in their matters relating to matrimonial issues and their allies, would be completely removed. The simple reason is that the parties involved in marriage dissolution would enjoy the fruits of their labour as the position of the divorced husband and wife would be properly placed. The legal effects, in addition to full understanding of their legal rights, would be adequately determined. These include among other things, observance of *iddah* as contained in the Glorious Qur'an (Q2:229), children's custody and maintenance as well as determination of their paternity.

Establishment of Independent *Sharī'ah* Panels

Of recent and upon the earlier demands of the Muslims in the area of our consideration, regarding the entrenchment of *Sharī'ah* into their judicial system, a renewed effort was made by the Muslims to establish on their own, different independent *Sharī'ah* panels to adjudicate upon matters relating to their lives. The Muslims swung into action consequent upon the historic re-introduction of the *Sharī'ah* in Zamfara State and other northern states of the country and refusal of the states in Yorubaland to yield to their request. The efforts of the National Council of Muslim Youth Organizations (NACOMYO) earlier on mentioned could not be glossed off in this respect. The Council mounted series of awareness programmes on the importance of *Sharī'ah* application among the Yoruba Muslims.[47] It is therefore to the credit of the Council that different Independent *Sharī'ah* panels were established.

The official launching of the Oyo State Independent *Sharī'ah* Arbitration Court took place at the Central Mosque Ibadan on May 1st 2002. On 11th December 2002, the inauguration of that of Lagos State took place at Abesan Mosque, Ipaja, Lagos. The Sharī'ah Committee of Ogun State was inaugurated on 3rd of June, 2003 while that of Osun State was inaugurated at the Osogbo Central Mosque on April 23rd, 2006.[48]

To the credit of members in different states mentioned above, people of sound Islamic legal education background were appointed to administer justice with the *Sharī'ah* in those panels. For example, in Lagos State, all the judges are degree holders in Law[49] and they operate like other *Sharī'ah* courts established by the Government in the Northern states of the country. It is interesting to note that the panels set up had a wider jurisdiction than even the early Muslims' demands whereby only matrimonial issues would be considered at those courts. Cases or matters relating to disputes emanating from imamship tussles and inheritance are being considered by the panels. Some criminal cases of self-confessed adulterers and consumption of alcoholic drinks were equally treated and they were publicly cained.[50]

Conclusion

In view of the above submission, it is our candid opinion that the establishment of *Sharī'ah* courts in these states, particularly states that are yearning for its establishment, is long overdue. To the Muslims, the *Sharī'ah* is divine in its origin, human in its subject matter and application, ideal in the principles, scientific in its methods, democratic in its spirit, comprehensive in the scope and dynamic in its nature. Thus the system adopted in the Northern States, where Muslims are given free hand to seek redress in the court of law in accordance with what they believe and practise especially on issues relating to their lives, should be adopted in the study area.

In conclusion, Islam is a religion in full harmony with the nature, life and man's social conditions and circumstances. It efficiently handles diverse problems and conjectures of marital relations between man and woman inside a family and a society. It presents in its attitude to life a perfect and flawless system. Thus Yoruba states wishing to do justice to matters of their lives should be given the opportunity to do so, in order to allow the much publicised freedom of religion entrenched in the constitution of the Federal Republic of Nigeria,[51] to be felt by all and sundry.

Notes and References

1. Abdur-Rahman I. Doi, *Shari'ah: The Islamic Law*, London, Ta-Ha Publishers, 1990, 2.
2. T.G.O. Gbadamosi, *The Growth of Islam Among the Yoruba (1841-1908)*, London, Longman Group, Limited, 1978, 4.
3. M.A. Ajetunmobi, "Shari'ah Legal Practice in Nigeria (1956 – 1963)," Unpublished Ph D Thesis, Department of Religions, University of Ilorin, 1988, 13.
4. H.A. Abdulsalam, "Matrimonial Issues Among Yoruba Muslims of Nigeria," Unpublished PhD Thesis, Department of Religions, University of Ilorin, 1997, 21.
5. E.I. Nwogugu, *Family Law in Nigeria*, (Heinemann Studies, n.d) xv.
6. J.N.D. Anderson, *Islamic Law in Africa*, London, OUP 1971, 56.

7. Raph Uwechue, (Ed.) – *Africa Today*, Africa Books Limited, 1986, 1160.
8. Raph Uwechue,
9. I.O. Oloyede, "Politicising the Divine, Theologising the Mundane: The Cross-Currents of Law, Religion and Politics in Nigeria" in B.O. Yusuf et.al (eds) *Topical Issues in Arabic and Islamic Studies: Essays in Honour of Late Professor A.A. Gwandu;* NATAIS, 2014, 2.
10. Raph Uwechue, *Africa Today*.
11. Bolanle Awe, "The Rise of Ibadan as Yoruba Power". Unpublished Ph.D Thesis, London, 1964, 1
12. Bolanle Awe, "The Rise of Ibadan as Yoruba Power", 3.
13. Raph Uwechue, *Africa Today*, 1161.
14. Bolanle Awe, "The Rise of Ibadan as Yoruba Power", 2
15. T.G.O. Gbadamosi, *The Growth of Islam Among the Yoruba*, 4.
16. T.G.O. Gbadamosi, *The Growth of Islam Among the Yoruba*.
17. T.G.O. Gbadamosi, *The Growth of Islam Among the Yoruba*.
18. T.G.O. Gbadamosi, *The Growth of Islam Among the Yoruba*.
19. A.A. Al-Ilori, *Al-Islam fi Naijiriyyah*, n.p. 1978, 33
20. Samuel Johnson, *The History of the Yorubas*, Lagos, C.S.S. Bookshops, 1921, 26.
21. A. Babs Fafunwa, *History of Education in Nigeria*, London, George Allen and Unwin. 1974, 57.
22. F.H. El-Masri, "The City of Ibadan" (ed) Lloyd, Mabogunje and Awe; London, Oxford University Press, 1973, 250.
23. F.H. El-Masri, "The City of Ibadan", 251.
24. T.G.O. Gbadamosi, *The Growth of Islam Among the Yoruba*, 5.
25. T.G.O. Gbadamosi, *The Growth of Islam Among the Yoruba*.

26. Richard and Lander, "Means to Explore the Sources and Termination of the Niger", *Journal of Expedition,* vol. II, 1961, 24.
27. H.A. Abdulsalam, "Matrimonial Issues Among Yoruba Muslims of Nigeria," 21.
28. H.A. Abdulsalam, 46, See also M.A. Okunola, "Interaction between Islamic Law and Customary Law of Succession Among the Yoruba"; Lagos, Faculty of Law, University of Lagos, 1984, 24.
29. A.R.A. Olaniyan, Comparative Studies of Islamic and Yoruba Laws of Inheritance, Long Essay, Department of Religions, University of Ilorin, 1982, 40.
30. A.K. Makinde, "The Institution of Sharī'ah in Oyo and Osun States, Nigeria 1890-2005. An unpublished Ph D Thesis, Department of Arabic and Islamic Studies, University of Ibadan, 2007, 40-58.
31. M.A. Ajetunmobi, "Sharī'ah Legal Practice in Nigeria (1956 – 1963)," 8
32. M.A. Ajetunmobi, "Sharī'ah Legal Practice in Nigeria (1956 – 1963)," 9
33. M.A. Ajetunmobi, "Sharī'ah Legal Practice in Nigeria (1956 – 1963)," 8
34. M.A. Ajetunmobi, "Sharī'ah Legal Practice in Nigeria (1956 – 1963)," 9
35. AbdulLateef Ahmad Adekilekun, *Oba Adetoyese Laoye the Late Timi of Ede,* Ede, Ilereke Printing Press, No. 6.
36. Y.Y. Ogirima, "Sharī'ah Controversy in Nigeria Re-examined." Long Essay, Department of Religions, University of Ilorin, 1982, 12.

37. M.A. Okunola, "Interaction between Islamic Law and Customary Law of Succession Among the Yoruba", 177
38. H.A. Abdulsalam, "Matrimonial Issues Among Yoruba Muslims of Nigeria," 29
39. M.A. Ajetunmobi, "Sharī'ah Legal Practice in Nigeria (1956 – 1963)," 6
40. M.A. Ajetunmobi, "Sharī'ah Legal Practice in Nigeria (1956 – 1963)," 7
41. M.A. Okunola, "The Relevance of Sharī'ah to Nigeria" in N. Alkali et.al (eds) *Islam in Africa,* Ibadan, Spectrum Books, 1993, 28.
42. T.G.O. Gbadamosi, "Sharī'ah in Nigeria: Experience of the Southern Nigeria." A seminar paper presented at the National Seminar on Sharī'ah held at Kaduna between 10th and 12th February 2007, 7.
43. The Constitution of Nigeria, 1979 see section 35(1) and as amended by that of 1999.
44. AbdulLateef A. Adekilekun, *Muslim Organizations in Nigeria*, Ede, Ilereke Printing Press, 1986, 84.
45. Matrimonial Causes Act 1970, see 2(1) which states inter alia that subject to this Act, a person may institute a Matrimonial cause under this Act in the High Court of any State of the Federation and for that purpose the High Court of each state of the Federation shall have Jurisdiction to hear and determine: (a) Matrimonial causes instituted under this Act".
46. M.A. Ajetunmobi, "Sharī'ah Legal Practice in Nigeria (1956 – 1963)," 25-26.
47. I.K. Sanni, "Independent Sharī'ah Court Enriching the Nigerian Legal System, Oyo State" as quoted by A.O.

Arikewuyo, "A Study of Independent Sharī'ah Panel in Osun State." Long Essay, Department of Religions, University of Ilorin, 2009, 77.
48. A.O. Arikewuyo, A Study of Independent Sharī'ah Panel in Osun State", 80-103.
49. Lagos State Chapter of Supreme Council for Sharī'ah in Nigeria, "Selected Judgements of the Lagos State Independent Sharī'ah Panel, vol. 1, Lagos, SCSN, 2005, v.
50. A.O. Arikewuyo, A Study of Independent Sharī'ah Panel in Osun State", 83.
51. The Constitution of Nigeria, 1979, 36 (i) and as amended by that of 1999.

CHAPTER EIGHTEEN

Distribution of Inheritance and Muslim Women in Kaduna and Kano States of Nigeria

Bello-Ja'afar, Hidayah
Department of Islamic Studies,
Federal College of Education, Zaria, Nigeria
+2348037919170; hbelloja39afar@yahoo.com

Introduction

The woman under the Islamic law (**Sharī'ah**) occupies an important position, which is better than that of womenfolk in many other civilizations. This is because at a tender age, she remains under the parental roof, and when she attains maturity, she is under the control of her father or her husband. The law vests in her all rights, which belong to her as an independent human being. As a female, young or old, she is entitled to a share in the inheritance of her parents along with her brothers. On her marriage, she does not lose her individuality; her property remains hers as of individual right.[1] This is unlike the case in other such religions and civilizations as Judaism, Christianity, Hinduism, Greek and Hebrew, where the woman is not accorded a specific share in inheritance. Islam stipulates the shares for both males and females from the property of their deceased relatives. This could be seen in the *Qur'ān* when Allah says:

> From what is left by parents and those nearest related, there is a share for men and a share for women, whether the property is small or large, a determinate share (Q4:7).

From the verses on inheritance, it is understood that the principles of inheritance laws are laid down in broad outline in the *Qur'ān*. Thus, the details have been worked out based on Prophet Muhammad's practices and those of his companions, as well as by interpretations and analogies of the jurists[2].

Kano and Kaduna States of Nigeria occupy a part of the area that was, before the British administration, called "Sokoto Caliphate", an area that was known and recognised as the seat of Islam and centre of Islamic education and administration[3].

Most of the people in the area of study are Hausa-Fulani speaking, and they are predominantly Muslims. They engage in agriculture, commerce, and small-scale industry. While most of them live in smaller towns and villages, others occupy several larger indigenous cities. However, many people of non-Hausa origins have become assimilated to Hausa nation through inter marriage and acculturation. Several customary practices exist within these two states. The traditional customs that are deeply rooted in the practice of the people tend to compete with their religious beliefs[4]. Thus, it could be said that the Islamic religious beliefs and practice of Muslims in Kaduna and Kano States are mixed with that of their customs[5].

In spite of the infiltration of the Hausa traditional beliefs and practices into Islam, most part of northern Nigeria partly apply the Islamic law except in areas that have not embraced the religion of Islam at all[6]. Consequently, the devolution of an interstate estate in most of northern Nigeria is based on Islamic law but with an admixture of the tradition and custom of the people. This is because after the advent of Islam, the Hausa rulers were not practising Islam properly as they were involved in all forms of syncretism. During those days, the rulers had neglected the proper practices of the **Sharī'ah** to the extent that some of them were openly hostile to its teachings. There were those who merely professed Islam by their lips but were fully engrossed in non-Islamic practices with various abuses and aberration in the administration of the Islamic law of inheritance[7]. Thus, the distribution of property among the Muslims and non-Muslims was unsatisfactory and ill defined. The right of inheritance among the people of these states was similar to that of the *Jāhiliyyah* (pre-Islamic) period because inheritance was mainly for the physically capable male relatives. Female and children were either totally denied or inadequately given a share from their deceased relations' estate. On this Kaura wrote thus:

> On economic plane, the inequality fought by Islam in redistribution of wealth in favour of women resurfaced. The rights of women to inherit in all circumstances were tampered with. Senior male members of the family appropriated inheritance to themselves. Uncanonical heirs like sons of nephews and uncles were made rightful heirs in place of women[8].

From this statement, Muslim women of these states had experienced all forms of ill-treatment, suppression and enslavement by men. Men denied them their rights to education, expression and inheritance.

Mīrāth and Women in Islam

The Qur'ān has specified that both male and female have right to inheritance. Allah says:

> From what is left by parents and those nearest related, there is a share for men and a share for women, whether the property is small or large a determinate share (Q4:7).

Therefore, Islam ensures the absolute right of woman to inheritance in different capacities as mother, daughter, sister or wife[9]. There are differences between the shares of male and those of female. But these differences are because the woman's needs must always be provided for adequately by her male relatives in her position as daughter, mother, sister or wife[10]. Hence, a Muslim woman's share of inheritance is completely hers and no one can make a claim on it without her consent.

The Qur'anic sharers (*'aṣḥābu-l-furūd*) are twelve in number and they are the first set of heirs to be considered in estate distribution. Eight out of the sharers are females. They are:

1. Mother, 2. Daughter, 3. Wife, 4. Son's daughter, 5. Full sister, 6. Consanguine sister, 7. Uterine sister, 8. True grandmother.

From the above listed female heirs, no other heir can exclude the first three. However, their shares can be reduced because of the presence of some other heirs that are closer to the deceased. In addition, it is one of Allah's favours and mercy conferred on the female that makes the number of female sharers to be more than that of male sharers. Allah also specifies their shares in inheritance without the interference of their male counterparts.

To clearly show the favours conferred on women, the female shares in inheritance can be grouped under the following;

a. When she gets half of what her male counterpart gets.
b. When she gets a share equal to that of a male.
c. When she gets a share greater than the male's.
d. When she inherits alone without her male counterpart inheriting[11].

Firstly, a woman gets half of what her male counterparts get in four instances as commanded by Allah when He says, "To the male a portion of two females" (Q.4:11). These instances are;

i. Whenever a daughter co-exists with a son (Q4:11).
ii. If a sister co-exists with a brother (i.e. full or consanguine) Q4:176.
iii. Whenever a deceased is neither survived by children, grandchildren nor two or more brothers and sisters, then the mother inherits half of what the father gets. The Qur'ān says "if no child survived the deceased and the parents are the only heirs the mother has a third" (Q4:11).
iv. The wife takes half of what the husband inherits if either of them survived the other. (Q4:12).

Secondly, she gets a share equal to that of a male. To this group, there are five instances.

i. The two parents get $1/6$ each, if the deceased is survived by son and daughter or two or more daughters or the husband and one daughter.
ii. The uterine brothers and sisters share $1/3$ equally and if it is either one sister or a brother, each has $1/6$.
iii. When the deceased is survived by uterine brother and sister, full brother, husband and mother. The uterine sister shares equally with the uterine brother and full brother.
iv. When a deceased is survived by mother, husband, uterine sister, and full brother, the uterine sister gets equal share with the full brother.

v. Uterine sisters and brothers get equal shares anytime they co-exist.

Thirdly, is when the females' shares are more than those of their male counterparts, when we consider the fractional shares in Qur'ān i.e. $\frac{1}{2}, \frac{1}{4}, \frac{1}{8}, \frac{1}{3}, \frac{1}{6} \& \frac{2}{3}$

i. The largest fraction stipulated in the Qur'ān is $\frac{2}{3}$ which is for the female heirs only i.e. two or more sisters or daughters.

ii. The half share which only one male inherits (i.e. the husband) when the deceased wife has no child/grandchild. But the female inherits half in four cases

    a. A lone daughter
    b. A lone son's daughter
    c. A lone full sister
    d. A lone consanguine sister

iii. The $\frac{1}{3}$ of the estate is for the mother when the deceased is not survived by a child or two or more brothers/sisters. Also, the uterine heirs share $\frac{1}{3}$ equally between themselves.

iv. $\frac{1}{6}$ is inherited by 6 females and 3 males. The females are:

Mother, grandmother, uterine sister, consanguine sister, full sister and son's daughter.

¼ is a share for only the spouses.
$\frac{1}{8}$ is only for the wife or wives.

From the above explanation, it is a fact that the female heirs get more shares than male heirs in most cases. For example, a man died leaving behind a wife, mother, two uterine sisters and two full brothers, with an estate worth N48, 000.

Wife ($1/8$), mother ($1/6$), uterine sisters ($1/3$), full brothers will share the residue.

    Uterine sisters 16000, each of them gets 8000
    Mother   12000
    Wife   6000
    Full brothers 14000, each of them gets 7000

It is a fact that at times the female gets more shares in inheritance than the male as shown in the example above; each of the uterine sisters will get more than what each of the full brothers gets.

Fourthly, when the female heir inherits and her male counterpart does not get anything from the estate. For instance, in a situation whereby a deceased is survived by a daughter, mother, a full sister, husband and a consanguine brother; the full sister will inherit $1/6$ of the estate while the consanguine brother gets nothing as the agnate; same is when the deceased is survived by grandmother, father, grandfather and a son. The grandmother will inherit while the grandfather will not.

From the foregoing discussions, it is clear that the female heir in the Islamic law of inheritance sometimes gets half the share of a male heir; or she gets the same share as the male; or she gets a share more in quantity than the male. Also, she may get a share while her male counterpart gets nothing. Therefore,

Chapter Eighteen	Bello-Ja'Afar, Hidayah, in Y.A. Quadri, E.W. Omotoye & R.I. Adebayo (Eds) Religion in Contemporary Nigeria London, Adoris & Abbey Publishers

for anyone to blame Islam for unequal shares between Muslim men and women seems to be a misconception[12].

Distribution of Estate in Hausaland (Kaduna and Kano States)

Kaduna and Kano States are predominantly Hausa settlements but there are other smaller groups scattered all over the states especially in Kaduna State. In essence, there are several customary practices existing within these two states. As earlier mentioned, the traditional customs that are deep-rooted in the practices of the people tend to compete with their religious beliefs. When Islam came, gradually it became syncretised, that is, Islam was mixed with already existing religious beliefs and practices in the region[13]. Thus, the Islamic religious beliefs are blended with the traditions and customs of the area.

Although the *Shari'ah* is the principal, legal status in Northern Nigeria as earlier said especially in civil matters (*al-aḥawāl ashakhsiyyah*) of marriage, divorce and inheritance, in reality, it has not completely replaced the customary law despite the influence of Islam. These customary laws of the Hausa and various ethnic groups in Northern Nigeria have for most past remained unchanged[14].

Most Muslim Hausa belong to the *Maliki* School of Law, and accordingly observe *Maliki* Law. This was because the Maliki Code was already in existence in the area and in West Africa in general. The administrations of inheritance vary among the peasants, among whom it is purely customary, the wealthy people in the villages (*attajirai*) to whom Maliki Law is partly applied and the ruling class among whom other practices are still obtained. In addition, the noble lineage practised yet another form of inheritance. Moreover, there is a difference between the method of inheritance in rural and urban areas respectively. To the rural settlers or peasants, farmland is the most important property while to the urban settlers; occupation, political status and family compound are of great significance[15].

Moreover, Hausa system of inheritance in most parts follows rules or conditions, which are not prescribed by law and which also vary. On this variation/ instability in methods used, Levy, R. observes that:

> Where family life is concerned in marriage, divorce and distribution of inheritance, the provision of *Shari'ah* (Hausa Sharia) would appear to be widely neglected...[16].

As regards inheritance, the Islamic Law (*Shari'ah*) is applied only where local custom has been replaced by the Islamic Code of conduct. According to the Hausa customs of inheritance, farmland is the most important property to the peasants that the women are mostly deprived of their share from it. This is because, man is expected to distribute his land to his sons as they marry and establish their household. The father farms with the aids of his sons to whom he allocates small plots known as '*gayauna*' which thereafter becomes theirs together with the produce. As sons mature, their father increases their *gayauna* portions from the old farm, while clearing more bushes with their aid for new family farmland. Moreover, when the son is ready to resettle outside the father's compound, the father gives his departing son final portion of the family plot[17].

At the death of the father, according to Hausa customs, the sons of the deceased are entitled to divide the farms amongst themselves. In practice, the eldest son runs the farm with the aid of his unmarried brothers. And in a situation where the deceased left only female issue, his brothers and their heirs or the heirs of his sisters may occupy the deceased's land in their own right. However, this is not right in the Islamic law because the law does not prevent the deceased's daughter from entering into possession of her deceased father's land, but in practice, the custom prevents her and that is what prevails[18]. Moreover, when brothers farm together in *gandu* (corporate property) and one died leaving younger offspring, the senior survivor assumes paternal responsibilities for the orphans together with control of their inheritance, which may be divided in future[19].

By custom, women are deprived of their share of inheritance. As such, on the death of the father, the most senior member of the family would take the overall properties left behind by the deceased. Such a person may be among the legal heirs or a non-heir like the uncles. He sits tight on the property claiming that it is the property of either his brother, sister or nephew. Thus, he uses the property as he wishes without any of the legal heirs challenging him. After his death, another powerful member of the family takes over the control of the estate[20]. On this, Kaura writes that such a person declares thus,

> This is the wealth of my brother and I am now in the position of their father. Then he would expend the heritage as he wishes; and nobody would challenge him in this act throughout his life. When he died, another (male member) who is strong would take over the heritage[21].

In addition, whenever a husband dies, his wife, mother and daughter will not be given anything from the property of the deceased. Instead, the uncles and their sons are made lawful heirs at the expense of the eligible heir. On this, Shaykh Dan Fodio was quoted to have said:

> And among (the innovations) is that inheriting by sons of uncles and nephews of the heritage despite the presence of rightful heirs and they would not be given anything.[22]

Despite the formal attachment of Hausa to Islam, their custom overrides the Islamic law of inheritance. For instance, court inventions of heritable estate have several features such as omission of land and economic trees or non-inclusion of compounds. Likewise, the dye pits, which are considered as important and productive form of immovable property, rarely feature in the inventories. On this Smith observes that:

> ...dye pits are tacitly left by the court for informal subdivision among male heirs. Such omission ensures that the estate administered by Hausa courts rarely made much value but consists mainly of self-acquired possession most of which are consumption goods (*tarkace*) used by the deceased[23].

The Hausa methods of inheritance incorporate *Shari'ah* law together with many customary practices, which deviate from this law[24]. Thus the religious injunctions on woman's share in inheritance are rarely recognised especially among the peasants because they feel that giving a woman a share of inheritance is unwarranted; she does not need it because she is always being taken care of by either her husband or any male relative[25].

Muslim Women and Inheritance in Hausa Tradition

The Hausa- speaking people have been profoundly affected by the impact of Islam over a prolonged period i.e., they have been Muslims for many centuries. Thus, at present, majority of the Hausa are practising Muslims though some of the cultures of the pagan minority (*Maguzawa*) had been fused with the teachings of Islam[26]

In the Islamic law, Hausa Muslim women should inherit half of the share of their brothers but in practice, they seldom do as earlier inferred. Moreover, according to the customs and norms, only the sons are entitled to divide the farmland, compounds and important immovable properties among themselves. As such, when a landowner left only female heirs, his brothers would occupy the deceased farmland in their own rights while the female children would be entitled to the proceeds of the farm land[27].

The Islamic law allows female inheritance while Hausa custom denies women the right to inherit valuable capital goods such as farm or compound house except when widows act as trustees to their children. This is because Hausa peasant farming has centered historically on an idealised unit of agricultural labour, which only involves the cooperation of the fathers and sons. In essence, this principle precluded not only female inheritance but farm division as well. In addition, there is a common reluctance among many Hausa families to allow their daughters' inheritance of real property; and this is accomplished by not dividing the estate according to the principles of Islamic law of inheritance. On this, the *Wazirin* Kano (vizier of Kano) was quoted to have told one district officer that, "Hausa customs did not allow inheritance of women under *Mohammendan* (sic) law"[28].

Moreover, government officials also discriminated against the women by altering women's inheritance rights and trying to control female independence. For instance, the Emir of Kano in 1923 forbade women from inheriting houses and farms. At times, the legacies of women were either claimed by male relatives, seized by village heads, or simply appropriated by others. In addition, houses and farms that did not pass to male inheritors would be sold by the treasury while the female heirs would only receive the proceeds of houses and farms that had been sold[29]. Islamic law does not prevent the deceased's daughter from entering into possession but in practice, the custom, described above, prevails.

On the denial of women of their rights to inheritance, Gurin observes thus,

> Here in Northern States, before the enactment of courts of law in 1956, most Alkali courts use to set aside farm and houses as reserved shares of male children before they did distribution[30].

From the ongoing discussion, it is clear that the inequality fought by Islam in the distribution of estate resurfaced among Muslims with the encouragement of some Emirs who claimed to be the protectors of the *ummah* and who enforced Islamic law. On this Kaura wrote that;

> The rights of women to inherit in all circumstances were tampered with, senior male members of the family appropriated inheritance to themselves. Uncanonical heirs like the sons of nephews were made rightful heirs in place of women[31].

It is only the males that take control of the heritage, while the woman is edged out of the inheritance of her parents or close relations. Therefore, the woman is not accorded her full right of inheritance in any position she is i.e. either as a wife, mother, sister or daughter. Hence, the Islamic law of inheritance is tampered with by the customs that denied the woman the possession and control of a deceased relation's property.

However, the denial of female her share in inheritance is mainly common on landed property and the male co-heirs are always the perpetrators of this practice. This is because the male co-heirs often take decision that are either contrary to that of their sisters or they may not even consult their female co-sharers on jointly owned properties[32].

Furthermore, the non-adherence strictly to the Islamic law on inheritance could probably be due to such reasons as;

1. Males have the feeling that women do not need landed properties since they are taken care of by their male relation at every stage of their lives or because Islam was not firmly established in some of the communities in Hausa land.
2. Or the *Ulama'al-su'* (the bad scholars) who failed to pursue the rights of women in their communities and even aided the denial of women their inheritance rights;
3. And finally illiteracy on the part of women prevented them from knowing their rights[33].

Nevertheless, the women in the urban areas are more likely to claim their rights in accordance with the Islamic law than their sisters in rural area who find the local customs and norms as predominant/prevailing in their area. Therefore, the position of women in estate sharing in Hausa land is determined and influenced by both Islamic law and the customs prevailing in the land.

Problems of Hausa System of Estate Sharing (inheritance)

Muslim women in Hausa land of Kaduna and Kano States have been subjected to practice that violated their inheritance rights. Thus, their allotted shares in the Qur'ān are either inadequately given to them or they are denied because of the influence of customary practice that prevails in the area. In essence, Hausa custom denied the women the right to inherit valuable capital goods such as farmland, compounds, dye pits. Nevertheless, the Islamic law permits and recognises their inheritance rights even in the presence of male heirs without distinction between the types of properties. For the Qur'ān says:

> There is a share for men and a share for women from what is left by parents and those nearest related, whether the property be small or large- a legal share (4:7).

The wrong distribution of a deceased's estate gave room to or caused many problems among the heirs. Some of these problems are as follows:

For the distribution of an estate an expert who possesses the knowledge of al-*Qismah* (identification of shares of landed property), plus mastery of the *fiqh* of inheritance and arithmetical calculations is more qualified to administer the estate. However, in most cases the administrator hardly possesses these qualities and qualifications; he is neither competent nor qualified to distribute an estate. Therefore, the administration of the estate would be done ignorantly and mostly with selfish interest. In addition, some heirs are favoured unjustly in the distribution of the estate by some judges, village heads or consultants.

Chapter Eighteen	Bello-Ja'Afar, Hidayah, in Y.A. Quadri, R.W. Omotoye & R.I. Adebayo (Eds) Religion in Contemporary Nigeria London, Adonis & Abbey Publishers

On this Allah says,

And whosoever disobeys Allah and His messenger (Muhammmad SAW) and transgresses His limits, He will cast him into fire, to abide therein; and he shall have a disgraceful torment. (Q4:14).

Furthermore, the omission of farmlands, economic trees, dye pits and some other valuable properties do make the estate to have less value because these items are set aside for the male heirs. This is against the command of Allah where He says, "to the male there is a share and to the female there is a share from what is left..." (Q4:7).

Deliberate refusal or delay in the distribution of estate by the guardians of the heirs is another common practice among the Hausa ethnic groups. This delay in distribution of estate stands as an obstacle on women's enjoyment of the favours conferred on them by Islamic system of inheritance. This is because some of the heirs do sell part of the estate and at times, real heirs are difficult to identify. So also is the devouring of the estate by local leaders (*masu anguwa*) as if they were the legal heirs.

The seizure and illegal control of an estate by either the eldest heir or a non-heir relation like an uncle without any one challenging him are also major problem that affects women in Hausa land. In addition, some distant relations (*dhāwwul-arhām*) of the deceased are included as heirs in the presence of eligible heirs who might not be given anything from the estate. This also creates problems for the heirs. The distribution of estate on *daki-daki* (hut by hut) basis makes the distribution of estate lack accuracy and consistency because the size and number of people of the *daki*-groups always vary.

Conservative reading and interpretation of the *Shari'ah* do pose problem to women in the distribution of estate because the laws would be interpreted in such a way that it is fused with the local traditions and is presented as religious commands. Such misinterpretation is always on the fractional shares (e.g. $1/8$ for wives $1/6$, for the parents and $1/3$ share of the mother) it is done in such a way that they do not consider if the deceased is survived by a child or not[34].

Normally a woman is denied her right to inherit farmland but if she is given, it is always in a very remote area and she would be given less than her prescribed portion, as earlier mentioned. Furthermore, the male co-heirs do make decisions that affect their jointly owned property, without consulting or considering the female heirs. In most cases, their decisions are always contrary to that of their sisters. Also the eldest son hardly takes judicious care of the estate and his co-heirs. Moreover, when the distribution is done, the female is always the last to choose. Also, few cases go to court because of the high cost of litigation and this impedes the right of women to complain on the inadequacies in the distribution.

The female's denial of her rights to inheritance affects her socio-economic security and puts her personality at risk. Widows are also denied their rights of succession without a justifiable reason; especially when she shows her interest in re-marrying outside her late husband's family. The sale of estate of deceased due to conflicts of interest between the widows on behalf of their children and that of the brothers of the deceased who are the traditional guardians of the children is also a problem.

Most of the problems mentioned above are caused by the denial of female inheritance by the Hausa customs because it is believed that the inheritance of real property and division of property according to Islamic law would reduce men's wealth and the control of female by the male i.e. she would be economically independent.

The injustice against women is not only supported but is also encouraged by some Emirs who are seen as leaders of Muslims and are expected to enforce Islamic law as well. For instance, Emir Usman bn Abdullah of Kano forbade women from inheriting houses and farmlands in 1923[35]. The same was the case of Iya Maiwana and Mamman Captain her brother's son.

Iya Maiwaina sued Mamman Captain who was her brother's son to the court of Emir Sanusi of Kano that she was not given a share of her deceased father's estate, who died thirty years earlier. The Emir's court dismissed the case that they should go and live peacefully since Iya Maiwaina did not claim her right when the distribution was made thirty years ago. Iya Maiwaina disagreed with the judgment and appealed to the Shariʿah Court of Appeal that she was denied her share of her father's houses and farms. The Northern Region Shariʿah Court of Appeal ordered that the Chief Alkali Court of Kano should redistribute the property to the eligible heirs i.e. Iya Maiwaina and Mamman Captain's father whose share would be shared by Mamman Captain and his four brothers[36].

Conclusion

Islam has not only given Muslim women equal right with men but has also elevated their position in the society and economically put them under the care of men. Indeed, there is no place in the Qur'ān where Allah obliged women to ensure any expenditure for herself or to any member of the family. At the same time, women have been given right of possession of any kind of wealth. To ensure the prevalence of these rights, Allah revealed to His Messenger the Law of inheritance, where the rights of every Muslim including the weak such as women, children, old people and the physically challenged are fully protected.

However, in the process of implementing the Law, it faced some issues and challenges. For instance, there are socio-economic challenges where women are denied their right to inheritance. There is also the problem of distribution of inheritance based on internal arrangement at home. Another problem is ignorance and selfish interest in the distribution by the Imams, Qudāt and ʿUlamā in connivance with some of the heirs. More so, inheritance distribution is sometimes done according to Hausa customs e.g. where the eldest son takes the whole estate and puts it under his care. At the end, he mismanages it to his personal satisfaction.

These problems can possibly be solved with some corrective measures like providing purposeful education especially Islamic education with special emphasis on science of inheritance. With the provision of such important aspect of education, all other problems will cease to exist. Many researchers on Kano and Kaduna States system of distribution of inheritance revealed that women are often being denied the right of inheriting houses and farmland. However, women especially in the urban areas are presently challenging this attitude in the courts.

Recommendations

Based on the findings from the study, the following recommendations are made:

1. The importance of knowledge of the science of inheritance cannot be over-emphasised. Therefore, every Muslim should learn the science of distribution of estate as commanded by Prophet Muhammad.
2. Delay in the distribution of a deceased Muslim's estate causes rivalry and hatred among the family members and consequently weakens the kinship. In line with this, Muslim rulers and scholars should educate and encourage the Muslims to distribute a deceased Muslim's estate adequately and timely among his legal heirs. This is to avoid internal crisis and all other related problems within the family.
3. Knowledgeable Muslims especially on the science of inheritance should handle the distribution of the inheritance. Otherwise, mis-placement of share and denying of Muslim women their legitimate rights will continue to prevail in the system of distribution.
4. Judges, legal practitioners, law lecturers, law students, Islamic studies teachers and students and the generality of Muslim community should acquire the knowledge of the procedure in the distribution of estate. And they should apply same correctly in appropriate cases. This will reduce to a greater extent all sorts of allegation of unjust distribution.
5. The judges in *Shari'ah* Courts should use *Ta'zirat* to punish whoever is found guilty of denying Muslim women their shares or giving them inadequate share of inheritance.
6. Muslim scholars should create awareness in the Muslim community either through radio and television programme, open air campaigns or during Friday

sermons, on the right of Allah against them on one hand, and the mutual rights they owe to one another, with regards to devouring of one another's wealth especially in the distribution of inheritance.

7. Muslims should go to *Shari'ah* Court to access justice because this will curtail many of the problems associated with the distribution of inheritance.

Notes and References

1. B.A. Awad, "Status of Women" in *The Islamic Quarterly a review of Islamic Culture*, (London: Islamic Cultural Centre, Vol. viii, No. 1 &2, 1964)
2. A.Y. Ali, *The Holy Qur'an Text, Translation and Commentary*. (Washington D.C.: The Islamic Centre, No.516, 1978), 181.
3. I. Sulaiman, *A Revolution in History: the Jihad of Usman Dan Fodio* (London: Mansell Publishing Ltd. 1986), 1.
4. Kari, Bergstrom, "Legacies of colonialism and Islam for Hausa Women: An Historical Analysis. 1804-1960" 2002. http://gencen.isp.msu.edu/documents/working-papers/cop.276 pdf. 23/03/2010.
5. "Customary Law Practice and Violence against Women" the position under the Nigerian legal System. http://www.vanatu.sus.ac.fj/so;-adobe-documents/usp%20only/customary. p.7 24/03/2011.
6. A.I. Doi, *Islam in Nigeria*. Zaria: (Gaskiya Corporation Company Limited, 1984), 21&35.
7. A.I. Doi, *Islam in Nigeria*.
8. J.M. Kaura, "Emancipation of women in the Sokoto Caliphate" in A.M. Kani and A. Kabiru Gandi (eds). *State and Society in Sokoto Caliphate*. (Sokoto: Usman Danfodio University, 1990), 79.
9. A.M. Gurin, *Introduction to Islamic Law of Succession (Testate and intestate)*. (Zaria: Centre for Islamic Legal Studies. 1987), vii.

10. B.O. Yusuf, "Feminism in the shade of the Qur'an" *Journal of the Nigerian Association of Teachers of Arabic and Islamic Studies,* (Vol5. No1, 2000), 78.
11. H.S. Taban, "Female share of inheritance is either greater or equal to the male's share" *Journal of Islamic Education.* (Baghdad: An-War Dajalah, 2012), 14-17.
12. H.S. Taban, "Female share of inheritance is either greater or equal to the male's share".
13. Kari Bergstrom, "Legacies of colonialism and Islam for Hausa women: An Historical analysis 1804-1960". (Working paper, October 2002). http://gencn.isp.msu,edu/documents/working-paper/wp276pdf. 23/03/2010.
14. Hussaina J. Abdullah and Ibrahim Hamza. "The Women and Land Studies" A paper presented at an international workshop on women and land in Africa organized by the Emory University School of Law. Atlanta, Georgia in collaboration with Associates for change Kampala, (Uganda, 1998), 5.
15. M.G. Smith, "Hausa Inheritance and Succession" *Studies in The Law of Succession in Nigeria.* J.D.M. Derret, ed. (London: Oxford University Press). http://ufas.us/smith/chapters/html. pp239-240, 26/04/11.
16. M.G. Smith, "Hausa Inheritance and Succession".
17. M.G. Smith, "The Hausa of Northern Nigeria" James L. Gibbs, Jr. Ed. *People of Africa* (New York: Holt and Rinehart & Wiston), 140-141. http://www.ufas.us/smith/chapters/html.26/03/2011
18. M.G Smith, " Hausa Inheritance and Succession", 249
19. M.G Smith, " Hausa Inheritance and Succession"
20. S.U.D. Keffi, "Practice and Procedure on Administration of estates under Islamic Law in Northern Nigeria". *Ahmadu Bello University Law Journal.* Zaria: Faculty of Law, (ABU, 2008, Vol.27-28), 279.
21. J.M. Kaura, "Emancipation of woman in Sokoto caliphate", 86.
22. J.M. Kaura, "Emancipation of woman in Sokoto caliphate".
23. M.G. Smith, " Hausa Inheritance and Succession", 251
24. M.G. Smith, " Hausa Inheritance and Succession", 87
25. Hussain J. Abdullahi and Ibrahim Hamza. "Land Studies" p20
26. Joseph Greenberg. "Some aspects of Negro-Mohammadan Culture-Contact among the Hausa West Africa", 51.

http://www.lawemory.edu/ifl/religion/wesafrica-html.westafrica.14/03/2010

27. Steven Pierce. "Farmers and prostitutes": Twentieth Century Problems of Female Inheritance in Kano Emirate Nigeria". *Journal of African History*, (U.K: Cambridge University Press. Vol.44, No 3. 2003), 486
28. Steven Pierce, "Farmers and prostitutes", 467
29. Steven Pierce, "Farmers and prostitutes", 467-468
30. A.M. Gurin, *An Introduction to Islamic Law of Succession. (Testate and Intestate)*, 2.
31. J.M. Kaura, "Emancipation of woman in Sokoto caliphate", 86
32. Ibrahim Naiya Sada, Fatima L. Adamu and Ali Ahmed. *Promoting Women's Right through Shari'ah in Northern Nigeria.* www.ungei.org/resources/files/dfid-promoting-women's-right.pdf, 24, 20/03/2011.
33. J.M. Kaura, "Emancipation of woman in Sokoto caliphate", 78.
34. Ibrahim M.S Maibushira. "Distribution of inheritance in Islam and Its application in Kano State". Unpublished M.A Thesis submitted to the Department of Islamic Studies. (Bayero University Kano, 1998), 276-280.
35. Hussaina J. Abdullah and Ibrahim Hamza, 15-16.
36. SCA/CV93/1962 (Shari'ah Court of Appeal) (Civil Case No. 93; 1962).

CHAPTER NINETEEN

The Evolution of *Izālatul- Bid ᶜah* Movement in North-Eastern Nigeria with Particular Reference to Bauchi and Gombe States

Aminu Umar
A.D. Rufa'i College for Legal & Islamic
Studies, Misau, Bauchi State, Nigeria.
babanwalle@gmail.com
+2348024073709

Introduction

The *Jamā ᶜatu Izā!atil bid ᶜah wa iqāmati-sunnah* (Society for the eradication of innovation and establishment of *Sunnah*), which uses the acronym JIBWIS or simply known as *Izālah* is a religious organisation founded in 1978 in Jos, Plateau State Nigeria.[1] The official registration of the association took place in 1985 during the military leadership of General Ibrahim Babangida.[2] Both in its objective and attitude, the *Izālah* was established to fight Ṣūfism which it considered inconsistent and alien to Islam. The *Ya'n Izālah* also condemned as *bid ᶜah* (innovation) a number of customs and traditions in northern Nigeria, such as exorbitant *Mahr*, extravagant expenditure during such ceremonies and celebrations like *Haqīqah* (naming ceremony) *Janāzah* and *Fidā'* (death rituals) practised by Muslims.[3] In the same way, the movement branded the celebration of *Mawlid* (the birthday of the Prophet Muhammad), visiting tombs of saints, and some aspects of intercession and *istigātha* (seeking succour) from other than Allah as non-Islamic acts.[4]

Although the launching of the *Izālah* as mentioned earlier took place in the late 70's, the actual person who laid the structure and framework for the movement was Shaykh Abubakar Mahmoud Gumi (1925-1992) a former Grand Kādi of Northern Nigeria and a former Nigeria's Hajj attaché to Saudi Arabia.[5] The audacity displayed by Shaykh Gumi towards Ṣufism on the Federal Radio Corporation of Nigeria, Kaduna, his writings (both in Hausa & Arabic) against the Qādiriyyah and Tijāniyyah *Ṣūfī* orders are essential elements in the later establishment of the *Izālah* movement.[5] Shaykh Gumi even evolved a method of sending his students and protégés to various towns and villages to preach what he considered to be undiluted pure Islam and discouraged people from perpetuating *bidʿah* such as *Taṣawwuf*.[6] It was these students of Gumi and many of those who subscribed to his views especially on *tasawwuf* that converged and formed the *Jamāʿatul izālatil bidʿah wa iqāmati-sunnah* under the leadership of Mallam Isma'ila Idris,(1932-1992) a retired *Imām* in the Nigeria Army from Bauchi State and a former student of Gumi.[7]

At the initial years of its establishment, members of the *Izālah* movement popularly called the *Ya'n Izālah* put followers of Sufism popularly called *Ya'n darika* under heavy pressure. In most cases, they engaged them in physical confrontation and skirmish especially in areas where the *Ṣūfī* seemed to be in the majority.[8] It was only in the early 1980's, according to Quadri, that the *Ṣūfī* brotherhoods started overcoming their shock by shelving their old disputes and forming a united opposition and counter offensive against the *Ya'n Izālah*.[9] This trend continued until the early 1990's when a crisis erupted within the leadership circle of the *Izālah* over leadership and finances, a situation that split the movement into two with each faction claiming to be the real and authentic founders and followers of *Izālah* teachings.[10]

The Origin and evolution of the *Izālah* movement

The circumstance surrounding the evolution of the *Izālah* movement has been a subject of divergent views by writers and analysts. One of the views held by some people especially the *Sufi* followers is that the *Izālah* movement was formed by late Shaykh Abubakar Mahmud Gumi. The reason advanced by the proponents of this view is that, when Shaykh Gumi with the assistance and support of Sir Ahmadu Bello (1910-1966) the Sardauna of Sokoto and the Premier of the defunct Northern region, founded the *Jamā ʿatu Nasril Islam*(JNI), his intention then was to manipulate it to propagate his anti-*Sufi* beliefs and ideas. Unfortunately, his intention could not be realised because of the composition of the membership of the organisation (JNI), majority of whom were Emirs, high ranking government officials, scholars and other important personalities. When it was clear to Shaykh Gumi that he could not make a head way with the JNI, though he could not forsake it completely, he then thought of forming another movement, the membership of which would consist only youths, and this led to the formation of the *Izālah* movement.[11]

The above view can hardly be accepted because when the *Jamāʿatu Nasril Islam* was founded in 1954, Gumi had not started his anti-*Sūfi* crusade probably due to Sardauna's personality who was a great grandson of ʿUthmān bin Fūdī. The fact that when the *Izālah* movement was founded, Shaykh Gumi had personally encouraged members of the *Jamā ʿatu Nasri'l- Islam, to* merge the *Izālah* members to its body, could not be a reason to assume that he was the founder of the

Izālah, because according to him, his reasons then was that the *Ya'n Izālah* were youths, versatile, vocal, educated and militant in their actions of propagating Islam and this would be of great assistance to the JNI in its Islamic propagation mission.[12]

The second opinion maintains that the founder of *Izālah* movement was a single person known as Shaykh Isma'ila Idris, a retired army *Imām* based in Jos. It was said that, the idea of the formation of the movement came to him, when he was still serving in the Nigerian Army as an *Imām*.[13] Isma'ila Idris himself was reported to have said:

> I am the soul founder of *Izālah*. *Izālah* came into existence from my personal efforts. Therefore, I belong to *Izālah* and *Izālah* belongs to me. There is no other person responsible to claim its ownership than me.[14]

To us, the formation of a public or religious organisation that comprises many people can hardly be attributed to a single individual, rather, it should be a joint effort of people with similar aim, as the name of the movement implies *"Jamā'ah"* which literally means society or group. Therefore, the formation of the *Izālah* movement cannot be a single effort of a single individual.

The third assertion maintains that the formation of *Izālah* movement was the outcome of the joint efforts of the students of *Shaykh* Gumi who agreed to converge together to support him in his war against Sufism and its practices, by forming or establishing a new organisation, which would be free from *Tariqah* doctrines and traditional dogmatism and which would be able to project the true image of Islam in Nigeria.[15]

The above view seems to have conformed to previous researches on this topic which proved beyond doubt that *Izālah* was a child of circumstances. The reason was that when

Shaykh Abubakar Gumi engaged himself in the propagation of Islam through his teachings, preaching and writings, he wrote his most controversial book entitled: *Al-'Aqīdatu's-Ṣaḥīḥa bi Muwāfaqati'sh-Sharī 'ah*. The publication of this book in 1972 generated a lot of arguments and controversies within the ranks and files of *Ṣūfī* Muslims in northern Nigeria, who saw the book as a direct assault to their *Ṣūfī* beliefs and practices. The trend of events that followed nearly claimed Gumi's life. This ugly situation aroused the interest of his students, followers, admirers and sympathizers to come together to defend him and his teachings and doctrines. This course of action eventually gave birth to *Izālatul-bid'ah* movement.[16] These youths assembled in Jos on 13th of March 1978 and inaugurated a new organisation named as *Jamā 'atu Izālatil bid 'ah*. Shaykh Gumi was said to have approved and blessed the move by adding 'wa *Iqāmatis-Sunnah* to the name of the organisation.[17]

The organisation was officially launched on the 13th of March 1978 in Jos, Plateau state capital with Alhaji Musa Maigandu as the chairman of the movement and Shaykh Isma'ila Idris as the chairman of the council of preachers.[18]

The Aims and objectives of the *Izālah* movement

Initially, after its formal inaguration, the *Izālah* movement had no formal constitution that clearly outlined or spelt out its aims and objectives. What could be said to be the main aim or objective of the movement was a denunciation of Sufism as disclosed and outlined by the leader of the movement, Mallam Isma'ila Idris in his small pamphlet written in Hausa language which he named; *"A Gane Banbancin Gaskiya da karya"* meaning "Differentiating the Truth from Falsehood". In the pamphlet, Idris presented the basic outline of his arguments against the *Ṣūfī* brotherhoods and attacked the *ṭuruq* especially on the issue of *shirk* (polytheism) thus: "All that the *tariqa* brotherhoods teach is associating somebody else with Allah in worship".[19]

The manifestos of the movement was only made known in 1982 when a formal constitution of the movement was drafted. Some of the aims of the organisation as spelled out in the constitution include:

i. to unite all Muslims as stated by God in the holy Qur'an: "And hold fast, all together, by the rope which God stretches out for you, and be not divided among yourselves;" And prophet Muhammad said "Believers are intact and undivided (one encourages the other);

ii. to enlighten the people about the activities of some so-called Muslims who have been distorting the true teachings of Islam.

iii. to alert all Muslims so as to be aware of books written by unscrupulous Mallams just to bring confusion into Islam.

iv. to show all Muslims that Prophet Muhammad (P.B.U.H.) before his death revealed the messages he received from God.

v. to make it clear to all Muslims that anybody who claims that Prophet Muhammad has been visiting him, should be regarded as a liar. This meant that the Prophet is still alive, while God in Qur'an said that "truly thou will die (one day) and truly they (too) will die (one day) and the

Prophet also confirmed that he would die and he did die. Also caliph Abubakar after the Prophet's death came out and said "Oh you who worship the Prophet, the Prophet is dead, but those who are worshipping God, God is still alive and he will never die".[20]

Some people have cited the above aims and objectives to buttress their assertion that the *Izālah* is an offshoot of Shaykh Gumi's ideas on war against the *Ṣūfī* orders as presented in his famous book *ʿAqīdatul Ṣahīha*.

The Relationship between the *Izālah* and the *Ṣūfī*

In Nigeria, the two main *Ṣūfī* Brotherhoods are the Qādiriyya and the Tijaniyya. The Tijaniyya brotherhood, however, is probably the largest numerical group in contemporary Nigeria.[21] The two brotherhoods have been very influential and have remained the cornerstone of Islam in Nigeria, perhaps due to the influence of the Sokoto *Jihād* whose leaders including Shaykh 'Uthman bin Fūdī were trained *Ṣūfīs* and wrote a number of works on Sūfism.[22]

Shaykh Abubakar Mahmud Gumi was the first scholar to attack the *Ṣūfī ṭuruq* on a dogmatic basis or platform. In 1972, he published his first major treatise against the *ṭuruq* entitled *al-ʿaqīdatu Ṣahīha bi muwāfaqat ash-sharīʿah*" (The right belief according to the shariʿah). The second edition with an English translation by Musa Abdul was published in 1976, and in 1978, a Hausa version with the title *"Musulunchi da abinda ke rusa shi,"* (Islam and the things that lead to its destruction) was published. Both books argue mainly on dogmatic level using quotations from the Qur'ān and *Hadīth*. The two books according to Umar provide the essentials of Gumi's critique against Sufism, namely that Sufism is not part of Islam because it emerged long after the fundamental principles of Islam had been perfected.²³ The book also condemns the origin of *Ṣalātul fātiḥ,* one of the important prayers of the Tijaniyya, as *bid ʿah* since it was not mentioned or referred to by the Prophet and his companions.

The above views as expressed by Gumi in this book, serve as a booster for Gumi's former students and protégés as it was later used by them after the formation of the *Izālah* organisation as the basis for their attack on the *Ṣufī* and their practices. However, the intensification of the conflict between Gumi's followers and the *Ṣūfī* began only when the *Izālah* movement, inspired by Abubakar Gumi's *ʿAqīdatul ṣaḥiḥa,* started its fight against the *Ṣūfī* brotherhoods at the grassroots level in 1978 and in so doing it did not merely criticise the network of the *turuq* on a dogmatic level but also turned to more intricate means of dispute where they produced a pamphlet in 1978 titled *Hujjojin da suka hana bin da'n darika sallah daga alkur'ani da hadisan manzon Allah.* The pamphlet summarises many of the criticisms leveled against the *Ṣūfī* orders namely that Sufism and the *Ṭuruq* are *bidʿah* that involve acts that lead to *kufr and shirk,* and which have to be destroyed. They particularly cited the treaties of the *Ṣūfī,* especially *Jawāhirul Maʿānī* as containing blasphemous statements, which according to them, is the basis for declaring the *Ṣūfī* as unbelievers.

On their part, the *Ṣūfī* basically try to depict Ṣufism as an integral part of Islam and their *ṭuruq* as absolutely orthodox in tandem with the *Sunnah* of the prophet. They also depict Abubakar Gumi and the *Ya'n Izālah* as representatives of the *Wahabiyya* who are ignorant in respect of the idea of Sufism and whose desire is only to cause *fitnah* and fragment the Muslim *Ummah*.

The *Ya'n Izalah* according to Quadri apply both peaceful and violent means in trying to force the members of the *Ṣūfī* brotherhood to renounce *taṣawwuf*, a situation that leads to serious public disorders in different towns and villages leading to loss of lives and property in some major towns and cities such as Kaduna, Funtua, Jos, Zaria, Kano, Gombe and Sagamu in Nigeria.[24]

The Split of the *Izālah* Movement

In his study on the *Izālah* movement, Umar listed certain factors which according to him, were accountable for the successful dissemination of the *Izālah* messages and its internal integration. He went on to forecast that:

> If these factors shall continue to obtain, then it follows logically that the movement will last. But if these factors cease to obtain, then it follows logically again, that the movement will wither away, or it may continue to exist in a weak, precarious and less vigorous way.[25]

In what one may describe as seemingly manifestation of these predictions, the *Izālah* later split into factions both at the national and within the local branches. One of the reasons or causes of the disintegration was leadership tussle that erupted within the leaders of the movement. The chairman of the organisation then was Alhaji Musa Mai Gandu while Shaykh Isma'ila Idris was the leader of the preachers. In 1990, as quoted earlier Shaykh Isma'ila Idris was reported to have claimed the sole leadership and ownership of the movement.[26]

One of the early *Izālah* members revealed that perhaps the logic of Isma'ila Idris was that since the *Izālah* was a religious organisation then, there was nobody competent to lead it other than an Islamic scholar.[27] The leadership of the movement therefore broke up into two factions. One was led by Shaykh Isma'ila Idris and backed by most of the *ᶜulamā'* based in Jos, and the second was led by Musa Mai Gandu, the National Chairman of the movement and backed by other *ᶜulamā'* such as Rabi'u Daura, the then Chairman Council of *ᶜulamā'* Kaduna State and other officials.

The second factor was allegation of corruption and financial impropriety that was leveled against Shaykh Isma'ila by some officials of the movement, who in 1991 questioned the sources of Shaykh Isma'ila Idris's money, which they considered to be too much for a preacher.[28] They also accused him of high-handedness in running the affairs of the movement and his unwillingness to take corrections and rectification on his views or ideas, no matter who suggests to him.[29] In June 1991 therefore, the Mai Gandu's faction issued a press statement suspending Isma'ila Idris and other officials from the movement thus;

> For reasons of dishonesty inconsistent with offices of religious leadership the chairman of the national committee of preachers {Isma'ila Idris}, his deputy {Usman Muhammad Imam} and the chairman of the national first aid group are dismissed.[30]

They also went ahead to dissolve all committees of the movement with a view to replacing them with caretaker committees. In direct reaction to this development, the Jos faction under Isma'ila Idris announced the removal of Musa Mai Gandu and his supporters from the *Izālah* official functions. As a result, the two factions started a bitter and hostile dispute and struggle that had continued to divide the *Izālah* movement in the whole country. Many efforts were made by various people to reconcile the two warring groups by late Shaykh Gumi and other well wishers but the efforts proved abortive. Even the death of Isma'ila Idris in 2000 did not end or minimise the dispute, as the two factions continued their antagonism towards one another. The dispute according to Lomier, acquired a rather bitter note due to stubborn adherence to doctrinal arguments by both factions leading to the mutual accusation of *kufr* and *shirk* by each side in order to discredit the other.[31]

Unlike other religious factionalisation and divisions, the split of the *Izalah* has shown one unique peculiarity. While others disagree on the basis of the fundamental beliefs that were significant to their existence, estrangement in *Izalah* appears not to have emanated from its central principles, rather disagreement surfaced from the charges of corruption and other issues as discussed earlier. The fact that each faction maintains the name, objectives and structures of the *Izalah* movement especially their attitude towards Ṣufism has clearly proved this point. However, some scholars have submitted that the way and manner in which the two warring *Izalah* factions condemn each other as unbelievers simply because of disagreements between them shows the extent to how *takfir* is being frivolously used by the Muslims.

After over twenty years of the split, in 2012, an attempt was made towards uniting the two factions in Bauchi during the condolence of one of the factional leaders, Shaykh Musa Maigandu. The two factions lamented the sad event and maintained the need to reconcile their differences and work for the upliftment of the movement's teachings and doctrines. A joint meeting of the two factions was therefore held in Sultan Bello mosque Kaduna on the 10th of December 2012 where the two factions formally reconciled under a unified leadership with Abdullahi Bala Lau as Chairman of the movement and Shaykh Sani Yahaya Jingir as Chairman Council of Preachers. Other positions were equally shared between the members of the two factions.[32]

However, the reconciliation of the *Izālah* appeared to be short-lived as another crisis re- surfaced in the movement over the issue of leadership. The former Jos faction still regarded and approved Shaykh Sani Yahaya Jingir the Leader of the Council of Preachers as the overall leader of the organisation, their reason being that as a religious organisation it is only the Leader of Preachers that is supposed to be the Leader. The former Kaduna faction on their part insisted that Shaykh Abdullahi Bala Lau is the overall leader of the organisation as this is what is obtainable in the constitution of the movement. Similarly, in 2013 the Kaduna faction during their national preaching in Yola accused the Jos faction, specifically Shaykh Jingir, of embezzling the movement's funds.[33] This, therefore, made the movement to re-split again with each faction conducting its activities separately since 2013.

The emergence of *Izālah* movement in Bauchi and Gombe States

The mission of the *Izālah* movement was said to have reached Gombe emirate the very year the movement was officially launched, that is 1978. According to one version, it began when two persons, the late Alhaji Baba Audu and Alhaji Musa Yola, after listening to the audio tape of Isma'ila Idris's sermon brought to them by some traders from Jos, decided to visit and invite him to Gombe.[34]

Another version says that there were some traders in Kumo Akko Local Government of present Gombe State who used to visit Jos and during one of their visits they brought the audio tapes of Isma'ila Idris's preaching. After listening to the cassettes, two people from Kumo, Alhaji Bābikir and Mallam Sulaiman Adamu, attended the formal inauguration of the *Izālah* movement in Jos and afterwards invited Isma'ila Idris to Gombe.[35] None of these versions can be authenticated. However, it is a fact, according to Abba that two people who were sympathetic of Isma'ila Idris's mission wrote a letter in May, 1978, to the police in Gombe seeking permission to invite Isma'ila Idris to Gombe.[36] The Police asked that a letter of undertaking be signed by at least ten prominent persons who would guarantee the peaceful conduct of the *wa'azi*. Among those who signed the letter were Alhaji Bello Sābon Kudi, Alhaji Bappa, Alhaji Shehu Usman (U.A.T.), Mallam Abdulqādir, Alhaji Ahmadu Haruna and Alhaji Mijinyawa Yakubu.[37] All of them were reputable and highly esteemed personalities in Gombe Emirate.

After the preaching session, some prominent members of the *Izālah* movement were arrested and detained for one month at the Bauchi Township Police station and then later at the Bauchi Central prisons where they spent eight months without trial.[38]

The *Izālah* movement in Gombe survived and thrived due to the doggedness of the members and also due to the financial support received from some prominent wealthy persons in Gombe. For instance, there was Alhaji Musa Mūri who was the first person to build a mosque for the *Izālah* in Shagon Goro Quarters in 1979. There was also Alhaji Ahmadu Haruna who built a big Jumuᶜat Mosque and a school for the

Izālah in Gombe. Others that assisted and sustained the *Izālah* project include Alhaji Bello Sābon Kudi, and Mallam Adamu Ibrahim Bajoga.[39]

According to Imam Lamido, the mission of the *Izālah* was largely accepted by the youths and the middle aged perhaps due to the *Izālah's* call for children to discard some traditional norms such as kneeling down for their parents, elders and or leaders when greeting them. This brought them in conflict with their parents some of whom drove the children away.[40]

In the early years, the *Ya'n Izālah* also clashed with members of the *Ṣūfī* brotherhoods, especially the Tijāniyya who were many in the Emirate. This was as a result of frequent condemnation of *Tasawwuf* and its adherents by the *Ya'n Izālah*. On the 19th -20th of June 1978 for instance, a fight ensured between the Tijāniyya members and *Ya'n Izālah* when the *Ya'n Izālah* were reported to have condemned the *Ṣūfī* members as unbelievers in one of their sermons.[41] However, two of our respondents in Gombe Alhaji Musa Yola and Shaykh Abdulmumin Ibrahim, gave a different story concerning this have all refuted this statement. According to them in June 1979, a certain preacher who was well known for his condemnation of *Ṭariqa* delivered a provocative and inciting sermon when he condemned members of the *tariqa* as *kāfirai*. This led to a bloody scuffle between the *Ṭariqa* members and the followers of the preacher resulting in the death of the preacher and destruction of valuable property.[42] Perhaps the ascription of the unfortunate incident to the *Ya'n Izālah* is due to their castigation of the *Ya'n Ṭariqa*.

The advent of *Izālah* movement in Bauchi State

Just like Gombe State, the mission of the *Izālah* reached Bauchi in 1978. According to Alhaji Abubakar Basharu (popularly called Shugaba Basharu), Isma'ila Idris was born and grew up in Bauchi Emirate where he studied under prominent scholars such as the late Chief Imam of Bauchi, Mallam Mahmood and Mallam Ahmadu na kan Kusurwa. So when the audio tapes containing the sermon of Ismā'ila Idris were circulating in Bauchi, he, Baba Shugaba, and many others such as the late Alhaji Bukar Birma, the late Alhaji Audu Mai Auduga and one Tijjaniyya Shaykh called Mallam Gidado Umar, converged and travelled to Jos in 1978 in order to have first-hand information of and to understand the mission and message of Isma'ila Idris. Perhaps after concurring with his mission and ideas, they promised to attend the formal launch of the *Izālah* which was then about to hold. They also invited him to Bauchi to launch the new movement and promised to assist him in spreading the new *Izālah* mission in Bauchi. After the formal launch of the movement in Bauchi, the pioneer leaders of the movement were chosen from these set of people that first visited him. Shugaba Basharu was chosen as the leader, Alhaji Audu Mai' Auduga, the Chairman Council of Elders and Mallam Gidado Umar as the First Chief Imam.[43]

As in Gombe Emirate, the *Ya'n Izālah* faced opposition, first from the traditional rulers and other *ᶜUlamāʾ* who saw the *Ya'n Izālah* as a threat to them, and second by the followers of *Ṣūfī* brotherhoods, especially the Tijaniyya under Shaykh Ṭāhir Usman Bauchi. They portrayed the *Ya'n Izālah* as a bunch of youths trying to foment trouble and *fitnah* in the predominantly Muslim and peaceful emirate.[44] This perhaps explains why the *Ya'n Izālah* faced a lot of obstacles such as assault and incarceration by the authorities. Perhaps when they realised that they might not be able to take over the control of the Friday Mosque in Bauchi, the *Ya'n Izālah* decided to build their own Mosque in 1979.

The Bauchi Emirate Council however, was said to have written a letter to the Bauchi State Commissioner of Police complaining about the new Mosque. Consequently the proposed Chief Imam Mallam Gidado Umar and other *Izālah* officials were detained and the Mosque was closed for weeks.[45]

Individuals who assisted in the promotion of *Izālah* activities in Bauchi included wealthy men such as Sule Makānike who donated his house in Gwallaga quarters in 1979 which was then converted to a Mosque. Also there were people such as Alhaji Bukar NTC (now late) and Alhaji Audu Mai'Auduga (now late) who each built a mosque and a school for the movement.[46]

One common feature of the *Izālah* mission in both Bauchi and Gombe is that at the initial years of their mission they faced detention and incarceration perhaps due to their defiance to the traditional institutions. While Mallam Gidado Umar the first Imam of the *Izālah* Jumuʿat mosque was detained in 1978, Alhaji Musa Yola and seven others were similarly detained in the same year. However, unlike in Gombe where the *Yan Izālah* at its initial years had serious clashes with members of the *Ṣūfī* brotherhoods especially the Tijāniyya due to the frequent condemnation of *Tasawwuf* and its adherents, in Bauchi no such cases were recorded as confirmed to the present researcher by both members of *Izālah* and *Ṭarīqāh*. This, perhaps as observed by Babangida, may be due to the few number of *Ṣūfī* followers in Bauchi Emirate compared to Gombe.[47] The other reason might have been due to the fact that the intense hostility of the people of Bauchi in general and the Emirate Council in particular towards the *Izālah* was enough to preoccupy and engage the *Yan'Izālah*. That notwithstanding however, the *Ṣūfī* in some of their fora or activities such as *Mawlid* celebrations used to denounce some of the *Ya'n Izālah*'s accusation against them by composing short poems and lectures. In 1982, the renowned *Ṭarīqah Shaykh*, Tāhir Usman Bauchi wrote a book titled *Gaskiya tā bayyana* (the truth has appeared) where he exposed what he termed the evils of the *Izālah* movement.

Another common feature was in the unpleasant reaction to the *Ya'n Izālah*'s mission by other Muslims in the two states. The *Ya'n Izālah* were accused of castigating and using unpleasant remarks against their parents for reciting *salatul fātih* during their *ʿaqīqah*, or refusing to bow to them as a mark of respect. This attitude made many parents to part ways with their children. One of our respondents in Bauchi revealed how he was driven out of his family house by his parents because of his refusal to quit the *Izālah*. Another narrated how his wife was forcefully separated from him by his in-laws for joining the *Izālah*. Similar treatments such as ejection from rented houses by landlords, and refusal by parents to give their daughters in marriage to *Ya'n Izalah* were all meted to them in the two states.

There are allegations that at the early years of the *Izālah*'s advent, there were cases of children who disowned their parents for subscribing to *Ṭarīqah* and for reciting *Ṣalātul Fātih* during their *ʿaqīqah* or cases of those who bought cartons of milk and gave them to their mothers in exchange of the milk they sucked from them. But according to Shaykh Gidado and Shaykh Ibrahim two prominent *Izālah* leaders, all these are baseless and unfounded allegations fabricated by their enemies. This could be true because all efforts to verify this allegations proved abortive as nobody could give a specific instance.[48]

Factors responsible for the spread of *Izālah* in Bauchi and Gombe States

As discussed earlier, majority of the people who joined the *Izālah* movement in the two states were youths and the middle aged. This might not be unconnected with the *Izālah*'s condemnation of some religious practices such as high bride price, marriage ceremonies, naming ceremonies, *idu'l -adha and idu'l –fitr* celebrations. Such condemnation was appealing to the youths and thus made the youths, especially the poor among them, to see in the *Izālah* doctrine a justification in the rejection of those extravagant social events.

Another factor that might have aided the spread of the *Izālah*'s mission was the hostility of elders especially parents against the *Izālah*. Some parents were said to have disowned and chased away their sons and sometimes even dissolved marriages of their children, some *Izālah* scholars used an opportunity to console the youths that their ordeal was an indication that they were on the right path because Muslims during the early mission of the Prophet of Islam also suffered similar predicament, but when they perseveredthey eventually became triumphant. This, according to Inuwa and Idris helped the *Yan'Izālah* in becoming more determined in their course.[49]

The enormous sacrifice through contributions and donation to the course of the movement by the *Ya'n Izālah* in these areas might also have been another reason for the progress of the movement. The *Ya'n Izālah* always encouraged their members to make contributions and sacrifices for the movement's progress. Two days of each week was dedicated for the collection of donations from members in every Mosque. Also a system of enforcing levy on member of the movement when there are some important events was in place. During the ʿidul-aḍḥā, members are encouraged to donate the hides and skins of their slaughtered animals to the movement. There is also a special committee of Zakāh and waqf in all the Izālah branches to which members are expected to give their zakāh. According to Mallam Yakub, this income base of the Ya'n Izālah has assisted and is still assisting them in carrying out their activities successfully.[50]

Another factor that assisted the spread of the Ya'n Izālah is their method of daʿwah. They used to organise mass preaching sessions called Wa'azi which they organised at national, states, local government and ward levels almost on monthly basis. This system or approach gives them the opportunity to carry their mission to all towns, villages and wards. In addition to that, the use of modern communication gadgets such as Sunnah T.V. and Manarah Television Satellite stations by the Izālah put them far ahead of other Muslim organisations in the dissemination of its mission.

The benefaction, good will gesture and support from some government institutions and politicians are also other factors that assisted in the advancement of the Izālah activities. Perhaps due to the fact that the Izālah movement has now become a strong human base to be reckoned with, the hostile attitude of government functionaries and traditional rulers towards the Ya'n Izālah had to change. Government functionaries started to attend some of the functions of the Izālah movement and made donations towards its course. The present Bolori Izālah Jumuʿat mosque which used to be the

Gombe polo ground was donated to the movement by the Gombe State Government. In Bauchi State, a large piece of land which contains the present *Izālah* Central mosque was allocated to the movement by the Bauchi State Government. More so, during the launching of what the *Izālah* leaders called Education Appeal Fund in 2011 in Bauchi, the sum of over 73 million naira was realised with highest donations from some North eastern states' governments.[51]

Conclusion

From the foregone discussion, it is our humble submission that the formation of the *Izālah* organisation can largely be attributed to the efforts of the students, followers, admirers, and sympathisers of Shaykh Abubakar Gumi. Even though Shaykh Gumi did not come out publicly to claim ownership of the *Izālah*, his preachings, teachings and writings especially his book *Al-'Aqīdatu's-Ṣaḥīḥa* generated a lot of ideas among his admirers to come together to form the movement with the sole aim of propagating and practising Islam as preached and practised by the Prophet of Islam and his companions. The movement suffered enormous opposition largely from the *Ṣūfī* and the traditional rulers due to their castigation of the *Ṣūfī* and the traditional Emirs. However, the *Ya'n Izālah*'s tenacity and determination through the establishment of their mosques and schools as well as the contributions from the well-to-do among them and the Government patronage in Bauchi and Gombe Emirates and the establishment of their separate satellite Television and Radio stations had greatly assisted them in the promotion of their mission.

However, it is our suggestion and hope that the misunderstanding between the two *Izālah* factions on one hand *and* the *Ṣūfī* on the other hand is uncalled for and should be amicably resolved so that peace and tranquility will prevail and the lofty teachings of Islam would be spread among the Muslim *Ummah* through good admonition and wisdom as enjoined by Islam.

Notes and references

1. For more detailed accounts of the *Izālah* movement and its founding in Nigeria, See Abubakar Gumi, with Ismaila Tsiga, *Where I Stand,* (Ibadan: Spectrum Books, 1992), 156. Ousmane Kane, *Muslim Modernity in Post-Colonial Nigeria,* (Leiden: Brill, 2003), 153. Roman Lomier, *Islamic Reform and Political Change in Northern Nigeria,* (Evanston, Ill: Northwestern University Press, 1997), 212. and Muhammad S. Umar, "Changing Islamic Identity in Nigeria from the 1960s to the 1980s: From Sufism to Anti- Sufism," in *Muslim Identity and Social Change in Sub-Saharan Africa,* (ed.), L. Brenner, (London: Hurst, 1993), 167, Azeez A. Olabiyi, "Izālatul-bid'ah movement in Nigeria (1973-2003)"
2. Razi Ben Amara ,"The development of the *Izālah* movement in Nigeria: its split, Relationship to Sufis and perception of Shari'ah Implementation*",* retrieved from http/www.sharia-in-Africa.net, (accessed June 12, 2011).
3. Moshe Terdman, "Clashes between Islamist and Sufis and its outcome: The case of Ya'n *Izālah* and the Sufi's in Nigeria" in *Islam in Africa newsletter* Vol.1. No. 6, 2006, 6, (accessed September 23rd, 2011), at www.e-prism.org.
4. See Y.A.Quadri, "A study of the *Izālah*: a contemporary anti Sufi Organisation in Nigeria," in *Orita, Ibadan*

Journal of Religious Studies (vol. XV11/2, 1985), 95. And Terdman, Moshe "clashes between Islamist and Sufis and its outcome...5.

5. For a full biography of Shaykh Abubakar Mahmood Gumi, see Abubakar Gumi, with Isma'ila Tsiga, *Where I Stand,* (Ibadan: Spectrum Books), 1992. and A.M. Sunusi Gumbi, *Rayuwar Shaykh Abubakar Mahmud Gumi* (Kaduna, 1986)

6. Razi Ben Amara, "The development of the *Izālah* movement in Nigeria: its split, Relationship to Sufis and perception of Shari'ah Implementation" (Accessed June 12th, 2011), at http/www.sharia-in-Africa.net. See also Y.A Quadri, "a study of the *Izālah* ...95-96

7. Ousmane Kane, *Muslim Modernity in Post- Colonial Nigeria,* (Leiden: Brill, 2003),124. and Roman Lomier, *Islamic Reform and Political Change* ...325 and also, Quadri, "a study of the *Izālah*...95-96

8. Ousmane Kane, *Muslim Modernity..,* 124. And Roman Loimeier, *Islamic Reform and Political Change*...324. See also Quadri, "A study of the *Izālah*..., 96.

9. Quadri, "A study of the *Izālah*", 97.

10. Quadri, "A study of the *Izālah* ... 97. For a chronology of the clashes between Ya'n Izala and the *ṭuruq* See Federal Government of Nigeria, Report of Tribunal of inquiry on Kano Disturbances, Lagos: 1981, Y.A Quadri, "*The Tijjaniyya in Nigeria: A Case study*" (Unpublished Ph D thesis, Department of Arabic and Islamic Studies University of Ibadan, 1981),123. and Ahmed, A.F."The *Qadiriyya and its impact in Nigeria*", (Unpublished Ph D Thesis, Department of Arabic and Islamic Studies, University of Ibadan, 1986), 98.

11. Azeez Adekunle Olabiyi, "*Izālatil-bid'ah* movement in Nigeria (1973- 2003)", Unpublished Ph D thesis, Department of Arabic and Islamic Studies, (University of Ibadan, 2006), 46-47.
12. A.M.Gumi, with I. Tsiga, *Where I stand,* (Ibadan: Spectrum Books Ltd, 1992), 162.
13. Danlāmi, Jibril Muhammad; "A critique of *Izālah* Activities in Abuja" (B.A Long Essay, University of Abuja, 1991), 12-13.
14. Olabiyi, p.10, quoting an interview he had with Shaykh Isma'ila Idris the (then) chairman of the council of preachers of *Izālah* on 29th of Feb. 1997.
15. Gumi, and Tsiga, *Where I stand,* 155
16. Gumi, and Tsiga, *Where I stand.*
17. Gumi, and Tsiga, *Where I stand.*
18. See Abubakar Gumi and Ismaila Tsiga, 156; Ousmane Kane, *Muslim Modernity in Post-Colonial Nigeria,* Leiden: Brill, 2003, 153; Roman Lomier, *Islamic Reform and Political Change in Northern Nigeria,* Evanston, Ill: Northwestern University Press, 1997, 212; and Muhammad S. Umar, "Changing Islamic Identity in Nigeria from the 1960s to the 1980s: From Sufism to Anti- Sufism," in *Muslim Identity and Social Change in Sub- Saharan Africa,* (ed.), L. Brenner, London: Hurst, 1993, 167. See also Azeez A. Olabiyi, (2006) "Izālatul-bid'ah movement in Nigeria (1973-2003)."
19. JIBWIS National headquarters (1980) *A gane Banbancin Gaskiya da karya* (n.p)
20. See constitution of the *Jamā'atu Izālatil bid'ah* Jos, 1985, 17.

21. J.N. Paden, *Religion and political culture in Kano*, Barkley, Los Angeles: 1973, 70.
22. J.N. Paden, 70. Also Quadri, *Tijjaniyya in Nigeria:* A case study" 187.
23. M.S.Umar, "Sufism and anti Sufism in Nigeria." M.A. thesis, Bayero University Kano, 1988, 198.
24. Y.A.Quadri, "A study of the *Izala:....*" 95.
25. M.S. Umar, "Islamic Revivalism Today: the case of *Jamā'atu Izālatil bid'ah wa iqāmat al-sunnah."* (B.A. Long Essay, University of Jos, 1983), 47.
26. Olabiyi, "Izālatul-bid'ah movement in Nigeria (1973-2003)," 10.
27. Interview with Dr. Ibrahim Jālo Jalingo the leader Council of Preachers JIBWIS National body on 10th May 2014 in Bauchi.
28. Kane, *Muslim Modernity in Post-Colonial Nigeria*, 131.
29. Kane, *Muslim Modernity in Post-Colonial Nigeria*, 124.
30. *Jaridar Amana*, a Hausa version of the National Concord Newspaper, (August 1991), 14.
31. Loimier, Roman: *Boko Haram: The Development of a militant Religious Movement in Nigeria*, in: *Africa spectrum*, 47, 2-3 137-155 (accessed on 16th January 2013), at www.africa-spectrum.org
32. Daily Trust Newspaper of 22nd December 2011, page 5 under the Caption "Izalah factions unite".
33. *Aminiya* Newspaper of 18th February 2013.
34. See Aliyu Sani Abba, et al, *Gombe state a history of the land and people*, (Zaria, A.B.U Press, 2000), 46; and also interview with Imam Abubakar Lamido and Shaykh Abdulmumin Ibrahim Chief Imam and Deputy Chief Imam of Bolori Juma'at Mosque respectively in Gombe on 23rd July 2012.

35. Abubakar, B. Muhammad, "The activities of *Izālatil bid ʿah wa iqāmatissunnāh* in Akko Local Government", (B.A. Long Essay, University of Jos, 1991), 85.
36. Abubakar, B. Muhammad, "The activities of *Izālatil bid ʿah wa iqāmatissunnāh* in Akko Local Government", 55-56.
37. Interview with Alhaji Musa Yola at his residence in Gombe, on 23rd July, 2015.
38. Interview with Alhaji Musa Yola
39. Interview with Alhaji Salisu Muhammad, Chairman JIBWIS Gombe State on the 14th of May 2013.
40. Interview with Imam Abubakar Lamido the Chief Imam of Bolori *Izālah* Juma'at Mosque on the 14th of May 2013, in Gombe on 15th May 2013.
41. See Federal Government of Nigeria, Report of Tribunal of inquiry on Kano disturbances, 1981 Lagos, 86.
42. Separate interview with Alhaji Musa Yola, and Mallam Abdulmumin Ibrahim in Gombe on 23rd July 2015.
43. Interview with Abubakar Basharu popularly known as Baba Shugaba (now late) a founding member of the *Izālah* on 18th August 2013 at his residence in Bauchi.
44. Interview with Mallam Gidado Umar yhe first Izalah Imam in Bauchi and Mallam Inuwa Dan'Asabe , Chairman of JIBWIS Bauchi state council in a separate interview on18th June 2013 in Bauchi.
45. Interview with Mallam Gidado Umar in his residence in Bauchi on 19th June 2013 and Imam Ibrahim Idris in Bauchi at the Gwallaga Juma'at Mosque on 15th June 2013.

46. Interview with some founding *Izalah* members in Bauchi in 2013 and also interview with Sheikh Abdulmumin Ibrahim in Gombe on 23rd July 2015.
47. Interview with Mallam Babangida Jahun one of the founding members of the *Izalah* movement Bauchi on 18th Aril 2013 at his residence in Bauchi; and Sheikh Abdulmumin Ibrahim in Gombe on on 23rd July 2015
48. Interview with Sheikh Ibrahim Idris and Mallam Gidado Umar in Bauchi.
49. Interview with Sheikh Ibrahim Idris, Alhaji Muhammad Inuwa Dan'Asabe at the Gwallaga Juma'at Mosque Bauchi.
50. Interview with Mallam Ibrahim Yakub at his recidence in Bauchi on 18th April 20013.
51. The event was held on 23rd August 2012 at the Babangida Square in Bauchi town.

CHAPTER TWENTY

Historical Development of Islam in Central and Eastern Delta of Nigeria

Abdulrazaq Kilani
*Department of Religious and Cultural Studies,
University of Port Harcourt, Nigeria.
abdulrazaq.kilani@uniport.edu.ng*

Introduction

The penetration of Islam into Niger Delta region of Nigeria has not followed the pattern that has been recorded in other parts of Nigeria. There are no records of itinerant Muslim scholars or any organised group who brought the religion to the area. What is however discernible is that inter group relations among ethnic groups of Nigeria most especially from the North to the creeks of the Delta using the course of the popular River Niger greatly assisted the contact of the two regions. The trade in yam by the Nupe to Nembein the central Delta has been recorded by scholars as among the factors for the contact. The Nupe people made earlier contact to the region as early as 16th century before the arrival of the Hausa and other Muslim ethnic groups.[1]

Niger-Delta is the most widely reported region in Nigeria both locally and internationally. The wide publicity the region has received in recent years is perhaps due to the political agitation fomenting in the region, enhanced by its strategic significance as the source of oil and gas. Niger-Delta is located at the southernmost tip of Nigeria, adjoining the continental shelf of the Gulf of Guinea. It accounts for 100% of Nigeria's oil production. It is the Delta through which the Water Systems of Rivers Niger and Benue empty into the Atlantic Ocean. The area covers about 70,000 km² and possesses huge oil and gas reserves. The areas covered in our study is the central Niger Delta which is made up of the present day Bayelsa State in Nigeria and the eastern Niger Delta which make up of the current Rivers State. The important towns in the areas include Port Harcourt, Bonny, Elele, Brass, Nembe, Ogbia, Okrika, Yenagoa, Ahoada, Bori, Ogbakiri, Choba, Emohua and numerous villages.

The Muslim communities in the Delta region are known through their languages and similarly economic and religious interests. Islam has offered them a collective identity as other ethnic groups like the Nupe, Fulani, Kanuri are collectively referred to as Hausa. Islam enjoys a considerable number of adherents in Niger-Delta more than the south Eastern parts of Nigeria. Although, there are no official records of Muslims' population in the Niger Delta however, Ogionwo[2] provided the following religious demography of the city of Port Harcourt (the most populous city in the region) based on questionnaires administered in 1974. Protestant 38.4%, Catholics 29.9%, African Traditional Religion 18%, Muslims 10.4% and others 3.7%. It should be succinctly stated that, many successes have been recorded by Islam in the region since 1974 to date which means that the Muslims are likely to have doubled the figure given by Ogionwo more than three decades ago. This could be juxtaposed by the number of mosques which is a verifiable index of the growth of Islam. In 1974, there were five mosques in Port Harcourt (the most important city in the region) while in 1988, it stood at eight mosques and by 2001, there are about 52 mosques of various sizes. By 2007, there are about 82 mosques and by 2015 about hundred mosques are recorded in the city and its environs. The arithmetic growth in the number of mosques is also recorded in other areas like Yenagoa, Bonny, Bori, Omoku, Ahoada, Buguma, Nembe and Brass.

The Dawn of Islam in the East and Delta Regions

The earliest mention of Islam in the Eastern Nigeria dates to around 1890 where Hugh Goldie and Mr Dean, both of the Primitive Methodist Missionary Society in Calabar made the following observation:

> A military station established at Ediba, a town beyond Ungwana, where a small detachment of Hausa soldiers under an English officer was stationed, greatly promoted the pacification of the river. The Hausa soldiers brought a new religion, Mohammedanism (sic) Islam, before the eyes of the people, and it was not long before Mohammedan traders from the Niger swarmed into Duke Town, and even up the river. The creation of a mosque has given a concrete form to the new influence. The strangeness of dress and habits of these newcomers, as well as the regular attention to their devotions, strangely impressed the natives, and they soon began to look upon them with a vague fear, which may in time become a great impulse to imitation[4].

Also, a notation from John Landers recordings shows that he noticed a Hausa trader in Aboh Kingdom during his travels with Clapperton in 1830 to 1832.[5]

The preponderance of migration in the ethno-historical discourse of African society cannot be underestimated. This explains why emergence of many societies in Africa is attributed to migration. In pre-colonial times, migration occurred largely in search of security, new land which is safe for settlement and fertile for farming[6]. Migration refers to the movement of people from one place to another, from one geographical region to another, which may be on a temporary or permanent basis. Migration can be international or internal (within a country, often from rural to urban areas). People migrate based on the prevailing conditions and the reasons for it vary from one person to another depending on the situation that brought about the decision. Migration is a selective process affecting individuals or families within certain economic, social, educational and demographic characteristics. Historical facts and oral tradition have shown that Africans are predominantly migratory people in nature and they are basically favourably disposed to this trend always[7]. The proponent of the Pushpull theory attributed to Tylor and Lee which is relevant to this study argues that people voluntarily migrate because it is in their best interest to do so; this theory implies that there are push factors that compel people to leave their home countries and "pull factors" in the receiving countries that attract them. This is an individualistic historical and very single-dimensional view of migration[8]. It is in this respect that the movement of the various ethnic groups that brought Islam to Niger Delta but pioneered by the Hausa is very significant.

Hausa Factor and the Establishment of Islam in the Central Delta

The contact of Islam with the central Delta of the present day Bayelsa State of Nigeria is attributed to the Nupe people commonly referred to as Hausa among the indigenous people of the region and they have been reported to have settled in Nembe for decades. Although, no written record has been found to locate the actual time but postulation from scholars put it around the 16th century.[9] The trade in yam was the first source of contact between the indigenes and traders of Nupe extraction who visited the area through the River Niger. The Nupe traders used their boats throughout trading periods, cooking and sleeping inside their boats until they finished their goods.[10]

The earliest example of notable Hausa names still found in Nembe is the popular Sambo family who according to sources originally migrated from Niger state as a yam merchant, bought land in Nembe and acquired citizenship of the town. Many great grandchildren of the Sambo family in Nembe do not know the migration of their ancestor from Nupe and astonishingly, they do not know of any link with Islam.[11] An interaction with a former student of the University of Port Harcourt whose surname is Sambo in the year 2000s yielded no clue as he did not even know the meaning of the name. The implication of this information is that as the migrant traders continued to bring their goods mainly yams, a new form of relationship was established between the host communities and the Hausa and Nupe traders which encouraged more people to embark upon the trading missions to the creeks of Niger Delta. The earliest among this group of traders during the pre-colonial era were the Sakwatawa. This tradition of trading mission to Niger Delta was continued during the colonial and independence Nigeria. On arrival, the traders ventured into the interior of the area carrying their wares and those with certain skills went about rendering such services as cobblers and butchers. Fishing was one of the occupations of the Hausa and they took advantage of the environment of the host communities to engage in fishing. The Hausa have been able to sustain their settlements in the two main towns of Nembe i.e. Ogbolomabari and Bassambiri or Sandfield.

In Yenagoa, the history of Hausa of Yenagoa dated back to 16th century. The Muslims who are commonly referred to as Hausa or Aboki are from Nupe in Niger State, Zuru from Kebbi, Gwari, Kataf and Bajju from Kaduna and the Kambari from Sokoto. It is apparent that most Hausa of Yenagoa are from North western axis of Nigeria which includes Sokoto, Niger, Kwara, Katsina and Kaduna states. In the contemporary time, the settlers from the north- west states are mostly cattle dealers while those from the North east supply most of the farm products in Swali market as well as other markets in Bayelsa state. Early Hausa settlement in Yenagoa area was around Ovom[12]. Other occupation of the Hausa in our contemporary time includes water vendor, motor cycle operators, cobblers and tailors. In Yenagoa, the major areas where the Hausa are found include Igbogene, Akenfa, Opolo, Yenizue-Gene, Amarata ,Gwegwe and Aritallin. In Ogbia, the Hausa started visiting Ogbia since 17th Century[13]. The main settlement of the Hausa is found in Ogbia main town and most of the settlements began during the colonial period through migration from already existing neighbouring Hausa community of Elele. In the contemporary time, the early Hausa immigrants are seen during the weekly market days where they trade different wares such as ear rings, wrist-watches and jewelries.

In Brass, a Nupe man using the River Niger started visiting Brass since 17th century even before the Hausa migrants stepped their feet on the area. What brought Nupe merchants to Brass was the supply of yams while Hausa merchants that came later traded in ornaments and jewelries. In

Kololuma/Opokuma area, Kaiama town has the highest number of Hausa merchants in this area and most of them are traders from Kano who started coming to the area as early as 16th century. They came to the area selling raffia clothes and peddling crocodile medicine for the local people.

Mahdi Adamu in his study of the Hausa factor in West Africa history posited that the Hausa people are considered as a highly mobile people and had established contacts with other groups in Nigeria.[14] Adamu explained that through their migration to the coastal region they subsequently developed social and economic relationship with their host communities. In this seminal work, Adamu pointed out that the Hausa migrants of pre-colonial Nigeria were not the seasonal labour migrants (*yancirani*) but were rather the long distance merchants (*fatauci*) and itinerant haberdasher (*yankoli*) and those engaged in that type of peripatetic scholars' apprenticeship known as *yawon almajiranci*.[15] As social exports, among the spinoff of Hausa migrations are their dress, language, music and religion[16]. In many communities, they provide services as needed by the different communities where they settle. The nature of service the Hausa provided to the Ikwerre of Elele contributed to the establishment of Islam in the Eastern part of the Niger Delta.

Islam in Eastern Delta

It is very difficult to say precisely when the first set of Muslims arrived the Eastern part of the Delta. However, as early as 1896 when Major Galway visited Elele, Mr. A. B. Harcourt reported the presence of Muslims at Elele in large numbers.[17] The Muslims settled at *Omuadai* compound of *Mgbuanyiam* village of Elele. They inhabited the area, which is called *Mbu-*

Osukpa. The Hausa Muslims were reported to have come on invitation of the people of Elele to help in killing marauding elephants that constituted a menace to farmlands in the later part of the 19th Century. The Muslims were able to achieve the aim for which they were invited (eliminating the menace of elephants on farmland) due to their superior weapons which consisted of bows and arrows with poisonous sharp points and local Dane guns. [18]

Apart from the popular "elephant factor" in Elele oral tradition, the Muslims might have settled down in Elele to engage in ivory trade which was buoyant at that time in European markets. The Muslims in Elele settled under the leadership of Malam Dadi who became the first *Sarki*. He was called *Eze Wosukpa* by the indigenes. He was succeeded by his brother Malam Muhammad Umar Dikko (d 1908). The next *Sarki* was Malam Dikko (also known as Dodondawa) while the indigenes called him Malam Ododo (d 1936). He was followed by Bawa Muhammad Dikko (1936-1939), Haliru Dikko (1941-1976) and the present Sarki Alhaji Saidu Dikko."[19] During the reign of Malam Muhammad Dikko (as *Sarki*), he was recognized by the colonial government as warrant Chief while Haliru Dikko (1941-1976) was appointed the Chairman of Ikwerre District Council at Choba.

The city of Port Harcourt was created in 1913 and the city attracted several European firms. There were national of countries like Syria, Lebanon and Nigerians who are Yoruba, Hausa and Fulani who were Muslims who came to Port Harcourt. The encouragement given by the government for people to come to Port Harcourt for labour in the Railway system spurred some people from Lagos to flock Port Harcourt who incidentally included some Muslims. Some

Muslims who have settled in Elele also took advantage of the booming business to move down to Port Harcourt. The Muslims in Port Harcourt started their religious activities as private individuals before they began their prayers in open places in congregation. The colonial government allocated two plots of land at 15/16 Victoria for the Yoruba while the Hausa were also given two plots at 41/42 Victoria Street to erect their Mosques. The two Mosques were constructed in 1933 with Planks. By 1935, the 15/16 Victoria Mosque was built with blocks[20].

In early 1940s, Muslim organisations with missionary zeal like Ahmadiyyah movement came to Port Harcourt to propagate Islam. In 1946, Alfa M. S. B. Dawodu, an Ahmadi missionary in Port Harcourt engaged in preaching tours of Port Harcourt and even challenged Gideon Urhobo, the founder of God's Kingdom Society in a debate which took place at Roxy Hall on Sunday 8 December, 1946 in Port Harcourt[21]. In 1954, the Muslim Council was established under the leadership of Alhaji Umar Kalio. He led the Muslim to the period of the civil war when the Muslims were persecuted by the "Biafran" soldiers. He was followed by Alhaji Ibrahim Alex Fubara (1976-79), Alhaji Ibrahim Minayellombo (1979-1984) and Alhaji Ahmed R. T Okiri who presided over the affairs from 1984 until his death in 2011. The Council has not been properly constituted due internal crisis that engulfed the Muslims over who becomes the new leader. The crisis has been precipitated by the Okiri family who have been making efforts to transform the Muslim leadership into a hereditary post by nominating one of their proxy to take over as the leader against the wishes of the generality of the Muslims in the state that chose Alhaji Hassan Welewa in a keenly contested *Shūrā* committee screening of 2012.

When the civil war broke out in 1967, most of the Muslims from the North and West of Nigeria left Niger Delta to their respective states. But in Elele, most of the Muslim stayed because, a considerable number amongst them did not know any state they could call theirs except Elele. The Muslims encountered their greatest problem during the civil war (1967-1970). The Biafran soldiers considered the Muslims of Elele who were Hausa-Fulani as the enemy of the Biafra cause; hence, an unmitigated misery through massacre was unleashed on the Muslims. The civil war caused a serious depletion in Muslim population in Niger-Delta.[22] The learned Muslims who could have continued expounding the tenets of Islam to new converts also left in large numbers thereby, creating a serious vacuum that could not be filled by any of the indigenes. The indigenous Muslims however were able to stamp their feet with some measure of authority albeit with their little knowledge of the faith they professed. By 31 September 1966 after the Friday prayer, the Muslim leaders announced to the worshippers to leave the region because it had become unsafe for them.

During the war, the Biafra Government bestowed a "Muslim identity" on Federal Nigeria in her press war for international attention and recognition. Hence, Islam was the main cause of the war. The "Biafra" Government viewed Nigeria as acting as a tool of the World Muslim League and in conjunction with the Nigeria Muslim organizations in a 'jihad' against Biafra. The Muslim identity ascribed to Federal Nigerian exposed the Muslim in Niger Delta like other minority groups into serious persecution. They suffered not only from the ravages of war but also from the Biafra forces that saw them as saboteurs to the cause of "Biafra". Many were captured, forcibly evacuated and killed and those suspected to be waiting for the arrival of federal troops were brutally executed[23].

In May 19, 1968, greater parts of the present day Rivers State was already liberated from Biafra hegemony and Port Harcourt became the Headquarters of the Third Marine Commando Division of the Nigerian army. Hence, the presence of 'Muslim soldiers' under the leadership of Major G. A. Bello became noticeable in major areas of Port Harcourt. The Muslim soldiers started gathering in open spaces to observe their ritual prayers. Apart from the 15/16 and 41/42 Victoria Mosques, which have been established in the early 1930s, the soldiers established mosques like Diobu Central Mosque (Mile 1), Elelewon, Rumuomasi and Rainbow mosques as praying grounds. After the end of the war in 1970, the soldiers transferred these 'praying grounds - Mosques' to the Muslim civilians who started arriving Port Harcourt for their commercial activities. One can safely say that the 'Muslim soldiers' were responsible for the consolidation of Islam in the region during the period of political interregnum.

Immediately after the war, Muslims started coming to Port Harcourt as civil servants in Federal establishments. When the National Youth Service Corps (NYSC) was established in 1973, Muslim graduates were sent to the region as part of the integration efforts of the government after the war and they contributed to the re-establishment of Islam in the various towns and villages of their primary assignments. Most of those graduates participating in the NYSC were members of the Muslim Students Society of Nigeria (MSSN) in their various higher institutions and they came to the region with the same proselytizing zeal inculcated in them by the Society. By the early 1980s the fear instilled in the minds of non-Easterners due to the civil war was reducing; hence, some Muslims started taking jobs in Federal establishments in Port Harcourt, Bonny, Warri and Yenagoa with the creation of Bayelsa in 1996. The period has also witnessed the establishment of many Muslim organizations like Islamic Propagation Centre (Warri), National Council of Muslim Youth Organization (NACOMYO), Al-Usrah, NASFAT, Al-Ithimam, FOMWAN, Muslim Students Society, Association of Muslim Professionals and Muslim Corpers Association of Nigeria.

The Growth of Islam in the Delta

The missionary effort of Muslim is technically called *Da'wah* and used in the Qur'an to mean inviting people to the right course and towards the cause of Allah or preaching righteousness (Qur'an 16: 125, 7: *55)*. Islamic missionary effort is a combination of "reform" *(Islāh)* and "renewal" *(Tajdīd)*. By reform it is undoing the harm that results from neglect of the religious code, and renewal, means the level at which prescriptive standards are applied after the removal of impediments[24]. Both *Islāh* (reform) and *Tajdīd* (renewal) are conjoined in the scriptural concept of *Amr bi'l Ma'rūf wa n-nahy an al-Munkar* (to enjoin good works and restrain from what is evil (Qur'an 13: 21-22).

The concept of *Amr bi'l Ma'rūf* is anchored on the following:

i) Muslims, apart from coming to the truth, are mandated to lead others to the truth (Qur'an 3:110; 22: 41; 9: 71; 3:104);

ii) The responsibility of proselytizing Islam is placed on the entire community *(fard kifāyah)*, hence, it is a communal and social responsibility and not a purely professional duty of the clergy because there is no priesthood in Islam;

iii) Balance and moderation are the main thrust of the work because the *Ummah* is a balanced one (Qur'an 2:143); and

iv) In carrying out the work, the perfect and noble paradigms of Allah from the Qur'an and His Messenger's *Sunnah* are to be followed.[25]

According to Molla, Muslim mission have been assisted in Christian areas by a number of factors:

> In order to become a Muslim there is no need for long periods of Catechism, no need to commit oneself to the payment of dues, no need to feel the rigours of Church disciplines which may not be fulfilled by the pastor himself, no need to send away your wives (if not more than four) and children from such wives.[26]

The growth of Islam in Port Harcourt in the form of conversion has been due to mental and spiritual factors, helped occasionally by material factors. According to Ejizu, conversion as a religious concept refers to change in the religious life and behaviour of people. Conversion therefore, usually implies a change from one religious state to another religious state. The change could be a permanent one, or it could last for only a period of time. Conversion could take place within the same religious system to which an individual or group already belongs or professes, or it could involve a change away from a religion to which one was previously[27].

The experience of Muslims in the Niger Delta in the proselytization of Islam is not as phenomenal like the earlier Christian Missionary enterprise in the region. The reason for the contrast is that, the Muslims do not enjoy supporting colonial power, no schools and medical care to be offered to the local people for inducement.

Conversion from one religion to the other is a system of personal and social orientation. A convert before his/her conversion, has been noted to experience a strong feeling of a spiritual crisis or dilemma needing an immediate solution. Consequences of conversion to Islam involve a transformation and a sense of relief and ecstasy. Scholars have provided insights to the growth of Islam in many areas of West Africa, which is also relevant to our study. Robin Horton account indicates that:

> Islam seems to have been fairly content with its catalytic role. It has been tolerant in allowing the individual to make his own particular selection from official doctrines. It has accepted that those who come to the mosque form a continuum rather than a band of total converts; and it does not nag excessively at those who lie towards the pagan end of the continuum.[28]

Horton's account for the growth of Islam represents the general and simplistic view in that to consider Islamic demands as not far different from those of traditional African religion or indigenous forms of worship in Africa is overstretched. What has been considered as Islamic practices are deviational practices of some clerics which Islam itself considers as repugnant but has been stubbornly practised by them for economic motives and gains. While Islam has accommodated some traditional ways of life, which are not considered repugnant to Islam, it however, rejects syncretism

Chapter Twenty	Abdulrazaq Kilani, in Y.A. Quadri, R.W. Omotoye & R.I. Adebayo (Eds) Religion in Contemporary Nigeria London, Adonis & Abbey Publishers

(takhlit). In the same respect, Islam does not demand a violent break, a complete and unconditional rupture with one's culture so long as such cultures do not contradict Islam. To describe Islamic growth generally as offering immediate value without displacing the old is indeed an inaccurate and distorted understanding of Muslim missionary methodology. According to Horton, Islam has had the edge in some areas because it was there first. However, in areas where Christianity was first, people opted for Islam enthusiastically as an alternative to the existing Catholicism, Anglicanism or the new wave Television Churches. It is this point among others that explains the reason for peoples' reversion and conversion to Islam in the Niger Delta region.

Apart from these intellectual insights of these scholars, the growth of Islam in Port Harcourt has been accentuated by the non-adoption of vernacular languages as a scriptural and canonical medium. The active participation of lay Muslims in ritual acts of worship like *Salat* means that Arabic phrases, however, imperfectly understood, remain on the lips of believers. The success of Islam as a missionary religion in Niger Delta is partly attributable to the perpetuation of the sacred Arabic. The Hausa, Yoruba, Fulani, Nupe and indigenous reverts can all read the book and mingle in worship together. There is to all one common authority and the ultimate umpirage – the Qur'an. Islam as a missionary religion has succeeded in providing a synthesis of language and religion. A preacher does not need to learn the myriad of dialects of the people of the Niger Delta in order to teach them Islamic rituals; likewise, the only task for a revert is to learn Arabic which is the language of the Qur'an and uniform mode of worship thereby attracting people to Islam.

The Muslim way of worship has been described by Morel as more African, than Christian way of worship, which is wrapped up in European clothes. According to him, "while Christian missionaries pride themselves in wearing European forms of dress, Islam adopts traditional attire for adherents".[29] There is a reciprocal interest in Islam express by people who see it as a means of achieving more prestige and better standard of living. Such people take significant steps toward conversion by adopting Muslim names, learning the Muslim greetings *(taslim)* and wearing long robes and caps. This attitude may be explained according to Jjomahand Bogardus by the contention that "an important religious group is chosen because of its social, economic and political powers".[30] This type of attitude began at the end of the civil war. A few years after the end of the civil war, have witnessed the ascendancy of some Muslims in the control of the political power of Nigeria. There has been an improvement in the academic profiles of Muslims in which some Muslims began to head important government Parastatals and Departments. This attitude also confirms the proposition that "social distance towards an important group diminishes in proportion to the magnitude of power possessed by that group".[31]

An important factor for the modest growth of Islam in Niger Delta region has been the enthusiasm and dedication of Muslims in operationalising their religion. The Muslims with ease rely on the local materials available, set up simple structure as mosque or a praying ground with no roof thereby making Islam visible and consequently facilitate the growth of Islam. Where they find it difficult to buy land in Port Harcourt, Yenagoa, Bonny and in other communities to build a Mosque, they lease land to erect one, though this is a financially tasking experience. The observance of ritual prayers in open places continues to attract the attention of non-Muslim neighbours who gather around the Muslims whenever any of the daily prayers is being observed or the *adhan* (call to prayer) is being made. The educative effects upon individuals and whole communities of Islamic rituals in the spread of Islam cannot be under-estimated. Muslims are often identifiable according to Peter Clarke, "by their dress, by what they eat or do not eat. They pray anywhere and in the open and thus make Islam a highly visible and public religion. Islamic ritual is the genius of Islam and has counted a great deal in the diffusion of Islam."[32]

The early history of Islam witnessed the construction of 15/16 and 41/42 Victoria Street Mosques in 1933. The period of the civil war marked another era with the establishment of Mile 1, Elelenwo, Rumuomasi and Rainbow town mosques by Muslim officers in the Nigeria Army. The major development in mosque histories in Port Harcourt between 1970 and 1980 was the establishment of Bori Camp mosque in 1970, Gambia Street Mosque in 1972 and the reconstruction of Mile 1 Mosque in 1973 as *Jumu'ah* Mosques. The tremendous expansion in Port Harcourt owing to the establishment of industries and institutions, led to the demand for more *Jumu'ah* mosques since the 1990s. Notable mosques in this category are Nigerian Ports (1994), Yam Zone (1994), Nigerian Port, Onne (1995), International Airport (1995), NNS Akaso (1995), University of Port Harcourt (1996), Anu Oluwa Po (Mile III), Polo Ground (1997) and NNS Okemini (1997). The creation of Bayelsa in 1996 witnessed the movement of more Muslims to the central delta and the construction of mosques at Amarata, Gwegwe and Aritallin.

Muslim-Christian Relations in Niger Delta

The relationship between Islam and Christianity in some parts of Nigeria has been characterised by intermittent conflicts because both religions want to expand. Tension and mistrust come from the feeling of unfair treatment by one side using state apparatus against the other. Nevertheless, the religious climate in Niger-Delta can be described as harmonious, despite the fact that the two religions are expanding and proselytising. There are no recorded hostilities between Muslims and Christians resulting in physical violence and thereby threatening the cordial relationship. Even though Muslims and Christians live together in harmony in Niger Delta, there have been tensions and rivalries between them. Nigeria as a country has witnessed internal security crisis occasioned by the adoption of *Shari'ah*, Boko Haram, ethno-religious crises in the North all have spiral effects on the Muslims in the Niger-Delta.

Internal security crisis implies the absence of freedom from danger to life and property and the decline of conducive atmosphere for the people to pursue their legitimate matters within the state. From 21 to 22 February, 2001, an unestimated number of people lost their lives in clashes between Muslims and Christians in Kaduna metropolis over the proposed introduction of Islamic criminal law. The Kaduna incident led to a reprisal attack in Aba, Umuahia (Abia state), Onitsha (Anambra state) and Okigwe (Imo state) and about 450 persons were killed[33]. The effect of the reprisal killings were felt in Rivers and Bayelsa States as many Muslims experienced periodic migration to the north and south-west of Nigeria for safety occasioned by internal security challenge.

The intervention of Rivers state government through sustained campaigns in the media protected the Muslims in the state from attacks when miscreants attempted to extend the reprisal killings in Aba to Port Harcourt in 2000, 2004 and 2005. During the 2015 general election, the atmosphere was so heightened that many Muslims temporarily relocated to other parts of Nigeria for safety.

The Muslims in the Delta to a large extent also face the backlash of morbid fear of domination competition from the indigenous ethnic groups from the region who view Muslims presence in the oil rich region from the same perspective the people in the region perceive other major ethnic groups like Hausa, Fulani and Yoruba as local imperialists who have only come to benefit from their oil wealth. Most officials in state establishments often times discriminate against indigenes of the states who are Muslims in the same way they treat migrant Muslims with contempt. Thus religion rather than being a cohesive factor has turned out to be a divisive factor for the Nigerian people. The current experience can be likened to what Ahmadu Bello, the Sardauna of Sokoto (d.1966) said when he lamented that:

> Religion which has become a cohesive factor in many societies has proved extremely divisive in Nigeria. In their search for religious sect, Nigerians have fallen back on prejudice, bigotry, extremism and parochial antagonism that only promote chaos, anarchy and disunity. [34]

Islam is seen by some non-Muslims like a 'close-circuit' meant for the Hausa-Fulani and some Yoruba. It is also not an exaggeration to say that a great deal of 'war of slogans' is waged against people willing to accept Islam by saying, 'accepting Islam is to be in the pay of the Hausa' (sic). Sincere

---

Chapter Twenty | Abdulrazaq Kilani, in
Y.A. Quadri, R.W. Omotoye & R.I. Adebayo (Eds)
Religion in Contemporary Nigeria
London, Adonis & Abbey Publishers

435

converts to Islam are often accused by their brethren of taking to Islam because of Muslim money or to become rich, as if a power exists in Islam that confers affluence on people.

The Muslims as a minority community live under perpetual media siege through the numerous church programmes on state television without the same opportunity being made available for Muslims. The Muslims have been consistently denied the opportunity to sponsor religious programmes in the

Rivers State Television (RSTV). In 2007, Al-Usrah wrote to the management of the media stations for courtesy visits in order to promote inter- religious harmony but the request was rejected and only the Federal Government's, Nigeria Television Authority (NTA) acquiesced to the request. In 1999 for example, the ratio between programmes on Islam and Christianity in the government owned Nigeria Television Authority at Port Harcourt was 1 to 27. There were 23 Christian programmes of 13 hours and 30 minutes from Monday to Sunday, as against 30 minutes weekly of programmes for Islam only on Fridays. On Saturdays and Sundays, when most families are at home, about four hours each day of Christian programmes are aired on the same station. By 2004, the 30 minutes programme for Islam has been removed giving Islam a complete blackout in all the media houses in the State.[35]

The emergence of Pentecostalism in the religious growth of Christianity in Nigeria has added a new dimension to the religious terrain in Niger Delta. Every available facility like hotel banquet halls, uncompleted buildings, empty classrooms and every available large hall have been taken over as churches by the Pentecostal groups in the scramble for souls. There are many para-church type of organizations that have been waging religious and psychological warfare against the Muslims in offices, hospitals, banks and schools. Among such organization include Fellowship of Christian Nurses, Hospital Christian Fellowship and Christian Bankers. It is not uncommon to experience as a patient in a hospital/clinic, a nurse advising the patient to leave the hospital and take a spiritual solution to a medical problem that has brought him or her to the hospital. Such nurses are also quick to recommend a church or a pastor to visit for spiritual intervention. Some medical Doctors are also involved in this unethical behaviour which most often is targeted at Muslim patients. In the same respect, in all government hospitals, Christian devotional worship of singing and dancing is imposed by these nurses every day on all patients most especially women (irrespective of their religion) who have come to the hospital either for ante-natal, post natal or as outpatients before they are attended to by the health officials. The preponderance of this unethical behaviour is due to Pentecostal teaching that sickness, disease and misfortune are not from God but of Satan and his demons.[36]

Appraisal of Islam in Niger Delta

A proper appraisal of Islam in Niger-Delta is a mixture of success and setback. It could be noted that most 'reverts' are Islamically dormant due to lack of Islamic education. This problem cannot be wholly attributed to the fault of the local Muslims, as it is also due to the lack of continuity and follow-up from the Muslim preachers. It appears that most preachers are only contented with conversion and reverts making the pronouncement of an intention to become Muslims. It is this situation that is responsible for the general ignorance among them. Furthermore, most teachers employed to reside in the communities often abandon their duty posts due to lack of water, light and other facilities found in the major towns and cities.

It is clearly discernible that many of the local Muslims cannot operationalise their new faith even after many years of becoming Muslim due to lack of adequate knowledge and education. The nominal or dormant attitude of many of them is not an indication of lack of faith but due to the widespread ignorance of Islam. In some communities with meager resources, mosques have been built on lands that are donated by individuals for such purpose, but few facilities are in place to provide continuing education and direction to the new converts. The village preaching tours through which most villages came in contact with Islam are voluntary and unorganised efforts of individual Muslims. While the majority of volunteers are always willing to participate on weekends, most of them are often handicapped by their official commitments on weekends, especially the industry workers. In the same vein, most Muslim activities are done in Port Harcourt, Bonny, Yenagoa, Ahoada, at the expense of the villages.

When Islam first came to Niger-Delta, it did remain as a stranger for some time, but with a strong doctrine combined with its specific culture, the Muslim community evolved through history and has become strong and viable through the combine efforts of all. As Hamilton Gibb points out, Islam:

> can be imagined by a triangle; the three angles are a doctrine, a culture and a history, and the three sides enclose a community. The triangle may be smaller or larger, the size of the angles may vary in relation to

one another; but the community always remains enclosed within them.37

In other words, Islam develops in different surroundings and environments. It tries to establish itself as part of the society where it is established. It may present different features under the influence of and in response to, local and social forces, but the spirit of the religion remains uniform. Islam in the region might have been influenced by Niger-Delta forces, although it nevertheless remains the same Islam that is found everywhere else in the world.

Islam, no doubt, is growing in Niger Delta, and the growth is not wholly unconnected with the global spread of Islam. The resurgence among the youth in the region *vis-à-vis* their style of *da'wah* should be appreciated in line with the global network of information available through television, radio, books and the Internet, which the youths have access to as compared to the traditional method of the older Muslims. There is no doubt that a lukewarm attitude exists between the old and the younger generation of Muslims in the region due to approach to Islamic propagation and doctrinal differences occasioned by the influx of salafiyyah*'aqidah* (creed) among the youths and professionals in the region. The way forward is cooperation among everyone and rather than the 'old' stigmatising the young as 'rabble rousers' or ignorant fundamentalists, the old can benefit from the youth on how to address modern challenges of the ummah and so also the youth have a lot to gain from the experience of the 'old' in the field of *da'wah* in Niger-Delta.

Conclusion

The many centuries of Islam in the Niger-Delta accentuated by inter group relations has come to some extent prove an integrative force, making it possible for the welding together of diverse groups into a community called the Muslim *ummah*. The Muslims have succeeded to a large extent in establishing a community based on the unity and equality of believers. The internal decadence within Muslims due to the syncretistic practices of some *'ulamā'* in Niger-Delta notwithstanding, the growth of Islam, *albeit* not a geometric one, cannot be denied. One of the important features of the planting of Islam in non-Muslim Communities is the inter-play of religion and culture. This feature has contributed to the association of diverse peoples in Niger-Delta region viz: Hausa, Fulani, Kanuri, Ebira, Nupe, Igala and Yoruba to an eventual assimilation into what is described as Hausa identity. Islam with its impressive ceremonies and ritual activities like *Salat* (ritual prayer), *sawm* (fasting), *hajj* (pilgrimage) and the Qur'an itself, have continued to excite the local inhabitants. The religion has survived to make impact in various aspects of human endeavours in view of the various challenges it has to contend with as a religion.

Notes and References

1. Luka, Nathaniel Bobby Gimba, "The Hausa in the Central Delta, in Historical Perspectives 1500-2011",Unpublished M.A. Thesis, Department of History and Diplomatic Studies, University of Port Harcourt, 2014, 24.
2. W. Ogionwo, *Migrant Families in an African City - A Social Survey of Port-Harcourt*, (Harvard: Harvard Centre for population, 1974), 75. Also, W. Ogionwo, *A Social Survey of Port Harcourt*, (Ibadan: Heinemann Educational Books, 1979), 21-22
3. Luka, Nathaniel Bobby Gimba, "The Hausa in the Central Delta", 13-14
4. Luka, Nathaniel Bobby Gimba, "The Hausa in the Central Delta", 13-14
5. Ojua, Takim Asu, Tiku Takim Oru, Chimezie Atama,, "Ethno- Historical Analysis of the Effects of Migration on African Family System", *Canadian Social Science*, vol.10, Number 3, (2014), 43. Available from: http://www.cscanada.net/index.php/css/article/view/4521
6. Ojua, Takim Asu, Tiku Takim Oru, Chimezie Atama, "Ethno- Historical Analysis of the Effects of Migration", 44.
7. Ojua, Takim Asu, Tiku Takim Oru, Chimezie Atama, "Ethno- Historical Analysis of the Effects of Migration", 46.
8. Luka, Nathaniel Bobby Gimba, "The Hausa in the Central Delta", 34.

9. Luka, Nathaniel Bobby Gimba, "The Hausa in the Central Delta." 34
10. This information was obtained from Dr Okorobia (Senior Lecturer, Department of History and Diplomatic Studies, University of Port Harcourt) on 20th May, 2014 and one of the descendants of Sambo family of Nembe.
11. Luka, Nathaniel Bobby Gimba, "The Hausa in the Central Delta", 32-33.
12. Luka, Nathaniel Bobby Gimba, "The Hausa in the Central Delta", 33.
13. Egbefo, Dawood Omolumen, "Aspect of Intergroup Relations in 21st Century Nigeria: Emblem of Ethnicity, Religious Fundamentalism and National Security Crisis 2000-2014". *International Journal of Arts and Humanities,* 4(1). 13(2015), 2.
14. A.H.M. Kirk-Greene, "Mahdi Adamu Hausa Factor in West Africa History, A Review", *Oxford Journal of African Affairs,* vol.79 Number 317 (1980), 606-608.
15. A.H.M. Kirk-Greene, "Mahdi Adamu Hausa Factor in West Africa History, A Review", 606-608.
16. E.W. Amadi, "Hausa Community in Elele", (Unpublished B. A. Long Essay, Department of History, University of Port Harcourt, 1984), 8.
17. Abdulrazaq, Kilani, "A Historical Perspective of the Penetration of Islam into Port Harcourt in Niger-Delta, Nigeria 1896-1998", *Journal of Religion and Culture,* Vol.1, Number 2, (2000), 13, also, Abdulrazaq, Kilani, "Islam and Christian- Muslim Relations In Niger-Delta (Nigeria)," *Journal of Muslim Minority Affairs,* vol. 20, Number 1, (2000), 129.

Chapter Twenty	Abdulrazaq Kilani, in Y.A. Quadri, R.W. Omotoye & R.I. Adebayo (Eds) Religion in Contemporary Nigeria London, Adonis & Abbey Publishers

18. Abdulrazaq, Kilani, "A Historical Perspective of the Penetration of Islam into Port Harcourt", 14.
19. Abdulrazaq, Kilani, "A Historical Perspective of the Penetration of Islam into Port Harcourt", 14.
20. Abdulrazaq, Kilani, "A Historical Perspective of the Penetration of Islam into Port Harcourt", 14.
21. Ilega, D.I., "Gideon M. Urhobo and the God's Kingdom Society in Nigeria". Ph.D. Dissertation, University of Aberdeen, 1982, 227.
22. Abdulrazaq, Kilani, *Minaret in the Delta, A History of Islam in Port Harcourt 1896-2007*, (Lagos: JJI Publishers, 2008), 46.
23. Abdulrazaq, Kilani, "A Historical Perspective of the Penetration of Islam into Port Harcourt", 15.
24. L. John, Esposito, *Islam: The Straight Path*, (Oxford: University Press, 1988), 118.
25. A. Ezzati, *An Introduction to the History of the Spread of Islam*, (Ghom: The Ahlul-Bayt World Assembly, 1994), 76-77.
26. See E.P.T. Crampton, *Christianity in Northern Nigeria*, (London: Geoffrey Chapman, 1975), 193.
27. C.I. Ejizu, "Conversion in African Traditional Religions".2012, 2. http://www.afrikaworld.net/afrel/conversion.htm retrieved 4/12/16
28. Horton, Robin, "African Conversion," *Africa*, vol. XLI, Number 11, (April 1971), 105.
29. E.D. Morel, *Nigeria: Its People and Problems,*(London: N. P., 1912), 27.
30. B. I. C. Jjomah, and Emory Bogardus, "Social Distance Scale: A Critic of its Application to the Africa Data," *The*

Nigeria Journal of Sociology and Anthropology, vol. 3, Number 1, 64-65.
31. B. I. C. Jjomah, and Emory Bogardus, "Social Distance Scale: A Critic of its Application to the Africa Data", 65.
32. P.B. Clarke, *West Africa and Islam*, (London: Edward Arnold Publishers, 1981), 261.
33. Egbefo, Dawood Omolumen, "Aspect of Intergroup Relations in 21st Century Nigeria", 10.
34. Egbefo, Dawood Omolumen, "Aspect of Intergroup Relations", 10.
35. Abdulrazaq, Kilani, *Minaret in the Delta, A History of Islam in Port Harcourt 1896-2007*, (Lagos: JJI Publishers, 2008), 225.
36. Abdulrazaq, Kilani, *Minaret in the Delta*, 226.
37. SeeA.R.I. Doi, "Islamic Thought and Culture-Their Impact on Africa (with Special Reference to Nigeria)". *Nigeria Journal of Islam, vol.*1, Number 1, (1970), 33.

Index

A
Abdullahi, Ango, 32, 229
Abdulsalam, H.A., 349
Adebayo, R.I., iii, v, 45, 73, 74, 241
Adebayo, Tajudeen, 199
Adebiyi,n Bishop Peter, 12, 16, 27, 28
Adeboye, Pastor E.A. Adeboye, 19
Adegboye, Pastor George, 175, 177, 179, 180, 191
Adelaja, Pastor Sunday, 20
African Traditional Religion, 11, 149, 274, 335, 339, 418
Akande, Lydia Bosede, 31
Akanni, Abdul Hakeem, 75
Akinfenwa, Olubusola Bosede, 47
Akinwumi, O. S, 61
Al-Haramain Islamic Foundation, 249, 250
Alkali, Nural, 35, 45, 102, 379, 384
All Christian Fellowship Church at Suleja, 80
Allah the Most High, 109, 110, 115
Almighty God, 33
Amalgamation in 1914, 12, 31
Amin, Idi, 26
Ansarud-Deen Society, 242
Arabic language, 201, 202, 203
Ashimolowo, Pastor Matthew, 19
Awolowo, Awolowo, 32
Ayoola, Adediran Amos, 135
Azikwe, Nnamdi, 32

B
Bakare, Pastor Tunde, 24
Balewa, Tafawa, 32
Balogun, H. O, 61
Barth, Karl, 142, 149
Bello, Sir Ahmadu, 181, 244, 245, 427
Bello-Ja'Afar, Hidayah, 367
Bidmos, M.A., 45, 111, 130, 131, 210, 225
Boko Haram, vi, 15, 22, 38, 52, 58, 61, 64, 65, 66, 67, 70, 75, 76, 80, 82, 95, 97, 99, 101, 113, 151, 154, 159, 160, 161, 162, 167, 168, 210, 214, 241, 261, 273, 434
Bonkie, Rev. Reinhard, 115
British colonial rule, 12
Buber, Martin, 138
Bulunkutu, Maiduguri, 64

C
Cameroon, 64, 261
Carthaginians, 201
Catholic Bishops Conference of Nigeria, 24
Celestial Church of Christ, 170
Charisma, 169, 170, 178, 197
Cherubim and Seraphim, 170, 184, 187
Christ Apostolic Church, 34, 160, 161, 170, 197
Christ Embassy, 175, 177
Christian Association of Nigeria, 25, 184, 191, 316
Christmas Day, 66
Church of the Lord, 170
Churches, vi, 33, 34, 38, 42, 52, 143, 169, 170, 174, 175, 176, 188, 195, 197, 292, 431
Crowther, Bishop Samuel Ajayi, 44, 169, 173

D
Da'wah in Islam, 82
Damaturu, 80, 161, 168
Dan Fodio, Uthman, 69, 377
Day of Judgement, 92
Day of Judgment, 122, 314
Deedat, Sheikh Ahmad, 115
Deeper Life Christian Church, 175, 177, 186
Doe, Samuel, 26
Durkheim, Emile, 49, 271

E
Economic and Financial Crime Commission, 135
Education in Islam, 226
Ehusani, Rev. Fr. George, 34, 44
Elisha, Kelly, 40, 46
Embassy of the Blessed God for All Nations, 20
Evangelism, 76, 190

F
Failed States Index, 13
False Spirituality, 18
Family Economic Advance Programme, 42
Fasting, 33, 40
Federation of Muslim Women Associations in Nigeria, 242
Fighting for God, 64

Fire and Miracles, 177
Fulani, 47, 107, 191, 202, 273, 350, 355, 368, 418, 424, 426, 431, 435, 440

G

Ghandhi, Mahatma, 50
Glorious Qur'ān, 77, 84, 85, 86, 87, 92, 94, 98, 102, 103, 122, 123, 129
Greek, 367
Gumi, Shaykh Abubakar Mahmood, 245

H

Hajj, 40, 231, 232, 233, 236, 237, 238, 314
Harry, Kehinde Young, 37
Hausa, 47, 51, 52, 64, 69, 76, 159, 202, 203, 273, 350, 351, 355, 368, 374, 375, 376, 377, 378, 380, 381, 382, 383, 385, 417, 418, 419, 420, 421, 422, 423, 424, 426, 431, 435, 440
Healing, 29, 188
Hebrew, 153, 154, 157, 165, 166, 367
Henslim, James, 53, 60
Herod the Tetrarch, 63
Hinduism, 367
Hutchinsen Encyclopaedia, 62
Huxley, Julian, 138

I

Igbo, 47, 329, 331, 342, 343, 350
Imo state, 323, 326, 336, 434
Independent Corrupt Practice and other related offences Commission, 135
Indonesia, 26, 252
Insecurity, iv, 15, 48, 56, 69, 151, 152, 159, 162, 164, 176, 277
Institute for Human Resources Development, 212
International Institute of Islamic Thought, 207, 254
International Islamic Charitable Organisation, 256
International Islamic Relief Organisation, 252, 260
Intra-Religious Unrest, 106
Isiala-Mbano, vii, 323, 324, 325, 326, 327, 330, 331, 334, 335, 336, 337, 338, 339, 340, 341, 342, 343, 344, 345
Islamic Brotherhood, 77
Islamic Development Bank, 246, 247, 248, 261
Islamic Educational, Scientific and Cultural Organisation, 252, 256

Islamic Research and Training Insitute, 247
Islamic Studies, vi, 61, 102, 199, 200, 204, 206, 207, 208, 209, 210, 211, 212, 213, 214, 215, 216, 256, 258, 367
Israel, 14, 15, 16, 19, 53, 151, 154, 156, 157, 162, 163, 286, 304
Izalah, 106

J

Je'adayibe, Gwamna Dogara, 9
Jesus Christ, 82, 142, 187, 188, 191, 194, 287, 290, 292, 303, 308
Jihād, 76, 77, 82, 85, 86, 87, 94, 98, 100, 102, 103, 104

K

Ka'aba, 64
Kalu, Ogbu, 192, 198
Kano, vii, 51, 52, 64, 67, 80, 115, 161, 207, 211, 231, 241, 255, 256, 269, 273, 367, 368, 374, 378, 379, 381, 384, 385, 423
Kanuri, 47, 202, 203, 350, 418, 440
Kastina, 269
Kimball, Charles, 48, 59
Kings International Christian Centre, 19
Kukah, Bishop Matthew Hassan, 12, 23, 28, 30, 111, 116, 131

L

Latter Rain Assembly, 175, 177

M

Macaulay, Herbert, 32
Madalla, 67
Madina, 63, 250
Maitasine riot, 241
Maitatsine, Muhammad Marwa, 64
Makkah, 63, 84, 88, 90, 232
Malaysia, 26, 236, 297
Maliki Code, 374
Marriage, 39, 229, 234, 237, 283
Martyrdom in Islam, 91
Miracle from the Qur'anic Narrative, 301
Moral, ii
Mosques, 33, 34, 38, 356, 425, 427, 433
Mountain of Fire, 34, 196
Movement for the Actualisation of the Sovereign State of Biafra, 100
Movement for the Actualization of the Sovereign State of Biafra, 15
Movement for the Emancipation of the Niger-Delta, 100

Musa, Yusuf Owoyemi, 297
Muslim Students Society of Nigeria, 242, 427
Muslim Women and Inheritance in Hausa Tradition, 378
Muslim-Christian Relations in Niger Delta, 434

N

Nasarawa State University, Keffi, 9
Nasrullahil Fathi Society, 242
National Council of Muslim Youth Organization, 359, 428
National Directorate of Employment, 42
National Joint Muslim Organization, 358
National Poverty Eradication Programme, 42
New Religious Movements, 170, 195
New Testament, 63, 174, 175, 178, 181, 287, 291, 292
Niger Delta, 75, 210, 417, 418, 420, 421, 423, 426, 430, 431, 432, 434, 436, 437, 438, 439, 440
Nigeria Customs Service, 212
Nigeria Police Force Headquarters, Abuja, 79
Nigerian Television Authority, 36, 180, 181, 183, 184, 185
Northern Ireland, 53
Nwazonobi, Patricia Ebere, 323

O

Obama, Barrack, 136, 147
Obasanjo, Olusegun, 137
Odudele, Rotimi, 269
Ogunkunle, C. O, 151
Olawuyi, Rev.Idowu, 175, 178, 182, 183
Old Oyo Empire, 351
Old Testament, 63, 156, 157, 165, 166, 283, 286, 287
Omotoye, R.W., ii, iii, v, 169, 177, 196, 197
Onaiyekan, John, 9, 11, 14, 27, 28, 30
Opoola, Elizabeth Omolara, 283
Organisation of Islamic Conference, 242, 261
Otokoto Hotel Amakohia, Owerri, 336
Owerri, 269

P

Polygamy in African Religion, 284
Polygamy in Christianity, 286

Pope John Paul II, 25
Port Harcourt, 418, 421, 424, 425, 427, 429, 431, 432, 433, 435, 436, 438
Positive Element of Faith, 57
Prayer, 34, 83, 164, 178, 189, 314
Prophecy, 147, 190
Prophet of Islam, 122, 130

Q

Quadri, Y.A., ii, iii, v, 94, 96, 102, 104
Qur'an, 36, 57, 145, 175, 252, 302, 360, 428, 429, 431, 440

R

Ramadan, 33, 40, 232, 251, 254
Redeemed Christian Church of God, 19, 175
Religious Bigotry, 110
religious disturbances, 51, 108

S

Salam Alaikum, 39
Save Nigeria Group, 24
Seko, Mobutu Sese, 26
Shari'ah, 207, 349, 351, 353, 354, 355, 356, 357, 358, 359, 360, 361
Shi'ah, 106
Shield of Faith Assembly, 178, 181
Shittu, A. B, 105
Shrines, 33
Sokoto caliphate, 349
Sokoto Caliphate, 65, 172, 196, 368
Southern protectorates, 349
Sufi Brotherhood, 106
Sunni, 106
Sword of Damocles, 62
Sword of the Spirits, 177

T

Tajdid, 77, 101
Taliban, 52
Taylor, Charles, 26
Terrorism, vi, 61, 62, 63, 69, 73, 74, 133
Tithes, 21
Transparency International, 14, 35
Traore, Karim, ii
Trinity Household of Faith Church, 182
Tutu, Bishop Desmond, 25

U

Umar, Aminu, 120, 121, 123, 391, 424, 425
Umrah, 232

United Nations Economic and Social Council, 252
United Nations International Children's Emergency Fund, 252
United State of America, 52
United States of America, 9, 52, 136, 254
University of Ibadan, 51, 182, 185, 196, 204, 210, 211, 212, 213
University of Lagos, 186, 207, 210, 212, 225

W

Walesa, Lech, 25
War Against Indiscipline, 140
Warfare in Islam, 87
World Assembly of Muslim Youth, 257, 258
World Declaration on Education for All, 199
World Trade Centre, 52, 259

Y

Yerima, Ahmed, 51
Yoruba, vi, 47, 51, 79, 145, 149, 153, 171, 195, 199, 202, 203, 210, 216, 273, 349, 350, 351, 352, 353, 354, 355, 359, 360, 362, 424, 431, 435, 440
Yoruba Muslims, 349
Yusuf, Muhammad, 45, 65, 66, 73, 77, 83, 95, 102

Z

Zakāt, 84
Zakizaki, Shaykh Az, 77
ZangoKataf crises, 51

www.ingramcontent.com/pod-product-compliance
Lightning Source LLC
Chambersburg PA
CBHW071434300426
44114CB00013B/1432